NERO'S KILLING MACHINE

MACHINE

THE TRUE STORY OF ROME'S REMARKABLE FOURTEENTH LEGION

STEPHEN DANDO-COLLINS

WILEY

John Wiley & Sons, Inc.

Published by John Wiley & Sons, Inc., Hoboken, New Jersey
Published simultaneously in Canada

For general information about our other products and services, please contact our Cus-
tomer Care Department within the United States at (800) 762-2974, outside the United
States at (317) 572-3993 or fax (317) 572-4002.

Wiley also publishes its books in a variety of electronic formats. Some content that appears
in print may not be available in electronic books. For more information about Wiley products, visit our web site at www.wiley.com.

Library of Congress Cataloging-in-Publication Data:

Dando-Collins, Stephen, date.
    Nero's killing machine: the true story of Rome's remarkable Fourteenth
 Legion / Stephen Dando-Collins.
        p.   cm.
    Includes bibliographical references and index.
    ISBN-13 978-0-471-67501-3 (cloth)
    ISBN-10 0-471-67501-6 (cloth)
    ISBN-13 978-0-470-04638-8 (paper)
    ISBN-10 0-470-04638-4 (paper)
    1. Rome. Legion XIV Gemina Martia Victrix—History. I. Title.
    U35.D3724 2004
    355'.00937—dc22

                                                          2004001728

Printed in the United States of America

10 9 8 7 6 5 4 3 2 1

CONTENTS

ATLAS

Southern Britain

Colchester

CATUVELLAUNI

Thames R.

NORTH
SEA

North
Foreland

KENT   *Medway R.*

CANTIACI   *Stour R.*

South
Foreland

Isle of Wight

Boulogne

BRITAIN

Area of Inset

Colchester

NORTH
SEA

USIPETES

Rhine R.

TENCTHERI

*Dover
Strait*

Isle of Wight

NERVII

EBURONES

SUEBI

ENGLISH CHANNEL

Boulogne

Sambre R.

Tongres

ATREBATES

Moselle R.

Trier

SENONES

Seine R.

TREVERI

VENETI

Paris

CARNUTES   Sens

Orléans

Alesia

GAUL

Dijon

Bourges   Bibracte   Besançon

BAY OF
BISCAY

BITURIGES

Saône R.

HELVETII

Geneva

Gergovia

Vienne

AVERNI

Rhône R.

Uxellodunum

Yar R.

Pyrenees Mountains

Narbonne   Marseilles

MEDITERRANEAN
SEA

NEARER
SPAIN

Britain and Gaul, 58–50 B.C.

©2004 by D. L. McElhannon

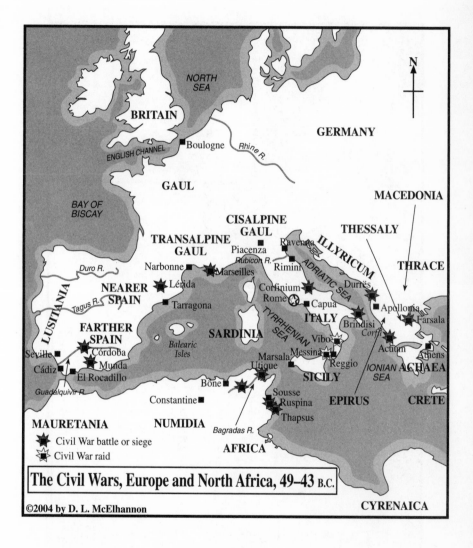

The Civil Wars, Europe and North Africa, 49–43 B.C.

©2004 by D. L. McElhannon

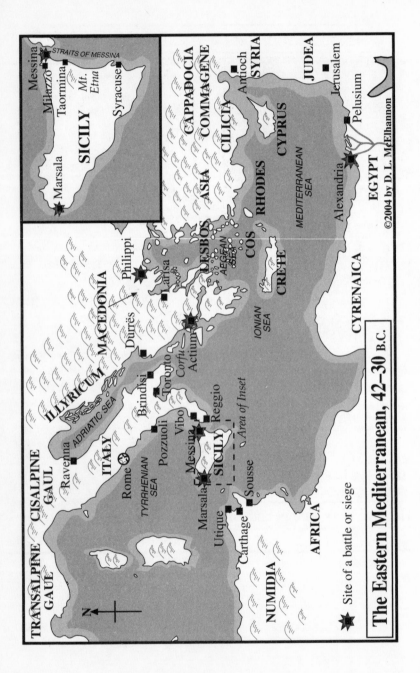

The Eastern Mediterranean, 42–30 B.C.

★ Site of a battle or siege

©2004 by D. L. McElhannon

Inset (SICILY):

Messina
Milazzo
Taormina
Mt. Etna
Syracuse
Marsala
SICILY
STRAITS OF MESSINA

Main map labels:

TRANSALPINE GAUL
CISALPINE GAUL
ILLYRICUM
MACEDONIA
Ravenna
Rome
ITALY
Brindisi
Durrës
Philippi
Larisa
Actium
Corfu
Toronto
Vibo
Pozzuoli
Reggio
Messina
Marsala
SICILY
Utique
Carthage
Sousse
Area of Inset
TYRRHENIAN SEA
ADRIATIC SEA
IONIAN SEA
AEGEAN SEA
LESBOS
COS
RHODES
CRETE
CYPRUS
CILICIA
ASIA
COMMAGENE
CAPPADOCIA
SYRIA
Antioch
JUDEA
Jerusalem
Pelusium
Alexandria
EGYPT
MEDITERRANEAN SEA
CYRENAICA
AFRICA
NUMIDIA

N

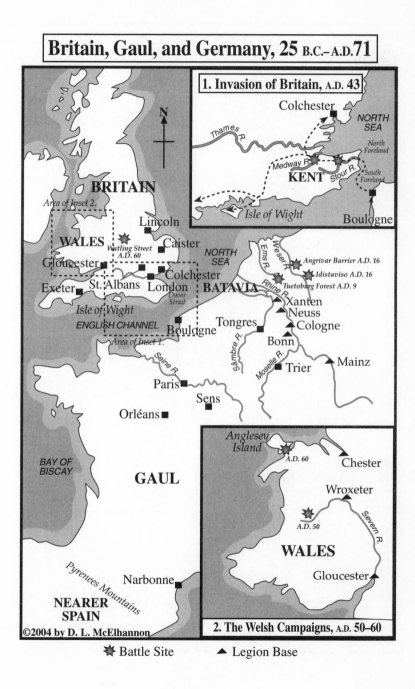

Britain, Gaul, and Germany, 25 B.C.–A.D. 71

1. Invasion of Britain, A.D. 43

Colchester

NORTH SEA

Thames R.

North Foreland

Medway R.

Stour R.

South Foreland

KENT

Isle of Wight

Boulogne

BRITAIN

Area of Inset 2.

Lincoln

WALES

Watling Street A.D. 60

Caister

NORTH SEA

Gloucester

Exeter

St. Albans

London

Colchester

Dover Strait

BATAVIA

Ems R.

Weser R.

Rhine R.

Angrivar Barrier A.D. 16

Idistaviso A.D. 16

Tuetoburg Forest A.D. 9

Xanten

Neuss

Cologne

Bonn

Trier

Mainz

Isle of Wight

ENGLISH CHANNEL

Boulogne

Area of Inset 1.

Tongres

Sâmbre R.

Moselle R.

Seine R.

Paris

Sens

Orléans

BAY OF BISCAY

GAUL

Anglesey Island

A.D. 60

Chester

Wroxeter

Severn R.

A.D. 50

WALES

Gloucester

Pyrenees Mountains

Narbonne

NEARER SPAIN

©2004 by D. L. McElhannon

2. The Welsh Campaigns, A.D. 50–60

✹ Battle Site   ▲ Legion Base

The Roman West, A.D. 66–395

©2004 by D. L. McElhannon

ACKNOWLEDGMENTS

This book would not have been possible without the immense help provided over many years by countless staff at libraries, museums, and historic sites throughout the world. To them all, my heartfelt thanks. Neither they nor I knew at the time what my labor of love would develop into. My thanks, too, to those who have read my research material as it blossomed into manuscript form and made invaluable suggestions.

I wish to record my gratitude to several people in particular. First, to T. R. Fehrenbach, for his support of this project when it was taking shape and for his generous words about the first book in the series. Thanks, too, to Stephen S. Power, senior editor with John Wiley & Sons, for his continued enthusiasm, support, and guidance and senior production editor John Simko. Then there is the wise one, Richard Curtis, my champion of a New York literary agent, who has gone into battle for me time and again.

And my remarkable wife, Louise, my muse, my shield, my countess. We are now into our third decade together, and never once in all this time has her faith in me, my writing, or my aspirations slipped. She has guided, goaded, and guarded me all through this time, and never let me lose sight of the goal. As Seneca said of his wife, Paulina, "Can anything be sweeter than to find that you are so dear to your wife that this makes you dearer to yourself?"

AUTHOR'S NOTE

This is the second book in this series of histories of legions of ancient Rome, the result of thirty-two years of research and writing. Prior to the 2002 publication of the first book in the series, *Caesar's Legion*, the story of the 10th Legion, never before had a comprehensive history of an individual Roman legion been published. In the process of those decades of detective work it was possible to identify the Augustan and post-Augustan legions raised between 84 B.C. and A.D. 231 and to compile detailed histories of many of them.

The works of numerous classical writers who documented the wars, campaigns, battles, skirmishes, and most importantly the men of the legions of Rome have come down to us. Authors such as Julius Caesar, Appian, Plutarch, Tacitus, Suetonius, Polybius, Cassius Dio, Josephus, Cicero, Pliny the Younger, Seneca, Livy, Arrian. Without their labors this book would not have been possible.

During the research for this series, light was shed for the first time on a number of issues relating to the legions, the most important of which was the reenlistment factor. The legions of Rome were recruited en masse, and the survivors discharged en masse at the end of their enlistment— originally after sixteen years, later, after twenty. Only on exceptional occasions, such as one described in this book, were replacements supplied to a legion before its new enlistment was due, to make up for battle casualties. By using the reenlistment factor it was possible to determine the exact years in which every legion and the Praetorian Guard underwent their discharges and reenlistments. This helps explain why particular units were crushed in this battle or that. In some, they were raw recruits; in others, they were weary men about to go into retirement after twenty years in uniform.

All speeches and conversations in this book are taken from dialogue and narrative in classical texts, and are faithful to those original sources. The exchanges at the officers' conference at Atuatuca in 54 B.C., for example, are as Caesar recorded them in his memoirs. Likewise, the prebattle speeches of Boudicca, General Paulinus, Civilis, and General Cerialis are just as Roman historians Tacitus and Dio wrote them.

For the sake of continuity, the Roman calendar—which in Republican times varied by some two months from our own—is used throughout this work. Place names are generally first referred to in their original form and thereafter by modern name, where known, to permit readers to readily identify locations involved. Personal names familiar to modern readers have been used instead of those technically correct—Mark Antony instead of Marcus Antonius, Julius Caesar for Gaius Caesar, Octavian for Caesar Octavianus, Caligula for Gaius, Pilate for Pilatus, Vespasian for Vespasianus, etc.

In the nineteenth and twentieth centuries it was fashionable for some authors to refer to legions as regiments, cohorts as battalions, maniples as companies, centurions as captains, tribunes as colonels, and legates as generals. In this work, Roman military terms such as legion, cohort, maniple, and centurion have been retained, as it's felt they will be familiar to most readers and convey more of a flavor of the time. Because of a lack of popular familiarity with the term "legate," "general" and/or "brigadier general" are used here. "Colonel" and "tribune" are both used, to give a sense of relative status. Likewise, so that readers can relate in comparison to today's military, when referred to in the military sense "praetors" are given as "major generals" and "consuls" as "lieutenant generals." In this way, reference to a lieutenant general, for example, will immediately tell the reader that the figure concerned was a consul. I am aware this is akin to having a foot in two camps and may not please purists, but my aim is to make these books broadly accessible.

Enough material exists, from sources classical and modern—detailed in the appendices of this work—to write a number of books on the more interesting of Rome's legions, and while growing armies of readers around the world, many of them new to Roman history, continue to enjoy these insights into the way the men of the legions lived and died, I shall continue to put together the legions' stories.

This is the story of the men of the 14th Legion, later called the 14th Gemina Martia Victrix Legion. For more than a century its legionaries bore the shame of a terrible baptism of fire, until the legion became Nero's killing machine and earned itself fame for a deed that would never be surpassed. These are the men who made Rome great. One or two extraordinary men, and many more ordinary men who often did extraordinary things. I hope that via these pages, you come to know them.

I

FACING THE BRITISH WARRIOR QUEEN

T he retreat was at an end. The Roman army had turned to face the enemy in a final stand, vastly outnumbered but determined to preserve honor if not life as it went down fighting the Celtic woman who had overrun most of Roman Britain in fewer than two weeks. She was Boudicca, war queen of the Britons. The Romans knew her as Boadicea.

The place, a tree-lined plain near the Anker River in central England. The time, a day in the late spring of A.D. 60. The contestants, a weary Roman army of ten thousand men, professional soldiers all, facing Boudicca's rampaging British army of as many as 230,000 rebels.

The queen stood in her chariot on the eastern side of the battlefield, addressing her vast army with the fire and passion of a born leader. Boudicca was in her thirties, recently widowed, with two daughters barely into their teens who, as Roman historian Tacitus tells us, now knelt in the chariot in front of her as she raged against the Romans.

Very tall, her thick, tawny-colored hair falling to her hips, dressed in a multicolored tunic and heavy robe and with a large golden necklace around her neck, that's how another Roman historian, Cassius Dio, describes her. Her voice, according to Dio, was sharp and harsh. There was a fierce, frightening look in her eye. She shook a spear in the air to emphasize her words as she addressed her fighting men in the curt Celtic tongue. Boudicca had just one major obstacle to overcome before eliminating Roman control of her country: a general who until now had refused to fight, leading a few auxiliary and militia units and a single Roman legion, the 14th Gemina Martia Victrix.

The 14th Legion had been founded more than a century before by Julius Caesar in the Roman province of Cisalpine Gaul, today's northern

1

Italy. Then, as now, its recruits were young conscripts. Over the years it had been granted several titles to add to its number, partly via amalgamation with another unit, partly from a battle honor. Now known as the Legio XIIII Gemina Martia Victrix, the legion had been stationed in Britain for the past seventeen years, normally based at Chester, or Deva as the Romans called it, on the border of England and northern Wales.

Today the legion was close to full strength, with five thousand men under arms serving a twenty-year enlistment. Right now, the youngest members of the legion were twenty-nine years of age, each with nine years' service under his belt. Men such as Legionary Publius Cordus, a conscript from Mutina—modern Modena in northern Italy—and his best friend, Gaius Vibennius. And Standard-bearer Marcus Petronius, a native of the town of Vicetia, present-day Vicenza. These men of the legion's senior cohorts were tough, experienced forty-nine-year-olds who had fought Germans along the Rhine and later stormed ashore in the A.D. 43 invasion of Britain.

Here, beside the river, in battle formation of three successive lines, the heavy infantry of the 14th G.M.V. now stood in their centuries of eighty men, eight across and ten deep, with a gap of three feet between each soldier and with a centurion occupying the front left position of each group. They wore the standard uniform and carried the standard equipment of the Roman legionary. Blood-red tunic. Segmented metal armor covering chest, back, and upper arms. Scarf, knotted at the neck, to protect against the chafing effect of the armor. Helmet equipped with neck protector and cheek flaps tied in place beneath the chin, its parade crest of yellow horsehair stowed away with leather shield cover, red woolen cloak, and other superfluous gear back at camp. Heavy-duty hobnailed military sandals. A sheathed dagger on the left hip, and, on the right, a twenty-inch *gladius*, the double-edged, pointed Spanish sword, universal sidearm of the Roman soldier for centuries.

In their right hands each man had several metal-tipped wooden javelins, the longest upward of seven feet long; the ends rested on the ground for now. The painted leather surface of an elongated, convex wooden shield four feet long by two and one-half feet wide on each man's left, its metal-rimmed edge resting on the ground, was emblazoned with Mars's thunderbolt, proud emblem of the legion.

The men of the 14th Gemina Martia Victrix Legion could see the British queen across the field as she moved from clan to clan in her chariot, delivering a prebattle pep talk to her tens of thousands of warriors. They saw, too, waiting like an expectant crowd at a football game, eighty thousand British women, wives of fighting men, lining the far end of the battlefield in a semicircle of booty-laden wagons and carts, there to watch the slaughter of this meager legionary army that was outnumbered as much as twenty-three to one, and eager to then rush in and strip the Roman dead and add to their treasure trove.

The disgrace of defeat was difficult for a proud, arrogant Roman legionary to contemplate at any time, but to be defeated by a woman, that would be the greatest disgrace of all. Greater even than losing the legion's eagle standard to the enemy, an ignominious fate the 14th had once suffered long ago. In this their darkest hour, the men of the legion looked to their commander in chief, who, like Boudicca, was moving among his troops, delivering an address, in his case from horseback, an address designed to bolster faint hearts and fire the will to win.

Lieutenant General Gaius Suetonius Paulinus—propraetor, or imperial governor, of Roman Britain—would have been well aware that he and his men might die before the day was out. Now close to fifty, he'd been a war hero in his younger days. Maturity had made him a resolute yet pragmatic man. Two years back he had come to Britain as the province's new governor, determined to impress the boy-emperor Nero by completing the conquest of Britain.

When news of the uprising behind his back reached him, General Paulinus had been campaigning in Wales with the 14th G.M.V. Suddenly all thoughts of imperial acclaim would have departed his mind. First he'd rushed east to meet the rebel threat. Then, realizing the scope of the revolt, he'd backpedaled, withdrawing ahead of Boudicca for day after day as he waited for the expected arrival of reinforcements, which never materialized.

In his withdrawal, General Paulinus had abandoned the settlements that would become today's cities of London and St. Albans, allowing them to be overrun by the rampaging Britons. Until, with further retreat pointless as most of the province of Britain was now in rebel hands, Paulinus had decided to make one last stand. At least he would show the emperor that he could die nobly, with his sword in his hand and his men fighting to the last gasp around him.

The Romans had a saying, "It's sweet and glorious to die for one's country." But just how willing General Paulinus's rank and file were to die to a man fighting the Britons is debatable. Still, Paulinus had every right to expect their discipline and esprit de corps to hold them together. These were men who had been hardened by years of daily training, by rigid Roman military discipline enforced by often brutal centurions. Arduous annual campaigns against wild tribesmen in the hills and valleys of Wales had molded the legion into a closely knit and chillingly efficient killing machine.

Professional soldiers such as Legionary Cordus and Standard-bearer Petronius would not have wanted to dishonor their legion by showing cowardice in the face of the enemy. Besides, they and their comrades had a score to settle with the Britons, for the torture and murder of former men of the legion in the first days of the uprising. Already, seventy thousand Romans and Romanized Britons had been slaughtered by the rebels.

Standing to one side of the men of the 14th G.M.V. were two thousand former soldiers of the 20th Valeria Victrix Legion, veterans of two decades' service, such as Gaius Mannius Secondus from Pollentia near Turin, who just months before had retired from the army to take up farming, only to be hastily recalled to the Evocati Corps militia several days back to serve behind the standard of their old 20th V.V. cohorts.

On the other side of the regulars of the 14th G.M.V. stood two thousand Batavian auxiliaries, lanky Dutch light infantrymen. Before being subdued by Julius Caesar and becoming his staunchest allies, Batavians had dyed their hair red and let their beards grow when they went to war, and, like their German cousins, each man had sworn to his gods never to cut either again until he had slain an enemy. Today the Romanized Batavians looked much like their legion counterparts, wearing helmets and protective leather jackets and armed with sword; dagger; spears; and a flat, oval shield.

A thousand cavalry rounded out General Paulinus's insignificant force, divided between the two flanks—troopers of the elite Batavian Horse Regiment, and the 1st Wing of the Thracian Horse. Steadying their nervous mounts would have been 1st Thracian Wing men such as Trooper Genialis from Frisia in Holland.

As General Paulinus, accompanied by his staff, rode back to his command position behind the lines, all eyes would have been on the British queen. According to Tacitus, she called to her warriors, "In this battle you must conquer, or die. This is a woman's resolve!" As for her male audience, she told them they could live, and be slaves of the Romans, if they so chose. But not Boudicca.

As her followers bellowed that they were with her, the young war queen wheeled her chariot around to face the Romans. The British warriors and the watching civilians broke out into a deafening cacophony of noise that rolled across the grass and assailed the ears of the waiting Roman troops. The war chants and battle songs of the many clans of the Iceni of Norfolk, the Trinovantes of Essex, and the other tribes of southern England that had flocked to join the rebellion mingled with their clan leaders' cries to the heavens beseeching the support of the Celtic gods, and the excited calls of wide-eyed women urging their men to cut the Romans to pieces.

Paulinus had briefed his officers on very specific tactics for both infantry and cavalry designed to counter the British superiority in numbers. Now he gave an order, and his personal trumpeter sounded "Prepare to loose." The trumpeters of each cohort, mere curly-headed boys, raised their G-shaped instruments and repeated the call. In response, every Roman legionary lifted his shield, stabbed one javelin into the ground and readied another, taking a throwing stance with one foot planted in front of the other and right shoulder back.

Boudicca was waving her chariots into the attack. They swept past the queen and her daughters—whose rape by Roman civil servants had in part sponsored this revolt. Not for almost two decades had British chariots taken the field against a Roman army. Away from the massed British infantry and cavalry the vehicles sped, a stirring sight as they surged across the plain toward the waiting, stationary Romans. At the same time, Boudicca sent the British infantry forward at the walk. The warriors went into battle yelling at the top of their lungs still, eyes flashing, faces contorted with hate, shaking weapons in the air or rhythmically crashing spears on shields with each forward step.

Tacitus says that instead of also advancing to meet the enemy, the usual battle tactic of the day, the Romans followed the orders of their general and stood stock still, with their backs to the narrow, tree-lined pass through the hills that had brought them onto the plain. With the roar of 310,000 British voices in their ears, feeling the ground begin to vibrate beneath their feet from the pounding of the hooves of the horses that brought the bumping, lurching British chariots closer with each passing second, the legionaries were silent. Eyes to the front, tensed, they waited for the next command. Having signed and sealed their wills the night before and handed them to their best friends for safekeeping, many a soldier now silently rendered the legionary's prayer: "Jupiter Best and Greatest, protect this unit, soldiers all."

Men in the 14th G.M.V.'s front ranks watched as chariots thundered toward them, streaming down one side of the tree-lined plain, the Roman left. They would have seen spearmen in the back poised to launch their first missiles with strong right arms. In those last seconds before battle was joined they also would have seen severed heads swinging from the sides of chariots; and it would have dawned on some that the bloodless, rotting faces dangling there were those of Roman officers of the 9th Hispana Legion, gory trophies from the last encounter between the rebels and the arms of Rome.

Many men of the 14th would have broken out in a sweat by now. Some would have paled with fear. One or two had probably lost control of their bowels. But they did not budge. Trusting in their officers, in their own training and the fidelity of their comrades, they suppressed their fears and waited for the Fates to unfold their destiny. In those final seconds before the morning saw its first bloodshed, the thoughts of legionaries would have gone to homes and families they hadn't seen in nine years or more. Legionary Cordus no doubt thought of his father, Publius, and the rest of his family back in Modena. Standard-bearer Petronius may have wondered how his father, Lucius, at Vicenza, might take the news of his son's death here on this British battlefield at the northwestern edge of the empire.

British spears were slicing through the air from the chariots, the first missiles landing short and quivering in the ground. But with each passing second more and more fell among the Roman ranks, most to be parried by rectangular, curved shields bearing the lightning-bolt emblem of the 14th G.M.V. and the razorback boar symbol of the 20th V.V., or the oval Batavian shields with their twirling Germano-Celtic motif.

Amid rising dust and flying clods of earth kicked up by the hooves of their horses, the leading chariots suddenly changed course, swinging to run along the Roman line from left to right, their spearmen letting fly every few seconds on this, their prime missile-launching run.

The Roman commander in chief issued a brief order. The legion trumpets sounded, just audible above the din made by the approaching enemy.

"Loose!" bellowed front-line centurions at the top of their lungs.

Roman troops heaved their first javelin, then quickly took up a second.

"Loose!" came the order again, and, once more, thousands of Roman javelins filled the air and then lanced down among the racing chariots.

Half-naked British charioteers and spearmen were falling from their vehicles, impaled by Roman missiles. Horses were going down. An out-of-control chariot tumbled end over end. The surviving chariots completed their pass and turned away, peeling off to the wing to permit the passage of the British infantry, who now broke into a run as they neared the Romans in a vast, surging mass.

Two Roman trumpet calls came in rapid succession now. "Close up," followed by "Form wedge." As one, legionaries drew their swords with practiced precision, then shuffled into three large close-order wedge formations, with the point of each facing the enemy. The 14th G.M.V. formed one large central wedge, the 20th V.V. veterans another, and the Batavians the third, one beside the other.

Now Roman trumpets sounded "Advance." As they went forward in formation, the men of the 14th would have been hoping that history would not repeat itself today.

For, once before, 114 years earlier, this legion had faced another foreign army beside a river. That disastrous day, in one of the most dramatic episodes in Roman military history, the 14th Legion had been wiped from the face of the earth.

II

WIPED OUT

With packs over their shoulders, the men of the 14th Legion were marching into Belgium. It was the late summer of 54 B.C., and the commander in chief of operations in France and Belgium—or Gaul, as the Romans called it—Lieutenant General Gaius Julius Caesar, was dispersing his legions for the winter. History would come to know the general as Julius Caesar. Fresh from celebrating his forty-sixth birthday, Caesar was completing the fourth year of a military campaign during which his forces had conquered central and northern France for Rome. Rather than also go to war with Caesar, most of the tribes of Belgium had hastily signed peace treaties with him, had agreed to accept wintering legions on their turf and to supply them with grain in return for peaceful relations.

Only just back from his second military expedition to Britain, Caesar had come ashore at the Pas-de-Calais and was basing himself at Amiens on the Somme River while his legions set up camps for the winter. For the first time, he was breaking up his army into groups of a legion or two, and spreading them across the conquered territories. Gaul had experienced a fierce summer that year; Caesar himself was to write that the wheat crop had been poor, and it was necessary to send his troops far and wide to find sufficient supplies to last the winter.

Under the command of Brigadier General Quintus Titurius Sabinus, with the younger Brigadier General Marcus Aurunculeius Cotta as his deputy, the 14th Legion was marching northeast from the Pas-de-Calais, heading for the Geer River in central Belgium, an area occupied by tribes classified as friendly, since they'd signed the peace treaty with Caesar. The 14th was accompanied by another five cohorts of unidentified infantry—perhaps from the 11th Legion, or auxiliaries—and a squadron of Spanish cavalry.

In the four years since Caesar had founded it in northern Italy—the Roman province of Cisalpine Gaul, as it was then known—the 14th Legion hadn't seen any combat. For four years the 14th had done nothing but guard camps, escort road convoys, and cut wheat to feed other legions.

Caesar was slow to trust new legions. Of the eight legions now making up his army, only five had his complete trust—the 7th, 8th, and 9th, legions raised in Spain in 65 B.C. by Pompey the Great; the 10th, raised by Caesar personally in Spain in 61 B.C.; and the 12th, raised by Caesar in Cisalpine Gaul in 58 B.C. As for the 11th and 13th, like the 14th, they were toiling to win Caesar's faith and the frontline role that brought glory, promotion, and booty to its legionaries. All in good time, their officers would have assured the frustrated troops of the 14th, the day would soon come when the legion would prove its worth to Caesar, would show their commander in chief that they were the equal of his favorite units.

The 14th was close to full strength. Its nominal strength was 5,940 enlisted men and 60 centurions—the lieutenants and captains who commanded the legion's centuries, maniples, and cohorts, subunits that were forerunners of today's platoons, companies, and battalions. The centurions reported to six tribunes, colonels generally under thirty years of age, members of the Equestrian Order and sons of Rome's best families. Often serving a tour of duty lasting just one year, most tribunes had little military experience, yet, at this point in Roman history, they ran every legion among them—on rotation, one tribune commanded the entire unit, while the other five each commanded two cohorts. Every two months, they rotated responsibilities. Within several decades, and with the coming of the imperial era, the role and power of the tribunes would alter drastically, with each legion commanded by a dedicated general of senatorial rank. But for now, the half-dozen tribunes called the shots, answering to whichever general Caesar chose to head their particular task force at the time.

The conquisitors, or recruiting officers, who'd conscripted the recruits for the 14th in northeastern Italy in the winter of 58–57 B.C. had enrolled healthy young men mostly between seventeen and twenty years of age. Roman citizens all, the 14th's draftees were recruited for sixteen years' service, signing a contract that bound both them and the State. Legionaries swore to serve the Senate and people of Rome; to obey their officers; to adhere to extremely tough service regulations; and, if necessary, to die for Rome.

In return, Rome was required to provide its legionaries with food, shelter, uniforms, basic gear and weaponry, and to pay them a salary, originally 450 sesterces a year, doubled by Caesar to 900 sesterces a year. Legionaries were forbidden to marry during their enlistment. Once enrolled in a legion they were no longer subject to civil law—the legion was their new family, and strict legion regulations with the penalty of death for major infractions governed their lives.

Leading the way into Belgium at the forefront of the 14th Legion's 1st Cohort was Chief Centurion Titus Balventius, who'd held his post as the most senior centurion of the legion for the past year. Farther back in the column, traditionally bareheaded and proudly holding aloft the silver eagle of the 14th, came Eagle-bearer Lucius Petrosidius.

In all, General Sabinus's detachment numbered about nine thousand infantry and cavalry, plus noncombatants, including officers' slaves and muleteers to drive the baggage animals accompanying the troops. The baggage train would have comprised at least a thousand mules—one per squad, minimum—and several hundred carts and wagons bearing artillery, ammunition, and supplies, the more bulky gear of the troops such as the tents and millstones of each squad, plus the pavilions, furniture, and plate of the senior officers and the equipment of the engineers, artillerymen, and armorers.

General Sabinus would have been in his mid- to late thirties. He had a mixed reputation. Two years earlier, when operating in Normandy, he'd been severely criticized by men under him, who'd accused him of acting timidly in refusing to venture outside his camp to fight an attacking Gallic force from the Venelli tribe. Caesar himself was later to write in Sabinus's defense, especially after Sabinus subsequently used a spy to lure the Venelli into a trap, after which he'd wiped out much of the enemy force.

Now, enjoying fine weather, the legionaries of the 14th and the other troops of Sabinus's force arrived in Belgium without incident and quickly built their fortified camp for the winter at Atuatuca, a then virgin site on a slightly elevated position a little way from the Geer River—the Jaar, in Flemish. Today the site is occupied by the town of Tongres, the Flemish Tongeren, twelve miles northwest of the city of Liège.

The camp would have followed normal Roman army specifications, as described by the Greek military writer Polybius, being roughly square and surrounded by a ditch at least ten feet deep and three across, and often with a wooden palisade on the outer side. An inner wall a minimum of ten feet high and three feet thick was created from earth dug from the ditch, topped by a wooden palisade of sharpened stakes. There was a gate, flanked by a wooden guard tower, in each of the four main camp walls. The tents of the cohorts were neatly arrayed along the camp's grid-pattern streets, as were those of the officers. According to Polybius, there was also provision for a market at the center of every legion camp. A broad, open space between tents and wall sufficient to prevent burning spears or arrows from reaching the tent line from outside the camp was occupied by the legion's baggage animals and cattle and, when in the legion's possession, chained prisoners of war.

In Caesar's time legionaries slept ten to a tent—originally leather, but by the first century made of canvas. In Gaul at this time, too, it was the habit of the legions to thatch the roofs of the little leather huts of their winter quarters as protection against the severe northern weather. The ten men in each tent made up a *contubernium*, a squad, the smallest subunit of the legion. With the emperor Augustus's reorganization of the Roman army two and one-half decades later, the contubernium would be reduced to eight men. But the nature of the squad never changed. Members cooked at their tent; there was no mess hall. And they marched, laughed, grumbled, fought, and died together as a tightly knit group.

Each officer had a tent to himself, with the commander occupying the spacious *praetorium*, the headquarters tent, which was both his quarters and office, with the tribunes and quartermaster quartered next door. Horse corral and store tents were set up in close proximity to the praetorium.

Guard duty rotated among the cohorts, with the guard cohort on duty reporting to the tribune of the watch and required to provide a set number of sentries for a variety of stations: a daytime picket outside the walls, ten men at each gate, more in the guard towers, on the walls, and at the officers' quarters and cavalry corral. On a trumpet call sounded from outside the praetorium, the watch changed every three hours. Daily, just before sunset, the tribune of the watch provided the commander with a register of the able-bodied men in camp and in return received the watchword or password for the next twenty-four hours.

The watchword was methodically distributed to the sentries on a wax tablet, the *tesserara*, by the *tesserarius*, the guard sergeant of each maniple. Anyone approaching the camp in the dark would be challenged by sentries, who would demand the watchword. Only with the arrival of daylight and the end of the last night watch at the sounding of the reveille trumpet call would sentries cease to issue their challenges.

To ensure that all guards were present and awake, each legion's cavalry unit provided a four-man patrol of the sentry posts every night, the troopers alternating as patrol leader for each of the four watches of the night while the other three acted as observers to ensure that he did his job. Their patrols were made at random, never at specific times, to catch offenders. And to ensure that sentries couldn't be tipped off about intended patrol times in return for a bribe, the patrol had to station itself for the night outside the tent of the centurion commanding the duty guard cohort. Sentries asleep on duty or absent without leave could be sentenced to death by a court-martial of the legion's tribunes

By paying their centurions a set fee, one legionary in four could take a furlough during the noncampaigning months. Men on leave frequently left their camp, but at Atuatuca General Sabinus kept all men in camp except those engaged in foraging.

With several idle months ahead of them, the men in the camp began repairing and replacing equipment, with specialists among their ranks employing their peacetime skills. Armorers labored over forges. Cobblers repaired footwear. Tailors were at work, too. The rank and file sharpened weapons, cleaned helmet plumes, polished bravery decorations, sewed gaps in shield covers. Every man took a turn grinding their squad's grain ration and cooking their daily bread for the main meal at night and a snack at lunchtime. Bread and olive oil were the staples of their diet, with meat an occasional supplement. Potatoes, tomatoes, bananas, and coffee were unknown to them. As they worked in the fall sunshine, sitting in groups outside their tents, the legionaries would have exchanged slanderous gossip about their officers and told crude jokes, as soldiers do.

One cohort in ten always was on guard, and there were daily drills and weapons practice for all ranks. This still would have left a good deal of free time. Wrestling matches probably were organized to keep the men amused and occupied. Board games were popular, such as Roman chess, which had a board with sixty squares, and another called twelve lines.

The one game that was the passion of all Roman soldiers at all times was dice, a game played for money and forerunner of today's game of craps. During the imperial era dice-playing was illegal, with the only time dice could be legally played being during the Saturnalia Festival in December. It's not hard to imagine groups of legionaries crowded around players at a dice board and a cry going up when someone rolled *basilicus*, the highest throw of the dice.

The peace of the scenic riverside setting at Atuatuca was not to last for long. Two weeks after General Sabinus had sent a cavalry dispatch rider to Caesar at Amiens reporting that his men had completed construction of their fortification beside the waters of the Geer and were settling in for the winter, "To arms" was unexpectedly trumpeted through the camp.

The cause of the problem was a Belgian king named Ambiorix. As its peace treaty with Caesar required, the local Eburone tribe, who lived between the Rhine and Meuse Rivers in a kingdom called Eburonia by

Roman historian Cassius Dio, had delivered a large quantity of grain to General Sabinus and the 14th while the legion's camp was under construction. The Eburones had two kings—Catuvolcus, who was old and ailing, and the younger, more active Ambiorix. It was King Ambiorix who supervised the handover of the grain at Atuatuca, and he'd eyed the growing Roman emplacement with distaste. He could see that the Romans were planning on a long stay in Eburonia.

Ambiorix soon came to hear that there were stirrings of revolt elsewhere in Gaul. The first manifestation was among the Carnute tribe, in territory to Caesar's rear between the Seine and Loire Rivers, southwest of Paris. The Carnutes assassinated their regent, Tasgetius, who'd been installed by Caesar two years earlier. As Caesar transferred General Lucius Plancus and his detachment south from Belgium to calm the Carnutes and identify and punish Tasgetius's murderers, more trouble brewed to the northeast.

The Treveri, a large and powerful German tribe whose territory straddled modern Luxembourg and eastern Belgium, with their capital, Trier, on the Moselle River, had been providing Caesar with top-class auxiliary cavalry for his Gallic campaigns. At the time Caesar considered the Treveri the bravest if not the best mounted troops in Gaul. But now, leading Treverans were plotting a revolt against Caesar. One of them, Indutiomarus, secretly sent envoys to neighboring tribes, urging them to join in an uprising.

Not long after making the grain delivery to General Sabinus, King Ambiorix the Eburone received a visit from one of these envoys. Inspired by the message from Trier, Ambiorix decided to ignite the revolt without waiting for the Treverans to give the lead. After convincing old Catuvolcus to go along with his plan, he sent messages to all the Eburone clan leaders, summoning them and their fighting men for a campaign against the Roman invaders.

The Eburones quickly answered the call. After just a few days' preparation, making ammunition and practicing rudimentary battle drills, the Eburone warriors quietly washed through the Belgian forests and arrived at Atuatuca. Without warning they overran and massacred a small 14th Legion wood-gathering party working a little way from the Geer River position. Before news of the massacre reached General Sabinus, ten thousand Eburones launched an assault on the fortified camp itself. As General Sabinus's legionaries dashed to take up defensive positions along the camp ramparts the sentries had just time enough to swing the camp's four gates shut.

Of Germanic origin, these Belgic tribesmen were undisciplined; disorganized; and, compared to the professional Roman soldier, untrained. But like all the Germanic peoples, they were warlike by nature and prided themselves in their individual weapons skills, ingrained since boyhood. What's more, as Caesar tells us, all the Belgae were quick to learn military lessons after observing the Roman war machine at work.

Their nobles were comparatively well outfitted in moccasins; ankle-length trousers, perhaps bearing one of the tartan designs then popular in the north of France; plus leather jerkins covered with protective iron mail; and iron pot helmets trailing long horsehair plumes. They came armed with Celtic swords, a foot longer than the standard Roman infantry sword but blunt-ended, and worn on the right side, as the legionaries did, plus large, flat shields made of planks of oak. The richer, more powerful nobles could be identified by the size of their personal bodyguard as well as by the size of their solid gold neck chains and bracelets.

Their followers weren't as well off. Like their leaders, they wore long trousers, but there the comparison ended. Often sporting mustaches, the fighting men of northern Gaul were bareheaded, with their hair gelled into upstanding spikes via a hairdressing of clay and lime. Although some had the protection of breastplates and carried swords, most were naked to the waist, and many were armed with just spears and stones. Shields were universal, but the least-well-equipped warriors of Gaul and Germany could only manage a wicker affair with a leather facing. These poor, uneducated subsistence farmers of Belgium were driven to war by strong clan loyalties forged through blood and marriage; by obligation to their nobles; by a hate of foreign invaders, be they Roman or German; and by the promise of rich Roman booty.

Caesar says that all the Belgic tribes employed a common tactic when assaulting a fortress. They would rain stones against defenders manning the walls; then, when the defenses had been thinned, and emulating the Roman army, they would send forward detachments under the cover of shields to undermine the walls at weak spots and force breaches through which they would then flood.

On this occasion the tribesmen's initial assault on the Atuatuca camp walls was easily driven off by a sortie by Sabinus's Spanish cavalry, who unexpectedly pounded out a swiftly opened gate and drove into the attackers' flanks while they were busy pelting the legionaries on the ramparts with stones of golf ball and baseball size.

As the tribesmen pulled back out of missile range and surrounded the camp, cutting it off from the outside world, King Ambiorix sent to the camp walls messengers who urged the Romans to send someone out to speak with their leader. "We have something to say that concerns both sides," Caesar says they called. "Something that can bring this fighting to an end."

In response, General Sabinus sent out two colonels to meet with Ambiorix. One was Gaius Arpineius, a member of the Equestrian Order and a friend of Sabinus. The other was Quintus Junius, a Spaniard and most probably commander of Sabinus's Spanish cavalry detachment. Colonel Junius and Ambiorix were already well acquainted; Caesar tells us he himself had sent Junius on a number of missions to Ambiorix in the past, missions that had resulted in the peace treaty that Ambiorix had now violated.

The two Roman officers would have been accompanied by General Sabinus's interpreter, Gnaeus Pompeius—no relation to the famous Pompey the Great. Gnaeus Pompeius appears to have later personally reported to Caesar in detail on this meeting and subsequent events, because Caesar was to repeat Ambiorix's words in his memoirs.

"I admit that I am greatly indebted to Caesar," the Eburone leader conceded to the two Roman colonels at the meeting. Caesar had, among other things, previously arranged the release of Ambiorix's son and nephew, who had been prisoners of a neighboring tribe. Yet, said Ambiorix, while he owed Caesar more than one favor, he had been forced into the attack on the Atuatuca camp by the will of his people, who were anxious to take part in a concerted uprising by all the tribes of northern Gaul and throw out the Romans while Caesar was absent. "But now having done my patriotic duty with my attack on your camp, and bearing in mind what I owe Caesar, I urge and implore General Sabinus, as my friend and guest in my country, to consider his safety and that of his soldiers."

The king went on to inform the colonels that a large force of German mercenaries had crossed the Rhine on their way to join the Gallic uprising, and they would reach Atuatuca within days. He then offered safe passage to Sabinus and his troops if they abandoned their camp now and withdrew to join other Roman forces to the west or south.

Surprised and alarmed by the news the colonels brought back, General Sabinus called a council of war of his senior officers to canvass opinions. The question he put to them was simple enough: should they stay, and risk being surrounded and either overrun or starved into submission, or accept Ambiorix's offer and abandon the camp?

The officers attending this meeting included Sabinus's deputy, Brigadier General Cotta, the cavalry commander Colonel Junius, Colonel Arpineius, and the five other tribunes of the 14th, as well as the five colonels leading the force's other unidentified cohorts. Also present were Chief Centurion Titus Balventius and the five other first-rank centurions of the 14th, including Quintus Lucianus, whose son was serving in the legion's ranks. They also may have been joined by Eagle-bearer Petrosidius, as eagle-bearers had influence with the troops and often were brought into councils of war by their generals.

As an authority on the Gauls, General Sabinus's interpreter Pompeius also would have been present. In his memoirs, Caesar rarely penned conversations or speeches verbatim relating to occasions when he was not present. But in this case he was to quote exactly what was said at the council of war, so someone present must have subsequently reported those words to him. Everything points to that again being interpreter Pompeius.

In the headquarters tent, as the officers discussed their alternatives, General Cotta, supported by the majority of tribunes and first-rank centurions, was all for ignoring Ambiorix's offer of safe passage and staying put behind the walls of the camp.

"We can resist any number of Gauls as well as a large force of Germans," Cotta declared. "We aren't short of grain, and before we do run short, relief will arrive from our nearest camps and from Caesar himself." Cotta felt certain that this uprising was localized, that Ambiorix was lying about a widespread revolt.

But General Sabinus could not believe that an obscure and insignificant tribe such as the Eburones would dare to make war against Rome on their own initiative. And he wasn't so sure that if he held out against a besieging army help would necessarily arrive—the other Roman camps also might be under siege and be in just as much trouble as they were. Sabinus thought that in staying at Atuatuca and inviting a siege the Romans might seal their own doom.

Some officers suggested that they wait and see if Ambiorix's prediction proved correct, banking on their hunch that the Germans would fail to appear, that Ambiorix was attempting to bluff the Romans into leaving.

"No, it'll be too late to do anything once the Gauls have put together a larger force, reinforced by the Germans," Sabinus countered. If they were to take Ambiorix's advice, they had to act on it without delay. "We only have a short time to decide."

The debate became an argument, which raged into the night. By this time the dander of the hot-tempered General Cotta was up. "What could be more irresponsible or unprofessional than to follow the advice of an enemy?" he wanted to know.

"That's irrelevant!" Sabinus snapped back. "It's the facts of the case that I'm looking at. It's inconceivable that Ambiorix would have taken this kind of action without being sure of his ground." In Sabinus's mind, a massive revolt was about to sweep all of northern Gaul, and it would be suicidal not to act on the advice of the Eburone leader and get out fast, before all avenues of escape were cut off by the rebels.

Cotta had yet to see any proof of a widespread uprising and was convinced that Ambiorix was trying to trick them into giving up their camp. But Sabinus, accused of being overcautious once before, was not prepared to make an incautious decision that condemned his force to being trapped here at Atuatuca.

"My policy is safe either way," the commander declared. "If nothing serious is under way we'll make our way to the nearest legion without any risk. If the Gauls are united and in league with the Germans, as Ambiorix says, this will be our only chance to escape. The plan recommended by Cotta and you others who differ with me might not involve danger now, but it certainly means a long blockade, and ultimately the threat of death by starvation."

With both men adamant that his was the wiser strategy, neither would give ground. As the hours passed, the tribunes swung their support behind General Sabinus, but Cotta and the centurions stubbornly held their course. For hour upon hour Sabinus tried to respect the opinion of his deputy, but finally, as the pair stood toe-to-toe in the flickering torchlight of the praetorium, red-faced and glaring at each other, the senior general's patience gave way.

"Have it your way!" Sabinus exploded, his voice so loud now that legionaries in the nearest row of tents across the main street from the headquarters could hear him. "I'm no more afraid of death than the rest of you. The men will understand. If this ends in disaster, it's you they'll blame, Cotta! If you'd only agree to my plan, by the day after tomorrow the men would have reached the nearest friendly camp instead of sitting here, isolated, like outcasts and exiles, to be massacred or starved to death!"

To the watching junior officers it looked as if their two generals were about to come to blows. Jumping up, they separated the pair.

"Generals, it's not important whether we go or we stay," said one subordinate. This was possibly Chief Centurion Balventius. Described by Julius Caesar as both brave and highly respected, Balventius would not only have been known to Caesar, but also twelve months earlier the commander in chief would have personally promoted him to chief centurion of the 14th Legion. "Just so long as we all agree on the one course of action," the middle-ranking officer now told his generals. "But if we go on arguing like this, there's no hope for our survival."

The two leaders were parted, and the torrid debate dragged on, until, as midnight arrived, General Cotta, exhausted and in tears of frustration, finally capitulated to his superior's will and gave up his objections.

General Sabinus's plan was adopted by the meeting. It was agreed that the 14th Legion and the other Roman troops at Atuatuca would break camp at daybreak, abandoning their fortified position and heavy equipment, and head west across open country into the territory of the Nervii, in present-day Flanders, to the camp of General Quintus Tullius Cicero. Younger brother of the famous Marcus Cicero the orator, General Cicero had joined Caesar's staff only that year, and commanded a single unidentified legion encamped fewer than fifty miles west of Atuatuca.

Traveling light and fast after leaving behind their heavy baggage and the bulk of their winter grain supply, it would be possible for the men of the 14th to cover the distance in forty-eight hours; legions are on record as not infrequently traveling twenty-five miles a day or more on forced marches.

An emergency order was quickly relayed throughout the camp: "Prepare to march at dawn." The troops stayed up the rest of the night, sorting out their gear, reluctantly parting with winter equipment, supplies, and personal treasures. In the hour before dawn, tents came down after the first trumpeting of "Prepare to march," as Roman army routine required. With the second sounding a long baggage train of pack mules was loaded with essential equipment and valuables by tense legionaries and anxious mule drivers. Carts, wagons, and the heavier loads they normally carried were being left behind. Then, on the third trumpet call, the *decuman* gate, or main gate, the camp gate that faced away from the enemy, was swung open, and the lead elements of the Roman force moved out. The countryside ahead of them was silent and encouragingly empty.

Roman legions literally broke camp. Normally, while the guard cohort removed gate hinges and other difficult-to-replace items, legionaries filed along the camp ramparts, each man taking a pair of stakes three feet long from the wall palisade and strapping them to his backpack, with the intention that when next they made camp each man would hand over his pair of stakes to the wall-building detail. In this way some twelve thousand wall stakes traveled with every legion on the march, ready to be used on the ramparts of the next marching camp. Last of all, the remaining woodwork—gates, guard towers, and the like—was normally put to the torch. But with orders to march light and to be ready to move as soon as the new day dawned, the men left the Atuatuca camp virtually intact.

As the first fingers of the new day's light stretched above the horizon, Colonel Junius's small Spanish cavalry detachment led the way west. General Sabinus had given no special instructions for his troops' disposition on the march. In general marching order, they carried their shields slung over their left shoulder, their helmets were hung around their necks, and a weighty backpack hung from a pole over each man's right shoulder. The legionaries, unhappy at giving up their camp without a fight, despondent about leaving possessions behind, trudged away from the Geer in silence and in loose formation, and, as Caesar tells us, already wearied by the lack of sleep the night before.

Sacrificing the protection of the fortified position, the Roman column straggled long and thin across the Belgian countryside with the baggage mules untidily spread the length of the march. Fresh in the minds of the common soldiers as they marched was the assurance of their officers that they had been granted safe passage by the Eburones all the way to General Cicero's distant camp.

The legionaries' immediate route passed through a thick wood. Two miles from Atuatuca, as the column tramped through a defile in the wood, and with the advance elements about to climb a hill up and out of the defile, thousands of yelling, threatening armed Eburone tribesman sprang from the trees and barred their way. At the same time, thousands more sprang from concealment in the Roman rear.

The column was caught between the two ambushing forces. Ambiorix himself appeared at the head of one, and waved his countrymen forward. With excited yells and bloodcurdling war cries, the Eburones rushed to the attack. Soon the Romans were fighting for their lives at both the front and the rear of the column.

Up front, the Spanish cavalry seem to have been quickly overwhelmed. At their head, Colonel Junius probably was among the first to die, tumbling from the saddle when both rider and steed were impaled after the air filled with spears. Several cavalrymen apparently fought their way through the close-packed Eburone ranks on the back of terrified mounts. Diving through the trees, they made their escape, swinging southeast and heading for the camp of General Titus Labienus, Caesar's second-in-command, in Trever territory. Frantically spurring on wounded horses, they literally rode for their lives along narrow forest tracks. With the Roman infantry swiftly deprived of mounted support, the Eburones employed both mounted men and foot soldiers against the ragged column.

General Sabinus panicked. Dismounting, he ran up and down the column, trying to organize cohorts into battle order. But his orders betrayed his fear, and time and again he changed his mind or contradicted himself. Meanwhile, General Cotta, who'd started the day morose and pessimistic, found his fire, and despite the vindication of his worst fears, quickly organized resistance in his sector. He was soon fighting on foot alongside the rank and file of the 14th as they strove to keep the Gauls from overrunning the column and chewing up strung-out individual Roman units piecemeal one after the other.

The order was passed up and down the column for all troops to abandon the baggage and concentrate in an *orbis*. This ring formation was notoriously a tactic of last resort for the Roman army, a desperate measure that sapped the confidence of legionaries and gave heart to the enemy. Even as the legionaries struggled to mass as ordered, the force's plight was made worse by legionaries dashing from their units to look among the straying baggage animals for their most cherished possessions before retiring to the ring. Their unmilitary efforts would have been accompanied by curses and bellowed orders from centurions telling them to resume formation, and cries of alarm from less materialistic comrades.

There was some hope among the men of the 14th that many Gauls would have pulled out of the attack and gone after the now unguarded baggage. But Ambiorix and his subchieftains passed the word along the entire Gallic line that no man was to leave the fight. There would be plenty of plunder for everyone once the Romans had been defeated, they said. The order was obeyed; the Eburones surrounding the Roman force ignored the lure of spoils and bore into the attack more fiercely than before, determined to finish off the legionaries quickly so they could take their rewards.

The battle raged all through the morning. The fifteen Roman cohorts, formed side-by-side in circular formation with the wounded and the non-combatant mule drivers and personal servants of the officers in the center, found themselves surrounded and increasingly hemmed in by the Gallic horde.

Every now and then a Roman cohort would make an organized and disciplined charge from the circle in an attempt to break up the attack. But each time, the tribesmen to their front rapidly retreated as a group ahead of the cohort, keeping out of range and drawing the Romans on, just as Ambiorix had trained them to do in the days leading up to the move on Atuatuca. Other tribesmen waiting for a gap to be opened up in the circle by a cohort's advance would attack at the site of the opening, aiming their missiles at the unprotected right sides of the exposed Romans in the circle. The cohort taking the offensive had no choice but to withdraw to their original place, to seal the hole they'd created.

Crushed shoulder to shoulder with their comrades, legionaries had little freedom of movement. At the same time, they made easy stationary
targets for the tribesmen who dashed in, threw their spears, or let fly with
their slings, then withdrew again. With each passing hour more men of
the 14th went down, many with crippling leg injuries that left them unable
to stand. The circle grew smaller; the number of legionaries able to offer
resistance grew fewer.

Sabinus was ineffectual as a commander by this stage. He had become
a mere spectator, standing behind the fighting line. The 1st Cohort of the
14th Legion was providing his bodyguard—a legion's 1st Cohort always
stayed with its general. And with a dazed look, almost of incomprehen-
sion, Sabinus would have seen the cohort's commander, Chief Centurion
Balventius, felled by a javelin that pierced both his thighs and pinned him
like a lamb on a spit.

He would have seen Centurion Quintus Lucianus of the 1st Cohort
making a desperate bid to go to the aid of his son, a legionary in his early
twenties, who'd been cut off and surrounded in a vain push forward by his
cohort. And Sabinus would have watched as both father and son were cut
down and killed.

Sabinus would have seen Brigadier General Cotta go down, dropping
his sword and shield and sagging to his knees, felled by a slinger's stone
likely to have been as big as a baseball, which Caesar says hit him in the
middle of the face as he urged a cohort forward at the charge.

As Roman hands reached out to help him, Cotta pulled himself to his
feet, dazed, and with blood streaming down his face. He would have
ripped off his helmet to determine the damage as subordinates crowded
around and a servant tried to stem the bleeding. Pushing the man away,
ignoring the blood, a ringing head, and blurred vision, General Cotta
slipped the elbow strap of his shield back in place, taking a firm grip on
the handle, took up his sword once more, and, seeing the anxious looks of
his men around him, told them in no uncertain terms to worry about the
enemy, not him. Caesar says that despite his wound, Cotta soldiered on,
continuing to rally his men, no doubt mixing encouragement and exple-
tives with alternate breaths.

With mounting casualties, the 14th Legion stood its ground and
fought off the tribesmen from an hour after dawn until past the middle of
the day. As two in the afternoon approached, General Sabinus seemed to
rouse himself. Through the melee he spotted Ambiorix in the distance,
addressing a group of his warriors. Sabinus called over his interpreter,
Gnaeus Pompeius, and instructed him to try to get through to the Eburone
king and seek a truce.

The interpreter, probably a native of Gaul who'd been granted Roman citizenship for his services to Rome and taken the name of her great general, would have swallowed hard as he looked across the field strewn with bodies to his assigned destination. How was he to reach that destination unscathed?

The Field Service Regulations of 1914 used by the British army during World War I state that an individual "who comes with a white flag" to communicate with the other side "has a right to inviolability." The white flag is today a universally recognized symbol, but in 54 B.C. there was no such thing as a white flag for soldiers seeking to discuss a truce or surrender. Romans did have a tradition of displaying an olive branch as a symbol of peace, but there wouldn't have been any olive branches handy at that moment. General Sabinus's envoy would only have had his prayers to protect him.

Interpreter Pompeius must have nodded grimly to the general. "I will do my best, my lord," he would have said.

Somehow, Pompeius did indeed manage to reach King Ambiorix unharmed, and conveyed his general's message. Ambiorix now called a cessation to hostilities.

"Tell your general he may speak to me in person," he told the interpreter. "I hope I can convince my men to spare the lives of the Roman soldiers, but whatever happens, I can personally guarantee that Sabinus himself will come to no harm."

The fighting stopped. Reluctantly the tribesmen held back, maintaining their positions around the trapped legionaries, some glaring at their opponents, others grinning in anticipation of finishing them off before the day was over. After the tumult of the preceding hours of battle, a chilling silence would have fallen over the battleground, broken only by the moans and the groans of the wounded and the dying.

The Roman interpreter returned to his own lines with the eyes of thousands of anxious legionaries on him. The Roman troops would have been wondering why the Eburone attack had halted, wondering what fate their incompetent general had in mind for them now. After Pompeius had brought him the Eburone king's response, Sabinus sought out the wounded General Cotta. He proposed to his deputy that the pair of them should go to Ambiorix to beg for their lives and those of their troops.

Cotta stubbornly refused to budge. "I will not go to discuss anything with an enemy who has not laid down his arms," the bloodied general declared.

Sabinus turned to the colonels and first-rank centurions still standing, and ordered them to follow him. He then pushed his way through the front ranks of the orbis, stepping over the dead and the dying, and strode across the bloodied grass toward the waiting Ambiorix. Interpreter Pompeius would have been close on his general's heels. Despite any misgivings they may have had, the general's subordinates could not disobey a direct order—the tribunes and centurions followed in Sabinus's footsteps. True to his convictions and his mistrust of Ambiorix, General Cotta resolutely held his ground, remaining behind with the troops.

Ambiorix eyed the Roman officers coolly as they approached. "Lay down your arms if you wish to speak with me," he commanded as Sabinus came up to him.

The Roman general meekly lay aside his shield and removed the sword belt that hung over his right shoulder, and dropped it to the ground. He then turned to the officers behind him and ordered them to do the same. Unhappily, his subordinates disarmed.

When the Roman officers' weapons lay on the grass, Ambiorix beckoned them closer. The Roman officers took several more steps forward. The Eburone leader then asked what the Roman commander had to say to for himself.

"I seek terms of surrender," Sabinus glumly announced. When Ambiorix indicated he should go on, Sabinus began to detail terms that would be acceptable to him.

From their lines, his troops could hear his words, some grateful that the fighting might soon be at an end, others frustrated and angry at the prospect of capitulating to these long-haired Belgic barbarians.

As the general and Ambiorix conducted a conversation, which was deliberately protracted by the king, tribesmen slowly closed around Sabinus, leering at the humiliated Roman commander. Someone gave a signal; perhaps it was Ambiorix himself. Spears plunged, swords struck, and to the horror of his watching men, General Sabinus fell dead at the feet of his chief adversary, victim of his own fear and gullibility.

The Eburone hordes let out a fierce, victorious bellow—their customary shout of triumph, Caesar called it. And even as the disarmed Roman tribunes and first-rank centurions turned and made a desperate lunge for their grounded weapons, the Gauls let out another guttural cry and charged forward. The defenseless officers were mowed down. The bodies would be stripped, with tribesmen scuffling over their valuable clothing, armor, fittings, and weapons, even as the battle continued close by. In the German tradition, the heads of the dead officers would have been lopped off, as trophies.

Meanwhile, a wave of triumphant Eburones fell on the men of the ragged orbis. Soldiers of the 14th, so full of the hope of life a few moments before as they witnessed apparent surrender negotiations—even if their perceived future had been as prisoners, probably sold as slaves across the Rhine to the Germans—were suddenly required to fight to save their skins once more. But they were too slow to overcome the double shock of their general's assassination and hopes dashed. The Belgic charge broke the Roman ring.

General Cotta went down fighting. He didn't take a backward step as scores of Eburones swarmed all over him. Around him, thousands of men of the 14th Legion also died fighting. And when no more Roman soldiers offered resistance, the tribesmen hacked defenseless noncombatants to pieces even as they begged for their lives. Just a handful of surrendered legionaries were spared; Ambiorix had plans for them.

Still, some men of the 14th Legion, perhaps as many as several hundred, were able to withdraw in reasonable order back to the camp beside the Geer that they had deserted that morning, and to shut the still-intact gates behind them. Their retreat was made possible by the fact that the majority of tribesmen turned to stripping the dead and rounding up the wandering Roman baggage animals. Led by bareheaded Eagle-bearer Petrosidius, these escapees included men of the 14th Legion's 1st Cohort who had retained their discipline in their determination to carry out their sworn duty to protect their legion's sacred eagle.

Petrosidius himself was cornered outside the camp walls by tribesmen intent on wresting the glittering silver eagle standard of the 14th from his hands. Throwing the eagle over the earth wall to colleagues who had managed to reach the comparative safety of the camp, Petrosidius turned, drew his sword, and raised his small, round, standard-bearer's shield. He took a few Gauls with him before he, too, was cut to pieces.

Those Eburones who persisted in harrying the last survivors of General Sabinus's force as they took refuge in the Atuatuca camp were insufficient in number to overrun it. The few remaining soldiers of the 14th Legion held off their wearying assailants until nightfall, when the attackers finally withdrew. Caesar says the Gauls both revered and feared the night, considering it the domain of their god of the underworld, from whom they believed all Gauls were descended. By the Gallic calculation, the old day ended at sunset, and the new day began with the arrival of night, so that Gauls spoke of the passing of time not in terms of days, as the Romans did and as we do, but in nights.

But the Gauls around Atuatuca didn't retreat far. In the night, the Romans sheltering in the camp would have seen thousands of Belgic campfires burning all around them, would have heard the laughter and victory songs of the celebrating enemy. The leaderless legionaries, seeing that all hope was gone, that no relief column would be coming to save them—no one even knew they were in trouble at this point—and determined not to allow themselves to be captured by the treacherous enemy and be tortured or sold into slavery, entered into a pact.

Next day, the Eburones who renewed the assault on the camp beside the Geer found no answering fire coming from the ramparts. Of the Romans who had taken refuge there the previous day there was not a sign. Tribesmen were soon warily scaling the undefended walls. Once inside the silent camp they discovered the reason for the lack of resistance. The fortress was occupied by a garrison of corpses. Every last proud legionary of the 14th Legion had fallen on his sword and committed suicide in the night.

III

RESCUE ON
THE SAMBRE

G eneral Titus Labienus was the first to hear of the extermination of the 14th Legion. Caesar describes how several survivors managed to escape from the battle during the day and find their way south to the post of Labienus's second in command on the Luxembourg border.

Labienus, in his late thirties, a wealthy noble from eastern Italy and a very astute general, sent Caesar a detailed, written account of the fate of Sabinus and his force, which he obtained by interviewing these escapees. Yet for Labienus, and subsequently Caesar, to be in possession of details of all of Ambiorix's conversations with the Roman leadership at Atuatuca, from initial parley to the surrender negotiations in the woods, the conclusion has to be drawn that interpreter Gnaeus Pompeius was among the survivors.

For the interpreter to have survived means he either escaped following the massacre, or Ambiorix set him free. Perhaps Pompeius played a secret and duplicitous role that resulted in the Sabinus disaster and for this reason his life was spared by the Eburones. We will never know.

Initially, Caesar was ignorant of the fate of the last men of the 14th Legion who managed to fight their way back to the camp at Atuatuca. Labienus's detailed report apparently went no farther than the bloody contest in the woods, perhaps terminating with the death of Sabinus and Cotta. Shocked and angered by the news that he had lost upward of nine thousand officers and men at Atuatuca, Caesar let his hair and beard grow in mourning, as Romans did after a close relative died, and vowed to revenge himself on Ambiorix and his people.

He didn't have long to wait before he discovered Ambiorix's location. A courier arrived from General Cicero in Nervii territory in Flanders bearing the news that his camp, fifty miles west of the site of the Sabinus disaster and built on rising ground not far from the Sambre River, was surrounded and under sustained attack. Cicero had a single legion under his command, probably the veteran Spanish 7th Legion, down to no more than five thousand men after several years of tough campaigning in western France and Britain. The attacking force, made up of the Eburones and seven other Belgian tribes, including the powerful Nervii, who'd flocked to the cause on the news of Ambiorix's bloody success at Atuatuca, totaled sixty thousand by Caesar's estimate.

Taking a leaf from the Roman book, and with the forced "advice" of a handful of Roman prisoners of the 14th and the other unit that Ambiorix had taken in the forest outside Atuatuca and kept alive, the attackers built extensive siege works, toiling under the cover of mantlets—sheds on wheels—and constructing impressive wooden siege towers, which they rolled up the incline toward the camp walls. To harry the attackers, General Cicero sent out legionary volunteers on commando sorties against the works.

A week into the siege, a message reached Cicero from Caesar, telling him the commander in chief was on his way, and urging Cicero and his legionaries to hold on. The message, written in Greek in case it fell into enemy hands, was carried by a Gallic courier who had to join in an attack on the camp walls so he could transmit the message, wrapped around a javelin, which he threw into a Roman guard tower.

At the same time, urgent dispatches went out from Caesar to other generals, ordering them to link up with him on a march to Cicero's support. Leaving behind his heavy baggage so his troops could move at speed, Caesar himself set off to the relief. With the Treveri menacing General Labienus in Luxembourg and preventing him from moving, Caesar reached Cicero's position with only five thousand infantry from an unidentified legion, perhaps his favorite 10th, and two thousand mixed cavalry.

The tribes had kept General Cicero's men cut off for weeks. They'd burned to the ground all his camp buildings, using bullets of red-hot clay slung over the walls and onto thatched roofs. And they'd caused heavy casualties among the defenders. But the Gauls hadn't been able to force their way into the Roman fortification. Now, with news from their patrols that Caesar himself was approaching, the Gauls terminated the siege, pulling out to march to intercept the Roman commander in chief.

Outnumbered almost ten to one, Caesar built a camp across the valley from the advancing Gauls and their German allies. They also pitched camp, with a stream separating the two distant troop concentrations. The tribesmen, daunted by Caesar's reputation, decided to wait for reinforcements before they took him on. In his memoirs, Caesar was to write that he took steps to give the impression that he had a lesser force than he in fact possessed, by building a camp smaller than usual. And to let the enemy think that he and his men were afraid of them, he erected elaborate additional defenses.

The ruse worked. Tempted by the possibility of killing Caesar himself, and expecting more of Caesar's legions to come marching into the valley any day to bolster his current small force, the Gallic leaders chose not to hesitate any longer. At dawn one morning, their thousands of massed cavalry splashed across the stream and came thundering all the way up to Caesar's position.

Caesar ordered his own cavalry to withdraw inside the camp. Then, to make it look as though he was afraid to come out again, he increased the height of the camp's main wall and sealed the camp gateways with walls of earthen bricks. Now the tribes' foot soldiers also flooded across the valley to surround Caesar's position. In response, Caesar ordered his men down from the ramparts. The astonished Gauls launched volleys of spears over the vacant walls. Meeting no response, the tribesmen prepared their arms and equipment for an all-out attack on the Roman position.

As their leaders carefully studied the defensive obstacles in their path, Gallic heralds were sent on horseback to yell over the trenches and walls of the defenses, offering clemency to anyone in Caesar's camp who defected by 9:00 A.M. After no defectors had appeared by that hour, the order went out for the tribes to launch a concerted assault on the Roman position.

It would be a methodical assault. Rather than try to file up to the walls via the narrow roadways to the four gates and be mown down by the defenders massed above the gates in towers and on ramparts, the plan was to go against the wall along its entire circumference. To achieve this, the Gauls would have to eliminate the trench system separating them from the wall. Tens of thousands of tribesmen lay aside their weapons and set to work dismantling the wooden palisade on the Roman perimeter. That done, they began to dig, shoveling earth into the Roman ditch. The plan was simple: when they had filled in the ditch, they would scale the camp's main wall from all sides at once.

The digging probably continued for an hour or two, until suddenly a Roman trumpet call sounded inside the camp. Perspiring Gallic diggers would have looked up with scowls. Then, suddenly, the apparently impregnable brick walls blocking each gateway tumbled outward. Thousands of legionaries charged out from all four camp gates in formation, followed by the Roman cavalry. Caught by surprise, unarmed diggers trapped outside the camp walls were trampled and butchered. The remaining tribesmen, who had been standing back in their bunched clans waiting to go against the wall, watched in disbelief as their comrades were overrun.

Panic thrives on numbers. Casting aside their weapons, the tribesmen of Gaul ran for their lives, heading for the protection of nearby woods and marshes, and pursued by the much less numerous Romans. Not one Gaul attempted to make a stand. Caesar was to say that his force didn't suffer a single casualty that day.

Among those tribesmen who escaped was King Ambiorix, who, with many of his Eburones, fled back to his home territory to the east. The uprising initiated by Ambiorix and that had seen the destruction of the 14th Legion dissolved in minutes there on the valley floor. But before they ran, the Eburones murdered their last captive survivors of the 14th Legion, the POWs from Atuatuca who'd been forced, under threat of death, to advise the rebels on siege tactics at the Sambre. Their bodies, with throats slit, would be found among the Gallic dead. The Eburones did take the prized silver eagle standard of the 14th Legion with them. The lost eagle was never recovered.

Later in the day, Caesar linked up with General Cicero and his beleaguered legion on the Sambre. Their position was surrounded by deserted Gallic siege equipment, while, inside, the camp was a fire-blackened ruin. Caesar says that when he paraded the haggard men of Cicero's legion to praise and reward them for their courageous defense, he found that nine out of ten legionaries of the 7th had been wounded during the siege.

From Eburone prisoners taken that morning Caesar heard the final chapter in the story of the annihilation of the 14th Legion, of how the Eburones had found the bodies of the legionaries who'd taken their own lives behind the walls of the camp at Atuatuca.

As he stood on a tribunal in front of the assembled men of Cicero's force, Caesar first praised them for their valor, for holding out for so long against such numbers. Then he told them about the disaster that had overtaken their comrades of the 14th Legion. He says that they were stunned by the news.

"The defeat of that legion was due entirely to the blundering rashness of General Sabinus," he quickly added. "You men have no reason to be concerned about it." But concerned they were. This was a Roman military disaster, a reverse of a magnitude Caesar's self-confident troops had not thought possible up to that time. Caesar tried to reassure them. "With the help of Providence your valor has avenged that defeat."

But in his heart Caesar would have known that no Roman could genuinely consider that vengeance had yet been fully extracted. He would have to do much more to wipe Sabinus's defeat from the minds of both friend and foe. To the former it was a black mark on his to date impeccable military record, an indication that he was fallible after all. To the latter it was proof that Caesar could err and could be beaten.

For hundreds of years to come, General Sabinus's fatal blunder in Belgium would still be spoken of in Roman circles as an example of foolishness ranking with the ill-fated expedition of Lieutenant General Marcus Crassus, father of Caesar's quartermaster, and onetime victor over the slave army of the escaped gladiator Spartacus; Crassus was to lose his life and his army to the Parthians at the crushing defeat of Carrhae in Iran in just the following year, 53 B.C.

Like their general, the men of the first enlistment of the 14th Legion would be remembered for the disgrace of defeat and the loss of their eagle. Unlike their general, they also would be remembered for their bravery— of the men who'd fought to the last, standing their ground, and for those last few who'd taken the noble way out, as Romans saw it, of taking their own lives rather than surrendering. It would give their successors who had to live with the shame of the legion's annihilation in Belgium a valorous example to live up to in decades and centuries to come.

As the winter of 54–53 B.C. loomed, Caesar sent urgent dispatches to Rome. One would have contained an account of the Sabinus disaster for the Senate, as well as a defense of his own role in it. But far from being put on the back foot by the destruction of the 14th Legion, Caesar was planning to take an unprecedented step, in a career dotted with precedents.

To begin with, he asked the Senate for new officers to be allotted to him—two generals to take the places of the dead Sabinus and Cotta, another general and colonels to boost the size of his staff to cope with his plans for the new campaigning season. Caesar also asked Pompey the Great for a favor. Caesar, Pompey, and Crassus Sr. had been ruling the Roman world for the past few years via a three-way military junta that historians have called the First Triumvirate. Even though he was a couple of years older than Caesar, Pompey was his son-in-law, by virtue of the fact that he had married Caesar's daughter Julia. The marriage had cemented the alliance of the two generals, an alliance that permitted Caesar to do as he pleased in Gaul, safe in the knowledge that he had Pompey's support back at the capital.

To the desolation of both her father and her loving husband, Julia would soon die in childbirth. Her death would begin the disintegration of the close friendship and partnership between the two generals. But in these late months of 54 B.C. that partnership still held firm. For reasons of friendship and patriotism, according to Caesar, Pompey quickly agreed to hand over recruits he'd recently levied in northern Italy, men he was entitled to draft under a Senate vote that empowered him to raise troops in all Roman provinces when he saw fit, recruits enrolled but not yet assigned to units.

The conscripts supplied by Pompey were soon joined by more men recruited from throughout northern Italy and southwestern Switzerland by Caesar's new generals, Silanus, Antistius, and Sextius. Before the winter was out, the three generals marched a total of eighteen thousand recruits across the alps to join Caesar. Twelve thousand of these men were formed into two new legions, the 15th and 16th. The remaining men went into a re-formed 14th Legion.

Never in recorded Roman history would an annihilated legion be instantly re-formed like this. Julius Caesar saw things differently from most men. Both stubborn and petty at times, he had neither the desire nor the intention to create a permanent reminder of his failure at Atuatuca by retiring the number 14. Caesar simply created a new 14th Legion, almost as if the ill-starred first enlistment had never existed. But Providence had been determined to scar the 14th Legion from birth, and not even Julius Caesar was to cheat Providence, as he was soon to discover.

IV

CICERO'S BLUNDER

K ing Ambiorix looked up in astonishment.

"The Romans are here!" was the cry from men who had been working outside in the spring sunshine and who were now rushing indoors, wide-eyed with terror. "The Romans are here!"

After the rout outside Julius Caesar's camp in the valley of the Sambre the previous year, Ambiorix had fled back to his homeland between the Meuse and the Rhine and kept his head down, exchanging messages with other tribal leaders throughout northern Gaul and biding his time as a new Gallic uprising came to the boil. The revolutionary Trever leader Indutiomarus had been tracked down and executed by Caesar's deputy General Labienus, who sent the rebel's severed head to Caesar. But that had only made the Treveri all the more determined to overthrow the Romans. The Treveri had brought together a new coalition of rebel tribes from the North Sea to the Rhine, enlisting Ambiorix as a member of their revolutionary council, and keeping him informed of developments.

As for Caesar, Ambiorix would have heard that the general had canceled his plans to return to Italy for the winter as usual, that before the winter of 54–53 B.C. was out he had led a force of four legions back into the territory of the Nervii to the west and ravaged the countryside. The Nervii had quickly surrendered to Caesar, but not before large numbers of cattle and prisoners were taken and handed over to his legionaries as booty. Caesar had then called a meeting of all the leaders of the tribes of Gaul at the town of Lutetia, capital of the Parisii tribe, modern Paris. Just four tribes apart from the Eburones failed to send ambassadors to the meeting—the Treveri, Carnutes, Senones, and Menapii. Now, at least, Caesar knew who his enemies were.

In the spring of 53 B.C., following the Paris meeting, Caesar marched into the territory of the Senones and the Carnutes, forcing them to submit. Then he turned his attention to the Menapii, who lived in close harmony with the Eburones on the northern border of Ambiorix's territory. Sweeping through the marshy Menapian homelands with five legions, burning their farms, confiscating their property, Caesar swiftly forced the Menapii to surrender.

Caesar hadn't forgotten Ambiorix. His very name seemed to taunt him and to haunt him. Repeatedly in his memoirs Caesar mentioned the man who had embarrassed him at Atuatuca, and stated his intent to rob the Eburone king of friends and allies before he went after him in person. After making the Menapii promise to hand over Ambiorix should he seek refuge with them, Caesar swung away and marched east, toward the land of the Treveri along the Moselle. His object now was to link up with General Labienus before the Treveri's German allies reinforced them for a spring offensive against the Romans, as had been agreed by the revolutionaries. That may have been the last that Ambiorix had heard of the Roman army. Until now.

When Caesar linked up with General Labienus, Caesar found that his able deputy had already decoyed the Treverans into a battle and routed them. Determined to teach the German tribes a lesson about the foolishness of messing with Rome, Caesar then built a wooden bridge of his own design across the Rhine, in ten days. The rapidity of this feat of engineering, involving a bridge forty feet wide built on piers sunk in the deep and fast-flowing Rhine—in his memoirs Caesar proudly details the construction technique he employed—still amazes engineers today. Caesar then crossed the Rhine in force.

At the time, the German tribes east of the Rhine were stunned to discover half a dozen Roman legions suddenly on their side of the great river. The powerful Suebi tribe at first assembled its clans to fight Caesar, but daunted by his reputation, they withdrew into heavily forested territory in central Germany and sent for help from other tribes. Caesar hadn't thought through what he wanted to achieve with this operation, which was nothing more than a demonstration of strength. After eighteen days east of the Rhine he pulled back across the river and tore down the eastern end of his new Rhine bridge so the Germans couldn't use it. Then, at last, he turned to settle the score with Ambiorix.

The wheat was beginning to ripen across northern Gaul as Caesar set off from the Rhine and headed along the forested tracks of the northern Ardennes. He marched with ten legions now, including the revamped 14th. To maintain the element of surprise, Caesar formed most of his cavalry into a flying column under the command of a young colonel, Lucius

Minucius Basilus, and sent them ahead at speed. They pushed west with orders not to light fires overnight to ensure that the Eburones had no warning of their coming.

Colonel Basilus's cavalry surprised Eburone farmers working in their fields. As the troopers swept through the wheat with javelins flying and swords flashing, some tribesmen were permitted to escape. Roman scouts followed the fleeing farmers at a discreet distance. As Colonel Basilus hoped, they led him to King Ambiorix.

Ambiorix had retired to his mansion in the forest. Caesar says that most Gauls built their houses in woods or beside rivers, or both, because the locations were cool in summer. Ambiorix's residence would have been a typical Gallic longhouse, its walls of wood and mud, the thatched roof pitched high as a protection against the weight of winter snow. There, Ambiorix had gathered many of his surviving retainers, all his many horses, his carriages and worldly worth, and had stockpiled weapons for the day news of the renewed Gallic uprising arrived.

"The Romans are here! The Romans are here!"

Panic seized Ambiorix's attendants as the Roman cavalry galloped into the clearing around the house. The king's men quickly barricaded themselves inside the building. As the auxiliary troopers dismounted and tried to force their way in the front, one of Ambiorix's bodyguards succeeded in finding a horse for his leader and slipping him out the back. Ambiorix, alone, rode away through the trees undetected, while his retainers and friends fought a desperate delaying action.

Caesar was not pleased that his adversary evaded capture. In his memoirs, he put Ambiorix's escape down to a great stroke of luck. Ambiorix was delivered from danger by "the all-prevailing power of Fortune," he said. The hunt for King Ambiorix, destroyer of Caesar's original 14th Legion, now became an obsessive quest.

Caesar arrived in central Belgium with his main legionary army, and trailed by a convoy of carts and wagons bearing the merchants, slave traders, pimps, and prostitutes who attached themselves to his baggage train wherever he went during the campaigning months. These camp followers—the lixae, the Romans called them collectively—were a necessary evil to Roman commanders. The women served the obvious purpose. Merchants traded in the marketplaces of the legion camps, buying the booty the soldiers acquired during each campaign—goods, chattels, animals, and prisoners—merchandise the traders would take away to sell at inflated prices in town marketplaces and at slave auctions from Gaul to Spain to Italy.

According to Plutarch, Caesar, during his eight years of active operations in Gaul, was to kill a million Gauls and sell another million into slavery. Some would be sold for life, others for twenty or thirty years, depending on Caesar's attitude to them or their tribe at the time of their capture. We don't know what price the prisoners were achieving for their sellers at this time, but two decades earlier, according to Plutarch, men being sold as slaves in the legionary camp of General Lucius Lucullus during his eastern campaigns went for four times the price of an ox.

As he reached the Geer River, Caesar learned that Ambiorix had sent messengers far and wide, telling his countrymen to disperse and hide. Some hid in forests, others in marshes. Others were taken in by friendly tribes, others still found refuge along the North Sea coast. But old Catuvolcus, Ambiorix's co-ruler, too weak to flee, took poison made from seeds and foliage of the yew tree, which contain a toxic alkaloid. Later Caesar was to learn that, as he died, the old man cursed his younger colleague for embroiling him in the failed revolt.

Ambiorix himself seemed to have vanished, and Caesar, now reunited with Colonel Basilus and his cavalry in the heart of Eburone territory, wasn't entirely sure what to do next. He had received a report that Ambiorix was heading for a hiding place at the western end of the Ardennes with the few Eburone cavalry he'd been able to muster. But the report could have been false, deliberately fabricated to lead the Romans away from the king, not to him. And Caesar knew it.

He decided to divide his army into three divisions that would conduct a wide-ranging reconnaissance in force. General Labienus would drive northwest, toward the coast, with three legions; General Trebonius would push southwest, with three legions; and Caesar himself would march down toward the Scheldt River and the western end of the Ardennes, with another three legions. To enable each force to travel light and fast, Caesar left all the legions' heavy baggage in the territory of the Eburones, guarded by one legion under the command of General Cicero. That legion was the new 14th. And the place Caesar chose for them to hole up was a deserted fort on the Geer River, the fort built at Atuatuca the previous year by the now dead legionaries of the first enlistment of the 14th Legion.

Caesar would later be criticized for installing the new recruits of the 14th Legion at Atuatuca. The majority of Romans, even the most educated of men, were highly superstitious. They believed in omens, in astrology, in ghosts. Caesar himself was a pragmatic man, and although he'd held the post of *pontifex maximus,* or high priest of Rome, since 63 B.C. and was responsible for overseeing the official auguries of the priests and magistrates at Rome, throughout his career, right up to and including the fateful last day of his life, he demonstrated a lack of interest in omens and signs. So the thought that it might be bad luck for the latest enlistment of the 14th to be quartered where their brothers had died so tragically seems not to have entered his mind. In his memoirs, Caesar was to excuse his choice of the site by saying he had several reasons. But primarily, he said, he chose it because the fortifications built the previous year were still intact and could be put to good use.

Agreeing that they would aim to complete their sweeps within seven days and meet back at Atuatuca in a week's time if they hadn't found Ambiorix, Caesar and his two divisional commanders set off, leading sixty thousand Roman legionaries and auxiliary Gallic cavalry in search of the Belgian leader. In addition to several thousand noncombatants, they left upward of seven thousand fighting men at Atuatuca—the six thousand new recruits of the 14th Legion, two hundred auxiliary cavalry, and hundreds of legionaries on the army's sick list—it seems that a severe gastric infection had been going through the more established legions since the winter, laying low large numbers of men who'd served for as many as eight years in their legions until then.

Caesar's chronic impatience as well as a fine tactical sense gave him a dislike for heavy baggage, which, although necessary to an army campaigning in foreign territory, slowed him down. It was a dislike his protégé Mark Antony would inherit. But while Antony would one day pay a heavy price for failing to adequately protect his baggage, in Gaul Caesar never left less than a legion with his. And even then, he kept his main grain supply with him. As he set off in search of Ambiorix, Caesar left just seven days' rations with the men at Atuatuca. And as he marched away, Caesar told General Cicero that to be on the safe side he was not to let anyone venture outside the camp over the coming week.

As the three forces disappeared from view, men of the 14th Legion industriously set to work repairing and improving the camp. But some superstitious souls in the ranks grumbled that it was bad luck to be garrisoned in this ill-starred place. And as it turned out, they were right.

A week passed. On the eighth day since Caesar marched away, General Cicero began to worry. There was neither hide nor hair of Caesar or his fellow generals. Not even a cavalry scout arrived to tell Cicero that Caesar was on his way back. Cicero had taken his commander in chief at his word, and he'd allowed his men to consume their seven days of rations. Now, on day eight, they had nothing left to eat.

Within hours of Caesar's departure, Cicero's men had begun to com-plain about being cooped up inside the camp. Despite these rumblings in the ranks, General Cicero had obeyed Caesar's orders to the letter, not even permitting a single servant to venture beyond the camp walls. Men grumbled that it was as bad as being blockaded by the enemy. Yet where was the enemy?

It was pointed out to Cicero that three miles from the camp a field of ripened wheat stood invitingly ready to be harvested. His officers recom-mended that rather than let the men starve, they could send out a large and well-armed foraging party to cut down the wheat and bring it back to camp. Cicero could see no reason why not, and the order was given to organize the foraging party.

Five cohorts of the 14th—three thousand men, half the new legion—were paraded for the mission, together with several troops of cavalry. In addition, three hundred experienced legionaries on the sick list, men from a variety of legions, had recovered sufficiently to also be involved, and these volunteers formed up in a separate detachment. The entire group would go out under the command of a young tribune of the 14th, Colonel Gaius Trebo-nius, who may have been related to the thirty-seven-year-old General Gaius Trebonius, who was leading Caesar's southern division at that moment.

The camp's decuman gate opened. It faced south, toward friendly ter-ritory. The cavalrymen would have appeared first, leading their short, neat Gallic ponies out the gate, then mounting up—unless an emergency com-bat situation existed, no man was permitted to ride in a Roman camp, not even a commander. Once settled in their saddles, which were equipped with four horns, two at the front and two at the back, and which provided such a secure seat that Roman horsemen had neither the need for nor knowledge of stirrups, and with an oval shield on their left arm, a short lance in their right hand, and a long cavalry sword, the *spatha*, on their hip, each trooper would have urged his steed forward and trotted off to patrol the route ahead.

On the heels of the cavalry, the five legion cohorts, then the sick-list detachment, came out the gate, marching ten abreast behind their various standards. They were followed by a flood of animals, as hundreds or even thousands of mules and packhorses were herded in the soldiers' wake by unarmed attendants—General Cicero also had decided that it would do no harm to allow many of the army's hungry baggage animals to be taken out to be exercised and to graze while the wheat was being cut.

With all four gates remaining open behind it, the column moved along a narrow bridge of earth leading out through the camp's outer entrench-ments, then passed through the congregation of tents and parked vehicles of the army's camp followers, who were never permitted to reside inside a legionary camp, and into the countryside beyond. From their tents, the traders would have watched the soldiers go. Some probably set off after them, to do a little business in the wheat fields if the officers gave them the chance.

In marching order, the legionaries had their shields and helmets slung over shoulders and around necks, while their gear included scythes for lopping grain, and sacks for its collection. It would have taken them upward of an hour to tramp over the low hill separating the camp from the gently swaying, waist-high field of wheat. Once there, they neatly stacked shields and javelins, squad by squad; then, with the cavalry and perhaps one legion cohort standing guard, the rest set to work in the sunshine.

After several hours of uneventful industry the reapers had filled their sacks and, led by their colonel, the men cheerfully set off back for the fortress. The cavalry proceeded out in advance as before, and the sick-party detachment and the baggage animals followed behind. It had been a profitable day's work, and the men were looking forward to the night's meal of steaming, fresh bread and olive oil.

Julius Caesar tells in detail of what followed. It started back at the camp.

"What is it? What's going on?" Wearing just his soiled tunic, Publius Sextius Baculus, chief centurion of the 12th Legion, staggered from a tent erected not far from General Cicero's headquarters, blinking as the bright sunshine met his red eyes.

The camp at Atuatuca was in an uproar. In various states of undress, raw recruits of the 14th Legion—some armed, some not—were running in all directions, many looking confused, the rest, terrified. The camp ramparts were unmanned. From the rear gate nearby came the sound of fighting—the ringing of metal on metal, the crunching of blade on leather and wood, alarmed cries, and, above it all, the yelling of German voices.

"Germans have surrounded us!" came one Roman voice in answer to Chief Centurion Baculus's question.

"Caesar has been overrun!" said someone else. "Our army has perished! And we're to be next!"

"It's this place!" another man cried. "It's haunted by the ghosts of Cotta and Sabinus. We're doomed!"

"That's right, we should never have been sent to this infernal place," a quaking young soldier declared. "We're destined to share the fate of our comrades of the first enlistment who fell here."

"Enough of that talk!" growled Baculus. "Where's the enemy?"

"They're in the camp!" came a yelping reply. "The place is already lost!"

"We'll see about that!" said the chief centurion angrily. "Here. Give me your shield." With that he yanked the long, curved shield from the frightened legionary's left arm. "And you, your sword!" he snapped to another man.

The recruit handed over his sword before Baculus swung around, determined to do what he was trained to do. Tall, skinny as a stick, he strode away, heading for the praetorian gate, pushing aside youngsters of the 14th who were milling around looking for someone to tell them where to assemble, which way to advance.

Baculus had been chief centurion of the 12th ever since it had been formed in northern Italy five years earlier. We don't know what his background was prior to that, but to receive such a senior appointment from Caesar suggests that Baculus had been marching with him for years. In 57 B.C., within months of his appointment, Centurion Baculus had been locked in a famous and desperate battle against the Nervii beside the Sambre River. With fellow centurions of the 12th dead and dying all around him, Baculus had been so severely wounded he'd been unable to keep his feet. From the ground, he'd stubbornly continued to direct and rally his men. Soon after he'd recovered from his multiple wounds, his legion had been surrounded in St. Bernard's Pass by Swiss tribesmen as General Servius Galba unsuccessfully tried to force a crossing over the Alps on Caesar's orders, and on that occasion Baculus had helped lead a breakout that saved the 12th from extinction.

Yet, to Baculus's chagrin, it had ultimately taken an epidemic, not a battle wound, to separate him from his legion. A week back, he'd been left behind at Atuatuca, suffering from the same ailment that had swept through the ranks of the older legions. But instead of soon recovering, like the three hundred men now out with the reaping party, Baculus had only become all the more unwell. So sick, in fact, that for the past five days he'd been unable to eat a thing. But Publius Baculus was a *primus pilus*, holder of the most senior and respected rank to which an enlisted man could then aspire. There were even a few centurions in Caesar's legions who were of Equestrian rank—knights—yet these men, too, deferred to Chief Centurion Baculus. Now, fired by pride, driven by adrenaline, the physically weak but single-minded Baculus reached the Atuatuca camp's rear gate.

What he found was a scene of carnage. The rear gate, like all the camp gates, had been left open during the day. Now, the ten men of the guard cohort who had been stationed there lay dead or dying in the gateway, surrounded by the bloodied corpses of big, bearded, long-haired German warriors. Beyond the gate, all the way to the entrenchment line, were more German bodies. Several horses lay dead in the entrenchments, their legs jutting grotesquely into the air. The legion sentries had done their duty before they fell, had prevented the attackers from entering the camp—the first Germans had obviously ridden all the way up to the gate before being slain.

Beyond the trench line, the tents of the camp followers were in mayhem as hundreds of heavily armed Germans ran amok, indiscriminately killing the defenseless noncombatants, men and women alike, and plundering their goods. As Baculus surveyed the scene, more Germans appeared on horseback on the far side of the thirty-foot-wide bridge of earth that cut through the entrenchments. Yelling excitedly, they pointed to the open gateway, where, to their glee, just the single pale chief centurion, devoid of even an armored vest or helmet, stood unsteadily in their path.

Baculus would have fought Germans on numerous occasions during the years Caesar had been campaigning in Gaul, and seems to have picked up a little of the German tongue in the process. According to Caesar, he heard the riders at the entrenchments call to each other: "It's true, just as the Eburone prisoner told us! There's no garrison at the Roman camp."

"Come on," said one of their leaders. "We can't let such a piece of luck slip through our fingers!"

They quickly dismounted, sent their horses away, drew their long, round-nosed German broadswords, and advanced, grinning, over their own dead toward Chief Centurion Baculus.

The centurion was bellowing at the top of his lungs, calling each centurion of the guard cohort by name, summoning them to his side, as giant Germans struck at him with overhead, two-handed swipes of their swords. Baculus parried the blows with his shield, then thrust the point of his own sword into faces and necks with powerful, short-arm jabs. One after the other, Germans dropped at his feet dead or reeled away with screams of pain and clutching at terrible face wounds. But still the enemy came on.

Baculus probably didn't even feel the pain of the wounds the Germans inflicted on him as he fought. But he would have seen and heard several centurions of the 14th's guard cohort now join him in the gateway with a handful of men. Shields raised and locked together, they quickly formed a barrier on either side of Baculus and began launching javelins into the ranks of the Germans, who continued to pour along the narrow embankment toward the gate.

The German attack slackened for want of numbers. Uncertain, warriors held back. At the same time, more legionaries of the 14th Legion arrived to form up behind the centurions at the gate. In the lull that now prevailed, Chief Centurion Baculus looked down, to see that his own blood was flowing. And then five days without food and his growing loss of blood combined to rob him of his strength. Baculus blacked out, and collapsed to the ground.

Willing hands reached down and dragged the unconscious chief centurion to his feet. Rather than break their shield line, the men of the 14th lifted him above their heads and passed him hand to hand to the back of the group, from where noncombatants carried him out of the firing line for attention to his wounds. We never hear of him again.

The Germans were spreading out. Repulsed at the praetorian gate, they galloped around the fortifications to the other three gates, all of which continued to stand open. But as they did, the example of Chief Centurion Baculus and the men at the rear gate gave heart to many of the raw recruits of the 14th Legion, who began to reinforce the guard details at the other gates and to man the ramparts at last, from where they could rain missiles down on the attackers.

Amid the struggle, cries of alarm went up from Germans congregating at the front gate. Men were pointing with concern to the south. Just above the top of a low hill in the distance the bobbing standards of an approaching Roman force could be seen.

Marching along with their full sacks of grain, the men of the reaping party heard the sounds of shouting coming from the direction of their Atuatuca camp. On Colonel Trebonius's orders, the cavalry galloped ahead to determine the cause of the tumult. Broaching the top of the low, grassy hill that separated the main body of the detachment from the camp, the troopers saw that the fort was under attack from a number of mounted Germans. The cavalrymen wheeled about and headed back to report to the colonel.

Seeing even the experienced men of the sick-list detachment looking unnerved by the cavalry's news, the inexperienced Colonel Trebonius ordered a halt to the march and called a hasty conference with his thirty or so centurions. As the raw recruits of the five 14th Legion cohorts waited anxiously for orders, the officers began arguing among themselves. Meanwhile, the noncombatants abandoned the baggage animals and flocked in a panic-stricken mass to the top of the little hill, thinking it offered some protection.

Colonel Trebonius was all for adopting a wedge formation, a textbook defense against cavalry, and then making a dash for the camp. Some men might be cut off, he said, but the majority should reach the camp if they all stuck together. In his twenties, the colonel appears to have been on his first posting. Probably only joining the legion that spring, he didn't enjoy the confidence of his centurions—they said it would be suicidal for untried infantry to attempt to cross so much open ground against mounted troops. The centurions advocated making a stand on the hill.

The Germans were pulling out of the attack on the camp. Thinking that the approaching standards must belong to Caesar's main army, they sent a group of riders to check them out. These Germans rode to the top of the hill, scattering the noncombatants clustered there, who ran back to Colonel Trebonius and his troops. Seeing the contemptuously small force of Roman infantry and cavalry halted beyond the hill, the Germans galloped back to their comrades. Soon, all surviving members of the German raiding party, numbering some two thousand men, had mounted up. Cutting down a few thousand Roman foot soldiers caught in the open sounded like good sport. Leaving their dead at the camp gates, the Germans charged in the direction of the reaping party.

As the sounds of pounding hooves grew louder, the centurions of the 14th ignored their colonel, ordering their cohorts to hurry to the hill and form up to make a stand. The old soldiers of the sick-list detachment thought this was crazy, and told Trebonius they were with him and his wedge-and-dash plan. The cavalry was undecided which option to take. Trebonius swiftly formed the three hundred experienced sick-list men into a small wedge, and just as the entire German cavalry force swooped over the hill and came in for the attack, the colonel and the wedge set off at the double for Atuatuca.

The Germans were confronted with a choice of objectives: the small, closely packed formation making an organized run for it and heading determinedly straight toward them, the much larger group forming up on the hill, the baggage animals roaming free, the sacks of wheat left dumped all over the river plain. The drive of the tightly packed wedge bristling with javelin points made the Germans part to the left and right of its advance. In the wake of the wedge, the auxiliary cavalry spurred their horses forward and followed close behind. Seeing the gap open up in the German line, many of the noncombatants now also made a dash for the camp through the same opening, as the Germans turned their attention to the Romans lining up in ragged cohorts on the hillside.

On the gentle slope of the hill, the remaining noncombatants tried to get as close as they could to the sacred standards of the legion's assembled maniples and cohorts, expecting the men around the standards to put up the fiercest fight of all. With civilians mingling in their ranks, cursing young legionaries of the 14th only became all the more agitated and undisciplined. All the while, their centurions were barking orders, trying to keep lines tight, shields raised, and noncombatants out of the way.

German cavalrymen galloped around the five surrounded cohorts, letting fly with javelins on the run or sweeping in with flashing swords, then pulling away again, leaving increasing numbers of legionaries dead and wounded. Legionaries on the hill now saw that Colonel Trebonius and the wedge had made it all the way to the camp unscathed, as had the cavalry. Most of the noncombatants who'd chosen that option also had gotten through. Angry that their centurions had made the wrong choice for them, groups of soldiers on the slope pulled out of the fight and made a run for the camp.

Before long, the organized ranks on the hill began to dissolve, as two-thirds of the men of the 14th Legion cohorts tried to make it to the camp. One large group at the forefront of the flight was soon caught by Germans in a dip and surrounded. The senior centurions in the group, realizing their error in not siding with their colonel earlier, were determined not to compound their mistake. They'd been promoted from junior grades in other legions to their present grades in the 14th on account of their bravery, says Caesar, and they were determined not to forfeit their reputations. Banding together, the handful of centurions made a charge up onto the rim of the depression, an unexpected offensive move that scattered over-confident German horsemen.

As Germans fell back in the face of the centurions' charge, a gap opened in their ring that gave many of the centurions' men the chance to break out of the encirclement and resume the dash for the fort. To their own surprise, these men reached the camp as their centurions behind them kept the Germans busy. But none of the centurions survived. Greatly outnumbered, they all fell as they made a last stand.

Back on the hill, almost the equivalent of two cohorts, a thousand men, hadn't budged, had retained their discipline and their formation. But now they were entirely cut off. With the group of centurions downed, all German horsemen now turned to concentrate solely on the men on the hill. The young legionaries found themselves outnumbered two to one, bunched up, trying to fight off drives through their ranks by German horses, to avoid the overhand thrusts of German lances, the decapitating swipes of German swords. No help came from the camp as their ranks were progressively chopped down. By late in the day, the thousand 14th Legion men on the hill had been wiped out to a man.

The gates of the camp had been closed. From the ramparts, the surviving men of the 14th Legion, bleeding, hungry, and humbled, watched forlornly as Germans stripped the corpses of their Roman friends and relatives on the battlefield, rounded up the straying baggage animals, and loaded up the abandoned wheat that had ultimately cost the 14th Legion so dearly. General Cicero probably couldn't bring himself to look. We hear not a word of him throughout the day's action. No orders came from him, no sallies were led by him—as Caesar would soon note.

The Germans withdrew to the woods behind the camp from which they had launched their attack earlier in the day. There, they had stored Eburone cattle and other plunder accumulated during this very profitable raid into Belgium. Leading their newly acquired Roman army pack animals, they turned their backs on Atuatuca and withdrew east, to recross the Rhine and victoriously return home.

As Caesar was to learn later from prisoners, the raiders were members of the Sugambri tribe, Germans whose homeland was to the northeast, between the Ruhr and Sieg Rivers. On hearing that the Romans had devastated the Eburones, the Sugambri had put together their mounted raiding party in the hope of mopping up some of the Eburone spoils, and crossed the Rhine in boats and on rafts thirty miles below Caesar's recently built and dismantled bridge. Described by Caesar as born fighters and bandits, the Sugambri had seized a number of roaming cattle and taken several Eburones prisoner before one of the captives had informed them that Caesar and his Roman army were campaigning well to the south and north, and that in Caesar's absence all the valuable property belonging to his army was being stored at Atuatuca.

None of this background was then known to Cicero or his men, and as the Sugambri returned home, the rumor quickly circulated around the Atuatuca camp tents that this German force had been part of a much larger Gallo-Germanic army that must have wiped out Caesar and the legions. So that night, when Colonel Gaius Volusenus, Caesar's regular point man, arrived at Atuatuca with most of Caesar's Gallic cavalry, few at the camp believed him when he said that Caesar and the legions were intact, unharmed, and close behind him. It took Caesar's return within the next day or so for the men of the 14th Legion to finally acknowledge that Volusenus had been telling the truth.

Caesar wrote in his memoirs that he took General Cicero to task for allowing the 14th Legion cohorts outside the camp, against his express orders. But apart from that—officially, anyway—he went easy on him, putting the loss of two 14th Legion cohorts down to bad luck more than bad leadership.

Caesar had a distinctly political motive for this. Cicero's brother, the famous orator Marcus Cicero, was one of Caesar's most outspoken critics in the Senate, and there was no point in antagonizing the elder Cicero unnecessarily. In person, Caesar was probably much more forthright with Quintus Cicero. Impatient as always, Caesar would have then moved on, mentally and physically. For the better part of his career he was quick to forgive most who disappointed him or let him down, and Caesar was to retain the younger Cicero on his staff for another year.

It's less likely that Cicero forgot the dressing down he received from his commander in chief after this second debacle at Atuatuca. By the time civil war broke out fewer than four years later, unlike a number of the generals who served with Caesar in Gaul, the younger Cicero would side with and march with Caesar's opponents.

Caesar had failed to achieve the objective of his expansive sweep through Belgium over the past week—the seizure of the fugitive King Ambiorix. Now, unhappy at that failure, smarting over the loss of a thousand men of the 14th, and with his spirits further dampened by the sudden arrival of heavy fall rains, he pulled out of Atuatuca, with the 14th now marching with the other legions. Sending the cavalry ahead, he made a punitive scorched-earth drive through Eburonia. Every Eburone village, every farm building, was put to the torch. Cattle were rounded up or slaughtered, crops not flattened by the rain were harvested and consumed as Caesar determined to punish the small, impertinent Eburone nation by starving it out of existence.

Often, reports came to Caesar from cavalry patrols that Ambiorix had been sighted, fleeing with just a mounted bodyguard of four men. But each time, the Eburone king would evade pursuit and disappear once more.

As the weather continued to worsen, Caesar sent the legions into camp for the winter of 53–52 B.C. and made plans to head south to Italy to conduct court sittings in Cisalpine Gaul and spend the winter there, as had become his custom. On Caesar's orders, two legions went to the Trever frontier in eastern Belgium; two went to central France, setting up camp in the vicinity of modern Dijon; and the remaining six pitched their tents in a huge new camp at present-day Sens in central France, sixty-five miles southeast of Paris. After their savaging at Atuatuca, the 14th Legion had earned Caesar's displeasure, and the unit probably was garrisoned at the main legion camp at Sens, out of harm's way. The men of the legion would have lapsed into depression, convinced that now they would be forever consigned to the rear. But they need not have fretted: Caesar would soon have a mission for the 14th Legion.

V

THE UPRISING

I n the second half of 44 B.C., at the request of Caesar's chief secretary, Lucius Cornelius Balbus, Aulus Hirtius, an officer who had been a colonel on Caesar's staff since 54 B.C., reluctantly sat down to complete Caesar's memoirs—his *Commentaries,* as they were known in his own time, or *The Gallic War,* as the book on his campaigns in Gaul came to be called.

By that stage the first seven parts of Caesar's memoirs had been published in Rome, receiving great attention and acclaim, even from Caesar's critics, such as the elder Cicero. When Hirtius sent his last chapter of *The Gallic War* to Balbus, his covering letter contained the protest that he was not qualified to write it. But write it he did. His work was not in the same league as Caesar's originals in either the literary sense or the military sense, yet it served its political purpose at the time. Like Caesar's own work it was pure propaganda, but with an even more one-eyed stance than Caesar had adopted. It's from Hirtius that we learn details of the last episodes of Caesar's conquest of Gaul.

Hirtius's eighth and final chapter took up where Caesar had left off, in the final stages of a 52 B.C. uprising against him in Gaul. Led by Vercingetorix, charismatic young leader of the Averni tribe of southern France, all of central Gaul had rebelled. There had been sieges and skirmishes, and a major reverse for Caesar outside the walls of Gergovia in the Auvergne Mountains, after which he and his legions, including the 14th, had been forced to retreat. And then there was Caesar's famous siege of Alesia on Mount Auxois, thirty miles northwest of Dijon. Destroying a Gallic relief force of as many as 250,000 men, Caesar's ten legions had then forced Vercingetorix and much of his army of 80,000 starving men trapped at Alesia to surrender. The Gallic Revolt, it seemed, had been crushed.

In late 52 B.C., as all the legions were settling into their winter camps in Gaul, the rebellion spluttered back into life. Caesar himself had decided to remain in Gaul for the winter, so he wouldn't be caught in Italy should there be further problems. He had only just set up his headquarters at Bibracte, on Mount Beuvray, twelve miles west of Autun, when intelligence reports arrived of fresh unrest among tribes to the west, with talk of a guerrilla war being planned. On December 29, leaving General Mark Antony in charge at headquarters, Caesar set off from Bibracte with his cavalry bodyguard and hurried west, picking up the 13th Legion and then the 11th Legion from their camps during his rapid progress.

In a minicampaign of forty days, Caesar surprised and overwhelmed the Bituriges with his two legions, taking numerous prisoners. Once he was satisfied that rebel ringleaders had been rounded up and the threat eliminated, he sent the two legions back to their bases as he himself returned to Bibracte.

In late February, just eighteen days after his return to Bibracte, Caesar was presiding over a court session when envoys from the Bituriges arrived to say that their people were under attack from the Carnutes, their neighbors to the north. Caesar promptly sent to the two nearest legions, units then camped on the Saône. The men of the 14th Legion, huddled around their campfires at Chalon, would have been surprised and delighted when ordered to prepare to march with Caesar at once to deal with the Carnutes.

According to Hirtius, the other legion summoned by Caesar together with the 14th was the 6th. This was the first mention of the 6th Legion in relation to Caesar's army in Gaul. Until 52 B.C., the 6th Legion was one of three legions based in eastern Spain with Lieutenant General Lucius Afranius, under the overall control of Pompey the Great, who governed all of Spain from Rome.

Plutarch says that a legion was temporarily transferred by Pompey to Caesar in Gaul as the result of an urgent request from Caesar, either just leading up to or during the period that Pompey was sole consul in 52 B.C. Plutarch adds that Cato the Younger complained bitterly that Caesar's request did not go through the Senate and that Pompey equally didn't bother to refer his loan of the legionaries to Caesar to the Senate.

That Pompey allocated the legion to Caesar in the face of the worrying southern advance of contingents of Vercingetorix's Gallic liberation army in 52 B.C. is obvious. We know from Caesar himself that the defenses of the Roman province in the south of France, the later Narbonne Gaul, were thoroughly stretched by rebel incursions in 52 B.C., with Caesar's cousin Lieutenant General Lucius Caesar raising a force of twenty-two militia cohorts to support local troops deployed by General Decimus Brutus Albi-

nus. Bringing experienced reinforcements from across the Pyrenees was a
sound move.

At the same time, Caesar had raised a new unit in Transalpine Gaul,
on his own authority. Suetonius says that none of its recruits was a Roman
citizen—Caesar didn't have to obtain Senate permission to raise units of
auxiliaries, noncitizens, which could be disbanded at any time. But then,
says Suetonius, Caesar unilaterally granted every man in the new unit
Roman citizenship, giving them rights under Roman law—another act to
severely ruffle feathers in Rome. Suetonius says that Caesar called the new
legion the Alaudae, from Celtic, meaning "crested larks," and said to have
been because of the men's long, trailing Celtic-style helmet plumes. Later,
during the civil war, he would allocate the Alaudae the number of Pompey's 5th Legion after he'd discharged that unit.

The arrival of the Alaudae and the 6th had brought Caesar's army up
to twelve legions. But before these two units could become engaged, the
Vercingetorix Revolt had been terminated at Alesia. But Caesar was in no
hurry to give the 6th back to Pompey, even though, as it hadn't served
with Caesar before, it was in his eyes no better than a brand-new legion
of raw recruits, like the Alaudae. He sent it to gather wheat at Macon until
the next spring, when it would be deployed with the rest of his legions as
required.

In the last days of February 51 B.C., the Spaniards of the 6th Legion
marched from the Saône, in the company of the excited young northern
Italians of the 14th, to join Caesar. After the two legions had tramped
into Bibracte, without heavy equipment and keen for action, Caesar took
charge of them and quickly led their cohorts northwest into the homeland
of the troublesome Carnutes.

This was not the ideal time for a military column to make a rapid tran-
sit across central France. Hirtius comments that the winter days were
short, the roads bad, and the weather intolerable. But the men of the 14th
and the 6th marched without complaint, wet and cold, swathed in their
woolen cloaks, driven by a determination to secure some glory and not a
little profit—after their unprofitable forty-day hike through Biturige territory a few weeks earlier, the legionaries of the 11th and 13th Legions had
been promised 200 sesterces each by Caesar in lieu of booty, their centurions, 2,000 sesterces each. The young men of the 14th would have had
ambitions for similar rewards.

As the 14th and the 6th slogged along poor roads and through dreadful weather to the Loire River, the Carnutes fled in all directions ahead of
them, deserting their towns, villages, and farms in terror. With Caesar's

cavalry and auxiliary troops chasing tribesmen from the district, the men of the 14th had no fighting to do. They marched into the deserted Carnute capital, Aurelianum, modern Orléans, and made themselves at home, helping themselves to possessions left behind by the townspeople in their hasty departure.

Caesar moved on to attend to other problems: reports had reached him that the Bellovaci, a Belgic tribe living around Beauvais, north of the Seine, was talking of taking up arms. Leaving General Trebonius in command at Orléans, Caesar told the 14th and the 6th that they could spend the remainder of the winter in the town. This meant comfortable accommodation for some men of the legion, who took over Orléans's empty houses. Thatched wooden shelters were quickly built over the tents of the remaining legionaries.

While these two legions put their feet up, Caesar led the 7th, 8th, 9th, and 11th Legions north of Paris to deal with the Bellovaci. In managing these winter operations, Caesar had shown a keen eye to a lesson from the past. Historically, Roman legions did not campaign during winter. Seventeen years earlier, General Lucius Licinius Lucullus had pushed his luck and his troops too far on a winter campaign in the East. Lucullus was a brilliant general who thought nothing of hardships, and in his single-minded determination to outmaneuver the armies of Mithradates the Great, king of Pontus, one of Rome's most formidable adversaries, he had kept his legions out of winter camp and incessantly on the march. Led in part by Clodius, Lucullus's brother-in-law, the general's men had mutinied—not once, but three times. After the troops refused to take another step, Lucullus had been recalled by the Senate and replaced by Pompey, who showed much more interest in the welfare of his men and still managed to beat Mithradates.

Caesar knew the lesson of Lucullus well enough. Three times in as many months now he had used different legions for winter missions limited in their goal and duration, calling out a fresh contingent each time he responded to rebel activity. Yet, for all this, the men of the 14th were not to relax for long—things were getting out of hand to the north. As the Bellovaci and five allied tribes massed for a major offensive, Caesar sent urgently to General Trebonius to bring up the 14th and the 6th, and the 13th, which was wintering in Biturige territory, to reinforce him. The 14th was on the march again.

Leading the Belgian rebels was Correus, king of the Bellovaci, together with King Commius of the Atrebates. For five years, Commius had been a loyal and energetic supporter of Caesar, even going to Britain as his ambassador and enduring capture by the Britons before Caesar's invasion of 55 B.C. had secured his release. Commius had sacrificed a great deal to lead four thousand of his men to war against Rome in the Vercingetorix Revolt the previous year. He'd been considered such a friend by Caesar that he'd also been given power over a neighboring tribe, the Morini. What was more, his people had enjoyed tax-free status courtesy of Caesar. Yet, like so many of Caesar's friends and allies throughout his career, Commius had turned against his patron.

Just prior to the Vercingetorix Revolt, after hearing from spies that Commius was a prime mover in the planning for a widespread uprising, General Labienus, Caesar's deputy, knowing how influential Commius could be among his fellow Gauls as Caesar's favorite, had decided to take preemptive action. Arranging a meeting with Commius, who was unaware that Labienus suspected him, the general sent along the troubleshooting Colonel Gaius Volusenus, then a cavalry commander with Mark Antony's forces, accompanied by centurions who'd been primed for their part in the mission.

At the meeting, as king and colonel conversed, Volusenus had grasped Commius by the right hand, as if in friendship. This was a prearranged signal. While Volusenus held the king's sword hand firmly in his two hands, one of his centurions drew a sword and went to cut Commius's throat. There was a struggle before Colonel Volusenus and his men mounted up and galloped away, leaving the king for dead. But they hadn't been thorough—the sword cut wasn't lethal. Commius survived, carrying an ugly scar and perhaps a damaged voice that would be a permanent reminder to him and to all who met him of the day the Romans tried to assassinate him.

Caesar and the Belgians now camped across a valley from each other. There were a few skirmishes as each side felt out the other, but as Trebonius approached from the south with his three legions, the six tribes sent away their noncombatants, then withdrew behind a wall of fire, which effectively prevented pursuit, to a new encampment on more favorable ground ten miles away. As Caesar set off after the rebels with the legions, he sent the cavalry on in advance, with auxiliary infantry in support.

Again Commius and Correus had a trick up their sleeves. Their waiting troops ambushed the Roman cavalry as it hurried after the rebels. But Caesar's mounted troops stood their ground and fought a battle that lasted for hours. News that Caesar was coming up with the legions reached both sides, news that inspired the Romans and demoralized the rebels. Belgian resistance wavered, then gave way. Thousands of tribesmen turned tail and fled, leaving more than half their number dead on the field. Correus, chief of the Bellovaci, was cornered. Offered his life if he surrendered, Correus refused, and cut down any man who advanced on him. In the end, he was shot with an arrow by a member of the unit of archers from Crete then serving with Caesar, and died there on the battlefield with his countrymen.

The surviving Bellovaci leaders and their allies now held a hasty conference. Seeing no other way out, they sent envoys to Caesar to arrange their surrender. Commius shunned the peace talks. After the previous year's attempt on his life he'd vowed never again to place himself in the presence of a Roman. Instead, he went into hiding.

Over the next few months there were a number of isolated outbreaks of hostilities as the Gauls' war of liberation went through its death throes. While General Labienus took two legions to finally subdue the Treveri, Caesar sent several legionary forces to western France to snuff out resistance there. One of these forces marched under General Gaius Fabius. The other, led by General Gaius Caninius, was made up of two legions, the 14th and the 6th, now working well together as partner legions. Here was an opportunity for the youngsters of the 14th to give Caesar reason to consider them more than just a B-grade legion.

Caesar himself still had a debt to settle—on his behalf, and on behalf of the 14th Legion. He returned to the land of the Eburones in Belgium, taking with him Mark Antony and the 12th Legion, supported by auxiliaries and cavalry. Hirtius wrote that in lieu of capturing Ambiorix, the best way for Caesar to gain the satisfaction that his honor demanded was to strip Eburone territory of its inhabitants and their means of survival.

Hearing that Caesar was tied up in the south, many Eburones had come out of hiding in the new year and returned to their farms. Now they were caught in their fields by the sudden arrival of Roman troops. Thousands were rounded up by Caesar's spring sweep through central and eastern Belgium. Some were killed, others sold into slavery. The last of the Eburones' cattle was plundered. Every building was destroyed.

Hirtius says that the plan was to cause Eburone survivors such grief that they would never permit their fugitive king to return. But the roundup was so complete that the Eburones ceased to exist as a nation. Before long, the Tungri Germans would be encouraged by Rome to settle in Eburonia. As for Ambiorix, he was never heard of again.

Perhaps, like Commius, king of the Atrebates, another resistance leader on the run, Ambiorix escaped to Germany or Britain. To begin with, Commius and his mounted bodyguard popped up in Belgium, making guerrilla raids on Roman road transport, only to ride into an ambush set by his would-be assassin, Colonel Volusenus, who had been given explicit orders by Mark Antony to find the Belgian king and finish the job he'd botched the year before.

The ambushed Commius and his few men wheeled around and made a suicidal charge at Volusenus. Taken by surprise, the colonel and his troopers fled. Commius overtook Volusenus and unhorsed him with a couched lance, which he drove clean through Volusenus's thigh before the rebel king made good his escape. Commius sought sanctuary with German tribes on the North Sea coast. Later, with a Roman price on his head, he crossed to Britain aboard a merchant vessel, to live out his days among Atrebate settlers in southern England. His sons would subsequently become leaders of this British offshoot of the Atrebate tribe.

Meanwhile, in western France, as General Fabius brought a number of tribes to heel, General Caninius and his two legions, including the 14th, hurried to help the people of Poitiers, Roman Lemonum, capital of the Pictones, longtime allies of Caesar, who were under siege from the rebel Andes tribe from the Anjou region. When he arrived, Caninius put his two legions behind the walls of a hastily built camp and wouldn't come out, later giving the excuse that his legions were understrength. The 14th was missing the two cohorts it had lost at Atuatuca a couple of years earlier, while the men of the 6th were fourteen years into a sixteen-year enlistment; natural attrition would have seen the legion reduced to about two-thirds of its nominal strength by this time.

The rebels made a cursory attempt to assault the camp before withdrawing after hearing that General Fabius and his two legions were coming up in support of Caninius. Fabius's cavalry overtook the retreating Andes tribe and cut to pieces twelve thousand of them. According to Hirtius, the Roman cavalry stopped the slaughter only when their horses were exhausted and the troopers' right arms were too tired to raise.

There would be just one last bloody episode, a test for the 14th Legion, before the war in Gaul was finally brought to an end and Caesar's conquest was complete.

VI

THE RULES
OF PLUNDER

O ver the past year, a small force of rebels not unlike the Confederate irregular cavalry that conducted harassing operations away from the main theaters during the American Civil War of 1861–1865 had been plaguing Caesar's supply lines in the south of France. Made up of slaves, outlaws, and bandits, according to Hirtius, and led by a Senonian desperado named Drappes, this group had raided Roman baggage trains and supply convoys with some success. Over the winter of 52–51 B.C. these raiders had linked up with the remnants of a force led by Lucterius, one of Vercingetorix's lieutenants, which had unsuccessfully attempted frontal assaults on Roman defenses in the south.

With their combined force numbering no more than two thousand men, Drappes and Lucterius learned that General Caninius and the 14th and 6th Legions were advancing south to mop up this last manifestation of Gallic defiance. Lucterius, a member of the Cadurci tribe, led his companions into his home territory. The two thousand rebels took a long baggage train laden with booty to the mountaintop town of Uxellodunum, near modern Vayrac in the Department of Lot in southwestern France. Prior to the revolt, Lucterius had governed the town, and now he convinced the townspeople to join him and his army of outlaws in resisting the Romans. As General Caninius and his two legions came marching down from the north, the town shut its gates and prepared its defenses.

The mountain terrain here was rocky and difficult to traverse, and General Caninius split his troops among three camps on high ground, then set them to work digging entrenchments around the mountain on which the town stood. While the work was still incomplete, Lucterius and Drappes led a party out at night to secure grain so they could comfortably outlast the longest siege. Collecting grain from sympathizers, they returned to a temporary camp about twelve miles outside the besieged town.

From there, Lucterius tried to slip back into Uxellodunum in the dead of night with one of several mule trains loaded with grain from around the district. General Caninius's sentries heard the mules in woods near the town, and a detachment the general sent out to investigate quickly captured the train and scattered the rebels accompanying it. Lucterius himself managed to escape, and disappeared. From prisoners, General Caninius learned of Drappes's camp, and flushed with his success, set off with one legion to take it. Emulating Caesar, he sent his cavalry and German auxiliaries ahead, and in a preemptive strike in the darkness they took the camp and all its occupants, including Drappes, before the general and the legion arrived on the scene.

Just two thousand armed defenders—a mixture of townsmen and rebels—remained in Uxellodunum, but they stubbornly refused to capitulate when Caninius victoriously returned with his prisoners, so the general recommenced his siege works. The next day, General Fabius also arrived below Uxellodunum, bringing his two legions, which took up entrenching tools and joined in the siege with the men of the 14th and the 6th.

Caesar was near Orléans in central France when dispatches from General Caninius brought news of the trouble in the south. Both Caesar and his opponents were well aware that his command in Gaul was soon to expire, and with politics at Rome currently in a state of flux, it was unlikely to be extended. The last rebels at Uxellodunum thought the Roman army might be forced to pull out if they could hold out until the next summer had passed, but equally, Caesar was determined to finally and decisively terminate all Gallic resistance while he still had an army at his command. Caesar hurried south to personally take command of the siege of the impudent little town in Lot.

His arrival, with the main Roman cavalry force, was a surprise to both sides. The town had by now been completely surrounded by entrenchments. Learning that the defenders were still reasonably well provisioned, Caesar blocked their main water supply, a river running around the foot of the mountain. This left a spring outside the town wall as the sole source of water for the occupants. Caesar then put a line of mantlets up the steep slope, to a place opposite the spring. Under cover of the mantlets his legionaries toiled at building a terrace. They then erected a siege tower ten stories tall, putting marksmen and artillery on every floor to make the approaches to the spring untenable.

The Gauls countered with two commando parties, one that set fire to Caesar's siege works, the other to attack any Roman who tried to put out the fire. This tactic worked well until Caesar sent a detachment around the mountain to attempt to scale the rocks on the far side. These legionaries had orders to make as much noise as possible, to give the impression that large numbers of Roman troops were somehow succeeding in climbing the almost sheer rock face. This trick succeeded, forcing the Gauls to call their commandos back inside the town to join the small number of defenders manning the walls at the rear. But the damage had been done: the wooden Roman tower crumbled in flames, and the townspeople were once more able to access the spring.

All this time, Caesar also had a party of miners digging through the mountain toward the rivulets that supplied the spring, and after weeks of work they were able to divert the water. The superstitious people of Uxellodunum, thinking that their spring had dried up through divine intervention, now gave up the fight in despair. The town gates opened. The defenders trooped out, piled their weapons in front of the waiting legions, and were clapped in irons. Drappes would starve himself to death while in custody. Lucterius was captured in the region by a Gaul, who handed him over to Caesar.

It was not an entirely satisfying result for the men of the 14th Legion. Because the town surrendered, under the Roman army's rules of plunder the legionaries couldn't loot the place, which was full of the fruits of the rebels' raiding activities over the past year. Only when they took a town by storm were legionaries entitled to plunder it.

Caesar, impatient to wrap things up so he could attend to political affairs in Rome, set free the two thousand Gauls who'd borne arms in Uxellodunum, but first ordered the 14th and the 6th to chop off the hands of every one of them. It was an act intended to deter other potential Gallic revolts. It worked. Following the capitulation of Uxellodunum, there were no more rebellious outbreaks in Gaul.

After spending the rest of the summer dealing peacefully with the tribes of Aquitania in southwestern France, Caesar sent his legions into winter quarters in Gaul—earlier in the year he'd sent the 15th Legion to Cisalpine Gaul to garrison towns near the border with Illyricum after the Adriatic city of Trieste had been attacked by bandits during the Vercingetorix Revolt.

The 14th and 6th Legions set up camp not far from Uxellodunum. Caesar himself returned to northern France, setting up his winter headquarters at Arras, the Atrebate town of Nemetocenna. This was King Commius's former capital, and that Caesar's occupation of it was a quite deliberate and symbolic act was emphasized by the fact that he brought cohorts from all his legions, including the 14th, there briefly for a grand ceremonial review before sending them back to their camps for the winter.

For the first time in eight years, Gaul was peaceful. For the 14th Legion, it was to be a winter without action, in contrast to the previous winter, and it's unlikely they welcomed the peace. This past year had seen the 14th playing an active part in Caesar's operations for the first time, and the men of the legion would have relished the opportunity for action, promotion, and the spoils of war.

Two thousand years later, toward the end of World War II, there was a saying current in the German High Command—"Enjoy the war, peace will be hell." A similar sentiment would have prevailed in the camps of the 14th and other legions during the closing stages of the Gallic War.

For now, with the tribes of Gaul abiding by their peace treaties, it was time for the men of the 14th to tally the booty that each legionary had acquired over the past year and to do some lucrative trading with the merchants who set up for business at their camp.

As for Caesar, the winter gave him time to plan his next career steps. His military victories had given him fame, glory, and wealth. His plans now called for victories in the political arena, engineered by favors, secret negotiations, and bribes, and backed by the steel of his legions if necessary.

In the spring of 50 B.C. Caesar returned to Italy armed with a firm political agenda. With his appointment as governor of Cisalpine Gaul, Transalpine Gaul, and Illyricum due to expire later in the year, he had decided to aim for power in Rome itself. According to Hirtius, Caesar's aim was to have both himself and his deputy, General Titus Labienus, elected consul. Caesar would be eligible for another consulship in two years, in 48 B.C. But first he aimed to increase his influence in what was essentially a hostile Senate.

He successfully campaigned for close friend Mark Antony's election to the prestigious priesthood of the augurs, and by December 10 Antony also was sitting in the Senate, as a tribune of the plebeians. The ten civil tribunes had the power of veto over Senate votes, making them powerful allies for politicians such as Caesar. Now he had three civil tribunes in his pocket. One, Gaius Curio, had been looking after Caesar's interests ever since Caesar had paid off his heavy debts a year or so earlier. Those debts had begun to mount, says Plutarch, when, as a teenager, Curio and his best friend, Mark Antony, had led a life of drinking, partygoing, and girl-chasing, and Curio had slid farther into debt as the years passed. Accord-ing to Dio, Curio had won his tribuneship through Pompey's influence. And initially, according to Appian, Curio, who was now about thirty-two, had been one of Caesar's most vocal critics in the Senate—until Caesar bought him off. According to Appian, Curio was just one of several mem-bers of the Senate bribed by Caesar that year.

Early in the year, before Caesar reached Italy, the Senate voted to send an army to the East to punish the Parthians for their defeat of the triumvir Crassus at Carrhae in 53 B.C. To support the legions already in the East, the Senate required Caesar and Pompey to each contribute a legion. Pom-pey had just one under arms in Italy, his elite 1st Legion. For years, he had camped the 1st outside Rome during the summer and sent it to the Puglia region southeast of the capital each winter. Nominating the 1st for the Parthian expedition, he now sent it up to Caesar in Cisalpine Gaul. Cae-sar was suspicious of the Senate's Parthian plan, but he sent the 15th Legion down to Rome with the 1st, replacing the 15th in the Cisalpine Gaul garrisons with the 13th Legion, from eastern France.

Now, inexplicably, the Senate called off the Parthian operation. But instead of sending the 15th back to Caesar, both it and the 1st were given over to Pompey's command. According to Hirtius, Caesar told him this was instigated by the ailing consul Gaius Claudius Marcellus, an old foe of Caesar's.

Pompey, until recently Caesar's son-in-law and firm ally, was under increasing pressure from powerful members of the Senate to clip Caesar's wings. Plutarch says that Pompey was prepared to agree to Caesar receiv-ing a new appointment as governor of Cisalpine Gaul and Illyricum, with an allocation of two legions, but was overruled. There were those, like Pompey's volatile father-in-law, Mettellus Scipio, who would be satisfied with nothing less than a complete stripping of the ambitious Caesar's power.

So as he sent the 1st and 15th Legions south into camp in Puglia, Pompey also sent his 6th Legion its marching orders. With all quiet in Gaul, it was apparent Caesar no longer needed a legion on loan from Pompey. Besides, the 6th Legion was about to end its sixteen-year enlist-ment—the men of the legion were due to be discharged and replaced by a new enlistment in the new year, and the place for that was back in home territory.

An unnamed general sent by Pompey arrived at the camp being shared by the 6th and 14th Legions in southwestern France, to lead the 6th back to Spain. According to Plutarch, when Caesar learned that the legion was preparing to leave, he had every single legionary of the 6th paid a bonus of 1,000 sesterces, more than a year's salary, in his name. Caesar had already decided on his future course, and if he had to buy the loyalty of Pompey's troops ahead of his bid for ultimate power, then so be it. So it was that in the spring or summer of 50 B.C., the men of the 6th Legion upped stakes, bode farewell to their campaigning partners of the 14th, and marched over the Pyrenees, back to General Afranius and their old base in eastern Spain, whence they had come two years earlier.

As the winter of 50–49 B.C. approached, Caesar sent orders to his legions in Gaul to move closer to Italy. The 8th and the 12th both crossed the Alps and set up camp in Cisalpine Gaul with the 13th. The remaining legions came down to the south of France. Three of them camped on the Mediterranean coast at Narbonne, under General Fabius. The 14th Legion was a member of this trio. From there, these units could stand in the way of Pompey's legions in Spain if they strove to march to Italy.

In late December of 50 B.C., Julius Caesar arrived at Ravenna, southernmost city of his province of Cisalpine Gaul, accompanied by the 13th Legion and his bodyguard of three hundred German cavalrymen. A few miles to the south lay the Rubicon River, the border with Italy proper. In the Senate, his minions were at work for him. "We had before us," Senator Marcus Cicero wrote to his friend Titus Atticus, "a speech made by Mark Antony on December 21 denouncing Pompey from the day he came of age, a protest on behalf of the people condemned [by Pompey's courts two years before], and threats of armed force."

On January 1, 49 B.C., Gaius Curio stood in the Senate and read an ultimatum from Caesar: if Pompey would give up his army, Caesar would give up his. If not, Caesar would advance into Italy with his troops and take what was due him. The Senate exploded in uproar. The course Caesar had chosen was to make him no less a rebel than men he had fought in Gaul over the past few years, men such as Vercingetorix, Ambiorix, and Commius. Their cause had been patriotism. For the sake of expediency and history, Caesar would cloak his ambitions in the same colors.

Considering Caesar's ultimatum nothing short of a declaration of war, the Senate overwhelmingly voted to appoint Pompey the Great as Rome's commander in chief and authorized him to put an army of 130,000 men into the field against Caesar if the rogue general did not voluntarily surrender his governorships and his legions. Curio, Antony, and their fellow pro-Caesar civil tribune Quintus Cassius disguised themselves and lit out of town to join Caesar and his troops in Ravenna.

Even now, Pompey didn't believe that Caesar would be as rash as to actually go to war with his own country. Pompey had recently been ill. Not yet fully recovered, he did not possess his usual acute powers of judgment. Confident he knew Caesar's mind, he thought he was bluffing. Besides, Plutarch tells us, the general who'd led the 6th Legion back to Spain from the camp it had been sharing with the 14th Legion had subsequently assured Pompey that from all he had seen at the camp of the 14th Legion, Caesar's troops had no interest in a civil war.

Pompey seems to have taken the general's view as his own, being convinced that when push came to shove, Roman legionaries would not go to war with Rome just because Julius Caesar told them to, and Caesar would be forced to back down.

VII

THE HILL AT LÉRIDA

Q uintus Fulginius was a first-rank centurion with the 14th Legion. In the spring of 49 B.C., sitting outside his tent in a camp on France's Mediterranean coast overlooking Rome's oldest colony in Gaul, the port of Narbo Martius, modern Narbonne, Centurion Fulginius would have been an unhappy man.

Over the years he had pushed his way up through the ranks to become the third most senior centurion in the legion. He was probably in or approaching his fifties, and before his enlistment was up, Fulginius could be promoted to chief centurion of the legion. But for Fulginius to achieve promotion, the 14th would have to see some action and provide the centurion with an opportunity to impress his superiors. Fulginius probably didn't care who he had to kill to gain Caesar's sanction—Gaul or Roman, it wouldn't have mattered. Talk of civil war had hovered on men's lips for months. As Pompey's new general of the 6th Legion had reported, the men of the 14th had not been enthusiastic about going to war with fellow Romans. But once Caesar had taken the irrevocable step of crossing the Rubicon, the men of his legions at Narbonne had grown impatient for action as they kicked their heels around camp waiting for orders.

Meanwhile, the men at Narbonne were hearing via dispatches from Italy that other legions were grabbing the glory. After surprising his opponents by his bold invasion of Italy with just the 13th Legion in the second week of January, Caesar had quickly pushed on down the eastern coast. In February, by the time Caesar reached Corfinium, traditional capital of the Marsi tribe, east of Rome, every town in his path had come over to him. At Corfinium, eighteen thousand Pompeians made a stand. Here Caesar had been joined by the 8th and 12th Legions, and after a week-long confrontation the town had capitulated.

The rapidity of Caesar's advance into Italy had taken the Senate completely off guard and put thousands of potential recruits in the rebel general's hands. At the same time, Pompey had managed to hurriedly raise just three new legions of raw conscripts in southern Italy. He quickly made a decision for which he would be criticized by historians such as Plutarch. Pompey would pull out of Italy with these untrained recruits and the men of the 1st and 15th Legions, which remained loyal to him. Rome's fleets also stayed faithful to the Senate, and with command of the seas, Pompey planned to go to Greece and rebuild the Senate's forces with the support of Eastern rulers who were in his debt. And when he was ready, he would take on Caesar.

Leaving Rome behind, Pompey, hundreds of senators, and the two current consuls had hurried south to the port of Brindusium, modern Brindisi. From there, Pompey evacuated across the Adriatic to Albania in two convoys. Caesar failed to prevent Pompey's Dunkirk-like escape with twenty-five thousand men. Still, once the final ships of the evacuation fleet left Brindisi on the night of March 17–18, Italy was Caesar's.

But Caesar didn't have the ships to go after Pompey, who landed his infantry and cavalry, together with most of the members of the Senate, at Durrës, in Albania opposite Brindisi, then marched across Greece to set up a base at Veroia, in Macedonia. What Caesar would do now was anyone's guess, and the men of the 14th at Narbonne would have been laying a bet or two on his next move.

The 14th wasn't alone at Narbonne. The 9th and 10th Legions were in camp here, too. That would have been the source of some satisfaction to Centurion Fulginius. The 9th and the 10th were classed as among Caesar's best legions. In fact, the 10th was notoriously Caesar's favorite. He'd raised it himself in western Spain twelve years earlier, and it had been at the forefront of many a victory for him since. Fulginius would have told himself that if Caesar was keeping the elite 10th Legion out of the action, he must have plans for it.

There was no use trying to wring information out of the generals and colonels—they didn't confide in the rank and file. The best grapevine in the army was the centurions' network. Fulginius would have chatted earnestly in camp with his six fellow first-rank centurions from the 10th, hoping to glean a piece of juicy information from them—men such as Titus Salienus, Marcus Tiro, and Gaius Clausinus. If anyone had inside knowledge, they would. Yet Caesar was never one to share his thoughts. His friends were often just as surprised by his actions as his enemies. So even the centurions' network would have been relying on gossip and speculation, just like everyone else.

By late March, Centurion Fulginius would have heard two pieces of news that were not good for Caesar but that contained a promise of action for the men of the 14th. The first was the story of Pompey's evacuation from Brindisi. The other involved General Titus Labienus, Caesar's loyal deputy of nine years. To the astonishment of Caesar's legions, Labienus—like Pompey, a native of Picenum—had gone over to Pompey and the Senate, taking most of Caesar's Gallic cavalry with him.

Caesar would tell his aide Aulus Hirtius that he'd heard reports that his opponents in the Senate had been trying to win over Labienus the previous winter but he'd not taken them seriously. This was uncharacteristically careless of Caesar. He was stunned by the defection of Labienus and a number of other friends and relatives including his second cousin, Lucius Caesar, and the young man he considered a son, Marcus Brutus.

All this time, another six hundred of Labienus's cavalry had been encamped with the legions at Narbonne. Away from Labienus's influence, they remained loyal to Caesar and stayed in camp with the legions. To make up for the troopers lost to Pompey, Caesar hurriedly sent letters to all the chiefs of Gaul, commanding them to send him fresh cavalry for the next phase of his operations. To replace Labienus as his general of cavalry, Caesar would promote his point man during the Gallic War, Gaius Volusenus.

The cavalrymen at Narbonne would have joined in the speculation with Fulginius and his 14th Legion colleagues about what Caesar had in mind. Some would have suggested that they would be involved in an amphibious invasion of Greece. Others would have reminded their comrades that there was the matter of Pompey's legions at their back to the west, in Spain. The career soldier goes where his orders take him, and Centurion Fulginius probably didn't care where he was sent, just as long as it involved active service. He would make the most of his opportunities; as the French say, where the goat is tethered, there it must browse. But just the same, the affluent Spanish provinces were close at hand, and offered rich pickings if towns and cities had to be stormed. Fulginius would have been justified in wondering why Caesar had placed the 9th, 10th, and 14th here at Narbonne if not to take on the Pompeians in Spain. He would have wished it were so.

Fulginius's wish came true. In April, the 9th, 10th, and 14th and the cavalry at Narbonne received orders to march west under General Fabius, to clear the Pyrenees mountain passes of Pompeian troops and open the way for full-scale operations by six of Caesar's legions against the Senate's forces in Spain.

*　*　*

As the Spanish sun beat down, Centurion Fulginius and his five fellow first-rank centurions marshaled their men of the 1st Cohort of the 14th Legion ten men deep to form the leading edge of the foremost of three lines on the left wing of Caesar's battle formation at the bottom of a small hill. So far, so good: no opposition troops in sight.

This low, bare hill, near the Segre River in northeastern Spain, overlooked a wooden bridge. On the far side of the river stood the town of Lérida, the Roman Ilerda. On this side, a Pompeian army camp occupied a hill. Split between town and camp were the men of five of Pompey's legions and forty thousand auxiliaries. The hill stood between them. If Caesar could occupy this rise, he could prevent supplies reaching the camp from the stockpile at Lérida. To achieve that objective he had led three of his six legions from General Fabius's camp on the Segre. One of those units was the 14th Legion.

The 14th's first battle line consisted of four cohorts; the second, of two cohorts. The last two of the below-strength legion's eight cohorts were in the third line. The two legions to the right of the 14th—one, a unit of new Italian recruits, either the 21st or the 30th, and on the right wing the 9th—had their cohorts split four-three-three through the three lines, Caesar's regular disposition.

Fulginius took up his post on the extreme left of the line and waited with a set, determined jaw for further orders and the opportunity to crown his career. There was an old Roman proverb, "From the foot, we recognize the Hercules." Many times before this day, in battles from Gaul to the Middle East, Fulginius had shown the proverbial foot. Now he was determined to be recognized as the hero.

Behind him, a legionary or two may have voiced the concern exercising many a 14th Legion man's mind at that moment—where was the cavalry support for their exposed left flank? Fulginius would have snapped at the grumblers that Caesar knew what he was doing, and to keep their lips sealed. He knew that speed of action had been Caesar's intent, to use the element of surprise. A cavalry maneuver may have alerted the other side. To take the Pompeians by surprise, he had brought up these three legions and formed them in battle lines below the small, vacant hill, without cavalry support.

In the open ground behind the first line, as was the custom, stood the trumpeters, the standard-bearers of the leading cohorts and maniples, heads clad in bearskin, and the bareheaded bearer of the sacred eagle standard of each legion. Caesar himself, accompanied by staff officers, watched from behind the 9th Legion's front line.

Caesar's opponent, Lieutenant General Afranius, had never been an inspired or an inspiring leader. He had even been labeled incompetent. Caesar would have been justified in expecting to outwit him. But the opposition commander on the spot was almost certainly Afranius's sometimes rash deputy, General Marcus Petreius, who had a wealth of experience fighting the tribes of Portugal. And he reacted quickly. General Petreius had several legionary cohorts from the 3rd and Valeria Legions formed up on guard outside the camp on the nearby hill. These were units he'd personally led in Portugal over the past year. Realizing Caesar's intent, Petreius had sent these cohorts around the back of the camp hill at the double, with orders to secure and hold the summit of the bare small hill.

Now, just as Caesar's troops had halted at the foot of the rise to regain their order prior to moving up the slope and occupying the summit, the leading elements of these Pompeian cohorts began to appear on the crest above the 14th Legion; they'd succeeded in climbing from the other side without Caesar seeing them.

Caesar probably cursed to himself when he saw that the opposition had reached his objective ahead of him, but he was here now, and by hook or by crook he'd dislodge the Pompeians from the hill and make it his own. He issued an order: "Front line of the 14th Legion, advance at double time."

Trumpets sounded, and the call was relayed to the left of his battle formation.

Perhaps Centurion Fulginius would have allowed himself a momentary smile as he heard the call. His prayers were being answered—action at last, and right under Caesar's very nose. The command rang out: "First Cohort, advance at the double!"

With a cheer, Fulginius and his legionaries, shield on left arm, javelins in their right hand, and hearts pounding, lurched forward and began to run up the hill toward the Pompeian legionaries waiting above.

The 3rd and Valeria Legions were both from Cisalpine Gaul, like the 14th. Over the years these legionaries had fought regular skirmishes with the wild Lusitanians and the mountain tribes from farther north who knew nothing of formal battle lines or unit tactics, and the Roman troops had adapted their offensive techniques accordingly, playing and beating the tribesmen at their own unorthodox game.

Now, instead of a formal Roman-style charge, the men on the hilltop let out a bellow and charged loosely and independently at various parts of the approaching 14th Legion line. The bemused men of the 14th came to a ragged halt as they met the charge.

"Close up! Close up!" came the order from Fulginius and fellow centurions.

The men of the 14th shuffled closer and locked their shields in front of them to create an impenetrable wall. There was little opportunity for them to use javelins, as the men on the other side pushed at the wall of shields, slashing and jabbing over the top of them with the short, pointed gladius, the Roman legionary sword, and javelins.

If they made no progress at one part of the Caesarian line, Pompeian centurions such as Titus Caecilius, chief centurion of either the 3rd or the Valeria, didn't suffer from the pride that caused some of their opposites on Caesar's side to shun the idea of even a temporary giving of ground. Instead, they would draw their men back, then lead another disorderly but determined charge at a different place. While some of the Pompeian troops paid attention the front of the 14th Legion's line, others swamped around the exposed flanks and began hacking away at the side of the line of the three leading cohorts.

Fourteenth Legion centuries at the front of the line were making a stand, and even forcing the other side back in places, but men at the rear began to panic, calling out that they would be surrounded and cut to pieces if they stayed on the downslope.

While Fulginius and his colleagues were yelling for their men to hold their ground and maintain order, others in the rear looked anxiously over their shoulders to see the eagle and the other standards of the 14th out in the open, ahead of Caesar's second line. Fearing for the standards, centurions in the rear ordered their men back to cover them.

The officers of the 14th Legion's second line now saw men from the advance guard withdrawing toward them, with Pompeians giving chase. Some second-line tribunes and centurions believed the advance guard would be overrun, and without waiting for orders from Caesar, they instructed the remaining five cohorts of the legion to break away from the general formation and pull back to higher ground, to their left.

Up on the slope, Centurion Fulginius wasn't giving an inch. Knowing Caesar didn't have a high opinion of the 14th after the legion's disastrous double birth, he was determined not to screw up this chance to show the commander in chief what he was made of. Around him, loyal legionaries also were standing their ground. But once troops behind them withdrew to the standards, Fulginius and his men were surrounded.

Spotting Centurion Fulginius's helmet with its transverse crest, symbol of his rank, Pompeian legionaries would have set their sights on the reward they would receive from their superiors for bringing back his head, and zoomed in on him. Fulginius would have put up fierce resistance. Perhaps he thought he could fight his way out of it, or maybe he resigned himself to the possibility of falling with his sword in hand, picturing a tombstone bearing an inscription like the one found on an anonymous Roman soldier's memorial: "Halt traveler, you're standing on a hero's dust."

Standing over on the right of the field with the 9th Legion, an exasperated Julius Caesar had seen his strategy dissolve before his eyes as the tide on the hill turned against the 14th. Now, too, with growing fury, he saw the rest of the 14th withdrawing. At the same time, more and more Pompeians were appearing on the hilltop and then running down to give chase to the withdrawing cohorts of the 14th.

According to Caesar, this sight caused panic to sweep through his entire force. He called out, urging the withdrawing cohorts to go to the support of the men trapped on the hill. But it was too late to turn the terrified men of the 14th. So now, ignoring the white-faced youths of the untried new legion at the middle of his battle formation, Caesar called to the men of the Spanish legion behind him.

"Ninth Legion, at the charge, follow me!"

The trumpets of the 9th blared the charge, standards inclined forward, and with a roar the hardened soldiers of the 9th followed Caesar at the run.

Afranius's chief centurion, Caecilius, and his 1st Cohort men, bearing in on the heels of the retreating 14th Legion cohorts and cutting down the rearmost men with glee, didn't hear the charge sound behind them. Only when Caesar himself appeared in his flowing scarlet general's cloak, the *paludamentum*, animatedly directing the thousands of troops of the 9th who were arriving on the scene with him, did they realize they were in trouble. Substantially outnumbered, and sandwiched between the 14th and the 9th, the Pompeians gave up the chase of the 14th and turned to fight their way out.

Pompeians on the hill, seeing in the dust cloud raised by the combatants the 9th Legion's charge change the battle in Caesar's favor, retreated. They didn't go back toward the camp whence they'd come, but instead took the shortest escape route available, dashing over the Segre River bridge to the safety of Lérida town.

Chief Centurion Caecilius and his Pompeians were still battling to break out. Some forced a way through the 9th Legion and ran to the bridge, with Caesar's men in hot pursuit. Many didn't make it, Chief Centurion Caecilius among them.

As the dust cleared, Caesar saw that most of the 14th Legion had reformed on high ground to the west, and that the Pompeian troops had given up the hill, the object of his original drive. The grass of the lower slope of the hill was stained with blood and covered with mangled legionaries, some slowly, painfully moving, some frozen in grotesque death poses. Most were men of the leading cohorts of the 14th Legion. Among the dead was ambitious Centurion Quintus Fulginius of the 14th's 1st Cohort.

Caesar later wrote that Fulginius was a man of "outstanding valor." The centurion couldn't have wished for a finer epitaph. Around Fulginius's body, and to the west in a trail leading toward the position where their legion now stood in silent, dejected ranks, were seventy dead legionaries of the 14th and six hundred wounded from the 14th and the 9th.

But Caesar had more urgent matters to attend to. In their enthusiasm for the chase, men of the 9th had surged over the Segre bridge and all the way to the walls of Lérida town itself, only to be cut off there. They were surrounded on a ridge outside the town for five hours before breaking out and escaping back to Caesar on the opposite side of the Segre. Both sides then withdrew to their respective camps with their dead and injured.

It had been a long and bloody day, for no good end. The bare hill remained a no-man's-land. Caesar, who notoriously fudged the casualty figures of later battles, gives no figures for 9th Legion losses outside Lérida, although he asserts that Afranius lost five centurions and more than two hundred legionaries. But Afranius claimed the day as a victory, and when news of the Lérida battle reached Rome, some faint hearts among Caesar's supporters decided they were on the losing side and hurried to join Pompey in Greece.

There was an old Latin saying, "It is not permissible to blunder twice in war." The men of the 14th Legion would have been familiar with the sentiment. They'd let Caesar down for a second time. Throughout his career men close to Caesar who let him down were often forgiven. But legions that displeased him didn't fare as well. Caesar hadn't blamed the men of this enlistment of the 14th for the original Atuatuca disaster, but the second disgrace had been theirs to wear, for five years now. Lérida had been their second chance to rid the 14th of the stain of Atuatuca. And they had failed themselves and their general.

Caesar was to make it perfectly clear that the 14th no longer had his confidence. After Generals Afranius and Petreius succeeded in a surprise breakout from Lérida, the 14th was the one and only legion Caesar left behind as he gave chase. There the brooding men of the 14th sat, watching Lérida town, with its pro-Pompey residents and its garrison of auxiliaries, while Caesar overtook Afranius, surrounded him, and forced him to surrender his entire force. Lérida town capitulated when it learned of Afranius's surrender.

As Afranius's five legions, including the 6th, were disarmed and discharged, Caesar sent General Quintus Cassius, the former civil tribune who'd been in his pay, into Farther Spain with the 21st and 30th Legions. He himself set off for Farther Spain via a different route, with most of the cavalry. As the 14th Legion camped at Lérida, Pompey's legions in the west, the 2nd and the Indigena, under General Marcus Terrentius Varro, surrendered without a fight. Pompey's control of Spain, and of seven legions, had been terminated.

As Caesar departed Spain, he issued orders for several newly raised legions currently in the south of France and northern Italy to march over the Pyrenees to reinforce the single experienced legion he'd assigned the job of garrisoning Nearer Spain—the 14th. Left behind in Spain, the men of the 14th Legion would have felt rejected and dejected. Of all the legions that had marched with Caesar for all the past five years, theirs was the only one he failed to take with him as he set off to continue the war elsewhere.

VIII

✿

SPITTING IN
SCIPIO'S EYE

Pompey the Great was dead, murdered by Egyptians as he went to step ashore at Pelusium in Egypt on September 28, 48 B.C. Just a day later he would have celebrated his fifty-eighth birthday. Seven weeks before, on August 9, Pompey's army had been defeated by Caesar's legions in Greece, at the Battle of Pharsalus, near modern Farsala in the Thessaly region. Most of Pompey's generals and eighteen thousand of his troops had fled west, escaping from Greece aboard ships of the Roman navy anchored off Corfu. Pompey himself had gone east, with just a handful of companions. As Labienus, Afranius, Petreius, Scipio, Cato the Younger, and other leading senatorial commanders sailed for North Africa, which was held by friendly forces, Pompey had sailed to Egypt, looking for support for a comeback from the Egyptians. Instead, they cut off his head.

The senatorial forces subsequently regrouped in Tunisia, electing as their new commander in chief Lieutenant General Quintus Caecilius Metellus Pius Scipio, Pompey's father-in-law and one of the divisional commanders at Pharsalus. Now, more than a year later, Caesar was conducting an amphibious landing in North Africa as he went after Scipio's army, determined to end armed opposition to his takeover at Rome. Meanwhile, in Spain, after it had missed the big one at Pharsalus, the 14th Legion had received the call to join this latest operation.

Caesar himself had been caught up in a struggle in Egypt that had delayed his pursuit of the senatorial leaders and given them the opportunity to rebuild their shattered army. After Caesar landed in Egypt with only thirty-four hundred troops, four days behind Pompey's fatal arrival, the Egyptians learned that most of Caesar's army had gone on strike after Pharsalus, demanding their overdue discharges and promised cash bonuses. With an army of twenty-two thousand well-trained troops, the Egyptians had decided to eliminate Caesar, too. So Caesar had taken their fifteen-year-old king, Ptolemy XIII, and his twenty-one-year-old sister Cleopatra hostage and barricaded himself inside part of the royal palace at Alexandria.

After nine months of bitter street fighting, and eventually reinforced—mostly by former POWs, Pompeian troops who'd come over to his side after being captured—Caesar had defeated Ptolemy's forces in the Battle of the Nile Delta. After installing Cleopatra, by now his mistress, on the Egyptian throne, he'd hurried north to Turkey to take on Pharnaces, son of the late Mithradates the Great, who'd invaded Armenia and Pontus while Caesar's back was turned. Decisively defeating Pharnaces and his war chariots at Zela, modern Zile, on August 3, 47 B.C.—after which he sent his famous "I came, I saw, I conquered" dispatch—Caesar had returned to Rome, to win back the legions that were still on strike, so he could lead them against Scipio in North Africa.

Caesar being Caesar, he'd talked his best legions into one more campaign, one more battle. But even then he would need all the experienced legions he could lay his hands on—Scipio had put together ten legions. In addition, Scipio had the support of four legions and 120 war elephants of King Juba of Numidia, a friend of Pompey and a backer of the senatorial cause.

Two and a half years had passed since the 14th Legion's poor showing at Lérida; it hadn't seen combat since. There had been only a brief police action in western Spain in the fall of 48 B.C., when the 14th had been a part of a force of thirty-five cohorts marched by the governor of Nearer Spain, Major General Marcus Lepidus, into Farther Spain to sort out a dispute between the locals and the governor there, Quintus Cassius, former civil tribune and brother of one of Pompey's admirals. Cassius had ripped off his subjects so much that two of his own legions, the 2nd and the Indigena, plus half of the new enlistment he'd raised locally on Caesar's orders to reconstitute Pompey's 5th, had rebelled against him.

Cassius had led his remaining legions, the 21st and the 30th, against the mutineers, and it had taken General Lepidus stepping in with his troops from eastern Spain, including the men of the 14th, to stop the dispute. Cassius withdrew to the hill town of Carmona, near Seville, then one of Spain's major citadels. After learning he'd been replaced as governor, he loaded a ship at Málaga with his ill-gotten gain and set sail for Italy, ignoring negative weather forecasts. Caught in a storm, Cassius and his gold had gone down in the mouth of the Ebro River just south of Tarragona.

Now, in the fall of 47 B.C., three legions marched through southern Gaul and Italy to reach Caesar's staging point in Sicily, to join his African operation. Elements of the 5th went first, joined by Spanish cavalry. The eight cohorts of the 14th Legion marched over the Pyrenees and into Gaul shortly after, with all their worldly goods. The legion hadn't been brought up to full strength since the second Atuatuca battle, and wouldn't be—it wasn't Roman policy to add new recruits to a legion before a current enlistment was discharged. For that reason, legions such as the 10th were now only about two thousand men strong. Only when their current enlistments were discharged would new recruits be drafted and each legion brought back up to the full nominal strength of six thousand men.

The 14th was accompanied on its march by the 13th Legion and the last cohorts of the 5th. Through southern France they slogged, over the Alps, down through northern Italy, across the Po River at Piacenza, and then on to Rome. From there, it was down the coast to Vibo, to embark on ships for the transfer across the Strait of Messina to Sicily, with a final march along the top of the island to the west coast embarkation point, Marsala, just as winter was beginning to bite.

As they marched, the thoughts of men of the 14th Legion would have been on Caesar's last attempt to invade North Africa. Two years earlier, while Caesar was conducting operations against General Afranius in Spain, Gaius Curio, the former tribune of the plebeians who'd been one of Caesar's spokesmen in the Senate, had led a landing in Tunisia by two legions, the 17th and the 18th. These were new units made up of former senatorial recruits who'd surrendered at Corfinium in February of 49 B.C.

Before that summer had ended, Curio and most of his men were dead, killed at the Battle of Bagradas River outside Utica, modern Utique, by forces under King Juba's deputy, General Saburra. Even the legionaries of the five cohorts that avoided the Bagradas River debacle hadn't survived after they surrendered; King Juba had executed every last one of them. Caesar had loaned Curio his chief aide, Colonel Gaius Asinius Pollio, as a sure hand to lead his cavalry, and it was Pollio who'd escaped to bring Caesar the news of the African disaster. As the Spanish say, Pollio, sent to fetch wool, had come back shorn. The fate of the men of the 17th and 18th was food for thought for troops of the 14th as they assembled at Marsala—King Juba's undefeated army was a key part of the large opposition force awaiting them in Africa.

Caesar had already been ashore in Tunisia for a month with elements of the 5th, 10th, 25th, 26th, 28th, and 29th Legions when, in the third week of January in 46 B.C., his second invasion convoy set sail from Marsala, carrying the 14th and 13th Legions and the last men of the 5th. It was not to be a pleasant voyage. For some, it would be their last.

Caesar was still short of shipping, particularly transports. Most of the merchantmen used by Curio for his 49 B.C. landing had fallen into opposition hands, so that Caesar now had only enough dedicated transports for his cavalry and limited quantities of supplies. So, for this operation, his infantrymen were put aboard warships. At least in that department Caesar was no longer a pauper. In addition to a small number of warships of his own based at Messina and Vibo, Caesar had added to his fleet when Admiral Gaius Cassius, brother of the infamous Quintus Cassius, who'd gone down at the mouth of the Ebro River, had come over to Caesar following Pharsalus, as had his colleague Admiral Decimus Laelius. Both brought a number of frigates and cruisers with them. According to the author of *The African War* at least forty capital ships were now involved in Caesar's North African operations.

The men of the 14th were packed onto the decks of the cruisers of the fleet while below them the ships' perspiring oarsmen heaved at their three banks of oars. Contrary to popular belief, the men who manned the oars in Roman warships weren't slaves chained to their stations. The wholesale use by Rome of punishment galleys as depicted in Lew Wallace's 1880 novel *Ben Hur* is a fiction. That was a phenomenon of the Middle Ages. Eastern potentates such as Herod the Great used prisoners as oarsmen, but the men who crewed Roman warships such as those now taking the 14th Legion to Tunisia were freedmen, former slaves, serving long enlistments with the Roman navy, men paid to row.

Standing cheek by jowl on the decks of the vessels of Caesar's small fleet, the men of the 14th Legion traveled light, under orders to leave behind their heavy equipment and personal belongings. Officers also were instructed to leave behind their horses and servants. Some of Caesar's officers considered this so much of a sacrifice that they would ignore the order, at their subsequent cost. To save space, the men of the 14th Legion even left their tents in Sicily. In North Africa, like the men who had gone before them in the first wave, they would have to sleep under the stars, trying to create protection from the elements by stringing their cloaks between branches of trees. They were assured by their officers that this primitive state of affairs wouldn't last long. This campaign would only be a short one, Caesar had promised; there was no need of "luxuries."

The convoy had to contend with the difficult winter weather that set in from November each year in these climes. Caesar's initial convoy in December had encountered strong adverse winds, but this second fleet met with even worse conditions. The cold, perpetually soaked legionaries sardined on warships' decks were racked with seasickness as the craft bucked through the waves. There would have been little opportunity to down cold rations of hardtack during the three days at sea, not that many legionaries would have the stomach for food. Vomiting over themselves and their neighbors, they would have prayed to the sea god Neptune that they might soon be permitted to land and be freed from their torment. All the ships would survive the storm. But for some men of the 14th Legion there would be another threat to contend with.

A number of the Senate's warships had reached North Africa from Greece and had been combined in a fleet under Admiral Marcus Octavius, who'd handled the Liburnian and Achaean Fleets on the Adriatic for the Senate. Off the Adriatic island of Korcula in 49 B.C., Octavius had captured Mark Antony's younger brother Gaius and the convoy carrying seventy-five hundred men of the 24th and 28th Legions as they attempted an amphibious landing in Croatia—probably aiming for Salonae, near modern Split, which Admiral Octavius had under siege. But Admiral Octavius had later been defeated in a naval battle in the Adriatic by Caesar's general Publius Vatinius. After his battleship sank under him, the wounded Octavius had swum to another ship, escaping to Africa, where the senatorial side's commanding general Scipio had placed him in charge of the Senate's naval forces.

As Caesar's second invasion fleet approached the Tunisian coast, Admiral Octavius was anchored in Tunis Bay with fifty-five warships—fast frigates and massive, heavy cruisers, most equipped with marines. Expecting Caesar to attempt to reinforce his initial landing force and so solidify his shaky foothold on African soil, Octavius prepared to set sail in search of Caesarian vessels as soon as the weather improved.

The gale broke up this second convoy of Caesar's, sending some ships too far south and others way to the north. As was demonstrated during World War II, a convoy's strength lies in numbers. On their own, ships become sitting targets. Now, in January of 46 B.C., Caesar's second African convoy was in tatters. Vessels lost contact with each other, and masters were forced to nervously proceed singly as best they could, hoping that enemy warships were still sheltering in port.

Still, for all the drama of the crossing, and despite the presence of opposition naval forces, most of the storm-tossed legionaries reached their destination safely. In dribs and drabs, the sick, weak men of the 14th and 13th Legions and several shiploads of 5th Legion men gratefully came ashore at Leptis, in Tunisia. Leptis was a walled port town at the heart of a prosperous olive-growing area, where the people still spoke Punic, the language of the old Carthaginian Empire. Caesar made it the landing point for reinforcements and supplies of grain, timber for building, and iron and lead for weapons and ammunition manufacture being sent across from Sicily in what became a series of regular convoys. Ten miles away lay the town of Ruspina, where Caesar sited his North African headquarters and where he was building up his forces. His opponent Scipio was training a large army farther south, along the Tunisian coast.

For the moment, Caesar assigned the newly arrived troops of the 14th and 13th Legions to garrison duty, to give them, he said, the opportunity to overcome the exhaustion caused by their seasickness. By this stage the men of the 54 B.C. enlistment of the 14th had served Caesar for more than seven years. Despite the failings that had earned it Caesar's past displeasure, the 14th was now described by Caesar's staff as one of his veteran legions, placing it in the same category as the famous 10th and the other Spanish legions, the 7th, 8th, and 9th. Compared to legions levied in Italy two years earlier, none of which had done anything spectacular in this war to date, and which on several occasions showed they weren't made of the same stuff as the legions that had fought in the Gallic War for Caesar, the 14th certainly was an experienced unit.

But not all the men of the 14th joined Caesar's army in Tunisia. Two ships of the second convoy failed to reach their destination. One carried centurions and four of the 5th Legion's six tribunes, including two brothers named Titius. Their ship and a number of others had been pushed well down the Tunisian coast, toward Cyrenaica, but once the storm abated, they were able to turn about and head for Leptis. In the process, they straggled past the enemy-held town of Thapsus, in full view of the garrison there.

The senatorial commander at Thapsus, Major General Gaius Vergilius, had a few sail-powered merchantmen and a single light, fast frigate at his disposal. Realizing that the opposition vessels would escape if he were to rely on sailpower to try to overtake them, he immediately boarded the frigate. Loading it with infantrymen and archers, he set off in hot pursuit. At the same time, he gave orders that the dinghies of his cargo vessels be loaded with troops who could wield an oar and be sent after him.

By urging his rowers to maximum effort, General Vergilius was able to overhaul the heavy, troop-laden ships with his frigate. Before long, the oarsmen in the small boats also soon caught up with the stragglers. Virgilius and his motley little flotilla proceeded to attack the Caesarian craft, but were beaten off by all but one. On board this last, surrounded vessel, cut off from the other troopships as they escaped north, a centurion convinced his superiors that the wisest course was surrender. It wasn't a good idea. The colonels were taken ashore and placed in chains at Scipio's head-quarters, where they were beheaded three days later—as traitors to the Senate and the people of Rome.

A second Caesarian vessel, a cruiser of the trireme class, was blown well to the north and found itself in Tunis Bay, the very lion's den. Hungrily, ships of Admiral Octavius's fleet swooped around it. Surrounded, the trireme's captain was forced to surrender. The cruiser was carrying two hundred passengers. The majority of these were legionaries of the 5th Legion, young men, teenagers many of them, from western Spain. They'd been drafted into the legion when Governor Cassius had re-formed Pompey's unit at Córdoba on Caesar's orders fewer than two years before. Apart from the Cassius affair, they had seen no action. The rest of the passenger list was made up of a crusty centurion and some seven-year veterans of the 14th Legion.

The prisoners were taken ashore at Utique. There, Major General Publius Attius Varus, the Senate's district commander, a man who always tried to play things by the book, gave orders that the captives be treated as prisoners of war and that no harm should come to them, and sent them to Scipio, his commander in chief. The POWs were duly marched down the coast to Scipio's camp outside Thapsus. There they were brought in a group before the dais of the general by a large escort from Scipio's legions.

Scipio was a severe man, long-nosed, with plaited hair and a beard in the Eastern style, a fashion he had adopted since residing in the East as the Senate's commander in Syria after escaping from Italy with Pompey in March of 49 B.C. He had a reputation for brutality, a reputation reinforced by the fate of the four captured tribunes of the 5th. But now he offered not only to spare the lives of the men of the 14th and 5th Legions standing in front of him but also to pay them if they changed sides and joined the senatorial army.

Details of the confrontation between Scipio and the POWs may have come from one of Scipio's officers, who related them to Caesar's men after later being captured, or from a 5th Legion recruit who survived what was to come. According to *The African War*, this is what transpired at that meeting outside Thapsus:

"I know that you haven't engaged in this wicked vendetta against your fellow citizens and all right-thinking men of your own free will," General Scipio told the prisoners as he glowered down at them. "You've done it at the instigation and command of that damned general of yours." He was referring to Caesar. After he'd informed them that he was prepared to spare them and take them into his army, he asked the legionaries what they thought of his offer, no doubt expecting them to express their gratitude.

The most senior prisoner, the centurion of the 14th Legion, a vastly experienced soldier who commanded one of the 14th's cohorts, now stepped forward. We don't know his name, but from his own lips we obtain sufficient information to calculate that he was at least fifty-three years of age, if not older.

"Thank you for your great kindness, Scipio," he began, his tone faintly sarcastic. "I won't call you 'General,'" he added, a deliberate comment that would have seen Scipio's eyes narrow. "Thank you for offering me my life and safety, even though I'm a prisoner of war and properly entitled to both. I might take advantage of your offer if it didn't involve completely criminal conduct!" The centurion's voice would have been raised by now, and the atmosphere would suddenly have become charged. "Do you really expect me to take up arms against Caesar, my own general, under whom I've commanded a cohort, and against his army?"

The centurion went on to say that he'd served in the Roman army for thirty-six years. In his younger days he would have fought in the East under General Lucullus, and later, under Pompey. But it was the latter part of his career of which he was most proud—for at least the past eleven years he had loyally marched for Julius Caesar. Caesar considered his centurions the backbone of his army and treated them with care and respect as long as they gave him their loyalty and fought bravely. In turn, most would have marched into Hades if he'd ordered them to.

"So Scipio, do you really expect me to take up arms against Caesar?" the centurion scoffed. "I won't. And what's more, I strongly urge you to abandon your plans, for if you haven't already realized who you're up against, you'll soon find out."

Laughter almost certainly erupted around him from his guards. After all, the centurion was in no position to boast. This would have only incensed the proud centurion even more than Scipio's offer, and before the furious Scipio could respond to his defiance, the centurion made an offer of his own.

"Choose from your army the cohort you consider to be your strongest. Pit it against me and ten men I choose from among my comrades now in your hands. Then you'll see, from our bravery, what fate lies ahead for your forces."

The indignant Scipio, arms folded, did not reply. Instead, he glanced over to the senior centurion of the guard detail and nodded. Two centurions moved forward and grabbed the brave centurion of the 14th by the arms and forced him to his knees in front of Scipio's dais. The officer in charge stepped up, drawing his sword. He lifted the prisoner's head, so his neck was straight. Then he raised his sword and swept it down.

Death by beheading was the right of every Roman citizen, but the execution was usually performed cleanly, with a sharp ax. No such privilege was afforded the centurion of the 14th. Just the same, as proven by modern-day experimentation by forensic archaeologists, General Scipio's executioner could have taken off the prisoner's head with a single blow of the gladius. One blow, or several, the result was the same: the head of the defiant centurion fell at Scipio's feet.

Scipio hadn't finished. Enraged by the centurion's audacity, he gave orders for the experienced legionaries of the 14th—these supermen their centurion had boasted of—to be separated from the youngsters of the 5th, taken outside the camp, tied to wooden crosses like slaves, and tortured to death. The youths of the 5th were distributed among the senatorial legions; like it or not, within a few months they would fight for Scipio against Caesar, at the Battle of Thapsus.

IX

LEFT BEHIND

The Battle of Thapsus was a disaster for the senatorial side. Some commentators suggest that as many as fifty thousand of Scipio's and Juba's troops died that day, April 5, 46 B.C. The author of *The African War* puts the figure at five thousand. Caesar's losses were a few hundred at most. Caesar's 5th Legion turned King Juba's war elephants on the flanks, the 10th Legion carved into General Scipio's left wing, and the senatorial line unraveled as the 14th Legion and other units in Caesar's center bore in. Ironically, Caesar, architect of the victory, was laid low by an epileptic fit early in the battle.

But it was a disaster mitigated by the fact that many senior senatorial officers and the substantially intact 1st Legion managed to withdraw up the coast to Utique, where Cato the Younger had command of the garrison and the fleet in the harbor. Scipio, too, escaped, commandeering the twelve frigates in port—light, undecked ships and the fastest craft available. Taking senators, staff officers, servants, and bodyguards with him, he set sail, intending to join Pompey's two sons, who were on Spain's Balearic Isles.

General Labienus, commander of the Senate's cavalry, also reached Utique. He and General Varus loaded the surviving men of the 1st Legion onto Admiral Octavius's larger, slower warships, and then they, too, set sail. Once Cato was certain that all who could escape had done so, and knowing that Caesar's army was advancing up the coast and would soon arrive outside the town, he calmly ate dinner with a few colleagues, then retired to his bedchamber. For a while he read—Plato's *Phaedo*, says Dio. In this dialogue, Socrates is in prison, discussing life and death prior to his execution. Cato would have consoled himself with Phaedo's statement that the souls of the dead exist in some place out of which they come again. His mind composed, Cato lay aside the book, unsheathed his sword, and fell on it, killing himself.

King Juba escaped back to Numidia, traveling by night and hiding in farmhouses by day. Barred by the townspeople from entering Zama, one of his capitals, where his wives and children were holed up—and the site of Hannibal's last great defeat on land a century and a half before—the king retired to an estate nearby. There he dined with General Petreius before the pair conducted a duel to the death, with the much more powerful Juba coming out the victor. Juba then committed suicide.

With a thousand men, General Afranius fled from his camp eight miles from Thapsus and headed west into Mauretania, accompanied by Lucius Cornelius Sulla Faustus, intending to reach Spain. Faustus, the son of the late dictator of Rome, Sulla, had married Pompey's daughter Pompeia, and she and their children accompanied him on the flight west. Afranius's party was eventually captured in Mauretania by Publius Sittius, a bankrupt Roman turned freebooter with an army of mercenaries for hire. Sittius was fresh from destroying the Numidian army of Juba's deputy, General Saburra, in a one-sided battle in which Saburra, slayer of Curio, also died. In return for a slice of Juba's former territory in western Numidia, Sittius handed his prisoners over to Caesar.

Caesar set Pompeia and her children free, and they sailed for Spain to join her family. But her husband, Faustus—whose name means "lucky"—and the hapless General Afranius were subsequently executed, along with Caesar's second cousin, Lucius Caesar.

General Scipio didn't escape far. Caught in a storm off the Algerian coast as they made for Spain, his twelve little frigates were forced into a bay off the town of Annaba, also known as Bône. There, to Scipio's horror, he found the fleet that had been supporting Sittius's operations in Numidia, also sheltering from the storm. These ships quickly surrounded Scipio's flotilla. Every one of Scipio's frigates was sunk, and all on board died. Scipio himself committed suicide before he could be captured. Perhaps the words of the centurion of the 14th flashed through his mind in his last moments: "If you haven't already realized who you're up against, you'll soon find out."

Caesar declared eastern Numidia a new Roman province, having divided the western half between the bandit Sittius and King Bogus of Mauretania, giving it the name Africa Nova, or New Africa, the original African province becoming Old Africa. The two would be combined to become the one province of Africa several decades later. While he was at Zama, auctioning off King Juba's belongings, Caesar appointed Major General Gaius Sallustius Crispus to control the two African provinces with the rank of proconsul, making him the most senior Roman official between Morocco and Syria, and installing him in Juba's former palace at Zama. History knows the curly-headed Sallustius better for his later career as the historical writer Sallust.

By June 13, Caesar was sailing out of Utique on his way back to Italy. In his wake, most of his legions were ferried back across the Mediterranean to Sicily, and from there to Italy. As far as he was concerned, the civil war was at an end, and he began planning a major military operation, the invasion of Parthia in the East. In part this was to be an act to restore Roman pride by punishing the Parthians for their crushing defeat of his fellow triumvir Crassus at Carrhae seven years earlier. But according to Plutarch, the operation was to be much more than just a raid of retribution: after defeating the Parthians, Caesar planned to march around the Caspian Sea, through the Caucuses, then conquer Germany and the lands bordering it, adding the entire area to his Roman Empire.

The half-strength 28th Legion was dispatched to Syria to commence preparations for the Parthian operation. The 5th, 7th, 8th, 9th, 10th, and 13th Legions went into camp in Italy, to embark for the East once Caesar had completed all the civil, political, and personal business he had planned. Four legions were left behind in North Africa: the 25th, 26th, 29th, and 14th. Some or all four legions moved into the camp previously built on the cliffs outside Utique by General Varus and set to work extending it.

To be left behind in Africa, a "veteran" legion stationed with three "new" Italian legions, would have been galling for the men of the 14th, like a high school student being put in a class of elementary school children. Certainly theirs was the most senior legion at the station, but that was little to be proud of—all the other senior legions that had taken part in the Battle of Thapsus had been earmarked for the next stage in Caesar's military career, and here was the 14th consigned to a backwater. Again. Just as it'd been placed in the center at Thapsus along with the new legions, rather than be entrusted with a wing. Apparently never to live down the disgraces of Atuatuca and Lérida, there they would sit, in Tunisia, while other legions fought the last great battle of the Civil War.

In Spain, supporters flocked to Pompey's two sons Gnaeus and Sextus when they landed from the Balearic Isles with Generals Labienus and Varus and the 1st Legion in the summer of 46 B.C. Despite the fact that the brothers were only in their twenties, the locally based 2nd and Indigena Legions defected to them. Then when Caesar sent his best legions to Spain to deal with these young upstarts, contravening his promise to his veteran troops of just one last campaign in Africa before he released them from military service, the 8th, 9th, and 13th Legions all defected to the Pompey boys as well.

In the end, Caesar went to Spain himself, and defeated the elder Gnaeus Pompey at the March 17, 45 B.C. Battle of Munda, south of Córdoba, a victory wrung from the jaws of defeat. Gnaeus, General Labienus, and General Varus were all killed. A little later, Caesar took Córdoba, and Sextus Pompey went into hiding.

With the end of resistance in Spain, the Civil War was finally over. The peace terminated all chances of the 14th Legion redeeming itself in Caesar's eyes, or so it would have seemed to the men of the 14th. Now they began to pin their hopes on being included in Caesar's rumored Parthian operation.

Again the 14th was to be disappointed, for a completely unforeseeable reason. But its day would come. It would be later, rather than sooner; but one day the 14th would be Rome's most famous legion of all. Before that day arrived, the course of Roman history would be changed, dramatically, in ways no one in 45 B.C. could have imagined.

It began with an event at the capital the following year. Toward the end of March in 44 B.C., the stunned men of the 14th Legion stationed at Utique learned that on March 15, the Ides of March, just four days before he was due to set off for Syria to launch his Parthian offensive, Julius Caesar had been assassinated while attending a meeting of his Senate at Rome.

X

ANTONY AND
THE ASSASSINS

O n the night of March 15, Mark Antony, the sole remaining consul now that Caesar was dead, dined with Gaius Cassius, leader
of the conspiracy to assassinate Caesar, as the dictator's corpse
lay across town in his mansion on the Sacred Way. Simultaneously, Marcus Brutus, another leading conspirator and Cassius's brother-in-law, dined
at the house of Marcus Lepidus, Caesar's former master of horse and chief
deputy.

After the murder, the more than sixty conspirators had congregated on
Capitol Hill, guarded by a troupe of gladiators in the employ of General
Decimus Brutus Albinus, one of the murderers. Antony began to negotiate
with them, and to show his good faith he had given his infant son Antyl-
lus as a hostage to the conspirators. That night, at the two dinners, a deal
designed to prevent Rome from lurching back into civil war was ham-
mered out.

The next day, March 16, Antony convened a meeting of the Senate,
which passed his motion that an amnesty against prosecution be granted
to all the assassination conspirators. On March 17, another Senate meeting agreed to government appointments for both conspirators and Caesar
supporters, including Antony.

That same day, another component of the peace deal was implemented.
The 7th Legion, which had been camped outside the city on Tiber Island
as it waited to escort Caesar to Syria for the Parthian offensive, withdrew
east to the town of Alba Fucens, modern Albe. At the same time, the
gladiators at the capitol marched for northern Italy as General Albinus
set off to take up his appointment as governor of Cisalpine Gaul. Now
there were no armed men at Rome to use the power of the sword to either

influence or prevent the return to republican democracy envisaged by Caesar's assassins.

Caesar's funeral took place in the Forum at Rome. Cassius had been against it; he'd wanted a quick, private affair, to make sure there were no public demonstrations. But to show good faith, Brutus, as urban praetor, had given his permission—funerals and burials normally had to take place outside the city. It was a mistake. Antony used the funeral oration to condemn Cassius and Brutus, inspiring Shakespeare's famous "Friends, Romans, countrymen" speech—and to incite a riot against the conspirators.

Cassius and Brutus had grabbed up their families and left town in a hurry. By July they'd set sail from Velia south of Salerno for a covert journey to the East, with Brutus leaving the ship at Athens and Cassius sailing on to Syria. Both then began gathering the resources they needed to raise an army to go against Antony.

Meanwhile, Caesar's widow, Calpurnia, had sent her husband's personal secretary, Quintus Faberius, to Antony with Caesar's seal and private papers for safekeeping, no doubt at Antony's suggestion. This enabled Antony to issue orders and appointments headed "Memoranda of Caesar," declaring they'd been decreed by Caesar before his death. To back his forged edicts with military muscle, Antony recruited six thousand men, all ex-legionaries, into a resurrected Praetorian Guard. This ancient corps, traditionally the protection force of the praetor and later the consuls of Rome, had fallen into disuse by the first century B.C. Using his authority as sole surviving consul to reform the Guard, Antony personally chose its members and had them swear loyalty to him.

Having created these paper and steel instruments of power, Antony should have been able to rule without hindrance, but now a new figure appeared on the scene, and the picture changed. Caesar's eighteen-year-old great-nephew Octavius arrived at Rome from Apollonia in Greece, where he'd been studying, accompanied by a close friend and fellow student, nineteen-year-old Marcus Agrippa. As the dictator's heir, Octavius not only inherited three-fourths of Caesar's estate but also legally took his name, becoming Gaius Julius Caesar Octavianus. Historians would call him Octavian.

Antony, Octavian's guardian, was obstructive when the young man tried to lay his hands on the money and possessions left him in Caesar's will. Antony tried to freeze him out of the picture, but he underestimated the youth. He was not alone; the influential Cicero was to write to his friend Atticus about Octavian, "I do not trust his age and I do not know what he is after."

But surprising Antony and many others with his ability, the teenaged Octavian courted and began to win key supporters, not the least being Cicero, who, month upon month, delivered stinging speeches in the Senate against Antony. According to Cicero, Antony was as bad as Caesar, and should have been killed at the same time as the dictator. Gradually public opinion turned against Antony.

By the late summer, when the Senate refused his demand to allocate him Albinus's province of Cisalpine Gaul, Antony chose to take it, and ordered five of the six legions stationed in Macedonia—the Martia, 2nd, 4th, 5th Alaudae, and 35th—to be shipped across the Adriatic, to Brindisi. In the fall, Antony marched the legions up the eastern coast of Italy to forcibly remove Albinus. The Senate met, and in the first week of February declared a state of emergency. Soon it would declare Antony an enemy of the state, in the same way that Caesar had been outlawed back in 49 B.C. A senatorial army was put together to relieve Albinus, commanded by the new consuls for the year, General Aulus Hirtius, Caesar's former aide and biographer, and General Gaius Vibius Pansa, one of Caesar's generals.

Two of Antony's legions, the Martia and the 4th, had lost faith in him after he'd decimated them for mocking him in an assembly at Brindisi, and they came over to the Senate, or, more precisely, to young Octavian, joining the 7th at Albe. To placate these legions, the Senate made Octavian a major general, but subordinate to Hirtius and Pansa.

To bolster the defenses at Rome while Hirtius and Octavian marched to Cisalpine Gaul and Pansa raised three new legions in southern Italy, the Senate sent orders for two of the four legions stationed in the two African provinces to sail for the capital. Which legions made the journey, landing at Ostia, is not recorded. But the 14th, despite its reputation with other units as an unlucky legion, would have been first choice as the most experienced legion at the station. The two legions from Africa landed and joined new recruits digging in on the outskirts of Rome in the late spring.

After General Albinus holed up at Mutina, modern Modena, with three legions, Antony arrived with his three remaining legions and surrounded the city with trenches. Reinforcements for Albinus were soon on their way from the south, but on April 14, Antony's 2nd and 35th Legions met and mauled the Martia and three legions of new recruits eight miles south of Modena as they were led north by General Pansa to join Hirtius and Octavian outside the city. Pansa himself was hurried away, mortally wounded.

Antony's jubilant troops hailed him *imperator* in the style of old, in recognition of the success, but that afternoon, as Antony was withdrawing, his legionaries singing as they marched, he was met on the road near Forum Gallorum, modern Castelfranco, by Hirtius with the 4th and 7th Legions. This time it was Antony's turn to be savaged, taking heavy casualties. Only nightfall, the marshes, and his cavalry saved him from total defeat.

That night, Major General Servius Sulpicius Galba, Pansa's deputy, wrote to his friend Marcus Cicero, telling him of the Castelfranco battle: "Two eagles and sixty standards of Antony's have been brought in. It is a victory."

A week later, an assault by Hirtius designed to break Antony's encirclement and lift the siege of Modena failed. Hirtius himself died in the attempt. But Antony suffered such heavy casualties that he abandoned the siege, withdrew north, and marched his men across the Alps into southern France. At the Var River near Nice, he was confronted by Marcus Lepidus, who had orders from the Senate to eliminate him. But led by the men of the 10th Legion, Lepidus's four legions from Nearer Spain and three from Gaul went over to Antony, and Lepidus had no choice but to do the same.

Caesar's former aide Major General Gaius Pollio soon arrived from Farther Spain with his two legions and threw in his lot with Antony. Pollio convinced General Marcus Plancus, who had three legions in Transalpine Gaul, to also desert the Senate. On top of that, Major General Publius Ventidius, a current praetor, enlisted three new legions of his own accord and promised to support Antony—who would soon reward him with a consulship. Potentially, an army of eighteen legions could now march for Antony.

Instead of going head to head with Antony, in the fall of 43 B.C. the pragmatic Octavian sat down to negotiate a deal. The end result was the Board of Three for the Ordering of State, or the Second Triumvirate, as historians would call it. Octavian, Antony, and Lepidus divided control of the Roman Empire among them, and agreed to a list of three hundred senators and two thousand knights opposing them who would be executed. At the top of Antony's murder list was Marcus Cicero.

All through this period of the spring and summer of 43 B.C. the 14th Legion and its fellow legion from Africa had sat just outside the capital, bored by the inactivity but amused by the sights and sounds of Rome that they could see and hear across the Tiber River from their camp in Julius Caesar's former gardens on the Janiculum Hill, today's Gianicolo. Now that the Second Triumvirate had done its deal, these two legions were ordered to pack up and return to Africa. They were to go in company with the general appointed by Octavian to take over the governorship of the two African provinces, Titus Sextius.

The governor appointed by Caesar in 46 B.C., Sallust, had gone back to Rome a year later, and replacing him as governor in Africa and the 14th Legion's commander had been General Gaius Calvisius Sabinus, who had commanded the 28th Legion in Greece for Caesar. The following year a new governor arrived, Major General Quintus Cornificius. Caesar's quartermaster in Albania and Greece in 48 B.C., he'd led the 11th and 12th Legions on a difficult campaign in Illyricum during 48–47 B.C. General Cornificius was still in the governor's mansion at Utique in Africa as the 14th Legion set sail from Italy to return to Tunisia.

Octavian's new appointee General Sextius had served Caesar during the Gallic War between 54 B.C. and 50 B.C. and had been one of the generals responsible for recruiting the fresh, post-Atuatuca enlistment of the 14th Legion in 54 B.C., along with the new 15th and 16th Legions. He'd also led the 13th Legion with distinction during the Vercingetorix Revolt. He was a man the legionaries of the 14th could respect.

General Sextius arrived at Utique with the two legions, sending General Cornificius instructions to hand over his command. But Cornificius stubbornly refused, declaring he didn't recognize the authority of the Board of Three and ordering Sextius out of his province. To solve the impasse, the generals went to war. The 14th and the three other legions of the Africa station found themselves roped into the conflict. Cornificius had the larger force, with the two legions that had remained in Africa plus numerous auxiliaries.

Cornificius's deputies laid siege to Sextius's forces at Cirta and Zama. But Sextius was reinforced by King Arabio, who'd recently overthrown King Bocchus of Western Mauretania and also killed the mercenary leader, Publius Sittius, absorbing Sittius's men into his own army. Arabio had served with the Pompeians in the civil war, but on Caesar's death he'd given his allegiance to young Octavian. With the king's help, the 14th Legion and General Sextius's other units drove opposition forces all the way back to Utique.

General Cornificius came out of Utique with his legions to do battle but was outwitted and outfought by the opposition cavalry and by a commando force of volunteers from the 14th and Sextius's other units, which scaled the sea cliffs to take the legion base outside Utique behind Cornificius's back. Cornificius died on the battlefield. Several of his deputies committed suicide. His leaderless legions broke up and withdrew inland; Sextius would pardon them and restore them to the Africa garrison with the 14th.

At last the 14th Legion had shone, even if only in a sideshow. Sure enough, the 14th had been unlucky—for Cornificius. Their success gave the men of the legion new confidence that they could restore the legion's reputation for good and all when orders arrived from the Board of Three shortly after the end of the Cornificius dispute for the 14th to be shipped to Italy for a major operation.

During 43–42 B.C. Cassius and Brutus took over the legions in the East that Caesar had readied for the Parthian operation and those left with Cleopatra in Egypt. Raising a number of others locally, they built an army of twenty-two legions plus thousands of auxiliaries and cavalry, and then led their men into Macedonia, equipping them from an arms cache Caesar had built up at Demetrias for his Parthian expedition.

Camping with twenty legions at Philippi in Macedonia, astride the Egnatian Way, the military highway linking East and West, the pair attracted many leading Romans who still cherished the ideal of a democratic Roman republic, men such as Major General Marcus Favonius, who'd stayed with Pompey till his death, and General Marcus Messalla, who would speak proudly of serving Cassius even after he'd reconciled with Octavian. There, Brutus and Cassius waited, daring Antony, Octavian, and Lepidus to take them on.

In the fall of 42 B.C. Antony and Octavian convoyed twenty legions from Italy to Greece. The 14th was one of those units. An earlier convoy had landed an advance force of eight legions that had skirted Philippi and occupied the mountain passes of Thrace in Brutus's and Cassius's rear, cutting them off from overland reinforcement and resupply and forcing them to rely on transport by sea via the nearby port of Kavala.

By the beginning of October, leaving one legion to guard their baggage, Antony and Octavian had arrived at Philippi with nineteen legions. More than one hundred eighty thousand men faced each other outside Philippi. Antony soon turned a commando action into a full-scale battle without consulting Octavian. The men of the 14th and Octavian's other units, lined up in battle order outside their camp, watched open-mouthed as Antony's units, including the 4th and the 10th, charged across the plain, cut through Cassius's troops, and successfully stormed his camp. This gave Brutus the opportunity to outflank Antony, savage the 4th Legion on his left wing, and then outflank Octavian's forces. Cutting through Greek mercenaries on Octavian's wing, Brutus seized the joint camp of the two triumvirs.

As Brutus's troops sacked the camp and murdered all the noncombatants sheltering behind its walls, the 14th and their colleagues were forced to abandon it and pull back. It was a chaotic day, and by the end of it, Cassius, having seen his camp taken by Anthony and in the confusion thinking all was lost, committed suicide.

Unbeknownst to Cassius, Brutus had inflicted heavy casualties on the triumvirs, but the loss of Cassius, an experienced and respected general, was a major blow to the morale of Brutus's troops. Both sides withdrew to lick their wounds, but three weeks later, Brutus's officers convinced him to again do battle with Antony and Octavian, and this time his troops were routed. Brutus retreated with just four legions, and when they refused to continue the fight, he, too, took his own life.

Among the officers who died with Cassius and Brutus during the Philippi battles was Marcus Cato, son of Cato the Younger and cousin of Brutus. Among those who survived was a twenty-two-year-old tribune in one of Brutus's legions, Quintus Horatius Flaccus, a farmer's son from central Italy, a young man with protruding ears and poetic ambitions who would become famous as the great poet Horace.

Now, at last, with the Philippi victory and the death of Brutus and Cassius, the triumvirs had unchallenged control of the empire. Now, too, as Octavian returned to Rome, Antony was able to cross over into Asia to take up command of the Roman East.

After Philippi, the 14th Legion was shipped back to Africa, which was now considered its home base. Marcus Lepidus, increasingly sidelined by his fellow triumvirs, was given the two African provinces by Octavian. The rest of the empire was divided between Octavian and Antony. General Sextius was replaced as governor by Lepidus's man Gaius Fuficius Fango, a former centurion made a senator by Caesar.

The following year, 41 B.C., the consul Lucius Antony, Mark Antony's brother, who had been on Antony's staff during the Modena battles two years earlier, unilaterally authorized Sextius to resume his African command, deliberately snubbing Lepidus. In a repeat of the Cornificius episode, Fango refused to vacate his position, out of loyalty to Lepidus. As before, two forces of indeterminate content—but including the 14th Legion on one side or another—went to war in North Africa. But even though both sides took the other's camp, Fango committed suicide, and General Sextius resumed command of the two African provinces and their once more combined military forces.

Over the winter of 41–40 B.C., with Antony in Alexandria sharing Queen Cleopatra's bed, in Italy his wife, Fulvia, and brother Lucius attempted a coup against Octavian. They had early success, attracting thirteen of the triumvirs' legions to them in the Perugia region, but as

Octavian surrounded the rebels with three separate legionary armies the coup dissolved. Fulvia fled to Greece. Lucius surrendered to Octavian, who pardoned him.

Wary of the loyalty of six legions that had supported Lucius Antony, Octavian sent them to Africa with Marcus Lepidus, giving the 14th a lot of company in 40 B.C. The 14th Legion's strength—five thousand men after the second Atuatuca battle—had drastically declined over the years via illness and battle casualties. Just a thousand men now remained in its ranks, to share their camp with the newcomers.

In Greece, Antony's wife, Fulvia, fell ill and died. Under Roman law, Antony could not marry a foreigner, so as much as he might have wanted to make Cleopatra his wife, in 39 B.C. he entered into an obviously political marriage, taking as his new bride Octavian's sister Octavia. It was a pragmatic way to shore up the alliance of the two triumvirs. The pair also redistributed the empire between them. Antony was to control all territory east of the Balkans as far as the Euphrates, while Octavian's domain would be the West. Lepidus, left with just Africa, was not a happy man. Dismissing General Sextius, Octavian's governor of Africa, he personally took charge of the 14th and the other units in Tunisia and Numidia.

Over the winter of 39–38 B.C., which he spent in Athens, Antony sent Major General Gaius Furnius to Africa to take several legions to Asia, which Furnius was to govern, in preparation for an offensive Antony was planning against the Parthians. It seems that Lepidus refused to hand them over, and Furnius continued on, empty-handed.

In late 38 B.C. the 14th Legion was due to undergo its first reenlistment since 54 B.C. With manpower stretched to the limit, four thousand men at most were enrolled for the 14th Legion in this 38 B.C. draft. Everything points to the new enrollment taking place in the legion's original Cisalpine Gaul recruiting grounds, the Veneto and Lombardy regions. As recruits of the new 38 B.C. enlistment went into camp in Italy to await transfer to Utique, Lepidus followed Caesar's practice, failing to discharge the thousand 14th Legion veterans in Africa, retaining them in service with promises of big rewards.

The delays—in permitting the veterans to retire, and in shipping the new recruits to Tunisia to join their unit—were the direct result of the ambitions of Pompey the Great's youngest son, Sextus, for in 38 B.C. Sextus Pompey threatened to disrupt Antony, Octavian, and Lepidus's club of three.

XI

SEXTUS, SEA BATTLES, AND SUICIDES

The 14th Legion was taking part in another amphibious invasion. This time they were sailing from North Africa to Sicily. To fight a Pompey.

By 36 B.C., Pompey the Great's youngest son, Sextus, was aged thirty, and he had been at war with Rome's Board of Three for years. Since he was sixteen, when the Civil War began, he'd never known a time when his life was not on the line. Nine years back, he had escaped from Spain after his elder brother Gnaeus's defeat at Munda and gone on the run. Following Caesar's death, Sextus had come to an accommodation with the Senate, in a deal worked out at the instigation of Mark Antony. This had seen Sextus paid reparations for the loss of his father's property and given command of a Roman fleet in the western Mediterranean. Little better than a pirate, over the next six years he'd been an irritation to the triumvirs as he used his fleet to create a power base west of Italy.

With his supporters in control of the islands of Corsica and Sardinia, where triumvirate troops had switched their support to him, he'd set his sights on taking over Sicily. It had been promised to him by the triumvirs to keep him quiet, but being Octavian's domain and at the heart of Roman commercial and military shipping routes, they'd never come through on the promise. After several failed attempts at a lasting negotiated peace, in 38 B.C. Octavian decided to rid himself of Sextus Pompey by force.

In two naval battles off Sicily that year, Sextus's admirals came off the better, and then storms drove many of Octavian's ships onto the rocky coastline of southwestern Italy, opposite Sicily. Octavian himself and a number of his shipwrecked sailors and soldiers managed to make it ashore on a remote stretch of the coast. The 13th Legion was just then marching over the mountains nearby, and came to Octavian's aid. Its legionaries shared rations with the shipwrecked men, provided shelter, and tended to injuries.

The 13th had undergone its scheduled reenlistment in 42 B.C. But instead of discharging its one thousand surviving veterans recruited by Caesar back in 58 B.C., Octavian convinced these men to stay in service for a few more years in return for big rewards. Just like Lepidus and the 14th. They were still waiting for their discharges and their rewards, which Octavian now indicated would come once Sextus was sorted out. For sort him out he must—as a result of Octavian's maritime disasters, Sextus was now able to occupy Sicily. And all the troops garrisoned on the island went over to him.

Octavian had lost more than half his ships to gale and enemy action. So he made a deal with Mark Antony, agreeing to swap thousands of his legionaries for 120 warships from the East. Octavia even begged another ten warships from her husband in exchange for a thousand of Octavian's Praetorian Guardsmen, men chosen by Antony in person. Antony kept his part of the bargain, but Octavian reneged on his.

Octavian now dismissed his naval commander, Gaius Calvisius—former governor of Africa and the 14th Legion's commander at the close of the Civil War in 45–44 B.C. In Calvisius's place as admiral in chief, Octavian appointed his dependable best friend, Marcus Agrippa. Made a consul and lieutenant general the previous year by Octavian, Agrippa had just returned from putting down an uprising in Aquitania, in southwestern France. This appointment of generals as admirals was the norm—Roman generals were expected to be as adept at sea as on land. If a good general turned out to be a great admiral, as proved to be the case with the multi-talented Agrippa, it was a bonus.

In the spring of 36 B.C., twenty-four-year-old Octavian and twenty-five-year-old Agrippa had finalized plans to retake Sicily from Sextus Pompey. Their joint army-navy offensive would involve twenty-four legions. Three-pronged, it would be an amphibious operation three times larger than anything Julius Caesar had ever attempted. Here, Octavian's talent for organization came to the fore.

Now, on July 1, 36 B.C., three separate convoys set out for Sicily. By far the largest convoy, a thousand transports escorted by seventy warships, sailed from Tunisia under Marcus Lepidus. Among the tens of thousands of legionaries being transported in Lepidus's armada were the thousand remaining men of the old enlistment of the 14th Legion, now two years past their discharges, accompanied by the three Italian legions of the Africa station, the 25th, 26th, and 29th, all of which still had three years of their enlistments left to run.

These four units were accompanied by the six legions transferred to Africa after Lucius Antony's failed coup attempt. A number of additional legions had been sent to Africa some time after 46 B.C., because twelve legions were being carried in the North African convoy, while another four waited back in Tunisia for the convoy's ships to unload and return for them. Lepidus's troopships also carried thousands of cavalry and auxiliaries.

As this massive convoy filled the waters off western Sicily, the second convoy—102 of Mark Antony's former vessels commanded by Lieutenant General Titus Statilius Taurus, Octavian's most trusted general after Agrippa—put out from Taranto, on the boot of Italy. Like Agrippa, Taurus had been a consul the previous year. Octavian's own fleet, of unknown size, sailed from Pozzuoli, on the Bay of Naples.

At first, all went well. The 14th Legion and its fellow legions of the Tunisian armada stormed ashore on the western coast of Sicily, unopposed. As Lepidus then besieged young Pompey's garrisons at Marsala and neighboring towns, his transports sailed back to Tunisia to collect the last four legions. But to the east, the two other invasion fleets were forced back to port by bad weather, which wrecked thirty-two cruisers and several frigates and damaged many more, although most passengers and crew were saved.

Meanwhile, Lepidus's troopships embarked the four waiting legions in Tunisia and again set sail. But this time, one of Sextus Pompey's fleets caught the convoy at sea—and devastated it. Two of the four legions in the convoy were close to wiped out in the savage ship-to-ship fighting. The other two legions managed to land and join Lepidus.

After pushing his commanders to repair his fleet within thirty days, Octavian tried for his eastern landing a second time. As Octavian put to sea, Agrippa, off the northern coast of Sicily, took his battle fleet against 155 opposition warships at Mylae, modern-day Milazzo. The Battle of Mylae saw Agrippa sink thirty of Sextus's principal ships, for the loss of five of his own, before the other side withdrew.

This provided breathing space for troop landings, enabling Agrippa to put three legions ashore on the northern coast, while despite difficult weather and nagging naval opposition, Octavian put three legions under Lieutenant General Lucius Cornificius ashore on the eastern coast, at Taormina. For four days Cornificius's units struggled inland over difficult terrain in the vicinity of the famous volcano Mount Etna, harassed by young Pompey's troops all the way, before linking up with Agrippa's legions at Milazzo.

In late August, Octavian himself landed at Tyndaris, on the northern coast, with several more legions. He had now put ashore a total of twenty-one legions, five thousand auxiliary light infantry, and twenty thousand cavalry. After Lepidus brought several of his units, including the 14th, overland from the western coast and joined him, Octavian advanced into the northeastern corner of the island and cut off Pompey at Messina. The men recruited for the 14th in northern Italy and the legion's veterans who'd come across from Tunisia were now able to link up. As veterans and recruits joined forces, the 14th Legion was close to full strength for the first time in eighteen years.

Sextus's strength lay with his naval forces. And he considered that Neptune, god of the sea, was on his side; so much so that he replaced his normal crimson general's cloak with a dark blue one, to show that he was a son of the sea. Now, confident of victory on water, he challenged Octavian to a naval battle. Although Octavian had experienced mixed luck on water, he accepted the challenge, gambling his future on the hope that his best friend, Agrippa, would bring him victory as he had at Mylae.

The Battle of Naulochus took place off the northeastern coast of Sicily on September 3, 36 B.C., with three hundred battleships and cruisers from each side doing battle just offshore. As the battle raged, the men of the 14th and fellow legions sat and watched the show from the clifftops. To distinguish one side from the other, the temporary wooden fighting towers erected on the decks fore and aft on each ship were painted a different color for each navy. Perhaps Pompey opted for blue for his ships, to match his cloak.

Neptune deserted young Pompey, for the day brought a stunning victory for Agrippa. Only seventeen of Sextus Pompey's ships escaped, dumping their fighting towers overboard and fleeing for the Strait of Messina. The rest were sunk, burned, or captured. Just three of Agrippa's ships were lost. Late in the day, as sailors and marines on Agrippa's warships raised a victory chant that rolled across the water, it was answered from the shore by the men of the 14th and the triumvirs' other legions.

Sextus's troops outside Messina quickly surrendered. But another eight rebel legions hurried from the northwest to support Sextus at Messina, now under siege from Lepidus and legions including the 14th. When Octavian's warships appeared off Messina, Sextus didn't wait for the reinforcements. He sailed with his last seventeen ships and headed for Asia, planning to throw himself on Mark Antony's mercy. When his legions arrived at Messina, only to find he'd deserted them, they opened surrender negotiations with Lepidus. Now the increasingly sidelined triumvir saw an opportunity for himself.

Accepting their surrender, Lepidus combined Sextus's troops with his own, then let all twenty-two legions now under his command sack Messina, supposedly on the grounds that the city had supported young Pompey. Once the legionaries had finished their pillage, Lepidus played a desperate card: having ingratiated himself with these legions, he called on them to swear allegiance—to him, and to him alone.

Octavian, only miles away and approaching fast, acted quickly to nip this insurrection in the bud, calling a meeting with his fellow triumvir outside Messina. In this first meeting, Lepidus haughtily offered to give Sicily and Africa to Octavian in exchange for Octavian's control of the rest of the West. Octavian refused, and angrily departed.

A day or so later, Octavian came unannounced to Lepidus's massive camp. Leaving his cavalry escort outside, he entered with a few staff officers and a handful of bodyguards, probably German cavalrymen, and passed along the tent lines of the legions, talking to Lepidus's men at their quarters.

Appian says that from the ranks he was greeted by cries of "Hail, Commander!"

Men who had served Sextus Pompey crowded around young Octavian to beg his pardon. According to Appian, in response Octavian declared that he was amazed these men weren't acting in their own interests. Taking the hint, standard-bearers hurried away and returned with their standards, forming up behind Octavian.

In his headquarters tent, an alarmed Lepidus received a report of what was happening outside. Hurrying from the tent, he called his bodyguard unit to arms, then came face to face with his fellow triumvir. In the tense standoff that followed, several of Lepidus's men threw javelins at young Octavian. One of Octavian's bodyguards was killed, and a javelin even glanced off Octavian's own breastplate. Shielded by his officers and bodyguards, Octavian withdrew.

Octavian's angry cavalry then surrounded a number of forts on the camp perimeter, wiping out Lepidus's men on duty at one fort. Soon the legionaries at all of Lepidus's outposts were going over to Octavian. Troops whom Lepidus sent to reinforce the outposts also changed sides. The rot had set in.

Many legionaries in Lepidus's force, including the men of the 14th, had never even seen Octavian before the day he appeared in their camp. Equally, a number, including veterans of the 14th, had firsthand experience of the weak and changeable Lepidus, going back as far as the Gallic War. It took just the sight of the fine-boned young Octavian for the troops to recognize the quality that set him apart from others, even though he had turned just twenty-five on August 6 of that year.

It was a quality put into words by Appian. When General Pansa was dying a slow, painful death in 43 B.C. from wounds he'd received from Mark Antony's troops outside Modena, he had said, according to Appian, that by his achievements, Octavian had demonstrated that he had "the divine force of destiny" on his side. Yet destiny smiles on many who are unfit or unready. It was not enough to be destiny's child. Octavian had a maturity that other men could not acquire in a lifetime. He wasn't even old enough to sit in the Senate. He was seventeen years short of the legal age at which a Roman could then be elected a consul. Yet his talents more than equipped him to rule the Roman Empire.

The temerity of this attempt on the life of Julius Caesar's heir galvanized Lepidus's men and Sextus Pompey's former troops. Over the next twenty-four hours they deserted Lepidus's camp in droves and went to Octavian. Desperate, Lepidus grabbed the standard of one deserting unit in an attempt to turn the tide. It may have been a standard of the 14th Legion—we aren't told which unit.

"Let go!" Appian says the standard-bearer demanded.

"I will not!" Lepidus replied.

"You'll let go when you're dead!" the standard-bearer growled, with his right hand on the hilt of his sword.

Lepidus got the message. He let go of the standard.

In the end, the 14th Legion and all the other infantry units changed sides, and then Lepidus's last supporters, his auxiliary cavalry, left him as well. The troopers even sent Octavian a message asking if he wanted them to kill Lepidus, but he wouldn't have it. Deserted by all supporters, the weak, insipid Lepidus went to Octavian, then tried to fall on his knees in front of his young colleague, blubbering and wailing as he begged for his life. But Octavian had him keep his feet and his dignity.

Lepidus was not only allowed to live, he also retained the lifelong appointment he had inherited from Caesar of *pontifex maximus*. But that was all. He would live in secluded retirement for another twenty-four years, just across the Strait of Messina, according to Suetonius, at a remote retreat popular with the Roman elite, Circeii, today's village of San Felice Circeo. Lepidus's father had taken on the Senate of his day, using force, only to be defeated by Pompey the Great and to die in exile in 77 B.C. Lofty ambition, poor judgment, and failed gambits seem to have been the destined lot of the Lepidus family.

As for Sextus Pompey, the following year, running out of friends and desperate to be taken to Mark Antony, he would finally surrender in Asia to Antony's young general and quartermaster during his recent Parthian campaign, Marcus Titius. Severe, by-the-book General Titius ignored Sextus's pleas for clemency and put him to death at Miletus. Some said Antony personally authorized Sextus's execution. Others say a deputy used his seal in his absence. One way or another, Sextus Pompey lost his head. And the influence that Pompey the Great's name had exerted on the Roman world for more than half a century died with his last surviving son.

Following the humbling of Lepidus outside Messina, Octavian called an assembly of his army, now including the legions that had marched for him, for Lepidus, and for Sextus Pompey. As was the custom, Octavian praised individual soldiers for their courage during the Sicilian campaign, handing out coveted golden crowns to men who had performed particularly meritorious acts of bravery, and paying part of the bonuses he'd promised every man before the operation began—he couldn't afford to pay them in full, but promised to do so as soon as he was able—and pardoning officers who had served with Sextus.

Now, voices called from the 13th and 14th Legion ranks: "Give us our discharge!" The veterans of the old enlistment of the 13th were six years past their due discharge date; those of the 14th, two years overdue.

But Octavian responded that he was not prepared to release any of his troops yet. When he went on to say that he planned to take his army on a campaign against rebellious tribes in Illyricum, the veterans of the 13th and 14th refused to serve any longer. They probably guessed he was thinking more about Antony than about Illyricum. Scowling down at them, Octavian reminded the two thousand veterans of the two legions of the laws and oaths that governed them as legionaries, and the punishment he could dole out to them. He meant decimation.

The men of the 13th and 14th weren't fazed by this thinly veiled threat. And Octavian, seeing men who had recently come over from Lepidus and Sextus being made uneasy by his tough attitude toward two of his own veteran legions, moderated his tone. "I'll distribute additional bravery crowns to you men," he said to the 13th and 14th veterans, "and your centurions and tribunes will have the purple-bordered full-dress toga of the Equestrian Order, and the status of decurion in their hometowns."

According to Appian, a tribune of either the 13th or 14th Legion, a Colonel Ofillius, called back a caustic response: "Crowns and purple are toys for children! Soldiers' rewards are land and money."

There was a rowdy chorus of agreement from the 13th and 14th ranks.

Incensed, Octavian stormed from the dais, and men of the two legions crowded around Colonel Ofillius, congratulating him on his forthrightness. But by the next morning, Ofillius had disappeared; he was never heard of again. Suspecting foul play and seeking protection in numbers, the legionaries now sent large delegations to Octavian to demand their discharge, their bonuses, and the land grants they'd been promised.

The disaffection of these two legions threatened to spread to the whole army, whose three previously disparate entities Octavian now held together with a slender thread of authority, as he knew only too well. Once he'd cooled off, he begrudgingly ordered the discharge of all two thousand veterans of the 13th and 14th, informing them pointedly that their discharges were granted against the wishes of their commander in chief. The retirees were shipped to Italy at once, to march home to Cisalpine Gaul. But Octavian only paid the men of the 13th Legion the bonuses he'd promised, because, he said, they'd served him loyally in the Modena battles seven years before—they'd actually served his superior, Hirtius—and had waited longer for discharge than the 14th.

The thousand discharged men of the 14th went home toting purses bulging with the savings from their military career, their pay and the profits from booty taken from Gaul to Messina, but bitter that they had been denied the bonuses and land granted other retiring legionaries. With Atuatuca, Uxellodunum, Lérida, Philippi, and Sicily behind them, they tramped up through Italy, crossed the Po River, and at towns, villages, and farmhouses across northeastern Italy, the ex-soldiers knocked on shocked relatives' doors for the first time in almost two decades. One of those 14th Legion retirees was Legionary Gaius Allius. He set up home at Ateste, modern Este, by the Adige River, where he married and settled down. There at Este, his wife would bury him sometime before 14 B.C. His tombstone survives to this day.

Back in Sicily, the men of the 14th Legion's new enlistment were presented with the silver eagle that had been carried by the legion since Atuatuca. Conscious of the dark cloud that had hung over the reputation of the 14th since 54 B.C., and that would have only been made worse by the last enlistment's rude discharge, the new recruits would have been anxious to prove themselves. Not only to Octavian, but also to the men of other legions who would have considered the 14th an unlucky legion, even a bad-luck legion, a pariah legion, despite the 14th's good work in Africa and Sicily of late. But as they were to find, bad reputations are easy to make but hard to shake.

Octavian's army was now huge. According to Appian, after reclaiming Sicily, Octavian found himself with six hundred warships, twenty-five thousand cavalry, twelve thousand five hundred auxiliaries, and forty-five legions, including the 14th. Within five years these forces would be involved in another civil war as Antony and his mistress Cleopatra, queen of Egypt, combined to take on Octavian.

Cleopatra was a fluent speaker of numerous foreign languages apart from her native Greek—the members of her Egyptian royal family were of Greek descent. She spoke another language with even greater fluency: the language of seduction. Plutarch was to say that Cleopatra knew a thousand different ways to flatter. No great beauty by all accounts, she had flattered her way into Julius Caesar's heart and bed. And she did the same with Mark Antony, winning him away from his new wife, Octavia, who, both Plutarch and Appian suggest, Antony genuinely loved. Octavia bore Antony several daughters, but Cleopatra also bore him two sons and a daughter.

With Cleopatra's emotional and financial support—based on the enormous Ptolemy fortune—Antony set out to dominate the Roman stage. His efforts to push back the Parthians saw mixed success. His failed invasion of Media in 36 B.C. cost him twenty-four thousand men, but his deputy, Lieutenant General Publius Ventidius, won major victories in Armenia that boosted Antony's reputation and ego. Antony punished his regional opponents, but he rewarded others, such as Herod the Great, who was cemented on the throne of Judea, with his land protected from the avaricious eyes of Cleopatra.

Not that Cleopatra fared badly from the partnership—in 34 B.C. Antony gifted all lands in the East formerly ruled by the great Greek king of Macedonia, Alexander, to Cleopatra and her children, a move that outraged many back home in Rome.

The five-year agreement of the triumvirs had been renewed in 38 B.C. When it came up for renewal a second time, in late 33 B.C., Octavian vetoed it, decreeing the dissolution of the Board of Three for the Ordering of State. It was all downhill from there. In the new year, Antony sent Octavian's sister letters of divorce, a move that swiftly destroyed any hope for a defrosting of relations between the two former ruling partners. Soon after, Octavian formally declared war—on Cleopatra, a foreign enemy.

Both current consuls went to join Antony; two hundred senators likewise fled to the East, to Antony. But the traffic wasn't one-way; several of

Antony's top men came back from the East to stand behind Octavian, including Marcus Titius, the general who'd executed Sextus Pompey four years back. If Octavian suffered from self-doubt, he didn't betray it. With the legions of the West solidly behind him, he and his brilliant deputy, Marcus Agrippa, made plans for a lightning campaign to destroy Antony and Cleopatra.

Immediately following the Sicilian campaign in 36 B.C., the new enlistment of the 14th Legion was transferred back to the 14th's regular station in Africa. There it stayed through four years during which the rivalry between Octavian and Antony blew up into war.

At their base outside Utique, the men of the 14th would have heard reports of the war as it flared up in Greece, and turned anxious eyes toward Egypt. Antony's dominion included Cyrenaica. Taking in today's state of Libya, it lay between the province of Africa and Egypt. Antony maintained seven legions in Egypt and Cyrenaica, and the larger part of that force was now camped in Cyrenaica under General Pinarius Scarpus.

Cassius Dio says that General Scarpus's troops had been positioned there in Cyrenaica to defend Egypt—against the 14th and Octavian's other legions in Africa. Equally, it's likely they were there in preparation for an invasion of Africa. Had Octavian not acted to forestall Antony's offensive operations by taking the war to him in Greece, it's likely that Antony would have ordered General Scarpus to invade Tunisia from Libya, in which case the 14th and the three other legions in Africa would have had a major battle on their hands. But it turned out that the center of operations was in Greece.

After first establishing a headquarters at Ephesus—modern Selçuk, in Turkey—in the spring of 31 B.C., Antony advanced twelve legions into Greece and set up a new headquarters at Athens before moving on to Patras, present-day Pátrai, creating a major supply base on the Ambracian Gulf on the west coast, at Actium, where his battle fleet and Cleopatra's Egyptian fleet met and concentrated. Combined, they had 230 battleships and cruisers here, and fifty transports.

In the summer of 31 B.C., Octavian appeared unexpectedly off the west coast of Greece with a battle fleet of four hundred ships, mostly fast frigates, escorting two hundred transports. As Octavian landed forty thousand legionaries and built a camp on the shore not far from Actium, Agrippa's warships beat off Antony's squadrons in several engagements, took Pátrai, and sealed off Antony's supply lines via the Gulf of Corinth.

Antony decided to withdraw to Egypt and regroup. Cleopatra now spoke in Antony's councils of war, influencing Antony's decision-making. They devised a breakout plan involving a sea battle, not a land battle. Off Actium on September 2, the couple succeeded in breaking out with eighty warships, but the rest were sunk or fell into Octavian's hands. Within a week, Antony's troops ashore surrendered to Octavian.

Following the Battle of Actium, Octavian discharged all Italians from both his and Antony's surrendered legions who were due to retire—fifteen legions raised by Caesar in 49 B.C. were now two years past their discharge date, and the four raised in 48 B.C. were a year overdue. Their men went home to Italy as Octavian marched on Egypt with the non-Italian legions.

The 14th Legion was able to sit out the rest of the war, for when the new year came, Antony's legions in Cyrenaica changed sides. Taken over by one of their colonels, the thirty-nine-year-old Gaius Cornelius Gallus, they marched across the border into Egypt, and at the port of Sollum destroyed scores of Antony's ships. As these units advanced on Alexandria from the west, Octavian came down through Syria with his army and entered Egypt from the east.

Pelusium, site of Pompey the Great's murder almost eighteen years before, and a major Egyptian military base, was quickly taken by Octavian. Plutarch quotes him saying in his thirteen-volume memoirs, which covered his life up to 29 B.C., that Pelusium was surrendered to him on Cleopatra's orders; in her heart, she had already deserted Antony.

Antony was by now like a bee in a bottle. Rushing to Sollum in the west, he made a failed surprise attack on Colonel Gallus and his own former troops before trying to talk them into coming back to him. Failing again, he dashed back to Alexandria to stand in the way of Octavian, whose advance reached the Egyptian capital in August of 30 B.C. Outside the city, after Antony's last infantry were wiped out, his cavalry surrendered.

On August 30, fifty-one-year-old Mark Antony took his own life, dying in Cleopatra's arms. Cleopatra had been secretly negotiating with Octavian for some time, but apparently horrified by the prospect of being paraded through Rome as a captive, she also famously committed suicide within days of Antony's death.

In Cleopatra's mausoleum, Octavian found a massive treasure—enough to pay his men everything he owed them and to finance a standing Roman army for years to come. In recognition of the fact that it was his conquest of Egypt that had made him, Octavian's seal for the next three years bore the image of an Egyptian sphinx.

The civil wars that had lasted, on and off, for the past twenty years were finally at an end. Octavian, sole ruler of Rome, rationalized the combined army he had inherited, abolishing a number of legions and combining others to create a standing army of twenty-eight legions. In this reorganization process the four thousand remaining men of the 14th Legion found themselves combined with new marching partners: Martians.

XII

PAIN IN SPAIN,
GLORY IN GERMANY

T In 30 B.C., at a stroke, the 14th Legion became the Legio XIIII
Gemina Martia—the 14th Gemina Martia Legion. (The legion
number was written as XIIII, not XIV.) Octavian's legion reforms
of 31–30 B.C. saw him reduce the legions that had marched for Antony
and himself from fifty-nine to twenty-eight. It was Octavian's intent that
never again would Italians have to serve in the ranks of Rome's legions.
That role would be filled by men from the provinces. From now on, only
troops for the elite Praetorian Guard and Rome's City Guard would be
recruited south of the Po.

To end up with twenty-eight legions, Octavian abolished a number of
units and combined several others. Those that were combined were called
Gemina or "twin" legions. In this way, the four thousand men of the
38 B.C. enlistment of the 14th Legion were combined with the thousand
or so remaining men of the Martia Legion.

All the legions of Octavian's new professional Roman army comprised
one double-strength 1st Cohort—5 double-strength centuries of 160 men
each, with a total of 800 men led by 6 "first-rank" centurions—and 9
cohorts each of 6 centurions and 474 men. Every legion also now had its
own cavalry squadron of 124 mounted legionaries and NCOs led by 4 decurions, or lieutenants, for scouting, screening, and communications.

The legion command structure also changed. Of the legion's six tribunes, five would now be young eighteen- to nineteen-year-old members of
the Equestrian Order, who served for six months as officer cadets of lieutenant colonel rank on the legion's headquarters staff. They then moved
on to appointments as prefects in charge of auxiliary infantry and cavalry
units. The sixth tribune with each legion was now a senior tribune, or full

colonel, who was the legion's second in command. By the reign of the emperor Claudius seventy years later, the promotional ladder was formalized so that a young officer first had to serve with auxiliary infantry units after his cadetship, then move up to command auxiliary cavalry before becoming eligible for appointment as a "broad stripe" tribune and deputy commander of a legion.

Each legion now had a dedicated commander of brigadier general rank—normally a new senator of thirty or so—who initially served for two years. In later decades this period would increase, with four-year postings not uncommon. We don't know the identity of the 14th Gemina Martia's first commander, but he would have been a young senator with extensive experience as a colonel during the war with Antony.

Each legion now had a number of auxiliary units permanently attached to it. In most cases, details of the auxiliary units in support of individual legions are sketchy, but in the case of the 14th Gemina Martia we know that by the next century its permanent auxiliary light infantry companions were eight cohorts from the Batavi tribe in present-day Holland, plus two *alae*, or wings, of cavalry, each of 480 Batavian auxiliary troopers.

Auxiliaries were noncitizens, they were paid less than legionaries, they served five years longer, and they weren't considered in the same class as legionaries because they lacked citizenship rights. There also were auxiliary units that served independently of legions, and they were generally assigned to garrison duty in peaceful provinces.

So that legions couldn't influence politics at Rome, Octavian required that from this point on, no legion be based in Italy south of the Po. That role was reserved for the Praetorian Guard, which was based in Rome and answered directly to Octavian. Legions were allocated permanent provincial stations, where they were required to conduct military campaigns in the warmer months and to go into local base camps over winter. Octavian stipulated that a maximum of two legions could occupy any winter camp. And no legion could be stationed in the province where it was recruited, to ensure it stood aloof from local politics.

To keep the army busy, to secure and expand the empire's borders and commerce, and to generate income from the sale of booty and prisoners, Octavian invariably had at least one field army conducting offensive operations in some part of the world. Within a year of the conquest of Egypt, which now became a Roman province under the command of a prefect, Octavian sent General Marcus Crassus with several legions on a successful campaign against tribes in northern Greece and along the Danube in present-day Bulgaria. He also sent the prefect of Egypt on an abortive and costly 24 B.C. expedition with three legions onto the Arabian Peninsula.

Legions also were involved in police operations in the Swiss Alps and to counter unrest among the mountain tribes of northern Spain.

In 27 B.C., the Senate offered Octavian the title of Augustus, meaning "revered." It was as Augustus Caesar that he was known for the rest of his long life and after it. By 23 B.C. he was granted the powers that made him king of Rome in all but name. Like Julius Caesar, he steered away from the title of king, but unlike Julius Caesar, he was a firm but benevolent pseudo-king. Neither Augustus nor his immediate successors were called emperor in their own day, but it's by this title that history came to identify him.

The new 14th Gemina Martia Legion was posted to the Rhine after the civil wars, under the overall control of Lieutenant General Marcus Vinicius, whose command was based in Gaul. All was quiet for several years, but in 25 B.C. they saw action. Germanic tribes of the northwestern Alps in present-day Switzerland had kidnapped and then murdered Roman merchants who had come to do business with them. In an undocumented operation, General Vinicius led several legions on a punitive raid against these Germans, which was bloodily successful in teaching the Germans a lesson.

As for Augustus himself, he had his sights set elsewhere. From the Rhine the men of the 14th heard that by early in that same year, 25 B.C., Augustus was involved in a major offensive against tribes in northern Spain, arriving there with cohorts of the Praetorian Guard to take personal command. That spring he launched a campaign involving the Praetorians and seven legions. It's likely that four legions operated directly under Augustus's command—the 1st, 2nd, 3rd, and 8th—with the other three marching under his deputy, Lieutenant General Gaius Antistius, for all four of these legions were to come out of this period honored with the title of Augusta, meaning "Augustus's," a title bestowed on them by Augustus personally for their valor under his leadership.

Augustus's early efforts against the Asture and Cantabri tribes in Spain's Cantabrian Mountains went badly. Accustomed to the set-piece battles of the Civil War, he was frustrated by the guerrilla tactics of the mountain tribesmen, who avoided close-quarters fighting and instead conducted hit-and-run raids. Taking seriously ill, Augustus was forced to withdraw to Tarragona, on Spain's northeastern coast. According to Suetonius, he was diagnosed with "abscesses on the liver." Too unwell for the rigors and anxieties of the continuing campaign against the guerrillas, he handed task force command over to General Antistius.

Later that same year, 25 B.C., General Antistius spread his Roman legions across northwestern Spain. Operating from three forward bases,

Antistius was able to lure the Spaniards into pitched battles. He and his deputy, General Titus Carisius, then followed on the heels of retreating tribesmen and took a number of their mountain fortresses, including Lancia, the Asturian capital. By the end of fall, peace treaties had been negotiated with the tribes. Augustus, still at Tarragona, celebrated a victory. As he returned to Rome at year's end he left his sixteen-year-old stepson Tiberius behind to organize spectacles in the legion camps for the entertainment of the troops.

On his return, the Senate voted Augustus a Triumph, for the success his generals had brought him in northern Spain and for the successful German campaign of General Vinicius and his legions—for which Augustus also was hailed as *imperator*. Augustus accepted the honors and trappings that went with the Triumph but didn't bother with the street parade, creating a precedent that would often be followed in future years when many generals were granted triumphal decorations but not the Triumph's public parade.

All this celebration proved a little premature. Before long the Cantabrian War flared again, and this time it would last for years. It began when the tribes sent messages that they wanted to present the Romans with grain and other gifts. A detachment of troops sent to collect the goods was massacred. The war was on again, off again for years until by 19 B.C. the conflict seemed at an end. Year by year, Roman commanders had captured numbers of Cantabrians, selling them into slavery for twenty years. But by 19 B.C. many of these prisoners had escaped back to the mountains. They stirred the nine Cantabrian tribes into rising once more, so that when Augustus's deputy, Marcus Agrippa, arrived in Spain on an inspection tour he had to lead a grueling counteroffensive. Angered by the cowardice of the 1st Augusta Legion in the initial stage, Agrippa stripped it of its Augusta title and transferred it to Gaul.

Agrippa's troops suffered numerous reverses before they eventually succeeded in overrunning the Cantabrian fortresses and wrapping up the war. Agrippa, determined to prevent any future uprising, had his legions execute most male prisoners capable of bearing arms. They then marched the remaining men and their women and children down onto the plain. The nine tribes of the Cantabri were reduced to seven and compelled to live on the plain, never again to return to the mountains.

The focus of Roman military operations now turned to Germany beyond the Rhine River. Between 12 and 9 B.C., Rome's offensive operations against increasingly hostile German tribes east of the Rhine were led by Drusus Caesar. Drusus was Augustus's nephew and adopted son and, ironically, Mark Antony's son-in-law, having married Octavia's daughter Antonia. His children would include two boys, the handsome Germanicus, named for his father's exploits in Germany, and the younger, slower Claudius, a boy with a clubfoot whom many considered mentally retarded.

Still only in his twenties, the dashing Drusus, vested by Augustus with the authority of a modern field marshal or five-star general, established two Rhine bases for his operations. One, Vetera, on the lower Rhine, became the present-day town of Xanten in Holland. The other, on the upper Rhine, was at a Celtic settlement at the mouth of the Main River, where a shrine to the Celtic god Mogo stood. Drusus named it Moguntiacum, after Mogo. It would become the present-day city of Mainz, capital of the German state of Rheinland-Pfalz. It was at Mainz that the 14th Gemina Martia Legion joined Drusus's army for the German offensives.

Leading as many as ten legions, including the 14th, Drusus used both amphibious and land operations to push deep into Germany year after year and subdue German tribes including the Frisii on the North Sea coast, and the Chauci, Cherusci, and Chatti east of the Rhine. Then, at the height of his success, the twenty-nine-year-old field marshal fell from his horse and broke his leg. Gangrene, it seems, set in. Drusus lingered, in agony, for a month, long enough for his devoted thirty-three-year-old elder brother Tiberius to ride four hundred miles from Pavia in Italy to the Rhine to be with him when he died.

Though devastated by his brother's death, Tiberius accepted the emperor Augustus's commission to take up where Drusus had left off. He would lead the 14th Gemina Martia and eleven other legions on nine campaigns into Germany, year upon year.

In 6 B.C. the 14th Gemina Martia Legion underwent its latest discharge and reenlistment. New recruits from northern Italy marched up to Germany to replace the retiring men. It was now regular practice for some legionaries to sign on for a second enlistment, and they moved up into the legion's senior cohorts, the 1st, 2nd, and 3rd, while the recruits filled the junior cohorts. Traditionally, the most senior officer at each post presented his legions' new cohorts with their standards. As the men of retiring cohorts marched away they took their old standards with them, to march behind them when recalled to serve in the Evocati Corps militia, as their discharge conditions required. Only a legion's eagle, now gold, as opposed to the silver eagle of republican times, never left the legion.

The legion's new cohort and maniple standards of 6 B.C. were seven to eight feet tall and topped by the emblem of an open right hand, symbol of power. Below that, a horizontal bar was inscribed with the legion's number and name, and the cohort number, and under that, the symbol of a goat, representing Capricorn, the 14th Gemina's birth sign. Next came a round ceramic *imago* of the emperor Augustus, and another of Julia Augusta, his wife. Farther down the wooden shaft were metal roundels and symbols celebrating bravery awards received by men of each maniple, and last of all a tuft of hay, representing the hay that had been twirled around the earliest Roman standards. Standards were sacred objects, purified by priests with perfumes and oils every spring in the Lustration Exercise prior to campaigning, and standard-bearers were expected to defend them with their lives.

The highest-ranking officer at Mainz in 6 B.C. was Rhine Army commander in chief Tiberius Caesar, and Tacitus indicates he duly presented the 14th with its new standards that year. He would have used time-honored words as he passed the standards to their proud bearers at assembly: "Under this standard you shall conquer."

In A.D. 4, the 14th Gemina Martia completed its latest campaign in Germany, a campaign led by Tiberius, who'd recently returned to his command after a lengthy reclusive sojourn on the island of Rhodes. It was a campaign that brought the complete submission of the Cherusci and Bructeri Germans. Under the treaty that terminated hostilities, the king of the Cherusci agreed to permit Roman traders to cross the Rhine each year to set up for business in the tribe's main market towns; to permit Roman legions free and unmolested passage through his cantons, or districts; to pay taxes to Rome; and to supply numbers of his finest, fittest young men to serve as auxiliary light infantry in the Roman army.

In return, Rome offered the Cherusci peace and commerce. Rome promised to protect the tribe from its enemies with Roman force of arms, and young nobles of the tribe were taken into the Roman army to command the Cherusci's own auxiliaries; given the rank of prefect, or colonel; and admitted into the Equestrian Order of Roman knights.

In compliance with treaty conditions, the king of the Cherusci's two sons crossed the Rhine to take up posts as colonels of auxiliaries in the Roman army. One son, Flavus, older than his sibling by several years, was posted with his Cheruscan cohort to the Army of the Upper Rhine at Mainz, where the 14th Legion was stationed.

The other son was twenty-two years old in A.D. 4. Many auxiliaries didn't begin their enlistments with the Roman army until age twenty-five, so the younger son of the king of the Cherusci may not have taken up his colonelcy until three years later. When he did so, he was stationed with the Army of the Lower Rhine, now based at the capital of the Ubii Germans at a settlement that became over time the city of Cologne. That son, who displayed great skill with a variety of arms, took a Roman name, Arminius. The name by which German history was to celebrate him, as Germany's first national hero, was his Cheruscan name: Hermann.

Within just a few short years, Arminius, a.k.a. Hermann the German, would give Rome and her emperor the shock of their lives.

XIII

BLOOD AND GUTS IN PANNONIA

T he men of the current-enlistment 14th Legion, now twelve-year veterans, were a long way east of the Rhine, slogging through Bohemia, near the present-day border between Germany and the Czech Republic. It was the spring of A.D. 6. This was the third successive year they'd driven deep into Germany.

The previous year, they'd penetrated as far as the Elbe River. Now the 14th was part of an army of twelve legions that was pushing back the Marcomanni, a fierce German tribe that had given Julius Caesar a hard time and that one hundred and seventy years later would battle the emperor Marcus Aurelius in the wars depicted in the movie *Gladiator*.

As always, at the end of the day's march, the legions built a temporary camp. And on this afternoon, as thousands of Roman troops were putting the finishing touches to the earth and timber fortifications, a dusty legion cavalry courier and his escort made their way past the outer guard pickets and rode up to the decuman gate. The courier dismounted outside the gate of the massive camp spreading on the edge of the Bohemian forest and reported to the centurion of the guard. "Dispatch for the commander in chief," he would have said, removing a scroll from his tubular leather dispatch case.

The centurion must have stiffened when he saw the seal on the trooper's dispatch—the yellowish Sardonychis, seal of the Palatium, the emperor's headquarters at Rome, bearing the image of Augustus. The courier would have been quickly taken to the tribune of the guard, then to the *praetorium*, next door to the tribune's quarters.

Field Marshal Tiberius Caesar, tall, with strong features, a hooked Roman nose, and a pasty complexion, would have read the dispatch with

110

a growing frown. He was forty-seven now, a vastly experienced soldier who had led many a campaign since he'd organized camp games for the legions as a teenager in Spain thirty years before. Perhaps he cursed as he lay the dispatch aside. He certainly wasn't happy.

At heart, Tiberius was a deeply insecure man. When Tiberius was only an infant, Augustus had forced his biological father, Tiberius Nero, to divorce the boy's mother, Livia, so Augustus could marry her. Tiberius and his brother Drusus had lived with their father until the elder Tiberius died, when his sons were nine and five. Augustus had then adopted the boys. In his late teens, Tiberius had been married by Augustus to Vipsania, daughter of his best friend, Marcus Agrippa. It was a true love match, and at first their marriage seemed to make up for Tiberius's unhappy childhood.

A decade later, everything changed. First the brother he adored had died in his arms. And then Augustus forced Tiberius to divorce his beloved Vipsania and marry Augustus's biological daughter Julia. The divorce broke Tiberius's heart. Worse, Julia was unfaithful to him within months. His only escape was to throw himself into military campaigning. Then, years later, back at Rome on leave, he'd stumbled onto Vipsania, who'd since remarried, in the street. He followed her through the streets, in tears. This encounter seems to have brought on a breakdown. Unable to face society, he went into self-imposed exile on the island of Rhodes—some historians think for as long as ten years, but possibly for only five.

When he returned to Rome, he came back a tougher though embittered man. He trusted no one, gave his affection to no one—to ensure that he could never be wounded again. Now all he did was obey orders and kill Germans. Yet even that was about to change—in one respect, anyway. The emperor had written personally to his adopted son, with orders to turn the legions around. A massive revolt had blown up in the Balkans, in the Roman provinces of Pannonia and Dalmatia. And to Tiberius fell the job of putting it down.

The subjugation of the Balkans had been commenced by Augustus himself back in 35 B.C. By 12 B.C. the task had been virtually complete. Pannonia and Dalmatia were annexed to Rome, covering much of modern Austria, Hungary, Slovenia, Bosnia, Croatia, and Serbia. For his A.D. 5–6 campaigns in Germany, Tiberius had withdrawn troops from Dalmatia and Pannonia and levied a number of Dalmatian auxiliaries, who joined him on the Rhine under Lieutenant General Messalinus, governor of Dalmatia.

Encouraged by the reduced troop presence, Bato the Breucian, a rebel leader in Pannonia, and another Bato, of Desidiatia in Dalmatia, had risen against the Roman garrisons. With much of the Adriatic coast opposite

Italy quickly falling into rebel hands, there was uproar at Rome, with the population in dread of an invasion of Italy itself.

Now, having read the dispatch from the emperor, Tiberius would have looked at his deputies, Lieutenant Generals Sentius Saturninus and Valerius Messalinus, both older men, as they and his other generals waited to learn the content of the dispatch. "This campaign is over," he would have told them grimly. "We march for the Rhine."

The Marcomanni king, Maraboduus, had been sending Tiberius envoys with gifts, seeking a peace treaty. Now Tiberius hurriedly sent to the king. They agreed on a treaty, and the Roman army pulled out of Bohemia. At Mainz, after recrossing the Rhine, Tiberius divided his legions. Three would go to the lower Rhine with the newly arrived Lieutenant General Publius Quintilius Varus, who would be based at Cologne. Four would be located on the upper Rhine with Lieutenant General Lucius Nonius Asprenas, a consul for that year who, like Varus, had been sent scurrying up from Rome by Augustus to help out until the Pannonian emergency was over. Five legions would march with Tiberius, who had orders to link up with more legions marching to Pannonia from provinces to the east.

Sending General Messalinus ahead with a fast-moving flying column, Tiberius then prepared to lead his legions south—the 14th Gemina Martia, 8th Augusta, 9th Hispana, 15th Apollinar, and 20th Valeria, backed by a number of auxiliaries, including troops from German tribes east of the Rhine. Among these German auxiliary units was a cohort of the Cherusci tribe led by Colonel Flavus, son of the chief of the Cherusci.

Bato the Dalmatian expected the Romans to come rushing down from Germany once they learned of the revolt, and he prepared an ambush for General Messalinus. After walking right into the ambush, the Roman advance force had to quickly backpedal out of trouble. But Messalinus set up an ambush of his own, and Bato's pursuing troops hurried straight into it. The survivors scattered, and Bato fled north, looking for his namesake.

By the time Tiberius arrived in Pannonia with the 14th and his four other Rhine legions, the two Batos had linked up at the Sava River, formed an alliance, regrouped their forces, and savaged Roman units that had moved up through Dalmatia from the south, aiming to join Tiberius at Sisak. The guerrilla war they would now wage would ultimately drag in fifteen legions and last for years. It was to be described by Suetonius as the most bitter in Rome's history to that time.

But even then it would not compare with what was about to take place behind Rome's back in Germany while the war was being waged in Pannonia—an event to shake the empire, and to set the 14th Legion at the start of the road to its greatest hour.

XIV

THE VARUS DISASTER

O ne late summer's evening at the beginning of September in A.D. 9, a banquet took place in the heart of the Chatti tribe's homeland in what today is the German state of Hesse. The setting was a pavilion in the camp of a Roman army of three legions likely to have been located outside the Chatti capital, Mattium, on the Fulda River, a little above the Eder River, the southern boundary of Chatti territory.

A palisaded town with meandering dirt streets and half-timbered buildings of rough lumber and mud—it would be centuries before Germans east of the Rhine built in stone—Mattium was possibly the forerunner of today's city of Kassel, whose name means stronghold. The symbol of the city of Kassel is Hercules, the Romanized version of Donar, the German god worshiped by the Chatti and other German tribes, and after whose Norse equivalent, Thor, the English-speaking peoples named the day of the week Thursday. Donar was a heroic, hard-drinking, hard-living hunter god, and his name would have been invoked more than once at this banquet outside Mattium.

Hosting the banquet was Lieutenant General Publius Quintilius Varus, Roman commander on the lower Rhine. The young colonels of Varus's legions, the prefects of auxiliary units, and their German guests were in good spirits as they reclined barefoot on dining couches around three sides of a low table, three diners to a couch, three couches of nine diners to each of the banquet's many tables. The general's cooks would have sent in up to a dozen courses of exotic dishes on rich silver plates, to be eaten with the fingers, accompanied by Falernian wine from Campanian vineyards south of Rome in silver goblets with Bacchic reliefs. Germans had a weakness for wine, preferring to drink it straight, unlike Romans, who diluted it with water. Roman writers refer to the Germans as heavy drinkers and bad drunks. As wine flowed in celebration of the end of the legions' campaigning season, the dining tent filled with ribald laughter.

At the high table, General Varus was enjoying his role as pseudo-ruler of Germany. He was, at a minimum, fifty-nine years of age; he may have been well into his sixties. He had been brought out of retirement for this job. Trusted by the elderly emperor Augustus, to whom he was related by marriage, he had been rushed to the lower Rhine to take command while Tiberius was away fighting the Pannonian War. The son of Sextus Quintilius Varus, one of Julius Caesar's assassins, who'd committed suicide after the Battle of Philippi, Varus had married Augustus's grandniece, gaining considerable political influence and great wealth during his years in public service. He was not without experience. A consul in 13 B.C., Varus had been governor of both Africa and Syria. In 4 B.C. he'd gained a military reputation after rioting broke out in Jerusalem on the death of King Herod the Great and the famous 10th Legion had been cut off in the city. Swiftly marching three legions down from Syria, Varus had dispersed the rebellious Jews and relieved the men of the 10th. But that had been a long time ago.

Reclining beside General Varus as his guest of honor was Segestes, king of the Chatti, described by Tacitus as a stately figure. Segestes was probably tall, possibly thin. He would have worn his hair long, in the German fashion, and was bearded. Perhaps his hair and beard were white, or gray, contributing to the king's stately appearance. It's likely he was advanced in years, yet with his only son probably in his late teens or early twenties, King Segestes may have only been in his forties.

At one table or another reclined that son, Segimundus, who was about to become a priest at the shrine of the Ubii Germans, in Roman territory at Cologne on the far side of the Rhine, in compliance with the Chatti's treaty obligations with Rome. The king's younger brother Segimerus also was present. According to Cassius Dio, Segimerus had ridden with General Varus all summer long; the Chattian prince was a highly trusted commander of a Chattian auxiliary unit attached to the general's army. Segimerus would have been accompanied by Catumerus, a senior clan leader of the Chatti.

Reclining at another table was a colonel of Cheruscan auxiliaries, Segestes' son-in-law Arminius, or as the Germans knew him, Hermann. The younger son of the king of the neighboring Cherusci, he was now twenty-seven years old, and had been serving with the Roman army for at least two years. He had not only been granted Roman citizenship, he also had been made a member of the Equestrian Order of knighthood. Members of the order had to possess a minimum personal wealth of 400,000 sesterces. A surviving bust, made of him west of the Rhine by a Roman sculptor, shows Hermann as a young man with curly, probably blond hair falling over his ears to his shoulders, a strong nose, a small chin, and an intense expression. He was then clean-shaven, in the Roman fashion.

Hermann would have joined in the banter and discussion. The talk would have been of Field Marshal Tiberius Caesar's ongoing campaign against the Pannonian and Dalmatian rebels. After years of reverses, Tiberius had at last turned the tide against the rebels. In siege after siege, the legions had gradually taken the rebel-held towns and strongholds and reclaimed southern Pannonia and most of Dalmatia. It seems that in these bloody, grinding sieges, three legions in particular had distinguished themselves to the extent that they would be awarded the official title of Victrix, meaning "Conqueror," by Tiberius on behalf of Augustus. The new Victrix legions were the 6th, the 20th Valeria, and the 14th Gemina Martia. By the time the 14th returned from the Pannonian War, it would march under the name of the 14th Gemina Martia Victrix Legion.

At the banquet outside Mattium, conversation would have included Tiberius's recent successful siege of the hill town of Andetrium in Dalmatia. News would have reached Mattium, too, that Hermann's elder brother, Flavus, had been seriously wounded in the campaign and lost an eye, after Tiberius gave his German auxiliaries the task of leading the difficult assault on the town's walls. And Hermann would have laughed when a haughty young Roman colonel lounging close by perhaps joked that now Flavus would look like Hannibal, the famous Carthaginian general of old, and Sertorius, the rebel governor of Spain who'd led Pompey the Great a merry dance for many a year—both of whom had lost an eye in battle. Another Roman colonel would have said that now Flavus would think he was Hannibal or Sertorius. There would have been a gale of laughter. And as Hermann laughed, he would have cast his steely eyes around the room, taking in the increasingly drunken company, until they came to rest on his father-in-law, who returned his gaze with a cold, sober stare.

According to Tacitus, Segestes despised Hermann. Nor did he have any time for Hermann's father, the king of the Cherusci—whose name has not come down to us. There was a time when, for the sake of German fraternity, Segestes had encouraged marriage between the two tribes at the highest level. One of the marriages between the Cherusci and Chatti he'd approved of had been that of Hermann's brother, Flavus, to the daughter of Catumerus of the Chatti. Flavus's wife now lived west of the Rhine with the Romans while her husband was fighting Rome's Pannonian War.

She would bear Flavus a son, Italicus, who would be raised at the Roman naval base city of Ravenna in Italy.

Hermann's own marriage had been a different matter. He had taken Thusnelda, Segestes' daughter and pride and joy, for his wife, with the emphasis on *taken*. Thusnelda had been betrothed by her father to another man when she and Hermann fell in love. In the spirit of the best romance novels, Hermann had snatched his sweetheart away from under her father's nose, and they'd eloped and married. Segestes' rage had only been intensified when Hermann's father gave his blessing to the match.

No doubt pressured by General Varus, Segestes had continued to recline at the same Roman dinner table as his son-in-law. But throughout the spring and summer, whenever he had the opportunity of a private word with General Varus—he accompanied the Roman army on its processional progress through eastern Germany—he warned him that Hermann was not to be trusted. But Varus put Segestes' accusations down to his personal enmity toward Hermann and ignored both the king and his warnings. Besides, Varus had developed a trust in and an affection for the young man. Dio says that Varus had come to consider Hermann his friend.

It's from Tacitus that we know most of what went on at this banquet. He credits Pliny the Elder's now lost twenty-volume *German Wars* as his major source. Pliny is likely to have questioned Germans who'd been present at the banquet when he himself was stationed at Mainz with the 2nd Augusta Legion in A.D. 41–42 as a young colonel of auxiliary cavalry. His nephew Pliny the Younger says he started writing his German histories while still stationed on the Rhine. One of Pliny's probable informants was King Segestes' son, Segimundus, who was to survive the turmoil of the next decade and spend his later life as a priest at Cologne. Pliny also may have interviewed senior German prisoners sent to live at Ravenna by their Roman captors.

When the banquet was at its height, King Segestes rose to speak. The diners reverentially fell silent, expecting him to offer a toast to their host. "From the time that Augustus Caesar gave me Roman citizenship," Tacitus tells us he said, "I have chosen my friends and my enemies with an eye to Rome's advantage, not from hatred of my fatherland. I believe that Romans and Germans have the same interests, that peace is better than war. I'm no traitor. Traitors are hated even by those they love, and I'm not hated by my people. But there are those here who are traitors, to Rome, to Germany, and to the peace!" He turned to Hermann, stabbing a finger in his direction. "This man is a traitor! Just as he has violated my daughter, he's planning to violate the peace with Rome, and bring misery to us all!"

Hermann responded with an amused smile. This only annoyed Segestes all the more. He raged that his son-in-law was plotting to drive all Romans from Germany. Then he said: "Arrest myself and Arminius, here, now. Arrest all the leading men of the tribes. I assure you the German people will do nothing without their leaders. Then you'll have the opportunity to sift the accusations and to determine the innocent and the guilty."

Cassius Dio says several of General Varus's subordinates voiced support for the king's warnings. Impatiently, Varus asked Hermann if there was any truth in the king's accusation, and he scoffed at any suggestion that he was in the least disloyal to Rome. Varus accepted Hermann's declaration of innocence without question. What's more, according to Dio, Varus berated Segestes and those of his own officers who supported his view, for being needlessly alarmist. "I will not have you slandering my friends," Dio says Varus told Segestes before apparently instructing the king to resume his seat and cease making claims that were obviously inspired by personal motives.

Tacitus says that Segestes considered Varus a "dilatory general," a man who both put off decisions and proceeded without due diligence. Insulted, and determining to take matters into his own hands, Segestes stormed from the banquet and from the camp.

Later, as Hermann left the banquet and made his way to his quarters in the town, Segestes was waiting for him, with armed Chattians. He was quickly overpowered, bound and gagged, then thrown into solitary confinement in Mattium. But members of Segestes' own entourage sympathized with the young prince, and they hurried to warn soldiers of Hermann's Cheruscan auxiliary unit of the fate of their commander. Hermann's men slid through the night, overpowered the guards, and freed their leader. With the complicity of Chatti leaders, Hermann in turn made Segestes a prisoner, locking him away in chains. Meanwhile, the Romans camped nearby slept the night away in blissful ignorance of the drama taking place behind the walls of Mattium.

The next morning at dawn, General Varus addressed a full assembly of the army, then allowed his adjutant—the "announcer," as he was called—to read his Orders for the Day. The army was to march for the Rhine, and their winter quarters. Soon the legion trumpets sounded "Prepare to March" three times. The camp was struck, the baggage train loaded, and then the lead elements moved out. The usual practice was for cavalry scouts to lead out. Then came auxiliary light infantry. Then more cavalry, followed by the road-clearing detail. Then the legions, probably two in the vanguard. Josephus records later in the century that standards were bunched in groups for the march.

In the vanguard rode the commander in chief and his staff and cavalry bodyguard. Next came the strung-out baggage train, loaded down with the 180 artillery pieces of the three legions, as well as ammunition, tents, grinding stones, officers' furniture and silver dining plate, supplies for the march, and the material acquisitions of a spring and a summer in foreign territory. The third of the three legions marched as a rear guard, with another cavalry detachment bringing up the rear.

The legionaries were in marching order. Their packs, each weighing up to a hundred pounds, were over their right shoulders, suspended from carrying poles. Their javelins were tied to the pack poles. Their shields, wrapped in protective leather covers, were slung over their left shoulders. Their helmets, hung around their necks, rested against their chests. With this load and a long baggage train they might make fifteen to eighteen miles a day, marching until noon, then spending the afternoon building a marching camp for the night and gathering firewood, fodder, and water. The next day they would do the same again. At this rate, and without major delays, they would reach the Rhine in a week or so.

Their destination was Cologne, due west. A permanent wooden bridge was spanning the Rhine at Cologne sixty years later, but in A.D. 9 a bridge of boats was probably in place. General Varus's intention was that by the time the Festival of the October Horse was being celebrated at Rome in the third week of October, the traditional end of the campaigning season, the legions would be snug in their quarters with their arms stored away until next spring, just as in the past two years. Varus himself would have planned to also spend the winter on the Rhine. Augustus didn't permit his generals to return home to their wives in Rome until their postings ended.

As the sun rose this September morning, Hermann was at the legion camp along with numerous other German auxiliary commanders to bid farewell to Varus and his men. The general had agreed to allow a number of auxiliary units attached to his command to spend the winter at communities throughout Germany—their hometowns in many cases. According to Cassius Dio, there were archers in Varus's column, specialists from Syria or Crete, and theirs were among the few auxiliary units that were to remain with him. When General Varus asked the whereabouts of King Segestes, Hermann would have blamed Segestes' absence on an overindulgence in wine the previous evening. Varus took his leave of the German officers, appointing a day the following March when they were to assemble at the Rhine to meet him, then pointed his column and his thoughts toward the west. As the Roman general rode away from Mattium, Hermann led his Cheruscan troops north, toward the home territory of the

Cherusci between the Weser and Ems Rivers. At the same time, Segestes'
son, Segimundus, set off on horseback with a small entourage to travel to
Cologne and take up his priestly duties. It was not a future he looked forward to.

The legions marching away from Mattium were trailed by a caravan of
camp followers—the traders, artisans, pimps, prostitutes, and their families
who habitually accompanied the army wherever it went, a body as numerous as Varus's army itself. When the last wagons of the camp followers lum-
bered over the horizon, smoke was still curling from the ruins of the Roman
camp, set ablaze by the legions, as they customarily did when abandoning
a camp. Chattian children would have played among the ruins, laughing
and chattering, looking for souvenirs of the Roman stay.

Segimerus, brother of Segestes, now paid a visit to the king to apolo-
gize for his continued imprisonment. The king was told he would be released once Germany had risen against Rome. Segimerus and his son, a boy
in his teens, then departed Mattium. With father and son rode only personal attendants—the Chatti had no cavalry. Their strength, says Tacitus,
lay in their highly disciplined infantry. As Segimerus's party galloped north,
large companies of Chatti infantry set off to follow them at all speed,
on foot.

Tacitus says that Varus's three legions were "unofficered"—that is, none
currently had a brigadier general at its command. Varus had either allowed
the generals to depart Germany early, to be replaced by new commanding officers who would come up from Rome in the new spring, or the
Pannonian emergency had caused such a drain on officers of general rank
that all three legions had been led that year by their senior tribunes,
which was rare but not unusual. The identities of Varus's three tribunes
are unknown.

As for Varus's legions, we know with certainty the identity of just one:
the 19th, an undistinguished legion. Originally a unit created from Pompeian troops who surrendered to Julius Caesar at Corfinium in 49 B.C., it
had sat out the Civil War on garrison duty in Sicily. It had been embroiled
in Sextus Pompey's Sicilian venture, on his side, and then in Lepidus's failed
gambit for power. At the time of Philippi it apparently was in the forces
of Antony and Octavian. Reenlisted in Cisalpine Gaul in 33 B.C., the
legion marched for Octavian against Antony before being based in Gaul
after 30 B.C.. Transferred to the lower Rhine, it served in the German
campaigns of Drusus Caesar between 12 and 9 B.C. and in the campaigns of

Lucius Ahenobarbus Domitius, who pushed into Germany between 7 B.C. and A.D. 1, resettling the Hermunduri Germans in Bohemia. By A.D. 1 General Domitius had been relying on diplomacy to try to win his way with Hermann's father, king of the Cherusci, as his legions built roads and bridges on the far side of the Rhine. Undergoing its 1 B.C. reenlistment in Cisalpine Gaul as usual, the 19th marched with the 14th and the ten other legions led by Tiberius Caesar into Germany between A.D. 4 and 6. They reached the Weser River and brought the Cherusci and Bructeri tribes to the treaty table before going on to penetrate as far as the Elbe and achieving the defeat of the Langobardi between the Weser and the Elbe.

According to numismatic evidence mostly, Varus's other two units have been identified as the 17th and 18th Legions. And ill-starred units they were. These had been the two legions wiped out under Curio in Africa in 49 B.C. Re-formed, the 17th and 18th fought at Philippi and Actium. Following the deaths of Antony and Cleopatra, both legions were retained by Octavian and posted to Aquitania. Together, the 17th and the 18th joined the 19th for Tiberius's operations in Switzerland by 15 B.C., before all three legions were transferred to the Rhine. By A.D. 9 the 17th was based at Neuss, the Roman fortress of Novaesium founded in 12 B.C.; the 18th at Vetera, today's town of Xantem in Holland; and the 19th at Cologne.

The men of the 1 B.C. enlistments of these units were required to sign on for twenty years, not the sixteen years of their predecessors—between 6 B.C. and A.D. 11 Augustus phased in twenty-year enlistments for all the legions. By the time they were marching away from Mattium in September of A.D. 9, each first-enlistment man had close to nine years of legion experience under his belt, while the men of the senior cohorts, including the double-strength 1st Cohorts, were a minimum of forty-nine years old. Being into the ninth year of their current enlistments, the three legions would have been understrength by a thousand men each, possibly more, as a result of battle casualties in the German campaigns; from the discharge of injured or infirm men; and through desertion. In all likelihood, the legionary forces now marching with Varus totaled about thirteen thousand men.

Normally the army would include a large number of auxiliaries, but Tiberius had built a series of forts along the eastern bank of the Rhine, and Varus had garrisoned them with many of his auxiliaries, including part of his complement of archers. He was also without the German auxiliaries he'd detached to various corners of Germany for the winter. His remaining auxiliaries numbered a few thousand men, including foot archers and cavalry from France, Spain, Luxembourg, Belgium, and Germany west of the Rhine.

Most of Varus's men would have now been thinking about cozy winter quarters, about banking their pay with their unit banker and totaling up their savings after another unprofitable campaign without a good fight or a hostile German town to pillage. Betrayal by their German allies would have seemed unthinkable, for to all intents central Germany apart from Bavaria and Bohemia was now part of the Roman world. General Varus thought it, his emperor thought it. It had been an impression given credence over the past two summers as Varus's army had trooped through towns and villages in German cantons where smiling locals had come out to watch the colorful Roman procession march by. It had been a picture of peace, of fraternity.

Three, possibly four days into the dawdling march to the Rhine, after several more auxiliary units had peeled off from the column to head for their winter quarters, a party of fast-riding horsemen reached General Varus with urgent news. There was trouble to the north, they advised. Cassius Dio says that Varus was informed there had been an uprising, north of friendly territory, in the homeland of the Chauci or the Angrivarii, on the other side of Cheruscan territory. Varus now turned his army around and headed north for the trouble spot. That he took his entire force with him indicates the message he received was from his friend and subordinate Hermann, and that he believed that a substantial force of rebel Germans was involved. Hermann may have even said that he and his Cheruscan auxiliaries had been surrounded and would be wiped out if not quickly reinforced.

As the Romans marched to the rescue, some camp followers pulled out of the column and continued toward the Rhine as fast as they could go, planning to take refuge at the forts along the eastern bank of the river until the army returned. But according to Dio, many civilians remained with the army. Varus took his complete baggage train with him, despite the urgency. There was no intent to travel light to save time. For some civilians, it appeared there would be safety in numbers if they stayed with the column. As for Varus, he wanted as much personal protection as he could get. Knock-kneed in his youth, he was now probably fat and unfit after lazy years in retirement and the easy perambulations through Germany of the past two seasons. As he swung north toward the Weser Hills, guided by the Cheruscans who'd brought him the message from Hermann, Varus sent away the last of the local German nobles who were riding with him, with instructions to urgently collect their fighting men. Varus obviously believed the force he had to counter was by no means small.

One of the German nobles who now rode away from the column was Colonel Boiocalus of the Ampsivari tribe. Prefect of an Ampsivarii auxiliary unit since the previous year, he was intensely loyal to Rome. On the way to round up his men, the twenty-six-year-old Boiocalus was overtaken by Cheruscans, arrested on Hermann's orders, chained, and imprisoned in a German village. Boiocalus soon escaped to the Roman side of the Rhine, but too late to warn of the revolt before it erupted.

General Varus was marching north as fast as he could go. In emergencies, a legion could march twenty-five miles every day for a week. There are times on record when they made forced marches of more than thirty miles a day. But that was when they were stripped for action. The journey ahead of Varus's lumbering, overburdened army, of forty miles or so, could have taken at least three days.

An army of thousands of German tribesmen lay in wait for General Varus and his legions in the Teutoburg Forest, which today still covers the westernmost escarpment of the Weser Hills. The Romans called it the Teutoburgium. Here, wooded limestone and sandstone ridges arc southwest from the Ems River for sixty miles. The works of Pliny the Elder and others provided Cassius Dio with details that enabled him to accurately describe the area. The mountains here were of irregular shape, he said, their slopes deeply cleft by ravines, with the trees of the forest—birch, spruce, and oak—clinging to the hillsides, growing closely together and extending to a great height.

A black sky shrouded the Weser Hills as rain that had begun as a shower that morning now drummed down and wild winds lashed the treetops. The rain would make the ground uncertain underfoot once the fighting began, but for now the storm would mask any sound emitted by the hidden men and their horses. The Germans waited, silent, tense. They were cold, wet, and ready for a good cooked meal after spending days without campfires that would have given them away. Most of all, they were ready to kill Romans.

And leading the German army was young Hermann. Just as Segestes had warned General Varus, his son-in-law had been secretly agitating among the tribes of the region for many months, urging them to join him in throwing the Romans out of their fatherland. The leaders had met in a council of German nations over the previous winter. Only one invitee had

refused to attend, the Marcomanni's King Maroboduus, who stuck by his
A.D. 6 treaty with Rome. The other tribes had entered into a war pact, had
made their plans, had given their vows. They'd been preparing ever since.

At that council meeting Segestes had spoken against going to war with
Rome, but Tacitus says he was unanimously outvoted by his fellow Chattians. Rather than simply denounce the plot, and be branded a traitor by
his own people and probably lose his throne, if not his life, Segestes had
attempted to preempt the war by convincing Varus to arrest Hermann.
Cut off the German wolf's head and the body will die; that had been
Segestes' plan. But now the wolf was leading the pack, and King Segestes
was in chains.

Thousands of fighting men of Hermann's Cherusci were here with
their prince. Whether Hermann's father was a party to the plot we don't
know, if indeed he was still alive. Certainly Hermann's mother would be
around for some years. The Chatti also were here in great number. In
Segestes' absence they were led by his brother Segimerus. According to
Dio, Segimerus and Hermann were the two principal architects of the
revolt. Three Chatti clan leaders also present would have been Flavus's
father-in-law, Catumerus, and Arpus and Adgandestrius, all future leaders
of the Chatti. The Marsi tribe was here at the Teutoburg as well. Unre-
lated to the Italian Marsi, these near neighbors of both the Cherusci and
the Chatti lived to their west, between the Lippe and Ruhr Rivers, and
probably were led by the man identified by Tacitus five years later as their
chief, Mallovendus. From well to the south, in Switzerland, came warriors
of the Cauchi tribe. The Bructeri from north of the Lippe were here, and
the Usipetes and the Tubantes, as well as Cheruscan near neighbors the
Fosi. Other tribes likely to have provided warriors were the Chamavi,
Ampsivarii, Angrivarii, Sugambri, and Mattiaci.

Seven years later, Hermann would muster an army of fifty thousand
men not far from here; something in excess of twenty thousand tribesmen
congregating in the Teutoburg this day in September of A.D. 9 is not unlikely. For months the tribesmen had been going through rudimentary tactical drills taught to them by men with experience in the Roman army.
And before they set out from their homes, every man would have gone to
a sacred grove and vowed to his gods not to cut his beard or his hair until
he had killed a Roman.

The Germans were broader, taller men than Roman legionaries. Germans lived on dairy produce and meat. It wasn't uncommon for them to
stand more than five feet, eight inches tall. By comparison, the Roman
soldier, with his daily bread and olive oil ration, averaged little more than

five feet four. Hermann was to take advantage of this height difference, placing the tallest warriors in his front ranks and arming them with the best weapons, to give the impression that all German fighting men were giants.

The principal frontline weapon of many tribes was a wooden spear up to twelve feet long. Behind the front line the second-rank men usually carried the *framea*, a short, metal-tipped spear used for both jabbing and throwing and which was common throughout Germany, Gaul, and Britain. Some came armed simply with wooden javelins, saplings whose business end had merely been sharpened and then hardened in a fire. Nobles also carried swords—some, large, blunt-ended broadswords; others, copies of the shorter Roman *gladius*. All tribes were equipped with flat shields, some of oak or linden planks, others merely woven wicker with hide covers. Shield shapes varied: the rectangular Chauci shield was four feet long; the Chatti shield, small and square. Nobles wore moccasin-style footwear, a tight tunic, trousers, and a cloak, and often wore their long hair tied in a topknot, the so-called Suebian knot. Their tribe members were only simply dressed; Chattians typically went barefoot and wore only a loincloth and short fur cloak.

The Teutoburg Forest had been chosen as the site of the ambush for a number of reasons. It prevented cavalry operations and also would make it difficult for the Roman infantry to employ their normal battlefield formations. The trees also offered concealment for large numbers of men. And there was a religious significance to the Teutoburg, with several groves sacred to the German tribes located in the forest.

The Roman column stretched for miles as it entered the Teutoburg and climbed up through the hill passes, guided by the decoy messengers. Progress was painfully slow. In the rain and swirling wind the advance road-clearing party was hard pressed felling trees, clearing the track, and bridging difficult stretches with felled trees and earth. As the downpour washed away earthworks, feet slipped and slid on leveled tree trunks, and the wheels of wagons became caught in gaps. Wet, cold, mud-covered, and miserable, legionaries often were called back to put their shoulders to vehicles in difficulty. The column stopped and started, straggling through the hills, with wagons and carts becoming interspersed with groups of troops, the servants of the officers, and camp followers. The scattered legionaries were in loose marching order.

Dio says that every now and then a high tree limb would be wrenched free by the wind and come crashing down. Marchers were struck, and pack animals bolted in terror, creating great confusion, according to Dio. And all the time, General Varus urged his troops to press on regardless: Rome's friends were in trouble, he said.

Watching from an elevated position, Hermann waited until the entire force was well into the hills before springing the trap. Then, with a yell, he rose and launched the first missile. Suddenly, shocked Roman troops discovered that they were flanked on both sides by thousands of adversaries in the trees, as clouds of spears sliced out of nowhere.

Centurions barked orders: "Helmets on! Uncover shields! Form ranks!"

Down the ragged column came the instruction to keep moving; no counterattack was permitted. But as casualties mounted, General Varus ordered a camp made. Under fire, the advance guard found a barely usable location, and while part of the column held off the Germans, the remainder furiously dug the trench and threw up the walls of a standard marching camp. As night fell, the legions and their cavalry and archer companions were able to take refuge in the camp. Their German attackers melted away, into the darkness.

Still convinced that he was needed on the other side of the Teutoburg, and apparently believing that his attackers here had been sent to prevent him from getting through to Arminius and his embattled troops, Varus was determined to press on. But next day the weather was so bad he held his position. Once the rain stopped, he waited for the muddy country in their path to dry somewhat. The pause gave him the opportunity to tend to his wounded; to organize a new order of march that would be adopted once the advance began anew; and, in a council of his officers, to plan defensive tactics. Dio says that in this conference it was agreed that the baggage train was slowing the column down.

Hermann held back on day two, waiting for the Romans to make the next move, as his men preferred to attack the column once it was in the open again, on the march. He also was waiting for expected German reinforcements.

On day three, with the sky clear and the ground dried out a little, the legions moved out in their units and in battle order. And they abandoned the vehicles of the baggage train. Wagons, carts, and their contents, including wooden artillery pieces, were burning furiously along with the guard towers and gates of the camp as the army set out. The pack mules and horses continued with the column.

Once the Roman rear guard was out of sight, Germans surged into the camp in the hope of salvaging spoils from the flames. By dallying at the burning camp they gave Varus enough time to break out into open country. German skirmishing parties still harried the column's flanks and rear, but, like flies, they were swatted away. The men of the legions became a little cheerier now that the going was much less difficult.

Toward the middle of the morning, guided still by the same Germans who had led him this far and whom Varus still trusted, the army's route took them back into the forest—and into another ambush. This time Varus launched counterattacks of infantry and cavalry into the trees. But Hermann had taught his men well. They dashed in, launched their missiles, then withdrew, using the same tactics Ambiorix's Belgians had employed against the 14th Legion back in 54 B.C. When legionary and cavalry units gave chase, they only bumped into each other and into trees. Hourly, Roman casualties increased.

To the struggling legionaries it would have seemed the Germans were more numerous than before. And it was true; Dio says that new contingents of tribesmen were arriving and going into action with each passing hour. Some had come to the Weser Hills after massacring Roman auxiliaries stationed among them. Others had a long distance to travel. Some bands had hung back to see which way the fighting went, and now that the Germans clearly had the upper hand, they were also committing to the fray.

Varus ordered a new camp to be built, but few men could be spared to dig. It was all the other surviving troops could do to keep the Germans at bay. Casualty numbers were soaring. Tacitus says that it was only a shattered remnant of an army that was able to make a stand at this camp. Deep in the forest to the south of modern Detmold and near the present-day town of Osnabrück, they struggled to build their fortification. The result was a pitifully low wall, little more than five feet high, fronted by a shallow ditch. At nightfall, the surviving Roman troops withdrew behind the defenses and the Germans pulled back for the night, surrounding the encampment so that no one could escape in the darkness. General Varus issued orders that with the morning the march must resume—if they stayed here, they would all die.

Overnight, the rain returned. A new storm blew up, so fierce that when, come morning, the advance guard tried to push on, they couldn't even maintain their footing. They fell back to the camp. The Roman column was trapped, and both sides knew it.

As the morning progressed and the rain tumbled down, wave after wave of tribesmen threw themselves at the camp walls, covering the rain-filled outer trench with wicker hurdles, then going against the walls with rough-cut ladders. The noise of battle, the yelling, the cheering, the screaming would have been deafening.

A spear pierced General Varus—in the leg, the shoulder, the neck, we don't know. Aides helped the general to the center of the camp. Dazed, bleeding, in pain, he gazed around the scene of carnage. The Germans were in the camp, cutting down legionaries and auxiliaries, slaying terrified, unarmed noncombatants who fell to their knees before them, pleading for mercy. In the sea of wild German faces Varus would have seen his charismatic young "friend" Arminius—Hermann—leading the assault.

The surviving bloodied, muddied men of the three legions clustered around their eagles, surrounded, trying to defend their standards. Their rain-soaked wooden shields were almost too heavy to hold up, says Dio. Progressively the Roman ranks were overwhelmed by sheer weight of numbers and cut down. Warriors of the Bructeri killed the eagle-bearer of the 19th Legion and the men who stepped up to take his place. With a victorious roar the Bructeri carried off the 19th's eagle. Before long, the Cauchi and the Marsi seized the eagles of the 17th and the 18th.

Varus knew he was doomed. Determined not to fall into German hands, he put his sword to his throat. Then, with a single stroke, says Tacitus, he drew the blade left to right across his neck. Varus toppled into the mud, drowning in his own blood. The colonels of the legions had bunched together with their staff. Once their general took his own life, all three followed suit. As the battle degenerated into a massacre, some men died in groups, while others met their end in the open, trying to run. Horses, too, perished—the steeds of the cavalry and the officers, useless in the mud and confined space, and baggage animals peppered by indiscriminate German missiles. As a few hundred Roman officers and men threw down their arms and gave themselves up, Hermann called for the slaughter to cease. The noise faded. Then there were just groans of the wounded, the relentless pounding of the rain. The Battle of the Teutoburg Forest was over.

The son of Segimerus looked down at the naked, muddy, bloody body of Quintilius Varus and sneered. The general's expensive armor and fittings had been ripped from his corpse; his tunic, too. Tacitus says that the teenaged Chattian insulted the body—perhaps with a kick, or maybe he spat on the dead man. Or, more gruesomely, he attacked his corpse with a knife. The boy's father pulled him away. A burly German then stepped up and swung a heavy blade, which decapitated the dilatory general. Varus's head was raised on the point of a spear. Tens of thousands of tribesmen roared their approval.

Severely wounded Romans had been put to death. The thousands of dead and the live prisoners were stripped. Surrendered officers were separated from enlisted men. Thin-stripe tribunes and first-rank centurions were divided from junior centurions. The prisoners were then made to dig large pits. The muddy earth from the pits formed a large mound, where captured Roman weapons and the eagles and standards of the legions were piled. The rank-and-file prisoners were forced into the slushy pits.

Hermann climbed onto the mound, and to tumultuous cheers and applause he praised his men for their courage, derided the defeated Romans, and spat on the captured eagles and standards. The severed heads of dead Roman officers were nailed to tree trunks. Gallows were set up for surviving junior centurions. They were strung up in front of their men and laughing, jeering Germans. Thin-stripe tribunes, officer cadets, mere teenagers, were dragged away in chains with the first-rank centurions. The men in the pits only realized the officers' fate when they heard their screams and smelled burning flesh.

The senior officers had been taken to a nearby sacred grove, a common feature of the religious observances of people throughout Europe, from Russia to Britain. A clearing in a forest, sometimes surrounded by a high palisade, the grove had a central altar, and often, tables where religious feasts took place. Women and children were banned, and foreign speech was not permitted, to avoid offending the gods. Julius Caesar wrote that in his time the sacred groves of some Gallic tribes were scenes of human sacrifice, with the victims placed inside giant wicker cages in the shape of a man. These cages were suspended over a fiery altar, where the victims were burned alive. It seems that this was how first-rank centurions of the 17th, 18th, and 19th Legions died, along with their young tribunes—sons of some of Rome's finest families, incinerated in cages prepared with relish in advance. The writer and philosopher Seneca, tutor and then chief minister to the emperor Nero, was to write to a friend half a century later, "Remember the Varus disaster? Many a man of the most distinguished ancestry, who was doing his military service as the first step on the road to a seat in the Senate, was brought low by Fortune." It was a road that came to a fiery end in the Teutoburg Forest.

After celebratory banqueting and thanks to their gods, most of the victorious Germans dispersed. The spoils from the defeated Roman army were borne away, to be divided among the tribes. The legionary prisoners were placed in chains and dragged to towns and villages throughout Germany and Switzerland, to become slaves. Thirteen thousand naked, butchered dead of the three legions were left where they had fallen.

Hermann led several thousand Germans west, to deal with Romans still on their soil. Over the next few days, all the forts but one along the eastern side of the Rhine were overrun. The exception, probably guarding the eastern end of the temporary bridge opposite Cologne, was apparently alerted by a handful of legionaries who'd escaped from the Teutoburg Forest. According to Dio, auxiliaries stationed at this fort included archers, and it was their bowmanship that helped save them. Surrounded by Hermann's men, the Roman colonel in charge led the fort's occupants in a breakout on a dark, wet night. It was from this group who escaped across the Rhine that the fate of Varus's legions became known to the Roman world. As soon as word reached him up the Rhine, Lieutenant General Asprenas rushed down from Mainz with several legions to secure the lower Rhine, immediately destroying the Cologne bridge. Now the Roman troops on the Rhine waited for the next move from the Germans, and the reaction at Rome.

Romans received the news of the Varus disaster with the same shock and disbelief with which the American nation received the news of the Custer disaster at the Battle of the Little Big Horn in 1876. The emperor Augustus was devastated. He didn't shave for months, mourning the lost legions as if they were his children. Suetonius says that Augustus was often heard to cry, "Quintilius Varus, give me back my legions!"

Eighteenth-century historian Edward Gibbon remarked, "Augustus did not receive the melancholy news with all the temper and firmness that might have been expected from his character." In fact, if Suetonius is to be believed, Augustus, like many at Rome, reacted with panic, expecting the Germans to now come flooding across the Rhine into Gaul and then Italy. Suetonius says the emperor temporarily dispersed the German Guard, his personal bodyguard unit, to Italian islands, suddenly distrusting all Germans.

To reinforce Tiberius, who was hurrying back to the Rhine from Pannonia with the 14th G.M.V. and several other legions with orders to secure the western bank of the river and make it the Empire's new northern frontier, Augustus put together a ragtag militia in Italy and sent it scurrying north. But the Romans' worst fears weren't realized. As it eventuated, Hermann's ambitions extended no farther than the Rhine.

Augustus didn't raise new enlistments to replace the Teutoburg dead. He retired the shamed numbers of the three destroyed legions and left the Roman army at twenty-five legions in all. The Varus disaster, as it became known, was a stinging blow to Roman pride that ranked with Atuatuca and Carrhae. The September day in A.D. 9 when General Varus's legions ceased to exist would never be forgotten. Nor would the man who stepped forward to take revenge on Hermann.

XV

MUTINY ON
THE RHINE

C aesar is here! Caesar is here!" The word ran through the ranks of
the 14th Gemina Martia Victrix Legion and the other legions
assembled at Mainz.

And there he was. Field Marshal Germanicus Caesar, great-nephew of
Augustus, nephew and adopted son of Tiberius, striding to the tribunal
with the purple, ankle-length cloak of commander in chief flowing behind
him. He was just twenty-eight. The men of the 14th G.M.V. had known
him since he'd arrived at Sisak in Pannonia in the spring of A.D. 7. He'd
been leading a force of militia hastily raised at Rome by Augustus after
Tiberius suffered setbacks against the Pannonian rebels and fear seized the
residents of the capital. Germanicus had then been only twenty-two, but
the Roman public already idolized him, and the very fact that he'd been
sent to help Tiberius had reassured a nervous citizenry that the rebellion
would now be quelled. Germanicus had won new admirers by leading a
flying column in Pannonia with dash—the only flying column commander to achieve substantial results. By the end of the war in A.D. 9, with
one Bato dead and the other in chains, Germanicus was storming town
after town in Dalmatia. After Pannonia, he'd served under Tiberius on
the Rhine. Only this year, Augustus had appointed Germanicus to take
over from Tiberius as Rhine commander in chief. Now, in late August of
A.D. 14, Augustus was dead, and the legions were in turmoil.

Germanicus stepped up onto the tribunal.

"Hail, commander!" the twenty thousand assembled legionaries of the
Army of the Upper Rhine boomed. But there was none of the applause
that usually accompanied his appearance on the tribunal. The men were
waiting to hear what he had to say.

As he surveyed the serried ranks of the 14th Gemina Martia Victrix, 2nd Augusta, 13th Gemina, and 16th Gallica Legions, the men studied him. He was well-built, athletic. He looked a great deal like his grandfather Mark Antony—square jaw, big mouth, curly hair, thick neck. But he had charisma Antony never possessed, with bright, lively eyes, a ready smile, and a common touch that made every legionary he met think he was special. Now, as he prepared to speak, his eyes rested on the men of the 14th G.M.V. Legion. They were the primary reason for his hurried ride up the Rhine from Cologne. It was their grievance that had inspired the entire A.U.R. to mutiny.

It all hung on the death of the emperor Augustus on August 19. He'd been seventy-seven when he finally died, at a house outside Naples. Few who'd known him as a sickly youth would have imagined he would live so long. Yet despite his age, no one had been prepared for his death, least of all the legions. It was as if the captain of the ship had died at the wheel. Now the crew was running around in confusion. Trouble had broken out immediately in Pannonia, where the legions stationed there, the 8th Augusta, 9th Hispana, and 15th Apollinaris, had killed their more brutal centurions and thrown out their other officers. They'd then prepared a list of demands. At the top of the list: drop twenty-year enlistments; the legions must return to sixteen-year enlistments.

Word of the mutiny quickly spread to the Rhine legions, and the men of the 14th G.M.V. had taken up the demands. The 14th's last discharge and reenlistment had been in A.D. 11, when the new enlistment period of twenty years had been introduced to the legion. The men who had signed up to serve a second enlistment in the 14th G.M.V.—an enlistment of twenty years this time—were now three years into their new enlistment, having served a total of nineteen years since originally joining. The second enlistment men of the 14th hadn't liked the idea of a twenty-year enlistment, but they hadn't relished the idea of life as civilians again either. So they'd signed on again. But now, after three years during which there had been no campaigning, no fighting, no booty, just chores, drills, the boredom of life around the post, with equally bored and frustrated centurions belting them with vine sticks for minor infringements of discipline, they'd had enough and were ready to quit.

The three other legions of the Upper Army had gone along with the 14th, although they didn't have as big an ax to grind. The four legions of the Army of the Lower Rhine, on the other hand, were of the same mind as the 14th—as they let Germanicus know when he'd arrived back at his headquarters at their Cologne base shortly after the death of the emperor.

He'd been supervising the annual tax collection in Gaul when he'd heard that Augustus was dead and then that his Rhine legions had mutinied.

There was another problem to complicate and destabilize the situation. While Tiberius had long been seen as Augustus's heir apparent, Augustus had never formalized his succession. To many in Rome, Tiberius had only to claim the throne for it to be his. But now the insecure Tiberius held back. He asked the Praetorian Guard and the German Guard to provide him with personal protection, and sent elements of both to forcibly settle the Pannonian mutiny—under his son and Germanicus's adoptive brother Drusus and one of the two prefects of the Praetorian Guard, Colonel Lucius Sejanus. But he didn't make any attempt to move into Augustus's Palatium or declare himself emperor.

In this power vacuum, with Rome leaderless and uncertain, Germanicus had returned to Cologne. He'd found the camp being shared by the 1st, 5th Alaudae, 20th Valeria Victrix, and 21st Rapax Legions in disarray. No centurions were on duty; all had been ejected by the legions. When he'd called an assembly, the men listened with just an occasional murmur as he'd extolled the military achievements of Tiberius. But when he asked why his legionaries had turned against their officers, they spoke up, complaining of the cost of buying furloughs from their centurions, yelling that they were badly paid, baring the scars from vine stick beatings. They were fed up, they said—with digging entrenchments, with lugging lumber and horse feed. This wasn't soldiers' work.

Most of all, they told him, they were unhappy at having to serve twenty-year enlistments. The last discharge and reenlistment for one of these legions had been in 4 B.C., and in 1 B.C. for the others. If they'd still been serving sixteen-year enlistments the conscripts of the 1st Legion could have gone home a year ago. The men of the other units, instead of being discharged in two years' time, still had another six to serve. Tacitus writes of the veterans of these legions complaining that they were exhausted after serving in thirty campaigns or more. One military campaign per year was the norm for the legions. The second-enlistment men of three of these legions had served thirty years by A.D. 14, while those of the 1st Legion had served thirty-three.

They swore that their complaints weren't directed at Germanicus—so much so that when one legionary declared that if Germanicus wanted to take the throne, the Rhine armies would back him all the way, there were loud choruses of agreement. Soon, thousands were voicing the same sentiment. Germanicus's face had clouded over. As the deafening shouts continued, he'd tried to leave the tribunal. But men broke ranks and surged around him, urging him to become their emperor.

When he'd declared that he'd rather kill himself than take the throne that was legitimately Tiberius's, his father's, a soldier of the 1st Legion had offered him his sword. Germanicus's staff had hustled their commander to the camp *praetorium*, and there, as the officers discussed courses of action, word arrived that the mutineers were sending messengers upriver to the 14th G.M.V. and their other brother legions of the Upper Army at Mainz, telling them what had just taken place. Germanicus's staff began to fear that all eight legions would go on a looting rampage throughout Gaul. There also was the concern that once the Germans on the far side of the Rhine came to hear about the mutiny they might be inspired to launch a raid across the river, or worse, a full-scale invasion. Some of Germanicus's officers were all for bringing in auxiliaries from camps along the Rhine and calling up fresh recruits from the allied tribes in the Gallic and German provinces to end the mutiny by force. But Germanicus wasn't prepared to contemplate a step he considered tantamount to launching into civil war.

Deciding to give the legions the one thing they wanted most, he drafted a letter. He agreed to unconditionally discharge and send into honorable retirement with their 12,000-sesterce retirement bonus all men who had served for more than Augustus's stipulated period of service—twenty years. This took in the second-enlistment men of all four A.L.R. legions. He would also discharge all who had served at least the original sixteen-year period of service—the balance of the 1st Legion—but these men had to stay in camp, on their legion rolls, available to serve behind their standards in emergencies.

The men at Cologne had soon accepted the offer and ended their rebellion. That had left only the legionaries of the 14th G.M.V. and the other legions at Mainz. This was why Germanicus was here now, looking out over their faces. He proceeded to require them all to swear an oath of allegiance to Tiberius as emperor. Tacitus says that as he spoke the words, the men of three legions readily repeated them and took the oath. But the legionaries of the 14th Gemina Martia Victrix remained silent and folded their arms.

Germanicus knew what was in their heads. Technically, the 14th didn't qualify for the unconditional discharge he'd granted the legions of the Lower Army—they'd missed out by one year. Fully aware of this, and confronted by the legion's hesitation, he thought on his feet. Germanicus now announced that he was extending the unconditional discharge and retirement bonus payment offer to the second-enlistment men of the 14th, regardless. Broad smiles appeared on the faces of the men of the 14th's senior cohorts.

"Do you agree?" Germanicus asked.

There was a unanimous shout in the affirmative. The satisfied men of the legion promptly swore allegiance to Tiberius. Now that all eight legions had sworn for Tiberius and returned to the authority of their officers, all problems seemed to have been resolved. Germanicus returned to Cologne, where he was joined by his wife, Agrippina—called Agrippina the Elder by historians—Augustus's granddaughter. They were a loving couple and, unusually for a Roman general's wife, she lived in camp with her husband. Most of their children were raised at Rome while they were away, at Germanicus's palace below Augustus's Palatium on the slopes of the Palatine Hill, but Germanicus and Agrippina always kept their then youngest child with them. Agrippina was to bear Germanicus nine children, and for years on end she was almost perpetually pregnant. Currently their youngest child was a boy, Gaius, born, according to Pliny the Elder, in A.D. 12 in Luxembourg, close to Trier and the Rhine. The boy had spent his first two years in legion camps with his parents, where he was adored by the troops. A legion tailor made the infant a tiny blood-red legionary tunic. A legion cobbler made him military-style sandals, *caligulae*. The Rhine legionaries soon gave the child a nickname that his parents liked so much they used it themselves: Little Boot. In Latin it was Caligula.

On May 18, Augustus had sent Caligula from Rome, where he'd wintered with his siblings, to rejoin his parents on the Rhine, accompanied by two of the emperor's personal servants and a doctor. By September, Agrippina, pregnant again after a hiatus of fewer than two years, was now with Germanicus at Cologne, along with Caligula, who had celebrated his second birthday on August 31.

Sometime toward the end of September, as the legions were just settling into their winter quarters, the peace was disrupted by the unheralded arrival in Cologne of a party of senators from Rome led by Senator Lucius Munatius Plancus, a consul the previous year. Senator Plancus announced that the Senate delegation had come to discuss the concessions Germanicus had made to the legions. Via the express riders of the Cursus Publicus, word had quickly reached Rome of the mutiny and of how Germanicus had settled it. Germanicus's chief of staff, Brigadier General Seius Tubero, described by Tacitus as an intimate friend of Tiberius, also had probably sent messages to Rome. The feeling in the Senate, the envoys now told Germanicus, was that he'd been too generous, and they'd come straight from the capital to investigate the situation for themselves.

Tiberius was behind this delegation. Fearful of rivals, he hadn't yet taken any step toward taking the throne. He held back, waiting to see what Germanicus would do. Not only was he jealous of the young man's popularity with the Roman people—he'd been forced by Augustus to adopt Germanicus and make him his heir—he also was fearful of what Germanicus might do with the backing of the eight legions on the Rhine. With the ambitious and manipulative Praetorian Guard commander Sejanus feeding his fears, Tiberius couldn't bring himself to believe that Germanicus was so selfless that he would turn down the legions' offer to make him emperor. Tiberius wanted an excuse to remove Germanicus from the Rhine command given to him by Augustus. But if Tiberius simply fired him, he knew the legions could revolt in Germanicus's favor. The senatorial delegation had come to the Rhine seeking grounds for the Senate to dismiss Germanicus in a way by which no blame could be attached to Tiberius.

Germanicus knew all this. And the last thing he needed was for the mutiny to flare up again and give the senators the excuse they were looking for. There were only two legions wintering at Cologne, the 1st and 20th V.V. The 5th and 21st Rapax had gone into winter quarters at Castra Vetus, Old Camp, sixty miles downstream. But these two were enough to ruin everything. Veterans of the 1st and 20th V.V. Legions, convinced that the senators intended canceling their concessions, gave way to their fears and attacked the delegation in the camp late at night. Senator Plancus had to hide in the tent of the eagle-bearer of the 1st overnight. The next day, Germanicus sent the delegation back to Rome with an escort, knowing that he would have to do something drastic to save his job.

He then told Agrippina that she and Caligula must leave Cologne for Trier at once. In the new year she would give birth to a daughter, Agrippina the Younger, and Germanicus had planned all along to send his wife into confinement in Trever territory, as he had when she was expecting Caligula, although not quite this early in the pregnancy. Agrippina didn't want to leave his side, but once Germanicus explained his motives to her, she agreed to go without delay.

When the legionaries saw their commander in chief's pregnant wife departing from the camp, taking their good-luck charm Caligula with her, they begged her to stay. But she continued on her way. Men then crowded around Germanicus, pleading for his wife and popular young son to be brought back. Nothing could be worse than entrusting mother and child to the Gauls, they said, swearing that no harm would come to the pair while they remained in a legion camp.

Germanicus, a trained and skillful speaker, then addressed them, and they listened in shame as he told them he had removed his wife and child because he genuinely feared for their lives. He had lost faith in these legions, Tacitus records him as saying. "After all, what haven't you dared over these past few days?" he went on. "What am I supposed to call you? 'Soldiers'? Men who threatened your commander's son? 'Citizens'? When you've trampled on the authority of the Senate?"

He spoke of the finest hours of Julius Caesar and Augustus. Descended from them both as he was, he said, it would be a strange and unworthy thing if he was turned on by the same legions that had served them. He reminded his audience that both these legions at Cologne had received their standards from Tiberius himself at their last enlistments—the 1st Legion in 4 B.C., the 20th V.V. in 1 B.C. He reminded the men of the 20th of the Pannonian War battles he'd shared with them, and of the rewards Tiberius had given them for their victories in those battles. What was he to tell Tiberius, he asked, about these men Tiberius himself had led? Men who now murdered centurions, threw out tribunes, and imprisoned senatorial envoys. He should have taken his own life the day he arrived back from Gaul, he said—then he would have died before learning what a disgraceful army this was. And then the troops could have chosen a general "who would avenge the death of Varus and his three legions."

Avenge Varus? Many a lowered head came snapping up. Germanicus must have decided on this course of action as he set Senator Plancus and his party on the road back to Rome. It was a dramatic and masterly way to kill two birds with one stone.

"Heaven help me," he said, "I will not allow the Belgians the glory and honor of rescuing Rome's name and subduing the tribes of Germany, even though they've offered." There is no proof that there had been any such offer. Germanicus was bluffing.

Tacitus says that Germanicus saw an immediate change in the expressions on the faces of the men around him. Roman legionaries were more than proud, they were also arrogant. They had little time for the auxiliaries attached to their units—noncitizens and foreigners—let alone their Gallic and Belgian "allies." How dare the Belgians offer to take revenge for the Varus disaster! If anyone was to do it, the legions would!

Germanicus's address didn't have the brevity of a speech by Julius Caesar or the construction of an oration by Cato. But it had the same power. His troops begged his forgiveness. Bring back his family, they called. Punish the guilty among their ranks. Pardon those who'd been led astray. And lead the legions against the Germans.

In reply, Germanicus said his wife would stay away until after she gave birth, but Caligula would come back right away. Agrippina would in fact soon return to Cologne, no doubt at her insistence, where Agrippina the Younger was born in the new year.

"As for everything else," Germanicus said, "you can settle matters yourselves."

Away the soldiers hurried—altered men, says Tacitus. They had experienced such a change of heart, says Dio, that of their own accord they arrested the ringleaders of the mutiny. The chief mutineers were dragged in chains to Brigadier General Gaius Caetronius, commander of the 1st Legion and most senior of the A.L.R.'s legion commanders. Preparations were made, and then the legions were called to assembly.

The men of the legions and the separated groups of semiretired veterans quickly fell in and came to attention as General Caetronius took his place beside Germanicus on the tribunal. The throng of accused mutineers was made to stand on a raised platform, in chains, facing the men of their own units, with centurions on either side of them.

An order rang out: "Draw swords!" All the assembled legionaries of the 1st and 20th slid their swords from the scabbards on their right hips. One at a time, mutineers on the platform were pointed out by young tribunes of their legion.

"Guilty or not guilty?" a lieutenant colonel called.

If the men yelled back "Guilty!" then the prisoner was thrown headlong into the ranks, and the troops, the man's former comrades, cut him to pieces. One after the other they were dealt with like this. The rank and file enjoyed the bloody business. Tacitus says it was like absolution for their sins, for their own mutinous acts or thoughts.

As the corpses were being hauled away, the second-enlistment veterans of the legions were ordered to collect their gear before marching up the Rhine to the province of Rhaetia, in present-day Switzerland, where they would settle in their retirement. This was nominally to protect the province from the neighboring Suebi Germans, but Germanicus wanted to separate these troublesome men from their legions as quickly as possible.

Germanicus wasn't finished. He summoned the centurions of the two legions to the tribunal, one at a time. Each man had to state his name, rank, birthplace, and length of service, list his bravery awards, then describe what courageous deeds he'd performed in battle, all in front of the watching, listening legions. The tribunes of his legion then gave their assessment of the centurion. The legions were then asked if they agreed. If tribunes and legions commended his energy and good behavior, the centurion retained his rank. But if charged with greed or cruelty, he was dishonorably discharged on the spot.

Germanicus sent a message to Lieutenant General Aulus Caecina, at the camp of the 5th Alaudae and 21st Rapax Legions farther down the

Rhine, ordering him to deal out similar punishment to the mutineers there. Caecina, a consul with Senator Plancus the previous year, had forty years' experience in the army. In his sixties now, the wily general called in the eagle-bearers, standard-bearers, and legionaries he could trust, read them Germanicus's letter, and told them to sort out the mutiny's ringleaders themselves. In the middle of the night, with swords drawn, the loyal troops went into ringleaders' tents and dealt out rough justice. A few days later, when Germanicus arrived at Old Camp, General Caecina showed him bodies in piles, hundreds of them, proof that his orders had been carried out, that the mutineers had been dealt with. Germanicus sadly shook his head. "This was destruction rather than remedy," he remarked before ordering the bodies burned.

The men of the 14th G.M.V. and other A.U.R. units escaped the bloody punishments. Yet, despite the executions downriver, or perhaps because of them, the result was as dramatic at Mainz as at the other legion camps. Germanicus had won back the respect, loyalty, and obedience of the soldiery. And he had created a thirst for action.

XVI

GOING AFTER HERMANN THE GERMAN

I n the half light of an October dawn, the army started rolling across the Rhine. A bridge of boats had been thrown across the river at Xanten in Holland. History was repeating itself. Xanten had been the jumping-off point for the German campaigns of Germanicus's father, Drusus Caesar, twenty-five years before. Now Germanicus was keeping his word to his troops: they were on the vengeance trail.

With their cloth standards fluttering, mounted auxiliary units under Germanicus's deputy commander of cavalry, Colonel Albinovanus Pedo, clattered across the narrow wooden decking of the temporary bridge and then fanned out into Germany to scout the way ahead. Pedo, in his late twenties, was a friend of the famous poet Ovid, and would himself become a noted poet, writing a popular epic poem about Germanicus's exploits. On the heels of Colonel Pedo's cavalry advance guard came the twelve thousand men still serving in the four legions of the Army of the Lower Rhine. The first-enlistment men of the 1st Legion had been recalled—as far as Germanicus was concerned, an emergency now existed. And they were happy to oblige, to strike against Hermann's Germans.

With the four legions marched thirteen thousand auxiliary light infantrymen in twenty-six cohorts. For the sake of mobility, the troops of the task force left their heavy equipment behind. Two millennia later, Germans would devise a term to describe the sort of rapid, devastating operation Germanicus had in mind: *Blitzkrieg*—lightning war.

*   *   *

The thousand or so men of the 14th G.M.V.'s senior cohorts had marched off to Switzerland along with the retirees of the A.L.R. legions, leaving the youngsters of the junior cohorts in camp at Mainz chafing for action through the fall of A.D. 14, for they knew the Lower Army was in Germany with Germanicus, and they wanted a piece of the action. Their officers had told them that they, too, would cross the Rhine in the new year, that Germanicus's current operation was just a feeling-out exercise. But the men of the 14th wanted to be the ones feeling out the Germans, with twenty inches of cold Spanish steel.

Once the task force returned, they came to hear all about the operation via couriers from the A.L.R., legion cavalrymen who'd been east of the Rhine with Germanicus. With great animation the couriers would have told crowds of envious A.U.R. men of a dash into Marsi territory. Germanicus had led his troops east through thickly forested territory between the Lippe and Ruhr Rivers—today one of the mostly heavily populated areas on earth. Back then it was mile after mile of towering oak, beech, and spruce. Scouts reported that in villages ahead the unsuspecting Marsi were preparing for the Festival of Tamfana, a major German religious feast. On a clear, moonlit night the A.L.R. legions had moved into position around Marsi villages as tribesmen feasted. Well into the night the Marsi drank beer brewed from barley and sang drinking songs. When the last Germans had staggered off to bed or fallen asleep at tables without posting a single sentry, Germanicus launched his attacks. Not one German survived. Leaving the blood-soaked, corpse-ridden villages ablaze, the legions had withdrawn into the night.

With daylight, Germanicus had split his force into four divisions and sent them advancing across a broad front for a distance of fifty miles, destroying every village and every living thing in their path. In the course of their rampage they found the Germans' Temple of Tamfana. That, too, went up in flames. By the time the fifty-mile limit had been reached, German refugees were fleeing east ahead of the Roman advance in the tens of thousands, with all the possessions they could carry. As Germanicus turned his army around and marched back toward the Rhine, Germans from three tribes north of the Lippe—the Bructeri, the Tubantes, and the Usipetes—were rushing to cut off the Roman withdrawal. They overtook Germanicus at the Caesian Forest but were beaten off the column's tail by the 20th V.V. A day later, the column had reached the Rhine and crossed to the western side. It had been a methodical, clinical trial run for the much larger operation Germanicus had in mind for the new year.

*   *   *

News of Germanicus's successful expedition across the Rhine was greeted
with joy and excitement by the people of Rome. For years the Varus disaster had gone unpunished, but now the young hero Germanicus had carved
up the Germans and come away without a single casualty. This was what
Romans expected of their generals and their legions.

Tiberius had by this time overcome his hesitancy. Learning that Germanicus was waging war east of the Rhine, he had finally taken the helm
at Rome. Now, with the news of the success against the Marsi, he delivered a speech in the Senate full of praise for his adopted son. But in reality he was annoyed that Germanicus had pulled off the German strike,
and even more annoyed when the Senate voted Germanicus a Triumph
for his success. Little did Tiberius or the Senate realize that Germanicus
had only just begun.

All through the winter of A.D. 14–15, Germanicus's chief of staff, General Tubero, and his team of staff and commissariat officers of the armies
of both the Upper and Lower Rhine made feverish preparations for a
major trans-Rhine invasion. This time Germanicus would go into Germany with all eight of his legions. It would be the single largest Roman
army to go into the field since Tiberius led twelve legions into Germany a
decade before. Germanicus's staff officers told him that the logistics of
such a massive operation would mean that the army would not be ready to
move until the summer. But an impatient Germanicus wanted to catch
the Germans napping a second time. Keeping his cards close to his chest,
he waited for the weather to improve, and for spies to bring back information from the far side of the Rhine on the temperament and disposition
of the Germans.

During this time, too, a senior officer arrived on the Rhine, sent by
Tiberius to "assist" Germanicus. Lieutenant General Lucius Apronius had
been a consul in A.D. 8, and was on intimate terms with the new emperor.
Germanicus knew that Apronius was Tiberius's man, and treated him
accordingly. With all the lieutenant generals he needed, he attached
Apronius to his staff. At least there he could keep an eye on him. He
would have known that General Tubero also was close to the emperor.
Now, he would have to watch his back from two directions.

As the spring of A.D. 15 approached and preparations continued for
the major summer offensive, an earlier operation was made all the more
urgent when spies brought Germanicus news that Hermann had once
more fallen out with his father-in-law, Segestes, who had resumed control
of the Chatti after the Battle of the Teutoburg Forest. The opportunity to

split the German confederation was too great to miss as far as Germanicus was concerned. Before the winter had ended, and as soon as the weather permitted, the young field marshal launched two simultaneous surprise attacks, planning to get in and out of Germany quickly before the spring rains made the rivers impassable.

This time it was the 14th G.M.V.'s turn. Germanicus personally led elements from all four legions of the Army of the Upper Rhine commanded by his close and trusted friend Lieutenant General Gaius Silius. Like General Caecina, Silius had been a consul the previous year, with Silius the senior of the two.

Since the retirement of the men of the 14th's second enlistment the previous fall, the legion now numbered fewer than four thousand men. Apart from their senior centurions, none of the 14th's troops had seen any action before now. Four years of training were about to be put to the test. From Mainz, Germanicus led the four A.U.R. legions and their auxiliary support across the river, again on a bridge of boats, and then quickly marched north into the territory of the Chatti tribe. At the same time, in a coordinated move, Lieutenant General Caecina led his four legions of the Army of the Lower Rhine in another crossing of the Rhine, at Xanten, via the customary temporary bridge. Heading east, Caecina's force traced the course of the raid of the previous fall.

Reaching the foot of the Taunus Mountains, Germanicus found entrenchments created by his father when he came this way many years before. There, Germanicus had the 14th G.M.V. and his other legions build a fort. It's probable that this fort was strengthened eighty years later during the reign of the emperor Domitian, as part of his Rhine defenses. If it's the same fort, it still stands today, added to over the centuries and called the Saalburg. Germanicus put Lieutenant General Apronius in charge of the Saalburg, with a small force of auxiliaries and orders to prepare roads and bridges in the vicinity for the army's return. Apronius would have fumed at being left behind—he would see or hear precious little from the rear, and be of no service to the emperor as a secret agent.

Taking the legions with him, Germanicus powered on east. His rapid advance took him as far as the Eder River. He moved so quickly that the tribes didn't have the chance to organize resistance. Many tribespeople tried to escape by flinging themselves into the Eder. Villages were burned and their occupants fled ahead of the men of the 14th G.M.V. and their A.U.R. companions as they marched up the southern bank of the Eder to where it joins the Fulda. Germanicus came to Mattium, the Chatti capital, site of General Varus's last banquet with the Germans. It had been abandoned by the Chatti. Germanicus allowed his troops to loot the town, then ordered its destruction. The men of the 14th G.M.V. would have watched approvingly as Mattium burned. Here, at last, they were beginning to repay the Germans for the slaughter of their comrades of the 17th, 18th, and 19th. After razing the town, Germanicus swung around and made tracks for the Rhine. General Caecina and his army covered his withdrawal, colliding with bands of Germans from both the Cherusci and Marsi tribes hurrying down from the north in support of the Chatti. These German warriors were so surprised to find a second Roman army on their doorstep and suffered so badly at the hands of Caecina's legionaries that they hung back after the initial conflict and didn't even harry the rear guard.

Now there was a surprise for the Romans, a pleasant one. As Germanicus was moving back toward the Rhine, Segimundus, son of King Segestes of the Chatti, rode up to the column. He carried, he said, a message from his father. Back in the fall of A.D. 9, Segimundus had just taken up his role as a priest at the temple of the Ubii in Cologne when the expected news of the battle in the Teutoburg reached him. He'd gladly ripped apart the sacred garland of flowers worn on the head as a crown of office and thrown off his priest's white robe, then slipped out of Cologne. He would have had a boatman take him across the river, after which he'd rejoined his people.

The men of the 14th G.M.V. and their colleagues watched with curiosity as the dejected young Chattian prince was made to dismount and disarm. He was then led to Germanicus. The message that Segimundus reluctantly brought the Roman field marshal, who was only a year or two his senior, was to the effect that old Segestes had long been an ally of Rome but had been forced to follow the will of the majority when the German tribes voted to go to war with Rome six years before. Now Segestes wanted to return to the Roman fold. And he had a prize to offer Germanicus Caesar: his daughter Thusnelda, Hermann's wife, who was in Segestes' "protective custody." What's more, Segimundus advised, Thusnelda was expecting Hermann's child. But there also was a small problem: having kidnapped his own daughter, Segestes was now surrounded and besieged by Hermann's Cheruscans at a stronghold in the hills. Not surprisingly, the Cheruscans were determined to secure the release of their leader's wife. Segestes begged Germanicus to come to his aid before it was too late.

In case this was a trap, Germanicus sent the king's son under escort to the western side of the Rhine. Then he swung the four legions of the Army of the Upper Rhine around and marched on Segestes' stronghold.

When he reached it, he found the situation just as the young man had painted it, with the wooden palisades of Segestes' fortress besieged by his fellow Germans. The attackers turned as the legions appeared, initially putting up a brave fight. But vastly outnumbered, they soon withdrew.

The gates of the stronghold opened and Germanicus strode in. At the king's residence, Germanicus was warmly welcomed by Segestes, who vowed allegiance to Rome and to Tiberius. At Segestes' command, his people brought in armor, weapons, and personal effects and piled them before the emperor's son. These, Segestes said, had belonged to General Varus and his officers, had been spoils of the Germans' bloody victory in the Teutoburg Forest six years before, brought back by Segimerus and his men as trophies. As Germanicus inspected the sad souvenirs, Segestes' pregnant daughter was brought in. Thusnelda, the young wife of thirty-two-year-old Hermann, was fiercely loyal to her husband and was equally defiant of Rome and her father. She glared at Germanicus as she stood proud and haughty in front of him with her hands tightly clasped over her bosom. She didn't cry, she didn't beg for her life.

Her father hurried to speak on behalf of both his children. "Please forgive my son, Segimundus," he said, "for the youthful error of his ways. As for my daughter, I admit she's been brought here against her will and that she has no love for Rome. It's for you, Caesar, to determine which fact weighs more importantly with you when you decide her fate—that she bears Hermann's child, or that she is my flesh and blood."

Germanicus didn't hesitate to spare Segestes and his family members, including Thusnelda, promising them safety in Roman territory on the far side of the Rhine. As the 14th G.M.V. and the other legions turned about and resumed the withdrawal, Germanicus took the members of the Chatti royal family and their retainers with him.

Both Germanicus's battle group and Caecina's screening force were able to pull out of Germany without incident, recrossing the Rhine to the Roman bank before the rains came and without any harassment from the disorganized German tribes. The 14th Gemina Martia Victrix returned from the operation without a scratch, and with a king, a prince, and the wife of Rome's public enemy number one. Not a bad week's work.

In the north, when Hermann heard that the Romans had captured his pregnant wife, he exploded with anger. Whipping up his own people into a frenzy for war, he sent envoys to neighboring tribes, calling on them to once more march with him against the invading Romans. Fearing that Germanicus would return, numerous German tribes answered the call. Men who had stood back from the uprising six years earlier now committed to war, among them Hermann's uncle, Inguiomerus, who had previously been well respected by Rome and had kept out of the politics of the Varus era. Now, as Inguiomerus became Hermann's deputy, the Cherusci, the Chatti, and their neighbors prepared for a renewed struggle against the Romans.

Meanwhile, as old Segestes and his family made a new home among the Ubii, with Segimundus resuming his priestly duties in Cologne, Hermann's wife, Thusnelda, was sent to Italy under tight security. She was confined at Ravenna, the Roman naval base on the Adriatic coast that housed numerous dissidents over the years, including Bato, the surrendered Dalmatian rebel. Thusnelda's sister-in-law, Flavus's Chattian wife, also lived at Ravenna with her son Italicus, but she and Thusnelda supported opposite sides in the war between Rome and Germany.

Even as the Roman people were marveling at Germanicus's pluck at snatching Hermann's wife and unborn child from under German noses, the Roman general was launching his full-scale summer offensive. This was in the form of a three-pronged attack. The first stage involved an amphibious operation launched from the lower Rhine town of Utrecht, Roman Traiectum, in Holland. Again the 14th marched with Germanicus, as he took the four legions of General Silius's Army of the Upper Rhine and part of the auxiliary infantry and cavalry by convoy from Utrecht across the Zuider Zee—Lake Flevo, as the Romans called it—into the North Sea. He then sailed along the Frisian coast before turning up the Ems River, the Roman Amisia, into the heart of Germany. Both Germanicus's father and Tiberius had followed precisely this same route when they invaded Germany in 12 B.C. and A.D. 5, respectively, so he couldn't be criticized back at Rome for going into uncharted territory and taking unnecessary risks—Germanicus would have been acutely conscious of limiting Tiberius's opportunities for criticism.

While Germanicus was slipping up the Ems, Colonel Pedo led a diversionary cavalry operation in the Frisian area of Holland and northwestern Germany. At the same time, the third prong was initiated by General Caecina. He crossed the Rhine from Xanten yet again, but now he marched his four A.L.R. legions northeast, heading for the Ems. Colonel Pedo then suddenly turned southeast and brought the cavalry overland, also aiming for a prearranged convergence at the Ems. With exquisite timing, all three forces linked up beside the river, deep inside German territory. Germanicus had brought together forty thousand legionaries, thirty thousand auxiliary infantry, and eight thousand cavalry on the bank of the Ems.

From here, Germanicus sent his cavalry commander, General Lucius Stertinius, with his entire mounted force as a flying column against Germans south of the Ems. The Roman cavalry army swept down through the homeland of the Bructeri, routing every German band that stood in their path. They moved so quickly that they caught the Germans trying to burn their own possessions before fleeing. In one village, General Stertinius's troopers discovered the sacred golden eagle of the 19th Legion taken by the Bructeri during the Teutoburg massacre. To Romans, this was a prize beyond value.

While the cavalry was laying waste to Bructerian territory, Germanicus marched the infantry from the river to the nearby Teutoburg Forest. This was a pilgrimage that Germanicus had been determined to make, to find the place where Varus and his legions had fallen and there pay his respects. There were a handful of men in his task force who'd escaped from the Varus massacre or from German captivity later and who were now serving with his legions. They guided the general to the place where Varus and his men had fought their last battle. The men of the 14th G.M.V. and their comrades found the well-preserved remains of a marching camp large enough to house three legions. Here Varus had dug in on the first, wet day of the battle. Climbing up onto the ridges, following the path taken by Varus's army as it struggled west under attack, they came to a large clearing in the thick forest where Varus had made his last stand. Here the hurriedly built walls of the last camp had partially collapsed. The ditch around the outside was not deep. It was clear that only a depleted force under extreme pressure had built this inadequate defense.

Germanicus and his silent, reverent troops trod the grass of the battleground as the wind washed through the trees and birds called agitatedly from the greenery. It would have been an eerie place, a place to send shivers down the spine. In the open at the center of this last camp lay the whitening bones of thousands of Roman legionaries, some piled in heaps, others strewn around. Tearful survivors pointed out where this had happened and that had happened. Skulls were found nailed to tree trunks. The troops located the pits where prisoners had been held temporarily, and, in adjacent groves, altars where the tribunes and first-rank centurions had been burned alive as offerings to German gods.

The 20th V.V. and 19th Legions had been recruited in the same part of northern Italy. And as they collected the bones for burial on Germanicus's orders, the men of the 14th could only guess that they might be handling the remains of a relative or neighbor of 20th V.V. men, or of friends of their own. Sad, angry, reflective—in other circumstances this might have been their fate and these their bones—they interred the remains. The name of just one victim of the Varus disaster has come down to us—fifty-three-year-old centurion Marcus Caelius of the 18th Legion; his brother would build a memorial to him at Xanten.

Germanicus himself turned the first sod of the mound raised over the mass grave. Once the burial was complete, he conducted gladiatorial games, traditionally and originally a funeral rite. The legionary contestants' weapons were wooden, and contests ended when one competitor yielded to another.

As the men of the 14th G.M.V. marched away from the Teutoburg, it would have been with a determination not to suffer a similar fate at the hands of the Germans. As they marched, too, to link up with General Stertinius and the cavalry, they drove uncoordinated German bands ahead of them. Germanicus had one last task to perform. He built a fort in Marsi territory on the southern bank of the Lippe and garrisoned it with a detachment of auxiliaries, naming it Fort Aliso. Now he could say that Rome had extended its reach east of the Rhine once more.

As the 14th G.M.V. and their fellow upper Rhine legions boarded the waiting fleet at the Ems, Colonel Pedo's cavalry set off to retrace their path via the Frisian coast, and General Caecina turned for the Rhine with the 1st, 5th, 20th V.V., and 21st Rapax Legions. Caecina was to follow a route called Long Bridges. This elevated roadway had been built through a marshy valley by Lieutenant General Lucius Domitius during his campaigns a decade earlier. It provided the shortest route to the Rhine, but Germanicus knew that this road was narrow and flanked by muddy quagmires, making it an ideal place for an ambush. So in sending Caecina this way, he urged him to make all speed.

Hermann knew all about Long Bridges, too. When his scouts saw the route that Caecina's four legions were taking, he hurried his Cheruscans ahead of the Romans, whose progress was limited to the speed of their fully laden baggage train. The Germans then moved into position in the hills around Long Bridges.

Germanicus was sailing back to Holland with the Army of the Upper Rhine. But as his convoy came down the Ems and reached the North Sea, his naval commanders warned that storms in these parts that accompanied the impending equinoctial change could wreck his ships if they were overloaded. So to be on the safe side, he put two of his four legions ashore on the coast: the 14th G.M.V. and the 2nd Augusta. These two units had been partners on the Rhine for years, sharing the same Mainz winter quarters and marching together each summer since A.D. 10. They weren't from the same region—the men of the 2nd Augusta were now recruited in the southeast of France. But the 14th's northern Italians and the 2nd's

Provençals worked well together. The name of the 14th's commanding general at this time is unknown, but Brigadier General Publius Vitellius led the 2nd Augusta. The senior of the two legion commanders and a friend of Germanicus, Vitellius was put in charge for this leg of the journey.

Germanicus instructed General Vitellius to march overland to the Weser River, where he would meet him and pick up his legions. The lightened fleet then headed out to sea, and the 2nd Augusta and 14th Gemina Martia Victrix Legions began their march along the coast, following the shoreline so they wouldn't become lost. At first, Vitellius and his force made good progress across the lowlands, following the seashore. But in the afternoon the weather changed dramatically. The sea rose, as it usually did at this time of year, and a strong north wind drove it onto the low-lying coastal strip. Fields for miles around were quickly inundated with water, and the legionaries found themselves waist deep, even neck deep in places. They struggled on, cursing, crying out to comrades for a hand, grabbing friends who stumbled. The men of the 14th G.M.V. and 2nd Augusta lost all their baggage animals in the swirling waters. With them went their food, their firemaking material, and their tents. As the heavily laden legionaries splashed on, some men were drowned, being sucked under by unseen quicksand or losing their footing and being washed away.

Toward the end of the day Vitellius managed to pilot the force to high ground, and there the two legions spent a miserable night, cold, wet, and hungry. The next day, from their elevated position, they could see dry land on their route ahead. As they pushed on, the weather improved, and faces lit up when legionaries saw their fleet at anchor in a cove ahead, waiting for them as Germanicus had promised.

West of the Rhine, with General Caecina's legions now several days overdue, concern began to rise in Roman quarters. A rumor flew that his army had been defeated and that a massive German horde was about to cross the Rhine. Preparations were made to destroy the Xanten bridge to prevent the Germans from crossing. Now, Germanicus's wife, Agrippina, who had been waiting at Xanten since her husband's departure, stepped in and refused to allow the bridge's destruction, certain that the legions weren't far away. Anxious for news, Agrippina crossed the bridge with her two-year-old son and personal servants, joining auxiliaries on sentry duty on the far bank. There, at the German end of the bridge, holding little Caligula by the hand, she stood looking anxiously east for signs of the returning army.

Finally, a week overdue, General Caecina appeared from the east leading his four legions. They came minus most of their baggage animals and carrying severely wounded men on hastily improvised litters. They were all bloodied, filthy, hungry, and tired. And they told of a desperate battle at Long Bridges when Hermann's Germans attacked them as they struggled along causeways and over broken bridges. Of being cut off and besieged in their camp. Of a brilliant scheme by General Caecina that enticed Hermann and his men into their camp and into a trap. A trap from which Hermann and his wounded uncle, Inguiomerus, only just escaped but that cost the lives of thousands of German and paved the way for the legions' escape.

Agrippina greeted Caecina's exhausted troops on her husband's behalf, with her little son at her side clad in his soldier's outfit. Aided by her women servants, she handed out clothing and medicine. She personally praised and thanked the soldiers as they trudged past, and she distributed coins among them. The tough legionaries grinned at the sight of mother and son—Caligula Caesar, as they called him—and blushed when their general's wife told them they were Roman heroes.

Within days, the seasick 14th G.M.V. arrived back from Germany. Germanicus's fleet brought all four legions of the Army of the Upper Rhine back into Utrecht, where he offloaded them and sent them to their winter quarters. Good news awaited Germanicus at Cologne. General Stertinius, his cavalry commander, had brought in Segimerus, new king of the Chatti, who'd surrendered along with his impetuous son, the youth who had insulted the body of General Varus. They were taken before Germanicus, who readily pardoned the father. But he had heard of the son's act in the Teutoburg, and hesitated at first. Before long Segimerus's offspring, too, would be spared, after being made to sweat on his fate for a time.

As the men of the 14th G.M.V. and 2nd Augusta settled into their winter quarters at Mainz, they were surprised to receive a visit from Germanicus himself. The commander in chief went around to the legions' wounded in their beds, talking to each legionary individually, asking him how he came by his wound, thanking him for his courage, applauding his feats. He encouraged every man he met, joking with them, revitalizing their fighting spirit, leaving them smiling. No general the men of the 14th knew of had ever done that before. By the time Germanicus had finished, there wasn't a man in his legions who wouldn't have followed him to Hades and back.

That wasn't all. Germanicus instructed the legions' centurions to compile a list of the equipment and personal possessions the men had lost on the last German campaign. He said he would personally reimburse every man for what he had lost. When the provinces vied with one another to compensate Germanicus for his losses, he took their horses and weapons, but he paid the men's compensation claims from his own purse.

Reverently Germanicus sent the regained eagle of the 19th Legion to Rome along with his campaign report. But still Tiberius managed to find fault—Germanicus shouldn't have buried the remains of Varus's troops, he complained. That would only dispirit his soldiers, he said, and Germanicus, who held a priesthood, had polluted himself with funeral rites—Roman priests weren't permitted to look at, let alone touch the dead. As for Agrippina's actions at the Rhine bridge, Tiberius was beside himself. For one thing, women and the army didn't mix. And Tiberius saw only a political motive in Agrippina's presence at the bridge as the men came out of Germany; he was convinced she was trying to win the legions' devotion to her husband and family. The more Germanicus tried to prove his loyalty by winning Tiberius and Rome glory in Germany, the more Sejanus, and then Tiberius, put a suspicious slant on everything the young general did.

Tiberius now asked the Senate to award Triumphal Decorations to three generals on Germanicus's staff. Two of those honored were Lieutenant Generals Silius and Caecina. The third was Lieutenant General Lucius Apronius—Apronius the spy. This was a deliberate signal to Germanicus from Tiberius, a literal finger in the air. For, while Tiberius could say he was rewarding all the lieutenant generals involved in the campaign, Apronius didn't have the accomplishments to merit the award—he had done no more than sit in a fort in Germanicus's rear. And everyone knew it.

Then Tiberius moved to reduce Germanicus's popularity with the army. He had received a petition from the businessmen of Rome asking for the 1 percent sales tax on all goods to be axed. Tiberius agreed, but on the basis that the state could afford it only if the period of legionary service was again extended to twenty years. After less than a year, the concessions granted by Germanicus to his legions and extended to other legions were removed by the emperor. But if Tiberius hoped that this would reflect badly on Germanicus, he was to be disappointed. The troops on the Rhine accepted the change without dissent.

The expectation at Rome was that Germanicus would launch a new campaign into Germany in the spring, and Tiberius didn't have a good enough reason to forbid him. Not that he ever forbade anything in the early part of his reign. Tiberius took care to frame his letters to his subordinates in the form of advice rather than instructions. The clever ones took the advice. And there was no reason to advise a cessation of operations in Germany, especially as the expectation around Rome would have been that in his next campaign Germanicus would bring back Varus's two remaining lost eagles. Instead, Tiberius apparently took up a suggestion of Sejanus. That winter, two Praetorian Guard cohorts were ordered to prepare to march from Rome to join Germanicus on the Rhine.

Traditionally, the Praetorian Guard stayed in Italy. Only if the emperor personally led a campaigning army did the Praetorians become involved in military operations in the field. So while officially the Praetorians were being sent to the Rhine to support Germanicus, there can be no doubt that the two broad stripe tribunes in command of the detachment had orders from Praetorian Prefect Sejanus to kill Germanicus should he attempt to lead his legions on Rome to take the throne for himself.

XVII

✦

SHOWDOWN
IN GERMANY

Smoke curled from armorers' forges. The noise of the camp was a constant din. As far as the eye could see, the pancake-flat Batavian "island" formed on the Dutch coast by the Waal and Meuse where the two rivers coursed to the North Sea was a mass of tents, men, horses, mules, wagons, and equipment. As they marched into the massive staging camp, home to seventy-four thousand troops, the hearts of the men of the 14th G.M.V. would have swollen with pride, and their impatience for combat would have intensified. Since the retirement of its two senior cohorts the 14th numbered some thirty-five hundred men, all now five years into their enlistment, all anxious to see some real action and teach the Germans a lesson.

Through the winter of A.D. 15–16 preparations had been going on for Germanicus's invasion of Germany. It was to be an amphibious operation. Germanicus had instructed General Silius at Mainz, General Caecina at Cologne, and his engineering officer, General Publius Anteius, to create a fleet of a thousand ships, mostly transports. He'd given them specific requirements—some ships had to be seagoing, with narrow stems and sterns and broad beams. Others were to be flat-bottomed craft that could navigate shallow rivers and be run onto the bank to disgorge troops quickly without damaging the hull, and then be easily refloated. One flotilla was to be equipped with steering oars at both ends, and with reversible rowing positions, so they could change direction in a hurry in narrow waterways. Many were to be decked over, to carry horses, supplies, and artillery. Some were to be warships, up to cruisers of the trireme class. Over the winter and spring, ships had been built by west bank Rhine communities all the way from the North Sea to Switzerland. Forests had been felled for the timber, tens of thousands of locals had been drafted into the Roman navy for the duration of the campaigning season, then trained to row and sail— on dry land, to save time, while their ships were under construction. Now the riverbank around the embarkation point at Utrecht on the lower Rhine was wall-to-wall ships. For months, wagons had rolled up through Gaul bringing grain, weapons, and ammunition for the campaign. Mule- teers brought fresh mules north for the baggage trains. From as far away as Spain, horse traders brought remounts needed by the cavalry to make up for the previous year's losses at Long Bridges and on the North Sea coast.

As spring arrived, Germanicus had sent legion commanders Brigadier Generals Publius Vitellius and Gaius Antius into Gaul to supervise the annual tax collection, as six legions moved down from Cologne and Mainz to the embarkation point. He'd left two legions of the Army of the Upper Rhine at Mainz for the time being, to give the Germans across the Rhine an impression of normality. But as a distraction, he'd sent General Silius across the river with a flying column of cavalry to spear into Chatti terri- tory. While Silius was away, urgent messages had reached Germanicus that Fort Aliso on the Lippe River east of the Rhine was under attack, so Ger- manicus had led elements from the six legions at Utrecht across the river to its relief. But the Germans pulled out as he approached, so he'd con- tinued east, drawn back to the Teutoburg Forest. Again he visited the site of the Varus disaster, only to find that the Germans had come behind him the previous year and knocked down the barrow he'd raised over the mass grave. This time, conscious of Tiberius's criticisms, he'd left things as he found them and withdrew.

General Silius, hampered by the inevitable spring rains that swept the region, had only minor success. Coming across a stronghold where Arpus, newly appointed king of the Chatti since the surrender of Segimerus, had hidden his wife and daughter and other members of his household along with his personal wealth, Silius was able to capture the lot, bringing loved ones and loot out of Germany. He'd then brought the two legions, auxil- iaries, and cavalry at Mainz downriver to join the invasion force.

Like enlistments before them, as the men of the 14th prepared their equipment for the operation, they would have speculated and wagered about their objective. Some would have tried to assess the significance of the fact that Chariovalda, king of the Batavi tribe, was joining the task force to personally lead the Batavian Horse, most famous of all Rome's cavalry regiments. Originally a clan of the Chatti, the Batavi had long ago fallen out with their German cousins. Ever since Julius Caesar had dis- covered the Batavians' talent for swimming rivers with their horses, in full equipment, they had been an integral part of the Roman army and often were associated with the 14th G.M.V.

Another source of great curiosity to men of the 14th and the other legions of the task force was Colonel Flavus, a commander of German auxiliaries, and Hermann's brother. A forbidding figure as he strode through the Utrecht camp—he'd lost an eye in Dalmatia in A.D. 9 at the siege of Andetrium, and the wound had severely disfigured his face—he'd served with the Roman army for at least twelve years and was highly decorated for bravery. Like Hermann, Flavus had been given Roman citizenship and membership in the Equestrian Order. Unlike Hermann, he preferred life as a Roman, was happy to be nothing more than a colonel. Wearing the knight's golden ring on his left hand and now commanding a cavalry unit, a more prestigious position than that of an infantry commander, Flavus seems never to have contemplated deserting to the German cause. The 14th's campfire generals would already have decided that Germanicus planned to replace Hermann with Flavus once the legions had quashed German resistance.

The rank and file would have noted that the suspect General Apronius was no longer on the Rhine. But in his place, two cohorts of the Praetorian Guard had joined Germanicus in Holland in the spring of A.D. 16. They were experienced men in their early thirties entering the eleventh year of their guard enlistment. Even more arrogant than the legionaries, they would have kept to themselves in camp. The men of the 14th wouldn't have liked them, would have questioned the need for them here. Germanicus himself seems to have taken the presence of the two thousand Praetorians in his stride. He intended that, under his command, they would not be idle.

Under a hazy summer sky the men of the 14th filed aboard ship with packs on their backs. All told, the task force comprised 28,000 legionaries; 2,000 Praetorians; 30,000 auxiliaries from France, Switzerland, northern Italy, Holland, Spain, and Syria; 6,000 men from allied German tribes; and 8,000 auxiliary cavalry, including 2,000 mounted horse archers. Once the troops were aboard, the thousand-ship convoy put out and made its way northeast through Drusus's Fosse, a canal built by Germanicus's father, and onto the broad waters of the Zuider Zee, heading for the North Sea with sails billowing. With the open sea giving the legionaries a fierce greeting, seasickness was rife in the rolling swells. Officers and men alike were grateful when the convoy reached the lower reaches of the Ems

River and the invasion force disembarked on the southern bank, where the fleet tied up. Using floating bridges, Germanicus crossed to the northern bank, choosing a campsite in the territory of the Angrivarii, a German tribe with a peace treaty with Rome.

But as Germanicus was marking out the camp, word arrived that the Angrivars had torn up their treaty. So he sent General Stertinius dashing north with a detachment of cavalry under Colonel Flavus and a unit of horse archers. As Angrivar villages burned, Stertinius's mobile force soon persuaded the tribe to return to the terms of the treaty. General Stertinius's mission to the Angrivars took him as far as the Weser River, and on reaching the principal town of the tribe, possibly the location that sponsored modern Bremen, on the Weser, forty-three miles from the sea—the Roman Bremum—he was amazed to be told that Hermann himself was on the far bank and wanted to parley.

Stertinius went to the Weser's southern bank, and sure enough on the opposite side stood Hermann, accompanied by other German leaders and their bodyguards. Tacitus describes what followed—in detail that must have come from General Stertinius.

"Has Germanicus Caesar arrived?" Hermann called across the river in good Latin.

General Stertinius nodded. "Caesar has come," he confirmed.

"Good," said Hermann. "We have been expecting him. Is my brother with you?"

"Colonel Flavus is here, yes," Stertinius replied.

"May I speak with him privately? Will you grant me that privilege, as a prince of my people? It's many years since we last saw each other, and I hear he was injured. I promised his mother I would try to see for myself that he was in good health."

Stertinius gave his permission for the meeting, but on strict terms. The brothers were to say what had to be said while standing on the two sides of the river. Both were to be unarmed, on foot, and alone. And they were to converse in Latin, so that Stertinius could monitor all that passed between them. Hermann agreed, but had a condition of his own: Stertinius had to withdraw his archers well back from the river.

Stertinius acceded, then returned to his waiting horsemen and Colonel Flavus.

"Talk to your brother," the general said to Flavus. "Convince him to surrender. Caesar will pardon him if he lays down his arms now."

Flavus dismounted, gave his horse to a trooper, stripped off his weapon belts, and removed his helmet, revealing a head of strikingly fair hair—his name means yellow. He then walked tensely to the river's edge with Ster-tinius as the archers withdrew. On the other side of the water, Flavus's brother sent his nervous bodyguards back to join the other leaders some distance away, then came to the river alone, equally unarmed. The broth-ers hadn't seen each other in ten years, not since Flavus left the Rhine with Tiberius to put down the Pannonian uprising in A.D. 6. Back then, Hermann was still a colonel of Cheruscan auxiliaries in the Roman army, and Flavus still had the use of two eyes.

"How did you lose your eye, brother?" Hermann began.

Flavus named the place and briefly described the battle.

Hermann nodded. "And what reward did you receive?"

Flavus replied that he'd been awarded a golden crown, a golden torque, and other decorations, and a salary increase.

"A crown, a neck chain, increased pay?" Hermann repeated. "The Romans buy their slaves cheaply these days."

"If that's all you had on your mind, we can end this now," Flavus snapped. "Nothing you can say can change the greatness of Rome, the limitless resources of Caesar, or the dreadful punishment that awaits those who oppose both and lose. As you are going to lose, brother. Believe me, if you fight Rome, you'll lose."

"Would you turn your back on your fatherland?" Hermann called. "On your gods, the gods who protect Germany's homes? On the freedom that's your ancestral right?"

"Save your breath," Flavus countered. "It's not too late for you to sur-render. I have influence with Caesar."

"And it's not too late for you to join me as ruler of your own people," said Hermann before lapsing into their native German language.

"Use the Roman tongue," Flavus said with a snarl, "or none at all."

Hermann reverted to Latin. "Our mother prays for you every day, as I do, that you'll cease to be a traitor. How does it feel to be the betrayer of your own people, brother? What mother deserves a traitor for a son? I ask you."

Flavus's eyes flashed. "Leave our mother out of this."

"She prays you'll see sense."

Flavus was becoming increasingly angry. "Surrender now. Caesar will forgive you. Caesar is merciful."

"Ha!" Hermann scornfully replied. "Pray that your mother is as forgiving."

"Germanicus Caesar didn't hesitate to show mercy to your wife and son," Flavus spat. He saw the look of surprise on Hermann's face and smiled. "You didn't know? Yes, little brother, you have a son. Born at

Ravenna. Born a Roman. A son you will never see if you die a deserter's death, with your severed head lying at your feet!"

Now Hermann's sore spot was exposed. "You pitiful specimen! You don't have the courage to stand up for your own people. Coward!"

"I'll show you who's a coward! Come over here and say that."

General Stertinius stepped up to Flavus and put a hand on his shoulder. "This is achieving nothing," he said. "Come away, Flavus."

Flavus angrily pushed the general's hand aside and turned to the cavalrymen standing a little way off. "Bring my horse! Bring my weapons!" he yelled.

Stertinius shook his head. "No! Enough." He guided the fuming Flavus back to their men. Behind them, Hermann remained at the water's edge, yelling insults after them and challenging his brother to fight. The general ordered Flavus to go, and detailed troopers to accompany him and make sure he didn't divert back to the river. Stertinius watched Flavus mount up and angrily ride away to the south, joining the waiting cavalry and archers, before he himself saddled up and followed with his escort.

As the Romans rode off, Stertinius would have cast a backward glance across the river. Hermann was still standing there, hands on his hips, glaring at them as they went.

After General Stertinius rejoined the main task force, Germanicus sent him with a large part of his cavalry to probe across the river and determine German dispositions. Stertinius split his mounted force into three groups commanded by himself; a first-rank centurion from the legions named Aemilius; and Chariovalda, king of the Batavians.

As King Chariovalda and his men penetrated deep into Germany, Cheruscans appeared at their front, then turned and fled. The king and his nobles eagerly gave chase, as if taking part in a wild boar hunt. Behind, the regular Batavian cavalry struggled to keep up and maintain formation. Suddenly Cheruscan warriors appeared from the trees to their rear and on either side of them. It was a trap. Now, too, the Germans the Batavians had been pursuing turned and charged. Chariovalda found himself fighting for his life.

Messengers from Chariovalda found Stertinius and Aemilius, and as they came to the rescue, the Cheruscans dispersed into the forest. But help arrived too late. Unhorsed, isolated from the regular cavalry, Chariovalda and the nobles with him had been filled with darts. In contrast, most of the Batavian troopers kept their discipline and their lives.

There would have been much celebration around German campfires that night. The Batavians had long been considered sellouts by other German tribes, and now their leaders had paid the price of collaboration. What was more, Germanicus Caesar had been stung. Many Germans took it as proof that he could be beaten.

As Germanicus advanced east with his main force and crossed the Weser, a German deserter came to him saying that Hermann was assembling an army farther to the south, in the Great Forest, a place sacred to Donar, the German Hercules. According to the deserter, Hermann was readying for a full-scale battle. Hermann, he said, had even chosen a battle site, beside the Weser. This information tallied with reports from Germanicus's scouts, who'd spotted campfires in the Great Forest and had heard the neighing of horses and the hum of thousands of voices on the chilly night air. Germanicus turned south, and set up camp several miles to the north of the Great Forest.

Germanicus himself was ready to take on Hermann, and his officers assured him the men were keen for battle. But he knew that tribunes and centurions tended to report what their commander wanted to hear. So that evening he pulled on a hooded camp follower's fur cloak that disguised his uniform and rank, and slipped out the back of his headquarters tent. Then, with just a lone, similarly disguised staff officer for company, he wandered around the streets of his huge camp at suppertime. Every now and then the general would pause at a row of tents and listen to the conversations around campfires. At every turn, he heard legionaries praise their general and express their determination to serve him well and repay the Germans for what they had done to Varus and his legions. Just as Germanicus was about to call it a night, he heard a voice calling from outside the camp walls. The general and his companion joined men who hurried to the ramparts, to see a bold German sitting astride a horse the other side of the entrenchments.

"In the name of Arminius, I promise rewards for all who come over to the German side," Tacitus says the horseman called in Latin. "To every man who changes sides, a German wife, a plot of land, and 100 sesterces a day for as long as this war lasts, if you give Arminius your loyalty."

"Don't insult our intelligence," came the voice of a legionary, perhaps a soldier of the 14th G.M.V. "Let daylight come, let battle be given! Then we'll *take* your land and *carry off* your wives!"

The men on the ramparts roared with laughter and chorused their agreement.

"This is a good omen, comrades," a legionary near the general declared. "The women and the lands of Germany are ours for the taking."

The horseman rode back into the night, followed by the jeers of the legionaries, his mission an abject failure. And Germanicus went to his bed secure in the knowledge that his troops were in the right frame of mind for what lay ahead.

According to Tacitus, that night Germanicus dreamed he was sacrificing a goat—Roman commanding generals customarily sacrificed to Mars prior to battle to ensure good omens. In the dream, blood sprinkled on his robe. Turning, he saw his grandmother Julia Augusta, who handed him a more splendid robe. He awoke convinced this was an omen of victory, that this was the day for battle. He would have shared both dream and conviction with his army at assembly that morning. Even as his troops received their orders, cavalry scouts were out, watching the German forces camped in the forest.

The place chosen by Hermann for the contest was just east of the Weser River on a plain named Idistaviso. The plain lay between ranges of low hills, with the Weser winding across it. The Great Forest ran along the eastern fringe of the plain, its trees so tall that their branches began way above head height. Grassland extended from the trees two miles to the Weser, rising up in the middle to gentle hills. On this summer morning, a breeze washed gently across the grass. All was peace and serenity. But then there was a sudden scattering of birds in the trees. Fifty thousand German tribesmen spilled from the forest and spread like locusts across the plain from the trees to the river.

Most German warriors wore neither armor nor helmet. They carried flat shields made of layers of thin boards painted with tribal motifs or of woven willow. Their twelve-foot spears quivered as the warriors ran excitedly to take up the positions their leaders had agreed on. The Germans had no unit organization like the armies of Rome. Each tribe had its clans, and each man formed up with his clan in his tribal group. As usual, the tallest men filled the front line—men of massive stature, according to Tacitus. Hermann and his Cheruscans occupied the high ground in the center of the plain. With Hermann, mounted, like his nephew, was Inguiomerus, who'd recovered sufficiently from the wounds he'd received at Long Bridges to join the fight.

Other tribes occupied the flanks, with some warriors lurking in the trees at the forest's edge. Most of the other tribes are unidentified, but after the encounters of the past two years they would have included Arpus and his Chatti, Mallovendus and the remnants of the Marsi, as well as the

Fosi, Usipetes, Tubantes, and Bructeri. The Cauchi from the south, who'd taken one of the eagles captured in the Teutoburg, were probably here. And young Angrivars, in defiance of their tribe's leaders and the latest treaty with Rome. Probably, Tenctheri and Mattiaci from the Rhinelands opposite Cologne were here, and Langobardi and Ampsivarii from just to the north, along the Weser and Hunte Rivers.

This was the largest concentration of German warriors since the famous victory over Varus and his legions. Hermann's army was more than double the size of the force that had defeated Varus. The Germans' spies had told them that Germanicus had fewer than thirty thousand legionaries with him. Discounting the auxiliaries as inferior and liable to run, and hoping Germans in the Roman lines would desert rather than fight their own countrymen, the German leaders were expecting to repeat the outcome of the Teutoburg Forest.

Now, mounted German scouts warned that the Roman army was approaching.

The legionaries of the 14th Gemina Martia Victrix Legion marched in perfect unison at the middle of the long Roman column. Apart from the sound of tramping feet, the rattle of equipment, and the occasional neighing of horses, there wasn't a sound from the Roman army as it came down the river ten men abreast. They'd been on the move for close to two and one-half hours, following the Weser from their overnight camp to the planned battle site.

The column was led by German and Gallic auxiliaries and foot archers. The four legions of the Army of the Lower Rhine came next. Behind them came Germanicus himself, with his staff, all on horseback. He was wearing his best helmet and armored cuirass, gold-plated and glimmering in the morning sun. A narrow red sash ran around his torso, just below his chest. Tied in an ornamental bow in the middle, it was the ensign of a Roman general. The rich purple cloak of a commander in chief trailed from his shoulders, flowing onto the back of his horse. His personal standard-bearer came close behind, holding high his square standard of purple cloth decorated with twelve golden fasces. Behind him rode Germanicus's personal trumpeter and the picked cavalry of the field marshal's bodyguard. The two cohorts of the Praetorian Guard assigned to him marched immediately behind.

Then came the 14th G.M.V. and the other three legions of the Army of the Upper Rhine, followed by the mounted archers, with the last of the auxiliaries and German allies forming the rear guard. The massed cavalry rode along the left flank of the column, to protect the infantry against attack from the trees. Baggage train and backpacks had been left at the camp with a guard of auxiliaries.

Fourteenth Legion men heard the Germans before they saw them—a hubbub of fifty thousand expectant voices, like a football crowd just before the kickoff. As they rounded a bend in the river, in step and in battle order, the 14th Legion caught sight of the Cheruscans milling all over the low grassy hills ahead, then saw the rest of the German warriors spread from one side of the river plain to the other in their path. Now, like an ancient precursor of the Mexican wave, twelve-foot spears that had till then been pointing skyward came down to the horizontal in sequence. The spears of rank after rank protruded over shoulders and out into the open in front of the German army like porcupine quills.

"Signal 'Extend,'" Germanicus ordered. His personal trumpeter sounded a trumpet call. His standard gave the same signal, perhaps rising and falling.

In concert with those of the other legions, the trumpets of the 14th Legion's eight cohorts sounded "Extend into Battle Lines." The legion's eagle, proudly sported by the 3rd Cohort since the 1st had been allowed to retire, and the standards of cohorts and maniples all inclined to one side. Without breaking step, the ranks of the 14th peeled away and formed up in deep formation in the army's third line. They had been assigned their battle positions back in camp at dawn, when Daily Orders had been announced. The men of the 14th and those of the legions ahead of and around them knew exactly where to go and what to do as they spread into three battle lines.

The legionaries could see, ahead, up on the hill, Cheruscans turning to their commander, calling urgently to him and waving their weapons around. The Roman troops had no idea what the Germans were saying, but even as they were dressing their ranks they could see great agitation up there on the hill.

Hermann had in fact instructed his Cheruscans to wait until he gave the word for them to attack, planning to hold his people back while the other tribes engaged the Romans before sweeping down off the hill to carry the battle by overrunning the embattled legions. That plan was about to go to Hades in a handbasket—Hermann's keyed-up tribesmen were chafing at being held back, were yelling to their leader that they should attack now, before the Romans had completed their battle formations. Some older Germans in the ranks who had participated in the defeat of

Varus seven years earlier would now have reflected that this disciplined, well-led Roman army bore no resemblance to the comparative rabble that had fallen to them in the Teutoburg Forest. But the youngsters, the firebrands, only saw Roman invaders and booty. And they jumped the gun. Against orders, first in their tens, then in their hundreds, then in their thousands, young Cheruscans lost patience and streamed down the slope toward the Romans with quivering spears at the ready, yelling at the top of their lungs. Hermann and his subchiefs tried to call them back, but it was too late. The rest of the tribesmen on the plain joined in. A wall of German warriors surged over the grass like the waters of a dam that had broken. A great deal now took place in seconds and minutes. From their position in the third line, the men of the 14th G.M.V. were able to see it all unfold.

General Stertinius had joined Germanicus, who, unfazed by the sight or the roar of the approaching horde, calmly turned to his cavalry commander. There was no need for detailed instructions; they had previously agreed on a tactical maneuver for this moment. Elite mounted units had already been separated from the rest of the cavalry, and every trooper had been given his instructions for the day.

"Go now, Stertinius!" Germanicus ordered. "I'll come up with the infantry in good time to support you."

General Stertinius nodded. He spurred his horse forward. Followed by his escort and trumpeter, and with his scarlet general's cloak flowing behind him, the cavalry commander galloped along his ranks of troopers, heading for the front and the Germans. It was nine o'clock in the morning, and the Battle of Idistaviso had begun. Now, 124,000 men would try to kill each other.

The Roman front line was composed of the leading auxiliaries. After a gap came the second line, made up of the four A.L.R. legions, with Germanicus and the two Praetorian cohorts in the middle. Behind this stood the third line, with the 14th G.M.V. and its brother legions of the A.U.R. in the middle and auxiliaries on the wings. Three battle lines, eight legions—the 1st, the 5th Alaudae, the 20th Valeria Victrix, the 21st Rapax, the 14th Gemina Martia Victrix, the 2nd Augusta, the 13th Gemina, the 16th Gallica. Now they waited for the onrushing Germans. Stock still, like statues, the sun glinting on their standards and the military decorations they had put on before they left camp. The yellow horsehair plumes on their helmets wafted in the breeze. This would be one of the last times that Roman legionaries wore plumes in battle; before long, plumes would be relegated to parade use only. The legionaries looked identical, their faces masked by their helmets and cheek guards. Same uniforms, same equipment. Only the motifs on shields varied from one formation to another: the legion emblems of Pegasus the flying horse of the 2nd Augusta; the eagle, boar, bull, and ram of other units; and the lightning bolts of the 14th G.M.V.

As General Stertinius reached the front of the cavalry column he nodded to his trumpeter, who sounded the "Charge." The signal was taken up by the trumpeters of individual wings. Letting out an exultant cry, upward of six thousand cavalrymen spurred their mounts forward to follow their commander. With a deafening pounding of hooves, the Roman cavalry formations swept along the tree line.

At this moment, one of the Germanicus's aides pointed to the sky. "Look, Caesar!" he called.

Germanicus looked up, as did everyone around him. Eight large birds were just then flying overhead. They were eagles. One for each of Germanicus's legions. As the Romans watched, the birds dipped toward the forest. It was an omen too good to ignore. Germanicus smiled. "Go!" he called to his troops. "Follow the Roman birds, the true deities of our legions." He ordered his trumpeter to signal the front line to charge.

As Germanicus's purple standard inclined forward in a slow arc to the near horizontal, the general's trumpeter blew the "Charge." The call was taken up and repeated by the trumpets of the front-line auxiliary cohorts. The air filled with the metallic notes. And with a throaty, determined roar, the Roman frontline light infantry surged forward.

Up on the hill, surrounded by mounted bodyguards and Cheruscan subchiefs, a furious Hermann cursed as his men ran to the attack. Knowing he had no alternative but to try to carry the day, despite the fact that his initial strategy had fallen in a heap, he urged his horse forward. With long hair flying, he galloped down the slope, heading toward the right wing, by the trees, the business wing of any battle, overtaking his running warriors. To his rear, his startled uncle and other companions galloped after him.

Immediately behind the charging Roman front line stood archers—Syrians, most likely, with pointy-topped helmets and fish-scale armor. On the order "Loose!" they let fly. The sky darkened over the mass of running Germans, and then hundreds of arrows fell among them. Germans tried to fend off the missiles with shields, but here and there screaming men fell with arrows embedded in eyes, cheeks, and throats, to be trampled by those behind them. Again the archers fired, and again. The Germans kept coming, and with a roar drove into the charging Roman auxiliary light infantry, many of them pushing through to the hapless archers, who had to discard bows and reach for swords.

In the midst of the fighting on the German right, Hermann felt searing pain. A lead pellet from a Spanish slinger had glanced off his skull. Blood ran down his face. Ignoring the wound, he rode into the nearest archers and began slicing them to pieces with his spatha, a cavalry broadsword. The bareheaded, bloodied, thirtyish rider in expensive Roman armor yelled instructions and encouragement to his countrymen as he drove through the archers. He came on to a solid wall of oval shields of auxiliary light infantry directly behind the archers.

Hermann had spent enough time in the Roman army to recognize the shield motifs of the auxiliaries opposing him: Gauls; Vendelici; Rhaeti from Switzerland; and Ampsivarii Germans led by Boiocalus, his former captive and since the Varus disaster a loyal subordinate of Tiberius and Germanicus. And, to his dismay, Chauci Germans from the North Sea coast, tribesmen who had fought alongside him at the Teutoburg Forest, but who had now allied themselves with Germanicus. With a sinking heart he swung his sword at heads and shields and arms, urging his men all around him to superhuman efforts.

As Hermann was engaged at the front line, the Roman cavalry pounding along the eastern flank of the battlefield had driven Germans at the edge of the forest out into the open to escape their drive. Now, as he galloped along beside the trees, General Stertinius put his right arm out horizontally, pointing to the massed ranks of the Germans on the plain. Behind him, preselected cavalry units, probably led by Colonel Pedo, wheeled away from the main formation, turning sharply to their right, and charged into the flank of the German army.

Stertinius continued on with the remainder of the cavalry. Once he'd passed the last ranks of the German concentration he, too, turned right. His force followed suit, curving around, into the German rear. As this occurred, legion trumpets sang another signal. Germanicus was moving forward with his second line, the initial legion line. So far, the Germans had only managed to come to grips with light infantry, archers, and slingers ahead of the legion lines. With Germanicus's frontline auxiliaries holding, just, his legions were moving up in support. The 14th G.M.V. and the other legions of the third line had yet to be engaged. As the men of the 14th stood waiting for their call to action, they saw a cloud of dust rise up behind the Germans—a sure sign that General Stertinius and his cavalry were plowing into the enemy rear.

At this point the German attack began to falter. Those tribesmen who had been at the timberline and who had run into the plain to escape the flanking maneuver of the cavalry had crushed in on their own people. The Germans in the plain, seeing the main cavalry force in their rear, tried to run to the trees to escape. Everywhere, Germans ran into each other or into Roman cavalry. There was no coordination, no direction, no plan. Panic set in. Self-preservation became the order of the day.

Hermann looked around and saw, shortly after its commencement, that the battle was already lost. Behind the frontline fighting, Germans were running blindly all over the battlefield with looks of terror in their eyes, throwing away their cumbersome weapons. Some, repulsed by the Roman cavalry as they tried to reach the trees, turned and fled to the Weser, flinging themselves into the river as troopers galloped after them. Reinforced by four legions, the Roman front line bulldozed forward. Pushing aside the huge German spears, legionaries forged in for close combat. The German line gave way.

Hermann knew that if he was going to save himself, now was the time. Using the blood running from his scalp wound, he smeared his face to disguise himself. To his right he saw the shields of the advancing Chauci German auxiliaries, saw that Germanicus's legionaries had yet to link up with them, and he had a desperate idea. He looked around, and saw Inguiomerus close by. "This way, Uncle!" Hermann called, riding toward the Chauci shields, and Inguiomerus urged his horse to follow. "In the name of our German gods and our German fatherland," Hermann yelled, "make way for the chief of the Cherusci, brothers."

A gap opened up in the Chauci line, and Hermann slipped his horse through it, then swung toward the trees. Inguiomerus and other chieftains quickly followed. The gap closed, the Chauci auxiliaries continued their advance. As Roman javelins began to fly in their direction, the German chiefs hugged the necks of their steeds and escaped into the trees. Behind them, their men, trapped between river, rampaging cavalry, and advancing infantry, were being mowed down like long grass. As any semblance of organized German resistance dissolved, the third-line legions were called up by Germanicus. Trumpets sang, and in step the 14th G.M.V. and its three fellow A.U.R. legions moved in for the kill.

Estimates of how many Germans died at the Battle of Idistaviso range between ten thousand and forty thousand. Tacitus says that Germanicus's army was still killing Germans by the time the sun went down. The men of the 14th and the other legions were given permission to pursue the enemy as far as it took to eliminate them.

Bodies covered the countryside for ten miles around the battlefield. Corpses floated downriver like logjams—Germans who jumped into the

Weser to escape were impaled with javelins or arrows from the shore or dragged under by the strong current. At one point, hundreds of tribesmen who crowded beside the Weser and tried to make a stand drowned when the riverbank gave way under them.

Other Germans climbed trees in the Great Forest, hoping to come down after dark and slip away. When these fugitives were spotted, Roman archers were brought up. The demise of the tree-climbers became a sport. Laughter echoed through the forest as bets were laid on each shot by bowmen looking for revenge for the loss of friends in the battle—Germanicus's few fatalities had mostly been among his frontline archers. Other tree-climbers too high or too well screened to be brought down by missiles were eliminated by chopping down their trees. Even if they were to survive a fall from one hundred feet or so there were plenty of Roman troops waiting on the ground to cut their throats for them.

In the Great Forest, too, Germanicus's troops found piles of handcuffs and leg irons left by the Germans. Prisoners told them these had been intended for use on the Romans when they surrendered after the defeat of Germanicus, in the same way that Varus's few surviving rank and file had been chained up and led away to slavery.

While Roman troops were piling up captured German weapons to form a giant trophy, Mallovendus, king of the Marsi, came humbly to Germanicus and surrendered. He was a broken man after the reverses suffered by his tribe over the past two years. Germanicus granted him his life but kept him handy. He had a hunch the king might prove useful in the near future, for, to Germanicus's frustration, Hermann had evaded capture. And Germanicus was determined to hunt him down.

XVIII

WRECKED

Years before, when the Angrivarii were at war with the Cherusci, the Angrivarii had built a massive earth barrier to separate the two tribes. To reach the barrier, it was necessary to pass through a forest between narrow hills. A small plain extended from the forest to the barrier, marshland spread directly behind it, and the Weser River was to one side. At the Angrivar Barrier, Hermann declared, he would have his revenge on the Romans.

In the days since the disaster at the hands of Germanicus at Idistaviso, the Angrivars had welcomed fugitives from the battle, again disregarding their treaty with Rome. And as Germanicus Caesar's Roman army advanced along the Weser, thousands of Germans flocked to the barrier— the Angrivars, as well as survivors who had fled from Idistaviso, and other tribesmen who had arrived to join the resistance since.

Since Idistaviso, another deserter had come to Germanicus with information. He told the Roman commander that Hermann was hiding out at the Angrivar Barrier, and offered to lead him there. Again Germanicus opted to go with a defector's story. He had good reason to—the informant soon confessed that he'd been sent by Hermann to lure the Romans to the Angrivar Barrier. And he told Germanicus of Hermann's plan for a trap not unlike the ambush in the Teutoburg seven years before. The value of good intelligence can never be overstated. As Germanicus's legions came up the Weser, their commanders knew precisely what Hermann had in mind.

Hermann had assembled several thousand mounted warriors—numbers of his horsemen at Idistaviso had managed to escape, and tribes to the north had provided more. As Germanicus approached the Angrivar Barrier with his eight legions, Hermann hid his cavalry in the woods some distance away. He planned to allow the Roman army to march into the forest and approach the barrier, then close the door on it by bringing his cavalry up from behind. Infantry would then attack from the barrier. Sandwiched between the two German forces, the Roman army would be trapped in the forest, just as Varus had been, and the Germans would wipe them out in the same way. It was a good plan, far superior to the loose and overconfident battle strategy devised for Idistaviso. And had it not been for the double agent, it may have worked.

Roman cavalry rode away from Germanicus's column as it approached the barrier. But this time, General Stertinius wasn't in command. It seems that General Seius Tubero, Germanicus's chief of staff, complained that he hadn't been given a chance for glory, that he was being kept out of the action. Germanicus knew how friendly Tubero was with the emperor and decided it would be politic to give Tubero a command for this operation. General Tubero led the cavalry off with orders to skirt around the concealed German horsemen and surprise them in their forest hiding place with an attack from their rear.

Meanwhile, Germanicus divided his infantry. One force, probably of four legions, including the 14th G.M.V. and the other A.U.R. units under General Silius, was to advance on the barrier through the forest, as if marching into the trap. Germanicus would personally lead the second division, of four legions plus the two Praetorian Guard cohorts, through the hills to the barrier. The force assigned to the forest met light resistance in the trees, and pushed through to the plain beyond, forming up and preparing to make a frontal attack on the barrier in full view of the thousands of German defenders manning it. Meanwhile, Germanicus and the second division made their way unnoticed along the hillsides, before launching a flanking attack against the surprised Germans on the barrier. Overcoming their shock, the Germans put up a hot defense, raining rocks and other missiles down on the legionaries. Devoid of scaling ladders or sophisticated siege equipment, Germanicus pulled back Then, while his slingers kept the Germans' heads down, he had his light artillery brought up—as many as four hundred scorpions. General Anteius's quick-firing catapults dropped any German who dared show his face above the rampart, and defenders were soon hunkering down below the horrendous barrage of flying bolts.

Germanicus announced that he would personally lead a renewed assault involving all eight legions. But before he gave the signal for the assault to begin, he handed his helmet to an aide. He would go into action bareheaded, so his troops would recognize him. He wanted his men to know he didn't expect them to go anywhere he wasn't prepared to go himself. He also wanted to be sure that in the heat of battle no Praetorian Guardsman put a sword in him with the excuse of mistaken identity, for he was going in at the head of the Praetorians, putting their vaunted reputation and arrogant self-confidence as Rome's highest-paid, most elite troops to the test.

With the last artillery volley slicing through the air on the command of "Shoot!" Germanicus, accompanied by the two thousand Praetorians, charged the barrier and started climbing. The men of the 14th G.M.V. and the other legions were close behind.

As the Romans reached the top of the bank they found the Germans lined up on the far side, waiting to repulse the attack. With their usual bloodcurdling war cries, the tribesmen surged onto Germanicus and his men. The fighting was intense. Hand-to-hand combat went on for hours. Germanicus recognized Inguiomerus flying from one part of the battle to another during the afternoon, striving to direct the German defense. But Germanicus never caught sight of the Cheruscan's nephew, leading him to assume that Hermann was heading the German cavalry force lurking in the distant forest.

In the end, weight of numbers told. Outnumbering their opponents, Roman troops eventually drove the Germans back from the barrier as more and more legionaries scaled the bank and joined their general. Pushed into woods, the Germans were trapped with their backs to the marsh. The men of the 14th and the other legions formed tight formations in the confined space, and with their shields pressed against their chests they struck overarm at the Germans' faces, as if their swords were huge daggers. As the Germans stood their ground, the legionaries stuck to their task for hours in the grueling, bloody contest.

"No prisoners!" Tacitus says Germanicus yelled. "Take no prisoners!"

The 14th G.M.V.'s centurions repeated the order. "No prisoners, boys!"

Late in the day, Germanicus ordered one legion to withdraw to the plain and entrench a night camp for the entire army. At nightfall, the killing stopped. The Germans had been dislodged from the barrier and slaughtered in their thousands in the woods. Under the welcome veil of darkness, surviving tribesmen fled for their lives. Their leader, Inguiomerus, also escaped. But the Battle of the Angrivar Barrier was his last hurrah—Inguiomerus wanted no more of fighting Romans, and went into hiding.

Germanicus withdrew his army to its camp. There, that night, he was joined by General Tubero and the Roman cavalry. Germanicus expected to hear that the cavalry had been as successful as his legions, and that Hermann was either dead or a prisoner. But he was disappointed. General Tubero had botched the cavalry operation.

All had begun well enough; Tubero had located the German cavalry just where the double agent had indicated. The Germans could have been led by Hermann himself; we don't know. Certainly, Tubero prevented the Germans from attacking Germanicus in the rear. But after some indecisive skirmishing he'd allowed the opposition cavalry to escape virtually un-scathed. Had Tubero deliberately fouled up? Did he set out to ensure that Germanicus didn't have the glory of taking or killing Hermann, which would have enhanced his already superstar image with the Roman public? Or was he simply inept?

Unimpressed by Tubero's performance, Germanicus promptly gave com-mand of the cavalry back to General Stertinius. Then, after forming a giant mound of German shields, swords, and spears, dedicating it to Mars, Jupiter, and Augustus, he sent Stertinius and the cavalry against the towns and villages of the flip-flopping Angrivars. The Angrivars soon threw down their weapons, surrendering unconditionally, and were grateful when Ger-manicus agreed to readmit them to the Roman fold as allies.

It now being the height of summer, Germanicus reluctantly conceded he wasn't going to lay his hands on Hermann. Not this year, anyway. He ordered a withdrawal back to base. Conscious of the storms that hit the North Sea coast of Germany and Holland at this time of year, Germani-cus detached two legions and sent them back to the Rhine via the over-land route. As it turned out, they were the lucky ones.

Green from seasickness, vomiting over themselves and each other, drenched from waves crashing over their ships, anxious legionaries of the 14th Gemina Martia Victrix tried to help steersmen and oarsmen maintain way in the monstrous seas, but their inexperience as seamen only meant that they got in the way.

The sky had turned black once the fleet reached the open sea; then a stinging hailstorm hit. The wind howled, the sea boiled, visibility was zero. Ships had difficulty staying together. For a time the wind shifted to the south, driving the fleet back the way it had come. Then the wind swung about and bore down from the northeast. As cold as ice and too strong to resist, it pushed part of the fleet toward rocky Frisian Islands shorelines. Other ships, including those carrying the 14th G.M.V., were driven way out to sea.

The legionaries of the 14th were bailing feverishly. All their transports were taking water. Spectacular engineers on land they may be, but the Romans built ships that leaked like sieves and had to be constantly caulked.

Now, apart from the normal leaks their crews had to live with, the ships returning from Germany were being filled by the waves crashing over them. Even with all hands bailing there was no guarantee that a ship was going to stay afloat. On every vessel, anything that wasn't essential was jettisoned—wagons, artillery, personal belongings, baggage mules, cavalry horses. If it wasn't battened down or couldn't say "Hail, Caesar!" it went over the side.

Even so, some ships went under. Others were wrecked along the German coast and on the Frisians. Several 14th Legion transports were blown all the way to Britain. Coming ashore there ready to fight for their lives, legionaries were taken in by British tribesmen and given food and shelter. Most of the legion's vessels were driven back up the German coast, some as far as Jutland. Their commander in chief was traveling in a big cruiser of the trireme class (with three banks of oars); Germanicus's flagship managed to find shelter in a cove on the Chauci coast between the Weser and the Ems.

The storm passed. Blue sky appeared. At Germanicus's anchorage, there wasn't another vessel in sight. Going ashore in a ship's boat, Germanicus stood for days on a promontory looking anxiously out to sea, blaming himself for this disaster, praying that he would soon see survivors. Eventually, ships began to appear—a few at first, then more with each passing hour, until the cove was crowded with craft riding at anchor or drawn up on the shore. Most ships had lost oars, some had lost crewmen overboard. Many craft had repaired ripped sails with the clothing of soldiers and crew. Some had to be towed in by others. As his grateful soldiers came ashore and camped on dry land, Germanicus had ships repaired, made up full crews from survivors, and sent them around the islands looking for shipwrecked soldiers and sailors. Large numbers were subsequently brought to safety.

Germanicus sailed back to the Rhine with the reduced fleet, his battered, leaky ships overloaded with men now, to find that the rumor had spread throughout Germany and Gaul, and inevitably to Rome, that the entire fleet had been lost. Ships of the scattered convoy continued to limp into Utrecht for weeks. To their credit, the Angrivars showed their renewed loyalty by ransoming shipwrecked Romans from German tribes farther up the coast and returning them to Germanicus.

The men of the 14th who'd been washed up on England's shores were shipped back across the North Sea by British chiefs friendly to Rome—in remembrance, they said, of treaties their ancestors had signed with Julius Caesar seventy years before. As the legionaries of the 14th G.M.V. came back from Britain, gossip would have begun to spread around other units.

The 14th's old reputation would have been resurrected by superstitious old hands with other legions—the unlucky 14th Legion; the bad-luck 14th. After all, the 14th had been just one of two legions caught up in the flood on the North Sea coast with General Vitellius; then it was swept all the way to Britain. Maybe the 14th was still a pariah legion, said the men of other legions. Angry legionaries of the G.M.V. countered with eye-popping stories of how in Britain they'd encountered and overcome sea monsters and mermaids, weird birds and creatures that were half man, half beast. The stories, in the telling and the retelling, became more and more fantastic. They seemed to effectively dampen the stories of the legion's unfortunate past. Before long, the men of the 14th would have begun to believe the tales themselves.

As the soggy legions marched back to their winter bases the length of the Rhine, and as Germanicus was reunited with his relieved wife, Agrippina, at Utrecht, word reached him that some German tribes were talking about launching attacks across the Rhine now that Germanicus and his army were sleeping with the fishes. He would show them who was sleeping with the fishes! The men of the 14th had hardly reached their base at Mainz when orders arrived for another operation in Germany.

Leading thirty thousand legionaries and auxiliaries and three thousand cavalry from the Army of the Upper Rhine, including the men of the 14th G.M.V., Lieutenant General Silius crossed the Rhine from Mainz for a raid against the Chatti. Simultaneously, Germanicus used the usual crossing point at Xanten, taking an army at least forty thousand strong from the Army of the Lower Rhine and spearing into Marsi territory. Germanicus took along surrendered Marsi king Mallovendus as his guide, and as they marched into his home territory the king pointed out a wood in which, he said, one of the lost eagles of Varus's legions was buried, guarded by only a small band of warriors. Germanicus sent one force to attack the Marsi guards from the front, and another to slip around to the rear to dig up the eagle. The eagle was recovered, although to which legion it belonged we aren't told. A monument was built at Rome later in the year to celebrate and commemorate Germanicus's recovery of two of Varus's lost eagles. The last of Varus's three eagles would be recovered from the Cauchi Germans twenty-five years later, in an A.D. 41 punitive expedition by the Army of the Upper Rhine led by Lieutenant General Publius Gabinius, who would be granted the title Cauchius by a grateful emperor for retrieving the lost eagle from the Cauchi.

As Germanicus drove east in the late summer of A.D. 16, German prisoners taken over these days told him that their countrymen were now in awe of him and his legions, having believed they'd all been lost at sea. The Romans, they were now convinced, were supermen. After several days, Germanicus, General Silius, and their supermen withdrew. This, at last, was the end to the A.D. 16 campaigning season.

When the weary legionaries of the 14th Gemina Martia Victrix sagged into their beds back at their winter quarters at Mainz, their centurions informed them that Germanicus Caesar would again make up for all equipment and personal belongings they had lost, again from his own purse. What was more, Germanicus had instructed the centurions not to bother checking the claims—he would trust his men to be honest with him. As the legionaries cheerfully began compiling their claim lists, the barracks talk would have been of one final campaign in Germany the next year. This time, said the men of the 14th, they would do Germanicus proud and bring Hermann back in chains!

XIX

❦

CLAUDIUS'S INVADERS

Twenty-seven years had passed since the 14th Gemina Martia Victrix Legion returned triumphantly from its A.D. 16 German operations. The legion hadn't been given a chance to invade Germany again. In the winter of A.D. 16, Tiberius recalled Germanicus to Rome, to put the glory of Hermann's final defeat out of his reach. He gave him a consulship, then sent him to Syria as commander in chief of the Roman East. There, in A.D. 19, Germanicus was assassinated—poisoned—dying in Agrippina's arms. A murder trial in the Senate ended when the accused, Gnaeus Piso, Governor of Syria, committed suicide. But like the historian Tacitus and most Romans, the men of the 14th G.M.V. would have gone to their graves convinced that Tiberius had ordered Germanicus's death.

Hermann died that same year, A.D. 19, also murdered by his own people. After Germanicus left the Rhine, on Tiberius's orders no more Roman armies marched into Germany. Hermann never again fought Rome. Instead he fought a Roman ally, defeating fellow Germans, King Maroboduus and his Marcomanni, to whom his uncle Inguiomerus had defected. For being overly ambitious, Hermann was soon assassinated by the Cherusci.

Tiberius Caesar died in A.D. 37, reputedly smothered by Praetorian Prefect Naevius Macro. Living out his last years a bitter, twisted recluse on the Isle of Capri, Tiberius had taken a liking to Germanicus's son Caligula, keeping the youth on Capri with him. On Tiberius's death, twenty-four-year-old Gaius "Caligula" Caesar succeeded him. Suetonius says Caligula's ascension to the throne was a dream come true for the Roman people, who held such fond memories of his father, Germanicus, and his late mother. Agrippina had died in A.D. 33 while being held by Tiberius on the Italian prison island of Pandateria. For the first seven months of his reign a reforming Caligula rode a wave of popular support before falling dangerously ill. When he recovered he was a different man—irrational, irrespon-

174

sible, jealous, paranoid, cruel, vindictive, murderous. Execution without trial became the norm during his reign. No one was safe.

Although, contrary to popular myth, Caligula didn't make his horse a senator, much of what he did was bizarre. The legions weren't immune from his craziness. In A.D. 40 he proceeded to France, summoning elements of the 14th G.M.V. and the seven other Rhine legions to the Channel coast. He was going to invade Britain, he said, and ordered the legions, their auxiliary units, and his Praetorian Guard and German Guard escort to line up on a Pas de Calais beach in battle formation, facing the water. Though Dio says as many as 250,000 men stood on the sands, the number would have been closer to 100,000. Caligula then had their trumpeters sound "Charge." As the mystified troops wondered what to do, their emperor issued a new order: the men were to collect seashells in the laps of their tunics, as spoils of Caligula's victory.

On January 24, A.D. 41, the last day of the Ludi Palatini Festival, Colonel Cassius Chaerea, the tribune commanding the Praetorian Guard cohort on duty at the theater at Caligula's Palatium that day—a career soldier who'd been a junior tribune on the Rhine under Caligula's father, Germanicus—and Colonel Cornelius Sabinus, Prefect of the German Guard, put Caligula and Rome out of their misery. The colonels cornered the twenty-eight-year-old emperor in a narrow passageway as he left a theatrical performance and was walking to the palace of his late father to meet Greek boys who were to sing a hymn in his honor at the festival. The officers' swords swiftly terminated the imperial malignancy.

Through the influence of the Praetorian Guard and the German Guard, Caligula's uncle, Germanicus's brother, the forty-nine-year-old cripple Claudius Caesar, was proclaimed emperor the following day. Unlike previous emperors, Claudius hadn't served in the army; he'd been a scholar. Within a year, the Governor of Dalmatia, Lieutenant General Furius Camillus Scribonianus, an old warhorse, felt that Claudius was so unsuited to the job he initiated a rebellion against him. Scribonianus's own 7th and 11th Legions soon turned against their governor and terminated the rebellion and Scribonianus. But the brief revolt had been a wake-up call for Claudius. He knew he would have to keep the army happy to keep his throne. One way to do that was by pulling off a bold military campaign, a conquest unlike anything any emperor since Augustus had achieved. And as he looked around for a suitable campaign, a British prince gave him an idea.

In A.D. 39 one of the sons of King Cunobelinus, Shakespeare's Cymbeline, had fled from Britain to France, banished by his dying father or on the run after fighting with his four brothers over control of their father's kingdom. Dio says his name was Bericus. Suetonius calls him Adminius, the Roman name given him once he settled in Italy and became of assistance to the Palatium. Caligula had formally received the surrender of Bericus, as if he'd captured him in battle—the "battle" that had resulted in the men of the 14th G.M.V. gathering seashells on the seashore. According to Dio, it was Bericus who inspired Claudius's British operation. He no doubt painted the new emperor a picture of minimal resistance and substantial profit should Rome send an army to his island. No doubt, too, Bericus had visions of being installed as Rome's regent in a conquered Britain. So it was that Claudius set in motion the invasion of Britain that Tiberius had once contemplated and Caligula had recently toyed with. Orders went out from the Palatium for the creation of a Britannic Fleet and for four legions and numerous auxiliary units to march to an embarkation point in France.

The 14th Gemina Martia Victrix was one of those four legions. And that was why, in the spring of A.D. 43, the legionaries of the latest enlistment of the 14th marched out of Mainz for the last time and headed for the French coast.

From the hill at Boulogne, gazing out over the embarkation camp on the French coast in the summer of A.D. 43, Major General Flavius Sabinus would have been both a happy man and an unhappy man. Son of a moneylender, grandson of a centurion in Pompey the Great's army at the Battles of Dyrrhachium and Pharsalus, but no relation to the Colonel Sabinus who'd murdered Caligula, he was about thirty-nine years of age.

Sabinus had good reason to be happy. He was to lead the 14th Gemina Martia Victrix Legion in the coming operation, and also had been appointed deputy commander of the task force, under Lieutenant General Aulus Plautius. And his younger brother, thirty-three-year-old Major General Titus Vespasianus—or Vespasian, as history knows him—was leading the 2nd Augusta Legion in the task force: he'd taken charge of the 2nd Augusta on the Rhine a year or two previously. Sabinus's unhappiness had two causes. First, the entire operation was on hold, delayed by a near mutiny of the troops. But worse, men from his own 14th G.M.V. were among the ringleaders of that dissension.

Forty thousand Roman legionaries and auxiliaries were in camp at Boulogne, a port the Romans originally called Gesoriacum, and later, Bononia. Just as General Sabinus's own command, the 14th G.M.V., had marched to Boulogne from the Rhine, the 2nd Augusta Legion, the 14th's old campaigning partner, had been detached from the Army of the Upper Rhine, coming down from Strasbourg. The 20th Valeria Victrix had come from its A.L.R. base at Neuss, while the 9th Hispana had marched up from its home at Sisak in Pannonia, escorting the invasion task force's commander, Lieutenant General Plautius, who, until that time, had been Governor of Pannonia.

Boulogne has a long history as an assembly point for invasions, in operations that suffered setbacks, delays, and sometimes premature termination. Julius Caesar used this site for the embarkation of two legions in his 55 B.C. British campaign. In 1066, William the Conqueror's invasion fleet would sail from Saint-Valéry-sur-Somme, just down the coast from Boulogne, after a false start from farther south. In the 1800s, Napoleon Bonaparte would assemble an army at Boulogne for an aborted British invasion. Then in 1940–1941, German landing barges filled Channel ports for Operation Sea Lion, an invasion of England that failed to proceed, while the German navy used Boulogne as a U-boat base.

The men of the junior cohorts of the 14th who came to Boulogne in A.D. 43 had joined their legion at its A.D. 31 discharge and reenlistment, when the 14th was brought back to ten full-strength imperial-era cohorts of 5,253 officers and men, including a general, 6 tribunes, a camp prefect, 60 centurions, and a cavalry squadron of 120 men and 4 decurions. Veterans of the A.D. 11 enlistment who'd fought Hermann and signed on for a second enlistment after their mandatory twenty years were up went into the 1st and 2nd Cohorts. Those 14th G.M.V. veterans were now a minimum of fifty-two years of age. Their comrades of the junior cohorts were in their thirties, with twelve years' service to their credit. That service had included occasional punitive crossings of the Rhine after one German tribe or another had caused trouble, but this British operation was the biggest thing the first-enlistment men had ever been involved in, and they would have arrived at the embarkation camp keyed up and raring to go. But the men of the 14th's senior cohorts had put a monkey wrench in the works of the entire operation: led by the 14th G.M.V., all four legions were stubbornly refusing to set foot in Britain.

Apart from the 9th Hispana, all these legions had served in Germanicus Caesar's A.D. 16 German campaign, although men of the second enlistment of just one of the three legions were still serving with their unit—the 14th Gemina Martia Victrix. The second-enlistment veterans of the 2nd Augusta and the 20th V.V. had retired in A.D. 40. These men of the 14th G.M.V.'s senior cohorts, legionaries with thirty-two years legion experience, had been wrecked on the shores of Britain on the harrowing return journey from Germany in the late summer of A.D. 16. And as they'd whiled away their time in the Boulogne camp waiting for this operation to commence, they'd told their first enlistment comrades wild stories about those traumatic days, about sea monsters and terrifying British creatures that were half men, half beast. And they reminded their wide-eyed younger colleagues that Britain was beyond the limits of the known world.

As an old Latin saying goes, no desire is felt for a thing unknown. And as the stories spread from the tents of the 14th G.M.V. to those of the other legions, the stories suffered from exaggeration, as rumors always do. Roman legionaries were highly superstitious at the best of times. Before long, thousands of them had confronted their officers and flatly refused to take part in an invasion of the unknown and mysterious British Isles. No amount of persuasion, cajoling, threats, or promises could change the minds of the troops, forcing an exasperated General Plautius to write to Rome confessing that his legions had gone on strike and couldn't be budged. Plautius had a friend at court—a handsome nephew was a favorite of Claudius's bed-hopping wife, Messalina, who dominated Claudius through his staff. Instead of replacing the general, the emperor sent his Chief Secretary, the freedman Narcissus, hurrying up to Boulogne to help him.

General Plautius ordered a parade of his army, then welcomed Narcissus onto the tribunal in front of the assembled legions. The wealthy and powerful Narcissus stepped up, wearing a purple-fringed toga granted to him by the emperor, and, at his waist, the sheathed dagger that was the symbol of office of the Chief Secretary. But before Narcissus could even open his mouth to address the troops, they began to heckle him. "Hooray for the Saturnalia!" they chorused.

It soon became a chant as legionaries gained full voice, no doubt smiling broadly. Their message was clear enough. During the Festival of Saturn each December, slaves were given a number of privileges, from permission to play dice legally to the right to wear their master's clothing. The Boulogne legionaries, Roman citizens all, were not prepared to give a hearing to a former slave who'd come to address them on behalf of his master, even if that master was the emperor. Humiliated, Narcissus left the tribunal.

Cassius Dio says that after Narcissus's failed mission, General Plautius was himself able to finally resolve the problem and convince the men to go forward with the mission. Just how he accomplished this is unknown, but it probably involved a hefty bonus payment. Narcissus would no doubt have come to Boulogne with just such a proposal, if not with the cash in question, but had been prevented from airing it himself.

Passing a giant lighthouse built by Caligula at Boulogne in A.D. 39–40 and modeled on the Pharos at Alexandria, a wonder of the ancient world— one of the few good things to have come out of Caligula's "British opera- tion"—the first transports of General Plautius's invasion task force set out toward the end of a late summer's day. From the accounts of Julius Caesar's landings ninety-eight years before, the men of the 14th G.M.V. knew to expect to be going ashore across the Strait of Dover the next morning.

After nightfall, a storm blew up. Rain pelted down. A strong north wind chopped up the water and drove the craft back toward France. Then, as the wind eased, a massive bolt of lightning was seen to flash across the sky from east to west, as if pointing the way for the legions. It was an omen not lost on the legionaries of the 14th.

Ignoring the beaches of Pevensey Bay farther west, which would attract William the Conqueror's invasion force in 1066, the new Britannic Fleet sailed up the Strait of Dover in the dark, following the low stretch of Kent coastline beyond Dover and its white cliffs; passing Deal, where Julius Caesar landed in 55 and 54 B.C.; and heading for the Isle of Thanet, near present-day Ramsgate. Back then, Thanet really was an island. Over the centuries the Wantsum Channel, the narrow waterway between the island and the mainland, silted up. Modern historians think that Lieutenant General Plautius's spearhead hit the beach in the vicinity of Pegwell Bay.

In the new day's light the ships slid into the shallows, and the 14th's men jumped over the sides and went wading ashore, packs on backs. The Celts of southern England had been alerted by traders from Gaul to Roman preparations at Boulogne, but when midsummer arrived and the Romans didn't, the British had decided it was a false alarm and went back to their farms and villages. The legions' strike had worked in their favor—the landing went ahead unopposed. So far, so good as far as the 14th was concerned.

Dio says the landing took place in three divisions. As only one land- ing place is thought to have been used, this suggests that the troops landed in three waves at Pegwell Bay. Splashing ashore with the 14th G.M.V. were the light infantry of the Cohortis Batavior, the Batavian Cohorts, eight of which now provided the 14th's regular auxiliary support.

One of their eight cohort commanders was a sandy-haired Batavian prefect of twenty-five who'd recently commenced service with the Roman army, Colonel Gaius Civilis. He was a grandson or nephew of Chariovalda, last king of the Batavi, who'd been killed by Hermann's men in A.D. 16. Rome had not permitted the crowning of another king since.

Also going ashore were the troopers of the Batavian Horse, plus a wing of the Thracian Horse multinational cavalry, and the Vettonian Mixed Horse, a Spanish *equitatae* unit, made up of both cavalry and infantry, commanded by Colonel Didius Gallus. The method of landing horses from transports in Roman offensive operations is unknown; perhaps via ramps, perhaps using mast booms and slings.

A troop of elephants had even been put on standby by the Palatium, but there's no indication it ever left its base at Laurentum, outside Rome, to take part in the operation. The nature of the terrain the invasion force would have to negotiate—often marshy ground frequently crossed by rivers—was not suited to elephant operations, as the Palatium knew from Caesar's Gallic War *Commentaries,* the guidebook for the operation.

Once ashore, the men of the 14th G.M.V. and General Plautius's other legions were permitted to remove helmets and stack shields and javelins, but otherwise worked in full equipment as they dug entrenchments to establish a secure beachhead and build a camp beside the Stour River, near modern Richborough. The safe harbor and camp here, named Rutupiae, would be used as a Roman base for supplies coming in from France for the next thirty years, before being superseded by other British ports.

These successors of the original, ill-fated 58 B.C. enlistment of the 14th Legion still came from the same part of the Roman world as their forebears, wore the same uniform, and carried similar weapons, although the A.D. 43 helmet had better neck protection, and instead of the mail-covered leather jackets of Caesar's and Augustus's days, the 14th's men now wore metal body armor, not unlike, in style and purpose, today's military and police body armor or flak jacket. This recently introduced *lorica segmentata* armor comprised curved metal segments fastened together by bronze hinges, covering torso and shoulders—the model for the armor of the knights of the Middle Ages. Shining in the sun, it would have made the legionaries look, to the part-time British warriors who were soon to come face to face with them, like gleaming machines from the underworld.

With a beachhead established, and leaving the 9th Hispana to hold the Rutupiae fort, General Plautius led the major part of the task force inland. Following in Julius Caesar's century-old footsteps, Plautius advanced toward the Thames, the river called the Tamesis by the Celts, with the

2nd Augusta on his left and the 20th V.V. on the right wing, and with the 14th G.M.V. occupying the center.

At first there was no contact with the Britons. The local people, of the Cantiaci tribe, took refuge in the swamps and forests of western Kent as the Roman army tramped though their wheat fields, and summoned help from tribes to the west and the north. When the British did commit to combat, it was under the command of two brothers, sons of the late Cunobelinus, king of the powerful Catuvellauni tribe. The boys' brother was the exiled Bericus, inspirer of the Roman invasion. Their great-grandfather, King Cassivellaunus, had fought and paid tribute money to Julius Caesar a century earlier.

One of the brothers was Togodumnus, who ruled from the old Catuvellauni capital, Camulodunon, "the fort of Camulos," named for the Celtic patron deity of the tribe, which was to become present-day Colchester, in Essex, north of the Thames. The other brother's Celtic name was Carodoc. History knows him as King Caractacus, or, more correctly, Caratacus, his Roman name. He ran the western part of his father's former kingdom from the town Romans were to call Calleva Attrebatum, near today's Silchester in Hampshire, in the heart of the Atrebates' tribal territory. We know nothing of Caratacus's appearance or background. We know he had a wife and daughter, and can guess that he and his brothers were perhaps in their twenties and thirties.

The rivalry between the five sons of King Cunobelinus that had led to the ejection of Bericus seems to have been a continuing thing. For, hurrying east, Caratacus didn't wait for his brother Togodumnus to join him with his warriors. Impatient for glory, he immediately took his Atrebate and Dobunni tribesmen against the Romans. King Caratacus's fighting men were equipped with just shields and short spears. They didn't possess armor or helmets, and the common warrior fought naked to the waist, often barefoot, and sometimes even buck naked to scare the daylights out of his opponents. Long-haired, often mustachioed, but not bearded, many covered their exposed skin with markings, like tattoos, in blue-green woad, a plant dye. The tribes had previously spent much of their time and energy fighting each other. Now they had to contend with a new, very different enemy.

All the Celts of southern Britain worshiped the Celtic war god Camulos, patron deity of the Catuvellauni tribe. And before they went into battle they swore a sacred oath to their god that they would not yield to the weapons of the enemy or to wounds they received in battle. Despite their oaths, Caratacus's men were soon on the run after being swiftly routed by the mechanical efficiency of the legions in the first engagement in Kent. Caratacus hastily withdrew, hoping to re-form his force beyond the Medway River.

As he pulled back, Caratacus lost one of his tribes, the Dobunni from the Gloucestershire region, which had been subservient to Caratacus for some time. Now, deciding they would prefer to be ruled by Rome rather than by fellow Celts, the Dobunni surrendered en masse to General Plautius. He hastily built a fort in his rear where auxiliaries were left to guard the Dobunni POWs, then pushed on.

Caratacus's brother Togodumnus now crossed the Thames and Medway Rivers with his Catuvellauni. Equally impatient, he left his chariots behind, apparently to be brought across the Thames on rafts, and swung southeast to attack the advancing Romans with his foot soldiers. In open country, against the drilled Roman machine, his loosely organized infantry force was easily repulsed by the 14th and its fellow legions, with heavy British casualties from javelin and sword. Togodumnus himself appears to have been seriously wounded in this contact. Carried away by followers, he was dead within days.

Togodumnus's warriors fled back to the Medway, where they linked up with Caratacus and his Atrebates and were joined by the chariots Togodumnus had left behind when he hurried to come to grips with the invaders. As Caratacus took overall command, General Plautius reached the Medway. The legions were greeted by the sight of thousands of warriors and hundreds of war chariots on the far bank—it's been estimated that Caratacus had sixty thousand to eighty thousand fighting men.

General Plautius gave the impression he was building a camp for the night, with extravagant activity from the men of the 20th Valeria Victrix Legion. At the same time, he discreetly sent the Batavian Horse downstream and Generals Sabinus and Vespasian upstream with the 14th G.M.V. and the 2nd Augusta. The Britons took no notice of the cavalry trotting away, not realizing that the Batavians were General Plautius's secret weapon. Out of sight of the two armies, the Batavians dismounted; then, hanging onto their saddles, they swam the river beside their horses in full equipment, as Batavian cavalry was traditionally trained to do. Once over the river, they remounted and came up the far bank, launching a surprise attack on the Britons. At first recoiling, the British regrouped and fiercely counterattacked the Batavians with chariots and cavalry. The Batavians deliberately wounded British horses, neutralizing chariots and destabilizing the British cavalry, but, vastly outnumbered, they became pinned down.

The men of the 14th, in the meantime, were crossing the river unnoticed in company with the 2nd Augusta, using a bridge of boats quickly thrown across the Medway by Roman engineers. The small, light boats had been brought along on the task force's baggage train for this very purpose. The forerunner of the latter-day Bailey bridge, Roman boat-bridges were strung across waterways with astonishing speed. As soon as they were across, the two legions then joined the battle from the north. The Britons not only held their ground as the 14th G.M.V. bore in, they also pressed back, hard. With the Batavians under severe pressure, legion commanders Sabinus and Vespasian threw their men into the fight as soon as each cohort funneled across the river. The 14th and the 2nd both straggled into the battle, cohort by cohort. Nineteenth-century military strategist Carl von Clausewitz wrote that when absolute superiority is not attainable, produce relative superiority at a decisive point. With their commanders going against that principle at the Medway, the men of the two legions were paying the price.

The fighting was bloody and no holds barred, and lasted all through the afternoon. For the men of the G.M.V., it became simply a matter of survival. Strong, gutsy leadership was all-important. The camp prefect of the 2nd Augusta, Major Publius Anicius Maximus, won several bravery awards during the British campaign, and almost certainly one or more of them came out of this torrid day's work beside the Medway. As the sun went down, the 14th G.M.V. and the 2nd Augusta found themselves penned beside the river, hemmed in on three sides. The Britons ceased their attacks but held their positions as the legionaries tried to dig a defensive trench line. It was a grim night for Generals Sabinus and Vespasian and the brothers' men, spent under arms and on the alert, without tents, bedrolls, or rations. It was made all the more depressing by the fact that General Plautius withdrew the bridge of boats. They were well and truly on their own.

With the arrival of the new day, General Plautius had the 20th V.V. build a new boat-bridge downstream, then sent that legion across to relieve the units pinned down on the northern riverbank. This time the Britons saw the Romans coming. Led by its commander, Major General Gnaeus Hosidius Geta, who'd three times defeated the forces of Moorish general Salabus in Mauretania the previous year, the 20th forced a bridgehead on the far bank under a hail of spears and against charge after British charge. It was tough going for the Powerful Conquerors as they fought to maintain their foothold on the far bank. General Geta himself only narrowly avoided being captured in one melee.

By sheer courage and determination General Geta's 20th V.V. held and expanded his bridgehead, from which they were able to break out later in the day and go to the rescue of the trapped legions upstream, which had fought off renewed British assaults throughout the morning and afternoon. Geta acquitted himself so well in this action that Claudius would award him Triumphal Decorations following the campaign, despite the fact that he was only a major general; uniquely, three of the four legions of the task force were commanded by major generals.

The bloodied Celts withdrew; the 14th, 2nd, 20th, and the Batavians linked up; and the legions followed hot on British heels to the Thames. The tribesmen easily crossed the broad waterway where the river entered the sea, knowing exactly where firm ground lay at low tide, leaving the Roman troops literally floundering in their wake. General Plautius again brought up his baggage train, unloaded his small craft, and lay another bridge of boats across the river in his path. At the same time, he again sent the Batavian Horse swimming across the waterway in his path, downstream. The repeated tactic succeeded: as Roman cavalry attacked the Britons from one direction and infantry from another, the tribesmen put a up a brief fight, but after taking heavy casualties, they lost heart and fled for the Essex Marshes, where the Thames entered the sea. Roman troops gave chase, only to become bogged down in the marshes. Finding danger in clawing sand and clay and hidden depths, the Romans pulled back.

The tribes had been devastated. As the will to continue the fight against this unstoppable Roman killing machine evaporated, King Caratacus, determined to continue resistance but deserted by his own people, fled west, taking his wife, daughter, and his two surviving brothers with him. In his wake, General Plautius decided to hold the line along the Thames with his main force, ordering General Vespasian to secure his left flank with the 2nd Augusta. As Vespasian's legion powered southwest, the 9th Hispana came up from the coast to join the 14th G.M.V. and the 20th V.V. at the Thames. Again the men of the 14th set to work digging a camp, this time on the southern bank of the Thames.

Vespasian and the 2nd Augusta swept along the southern coast of England, fighting thirty battles, mostly short, sharp sieges of hill forts, taking twenty towns, including Caratacus's capital, Calleva, plus the Isle of Wight, and forcing the surrender of the tribes of Somerset and Dorset, the Regni and the Durotriges. The young ruler of the Regni, Cogidubnus, a descendant of Commius, the Atrebatean king who fled to Britain after going against Julius Caesar, became a faithful ally of Rome, and would remain so for the next fifty years. King Cogidubnus would have been among envoys who now went to British tribes to the north and west to convince them to come to terms with the Romans.

By the fall, with General Vespasian in control in the south and a number of tribes beyond the Thames indicating they were prepared to submit, General Plautius sent a message to Rome, a message the emperor had been waiting for. Claudius now set off for Britain, departing Rome in a fleet of lavish barges rowed down the Tiber to Ostia and waiting warships of the Tyrrhenian Fleet from Misenum. Accompanying the emperor on the barges was a large entourage of senators and sycophants, as well as Claudius's private secretary, Posides, and Xenophon, Claudius's personal physician. At the same time, Praetorian Prefect Colonel Rufrius Pollio marched several cohorts of the Praetorian Guard and the German Guard down the Ostian Way to join the fleet.

Officially, Claudius was coming to take personal command of the offensive. But the fighting was over. All that was left for him to do was accept the surrender of the conquered tribes. His course from Ostia took him across the Mediterranean to Marseilles, where his storm-tossed party landed and continued overland, through France and Belgium to the Rhine, and from there to Boulogne for the Channel crossing.

Silent, as rigid as statues, in full parade dress with helmet plumes and shining bravery decorations, the men of the 14th Gemina Martia Victrix Legion, 20th Valeria Victrix Legion, and 9th Hispana Legion stood at attention in their cohorts outside Colchester.

Suetonius says the legions sacked the town, and it appears that once the tribes north of the Thames agreed to surrender, the legions crossed the river and moved inland to take the dead Togodumnus's Catuvellauni capital. Dio says that Claudius led them across the Thames and on the short march north to the town.

Flanked by lanky soldiers of the German Guard and the Praetorian Guard, the emperor Claudius took the surrender of British rulers—eleven of them, according to the inscription on the Arch of Claudius erected at Boulogne nine years later to commemorate the British campaign. They would have been leaders of the Cantiaci, British Atrebates, Regni, Durotriges, Dobunni, Catuvellauni, Trinovantes, Coritani, Cornovii, Dumnonii, and the Parisii of Yorkshire—emigrants from along the Seine River in France.

One after the other the British leaders came forward; prostrated themselves in front of the Roman emperor, Lieutenant General Plautius, and the host of senators who'd come with the emperor; swore allegiance to Claudius Caesar and to Rome; and signed a peace treaty. That treaty permitted the kings to retain their thrones, but required them to pay annual taxes to Rome, to disarm their populations, and to provide their tribes' finest young men to serve as auxiliaries. Within fifty years there would be at least thirteen British auxiliary infantry units, the Cohortis Britannor, as well as British cavalry, serving in the Roman army. With the sealing of the treaties, Claudius proclaimed Britain an imperial province of Rome, with General Plautius its first propraetor and Colchester the provincial capital and governor's seat.

After spending just sixteen days on the island, Claudius went home. He arrived back in Rome early in A.D. 44, six months after he'd departed, bringing thousands of British prisoners captured in the initial advance and the 2nd Augusta's southern sweep. The Britons marched in chains through Rome's streets in the Triumph celebrated by Claudius that summer for the British victory. Subsequently sent to the amphitheater, British prisoners would still be fighting in gladiatorial contests at Rome two years later.

Claudius gave out numerous awards for the campaign. When General Plautius returned to Rome at the end of his posting several years later he celebrated an Ovation, a lesser form of Triumph where the awardee rode through the streets of Rome on horseback rather than in a golden quadriga. Plautius was the first to receive an Ovation in many years. General Geta received his T.D.s for the Battle of the Medway. And for his all-conquering southern coast sweep, General Vespasian was likewise granted Triumphal Decorations, even though he, too, was only a major general. But taking the shine off their awards was the fact that Claudius also awarded T.D.s to senators who'd merely accompanied him to Britain and played no part in the fighting.

The 2nd Augusta pushed on to the Exe River in Devon, turning the capital of the Dumnonii tribe on the eastern bank of the river into the Roman town of Isca Dumnoniorium, the later Exeter. By the end of the year, all four invasion force legions had spread across southwestern England and established permanent bases along a frontier line thirty miles deep, from Dorset to the Humber Estuary. To the north of the 2nd Augusta, the 20th V.V. established a base called Glevum, which would become today's city of Gloucester. The 14th G.M.V. was based above the 20th at a number of frontier forts spread through present-day Derbyshire to Nottinghamshire. Digging in on the 14th's northern flank, the 9th Hispana would make its forward headquarters at Lindum, today's city of Lincoln.

The 14th G.M.V. faced west, toward the wild valleys of Wales, home to fierce tribes the legionaries had yet barely heard of. They would come to know of them soon enough. King Caratacus and his family reached Wales, taking with them the king's household but leaving behind most of the horses, arms, and possessions that had once been symbols of Caratacus's power. These spoils of war fell into the hands of the 2nd Augusta as the legion took over Calleva, demolished Atrebatian mud huts, laid out grid-pattern streets, and planned grand public buildings in stone. In Wales, the tribes not only welcomed Caratacus, they also made him their war chief, as he swore to repel the invaders.

Meanwhile, the men of the 14th G.M.V. and the other legions of Plautius's task force had a mental readjustment to make. After decades at their old postings they now had to turn their backs on places, sights, sounds, weather, and people they had known intimately. Old lives, business investments, illegal wives, and illegitimate children had all been left behind, and there was no going back. The legions' places at their previous stations had already been filled by the transfer of units from elsewhere in the empire.

For the 14th Gemina Martia Victrix, after a solid if unspectacular performance in the invasion, this was where their future lay. Britain was home.

XX

CATCHING KING CARATACUS

T his, the legionaries of the 14th told themselves as they marched down the lush Welsh valley toward the British army in the summer of A.D. 50, would be the final battle. The 14th Gemina Martia Victrix Legion had been chasing British resistance leader Caratacus around Wales for six years. With the legion due to undergo its twenty-year discharge in the new year, the latest Governor of Britain, Lieutenant General Publius Ostorius, was determined to finally eliminate Caratacus while he still had these experienced G.M.V. men under his command. For the 14th's legionaries, it would be a fitting way to bow out before they hung up their swords.

Already, the men of the legion's senior cohorts had been detached from their unit. Veterans of around fifty-nine years of age, with thirty-nine years service in Germany and Britain to their credit, they'd originally been drafted back in A.D. 11 when Germanicus was just arriving on the Rhine. Now, to free up the 20th Valeria Victrix Legion cohorts that General Ostorius had been holding back at Colchester to provide a legionary presence at the province's capital—cohorts made up mostly of youngsters—the Palatium had decided to make Colchester the first military colony in Britain. And its first citizen settlers would be the retirees of the 14th G.M.V. Legion.

That settlement process had already begun. The second-enlistment men of the 14th's senior cohorts now occupied the permanent camp on the western outskirts of Colchester, allowing the youngsters of the 20th V.V. to join the rest of their legion for this campaign in Wales. And in the new year, once the Welsh campaign was at an end, men of the 14th's junior cohorts who chose to retire at the end of their twenty-year stint would accept their 12,000-sesterce discharge bonus, withdraw their accumulated savings from the legion bank, receive their bronze record of discharge and a land grant title, and join their comrades in well-earned retirement at Colchester.

The idea of making Colchester a colony would have come from the emperor's latest wife. Of Germanicus Caesar's nine children, just two, daughters both, had outlived Caligula: Julia, born on the island of Lesbos as Germanicus and Agrippina sailed to the East in A.D. 17, and Agrippina the Younger, born at Cologne in A.D. 15. Claudius had executed Julia, for supposedly plotting against him. But Agrippina had an altogether different fate. She won the heart of her uncle, Germanicus's brother, after he had executed third wife Messalina for her infidelities. Pushing legislation through the Senate that made it lawful for an uncle to marry his niece, fifty-eight-year-old Claudius had wed his thirty-four-year-old, twice-married niece, Agrippina, in A.D. 49.

Agrippina was soon playing a leading role in Palatium policymaking. She suggested establishing a military colony at her birthplace on the Rhine, to accommodate the men of the 16th Legion's A.D. 51 discharge and to provide Cologne, which had lost its military garrison back in A.D. 30, with a local Evocati militia force of retired legionaries as a defense against threats such as a recent trans-Rhine raid into the area by the ever troublesome Chatti. That colony, created on the Rhine in A.D. 50, was named jointly in honor of the emperor and his new wife—Colonia Claudia Ara Agrippinensium, shortened over time to Colonia Agrippinensium, eventually mutating into Cologne.

But before they headed for the new colony of Colchester and a new life as citizen settlers, the intending retirees in the 14th G.M.V.'s junior cohorts had to overcome Caratacus and his defiant Britons. The 14th now marched with a new commander, identity unknown. Major General Sabinus had been recalled to Rome after three years in Britain to become a consul, and now he was governing Moesia, modern Bulgaria.

As the 14th Legion's men advanced down the Welsh valley with the rest of General Ostorius's army, they could see frantic activity in the tree line ahead. What they couldn't see were thousands more Britons skulking in the forest and preparing to give them a hot welcome. Marching with the 14th G.M.V. was the 20th V.V., commanded by Gaius Manlius Valens. He was forty-four, unusually mature for a brigadier general. But Claudius regularly appointed older men to commands, perhaps to show that rather than youth, maturity, like his own, was what Rome needed in responsible positions. And Valens had a reputation for vigor.

The 14th's usual companions, the Batavian light infantry and the Batavian Horse, were there, and probably four cohorts from the 2nd Augusta Legion. The 2nd also had a new commander, identity unknown—General Vespasian had been replaced by A.D. 48. There were possibly also cohorts of the 9th Hispana Legion from the north. That unit's commander, Brigadier General Caesius Nasica, was well advanced in years and a lazy campaigner who sent his subordinates to do his job. While he remained in Lincoln, his senior tribune or camp prefect would have led the 9th Hispana detachment.

Tacitus describes task force commander General Ostorius as a fine soldier. From the beginning of his appointment as Governor of Britain in A.D. 48, Ostorius had set out to subdue the tribes of Wales, where Caratacus was still at large and mounting regular raids on forts along the frontier. The general had quickly extended the frontier thirty miles into Wales and set up new bases, including one for the 14th G.M.V. at Viroconium, present-day Wroxeter, on the Severn River. Jumping off from these new forward bases, the legions had quickly conquered the Cangi tribe of central Wales. The general himself penetrated almost to the Welsh coast, with Ireland not far away across the Irish Sea.

But the years that followed had been filled with distractions and frustrations. First there'd been internal strife among Rome's northern allies the Brigantes of Yorkshire. Once Ostorius had settled that and left auxiliaries with Queen Cartimandua, longtime ruler of the Brigantes, to secure the peace and maintain the alliance, he'd refocused on Wales, the Silure tribe, and Caratacus and his shoot-and-scoot campaign.

It had been galling to the men of the 14th G.M.V. after they'd achieved so much early in their British campaigns to be tied up in small-unit actions without victory, booty, or glory, year after year. Then, while going dejectedly into winter camp in A.D. 49, they'd heard an amazing story that lifted their spirits. That summer, Lieutenant General Lucius Pomponius of the A.L.R. had pursued Chatti raiders deep into Germany, and at a Chatti camp his troops had found a group of slaves, elderly men of sixty-nine or so who greeted them as brothers. These were survivors of General Varus's massacred 17th, 18th, and 19th legions, prisoners of the Chatti for the past forty years. The repatriated men were not permitted to set foot in Italy, due to the shame of their A.D. 9 surrender.

Determined to corner Caratacus once and for all, General Ostorius had implemented a troop buildup that lasted into May of A.D. 50, when he'd launched the current offensive, driving into southern and central Wales. Using his usual hit-and-run tactics, Caratacus led Ostorius's force a merry chase in South Wales for weeks before drawing the Romans up into the north, home of the large Ordovice tribe. There he'd prepared an ambush along the lines of Hermann's Teutoburg trap, convincing thousands of men from surrounding tribes to join him. As Caratacus lured the legions north with his skirmishers, his main body assembled in the hills. Totaling possibly as many as thirty thousand, these Celtic warriors would have come from the Ordovices, the Deceangli, the Demetae, the Cornovii, and the tribe Tacitus describes as the fiercest in Britain, the Silures.

The location chosen by Caratacus for his ambush is thought by some historians to have been in the Severn River valley in the vicinity of Llanidloes, in central northern Wales. As the men of the 14th G.M.V. and the other Roman units came down the valley, they saw a river of varying depth slicing across their path. Beyond that, Caratacus had built a tall wall of stones along the lower, exposed slopes of the surrounding, thickly forested hills. This wall seems to have been in a U shape, designed to wrap around any force coming down the narrow valley, so that they had only one way out, to their rear. Caratacus probably intended sealing off the open end with a sudden materialization of troops once the Romans had been sucked into the trap.

The tribes formed up in their clans in front of the wall and waited, with more tribesmen lurking out of sight in the trees above the wall. Caratacus had only infantry at his disposal—no chariots, no cavalry—so he was intending to fight an infantry action in a fixed position, which eliminated the Romans' cavalry advantage.

The G.M.V. men would have felt confident of success here. They knew their force was twenty-two thousand strong, with eleven thousand legionaries from four legions and a similar number of auxiliaries. And they would have wondered why, after evading the Romans for six years by using guerrilla tactics, Caratacus was committing to a full-scale battle. Not that the 14th minded. If Caratacus wanted to invite disaster, they would gladly deliver it.

Perhaps, as young Gnaeus Pompey had found back in 45 B.C. in Spain, there comes a time when the patience and resilience of your supporters run out and they demand a decisive battle. Later events suggest that an aspiring war leader among the Silures, Caratacus's hosts for the past six years, may have delivered Caratacus an ultimatum to give the tribes a decisive victory over the Romans or move aside.

As for General Ostorius, Tacitus says that he was both confounded and daunted by the sight of the Britons massed in front of the stone wall. As the men of the 14th G.M.V. and their comrades came down the valley in marching order, Ostorius refused to issue the command for battle to be joined. His men began to mumble complaints. With the ragtag British force calling them on, scruffy tribesmen without helmets or breastplates shaking their weapons at them and beckoning, and with the chiefs of the tribes moving among the Welsh and exhorting them to fight or die, legionaries of the 14th began to call out to their general, demanding he send them to the attack. All the legions joined the call. Even centurions and tribunes called for action. But they were all ignored.

With the river directly in front of his column, the general ordered a halt. He then cautiously sent scouts ahead to study the lay of the land and report back. His waiting legionaries grew more and more restless, eyeing the increasingly agitated tribesmen on the slopes across the valley as Caratacus himself became clearly visible, riding back and forth among the different bands, firing them up. Tacitus says that Caratacus invoked the names of long-dead British forefathers who fought Julius Caesar to give his people the strength to recover their freedom from the invaders. And in response, the pumped-up tribesmen cheered and applauded.

The frustrated men of the 14th watched as the cavalry scouts returned. They saw the scouts dismount and speak animatedly to General Ostorius and his staff, pointing to the river, to the wall. A groan ran through the ranks as Ostorius still didn't give the order for the attack and instead convened a meeting of his senior officers. Impatiently the men in the ranks watched as the generals and colonels and first-rank centurions huddled, deep in conversation. The scouts had painted a vivid picture for General Ostorius of the terrain ahead, indicating the best places to ford the river, the most accessible routes for an assault on the stone wall. The general passed on this information to his officers and told them how and where he wanted the army to go about the task that lay ahead. As the officers were returning to their units, the general's purple standard went up, the signal for battle. At last. The trumpets of the legions sounded "Battle Order." A cheer rang out from the thousands of legionaries.

Prefects and centurions barked orders, trumpets sounded, standards inclined to left and right. For a moment it looked as if chaos reigned, as men and horses moved in a flurry of action this way and that. And then order emerged as two battle lines formed up facing the Britons, extending across the valley. Auxiliary units filled the front line. A hundred yards back, the legions formed a second line, in depth. At the double, the men of the 14th G.M.V. moved into position and neatly dressed ranks. In their centuries, their maniples, and their cohorts, each separated by a gap, they were soon standing stock still, shields raised, javelins at the ready.

As the cavalry formed up on the wings, General Ostorius took up his position in the middle of the second line, on foot. He gave an order. The general's standard inclined forward. Trumpets sounded "Advance at Marching Pace." Ostorius's army stepped out. Following the advice of the scouts, the Roman troops funneled to the best fording places at the river. Once his men had splashed across and re-formed their battle lines on the other side, the general's standard dropped, and frontline trumpets sounded "Charge!" With a roar, the Batavians and other auxiliary light infantry of the front line dashed forward. The legionaries of the second line held their position.

Throwing light javelins as they ran up the slope toward the British line, the auxiliaries came under a hail of stones and spears. Some men fell, bleeding, screaming in pain, or dead. But most drove on. The tribesmen in front of the stone barrier hurriedly retreated to the wall after they'd loosed off all their ammunition. Using ladders that they drew up after them, they scrambled onto the top of the wall. Now they were joined by thousands of tribesmen waiting in reserve in the trees. As the auxiliaries reached the wall, the reinforced tribesmen on top rained missiles down—spears, stones, anything they could lay their hands on. Among those wounded at this point was, in all likelihood, Colonel Julius Civilis—the Batavian cohort commander received a severe battle wound to the face while serving in Britain.

A trumpet call was repeated up and down the legionary line: "Form Testudo." The men of the 14th closed up and locked their curved shields together, some at their sides, some over their heads, as they were trained. Then another trumpet call: "Advance to the Attack." The auxiliaries parted, and the legionary cohorts came pushing through their ranks in tortoise formations. Under cover of the testudos, and with missiles clattering down over their tortoise "shell," legionaries industriously began removing stones from the bottom of the wall. In perhaps just ten or fifteen minutes, the tough, no-nonsense soldiers of the 14th Gemina Martia Victrix and their less experienced colleagues pulled down part of the wall.

Centurions bellowed orders, then led a charge. A crimson tide of legionary uniforms flowed up and over the shattered wall from one direction; the auxiliaries scrambled forward from another. In hectic hand-to-hand fighting, the tribes' front ranks were broken, and the Britons behind them fled up into the trees. In the heights, some tribesmen re-formed and tried to make a stand. The auxiliaries came up and kept them under constant javelin fire from one direction while the legions closed in for in-your-face combat from another. Between them, they slaughtered every Welshman who resisted.

The tribes were routed. Thousands died, many surrendered. Caratacus's two younger brothers were among the numerous chieftains who threw down their weapons and begged for their lives. Among the trees, legionaries found the tents of the British camp, where Caratacus's men had gathered and waited for the Romans to come to them and no doubt shared many a lurid tale about what they were going to do the men of the 14th Gemina Martia Victrix and the other legions. In this camp, the legionaries found the terrified wife and daughter of Caratacus. Like Caratacus's brothers and the other captives, his family was spared by General Ostorius.

The British resistance leader himself escaped, desperately fleeing through the forest, to hide in the hills and think about what had been and what might have been. Caratacus would not be heard of for another twelve to eighteen months. In the interim, he probably hid out on Anglesey Island, off the northern coast of Wales, with Druid priests who were notorious for sheltering fugitive British partisans.

With the Severn victory, men of the 14th G.M.V. were able to take their discharges. In early A.D. 51, those men of the A.D. 31 enlistment who chose to leave the legion marched to Colchester to join the veterans of the 14th's senior cohorts and to accept their retirement benefits. With the legion down to about forty-five hundred able-bodied men by A.D. 50, some three thousand men from the first and second enlistments would now go into retirement, with the remainder volunteering to sign on for a new enlistment and automatically moving up into the legion's senior 1st, 2nd, and 3rd Cohorts.

To make the transition from soldier to settler as swift as possible, the pragmatic General Ostorius forced thousands of British tribesmen living around Colchester from their farms, distributing their lands to the retiring 14th G.M.V. legionaries. The size of the legionaries' land grants is unknown. It had been sixty acres per man after the Jugurthine War of 111–105 B.C., but that had been before the days of 12,000-sesterce retirement bonuses, so smaller land grants may have become the norm in the imperial era.

That spring of A.D. 51 a new enlistment of recruits arrived to join the 14th G.M.V. Legion, replacing the recent retirees and the casualties suffered over the past twenty years to bring the unit back up to full strength. As usual, the new recruits had been enrolled in northern Italy. Some were volunteers—the hungry and the homeless, says Tacitus. Most were conscripts, such as Publius Flavoleius Cordus from Modena and his soon-to-be best friend, Gaius Vibennius. Then there was Titus Flaminius. And Marcus Petronius from Vicenza. They had no time to overcome their long march from Italy, or their crossing of the stormy Channel, or the final march to Wales. They were thrown straight into the thick of the Welsh campaign. General Ostorius, who'd been voted T.D.s by the Senate for his victory on the Severn the previous year, was embarking on a drive into South Wales this campaigning season, with the stated intention of wiping out the numerous and defiant Silure tribe once and for all.

The next two years did not bring the sort of success the general had experienced at the Severn battle. The Silures had found themselves an energetic new leader, one who reverted to guerrilla tactics. But instead of the stinging, hit-and-run style of attack that Caratacus had specialized in, this unidentified Silurian leader planned operations in strength against isolated targets that he quietly encircled, cut off from the outside world, then assaulted in ferocious attacks that had the goal of their annihilation. The camp prefect of the 20th V.V. was killed when his fort was surrounded. Eight centurions and a number of the best 20th Legion rank and file died with him before the raid was repulsed. A foraging party was wiped out, and the cavalry dispatched to their aid was forced to retreat. Two auxiliary cohorts cut off for a time went close to going over to the Silures, tempted by offers of payment for deserting. For all Caratacus's fame, his replacement, this anonymous "Silurius," was succeeding where he had failed.

Then General Ostorius died, apparently of natural causes. Perhaps it was a sudden heart attack. Or perhaps a terminal illness had been invading his body all the time that Publius Ostorius was invading Wales. With the Welsh campaign halted while the Palatium chose a new propraetor, then sent him out from Rome to take charge, the legions pulled back, returning to their bases along the Welsh frontier. And there they heard that Caratacus had been captured at last.

In A.D. 52, exhausted, dispirited, and no doubt in disguise, Caratacus arrived at one of the chief towns of the Brigantes, either Aldborough, the Roman Isurium, or Eboracum, the future city of York. Finding his way to Queen Cartimandua, he begged for help in a continued war against Rome—in the name of their common gods, their common cause, and in defiance of their common foe. The queen didn't quite see things that way. Conscious of her treaty with Rome, and of the Roman auxiliary troops stationed at her capital, she clapped Caratacus in irons and handed him over to the colonel commanding the auxiliary detachment. The Battle of the Severn had been Caratacus's last stand.

King Caratacus was taken to Rome, and that summer of A.D. 52 was paraded like a sideshow attraction. Tacitus says that his fame had spread throughout the Roman world, this guerrilla leader who had evaded capture for so long. Even at Rome, Tacitus says, the name of Caratacus was no obscure one. A vast crowd came to the Field of Mars outside the city walls to witness a show staged by the emperor, eager to see "the great man who for so many years had defied our power," as Tacitus puts it.

Cohorts of the Praetorian Guard were drawn up on the flat outside their barracks, fully equipped with shields and javelins as they were allowed outside the city. Claudius was resplendent in gold-plated armor and the crimson cloak of a Triumphant as he and his wife, Agrippina the Younger, sat enthroned in front of the Praetorian standards. Members of Caratacus's household were led by in chains, their heads bowed. Next came carts bearing the spoils of General Ostorius's campaigns, the ornaments, torques, and gold that Caratacus had acquired from other British tribes as tribute in peace and spoils in war. His brothers came next, followed by his wife and daughter. Finally, Caratacus himself was paraded before the wide-eyed Roman public. Yet, unlike the Celts who had gone before him, the British king held his head high, undaunted.

Claudius permitted his captive to deliver a speech, a plea for his life. But Caratacus didn't beg. Bravely, he stood by his right to defend his homeland. "Just because you Romans choose to lord it over the world," Tacitus records him saying to Claudius, "does it follow that the world has to accept slavery?"

The emperor spared Caratacus and his family. They would spend the rest of their days in Rome, under house arrest in one of the imperial mansions. Cassius Dio says that while being conducted on a later guided tour of the city, Caratacus asked why people with such magnificent possessions would want the humble tents of the Britons. On the day of their exhibition and pardon, once Caratacus and his family members had been released from their chains, they were required to kneel and pay homage before Claudius and his empress, Agrippina. Enjoying these proceedings from a royal enclosure were Claudius's twelve-year-old son Britannicus, and Agrippina's fourteen-year-old son, who had been adopted by Claudius and made his heir. Accompanied by Lucius Anneius Seneca, his tutor of the past three years, Agrippina's boy was wearing a full military uniform and the scarlet cloak of a general who'd been awarded a Triumph, just like the emperor. Only the previous year, Agrippina's son had been given the title Prince of the Youth of Rome. The young man had grown up with the name Lucius Domitius Ahenobarbus, but that was about to be changed, to recognize the fact that he was Claudius's adopted son and heir. In full, he became Nero Claudius Caesar Drusus Germanicus. Or, as history would know him, just plain Nero.

XXI

BOUDICCA
THE TERRORIST

A pattern of garrison duty had emerged for the youngsters of the A.D. 51 enlistment of the 14th Gemina Martia Victrix, men such as Legionaries Cordus, Vibennius, Flaminius, and Petronius. The Roman governors who immediately followed General Ostorius preferred to contain the Welsh tribes rather than go after them. There was just an occasional probe west during summer, with long months spent in permanent wooden barracks, meaning there were few opportunities for the glory or the booty the old-timers boasted of when they were sitting around in camp and talking nostalgically of past campaigns.

During this period the 14th's Marcus Petronius was promoted to standard-bearer, equivalent to a modern-day corporal. Standard-bearers also acted as bankers to the men of their subunits, keeping a record of their savings in liaison with the legion's camp prefect, who was paymaster and bank manager. A legionary didn't have much on which to spend his pay, booty, and bonuses. Some invested in local businesses. Others spent on whores. Some drank themselves poor when on leave. Others didn't have to leave camp to go broke, gambling away every penny on illegal dice games and distant chariot races.

Rome's race results were posted in camp when the latest handwritten copies of the *Acta Diurnia*, Rome's *Daily News*, arrived. Via the *Acta*, too, they learned that at noon on October 13, A.D. 54, Claudius had been pronounced dead at the Palatium and that seventeen-year-old Nero, grandson of the still revered Germanicus Caesar, had been proclaimed emperor. What they wouldn't have read was that Agrippina had poisoned Claudius so her son could become emperor. Nor would they have read over the next few years that while Nero's chief advisers, Seneca and Praetorian Prefect Afranius Burrus, steered Rome on a steady, progressive course, Nero's

198

mother had tried to control her son, even offering herself as his bed partner to manipulate him.

In A.D. 59, the men of the far-flung legion read that the emperor's
mother had been executed at Anzio by officers of the Tyrrhenian Fleet
after it was discovered that she'd sent an assassin to kill Nero. But the
legionaries heard the rumors that soon abounded, that Nero, determined
to marry Poppaea, attractive wife of his best friend, Marcus Otho, against
his mother's wishes, had arranged for Agrippina to be murdered to rid
himself of her interference. And that the guilt of his bloody deed had
begun to affect his mind.

At about the same time in A.D. 59 that Nero's mother died and lost an
empire, another woman, in Britain, lost a husband and became a queen.
She was the widow of Prasutagus, king of the Iceni tribe. Her Celtic name
was Boudicca—appropriately, it meant "Victory." The Romans called her
Boadicea.

Boudicca's tribe occupied modern Norfolk and part of Suffolk in the
East Anglia region of England, north of Colchester. Boudicca probably had
married Prasutagus in the late 40s A.D., after the Roman invasion. If she'd
wed in her early teens, as Roman women often did, she may have been
only in her twenties by A.D. 59. More probably, she was in her thirties.
Tacitus says she descended from noble ancestry. Either her father was
an Iceni noble or she came from the nobility of another tribe such as
the neighboring Trinovantes and was given in marriage to Prasutagus to
cement an intertribal alliance.

Boudicca had borne Prasutagus two daughters, who by A.D. 59 were still
not of marrying age, were virgins approaching teenagerhood. We don't
know Prasutagus's age or when he took the Iceni throne. Tacitus says that
by the time of his death, which was apparently due to natural causes, Prasutagus was famed for his long prosperity. A reign of twenty years or more
is not unlikely.

The Iceni were farmers, cultivating wheat and vegetable crops and
running livestock, including horses. As in Gaul and Germany, and just as
with the Plains Indians of North America in the nineteenth century,
a Briton's prestige and worth were tied up in the number of horses he
owned. In times past, too, each noble would have possessed a British-style
chariot, another symbol of his position in society.

Tacitus says that the Iceni didn't participate in resistance to the
A.D. 43 Roman invasion, neither fighting the Romans nor surrendering to

them. They later signed a treaty that gave the Iceni the status of Roman allies, although they weren't exempted from taxation, like some allied nations in Europe. Partial Iceni disarmament, including destruction of the tribe's war chariots, would have been a Roman treaty requirement.

The tribe enjoyed mostly amicable relations with the Roman authorities. As the price of peace they paid taxes and supplied young men to serve as auxiliaries in the Britannic cohorts of the Roman army. And instead of sending their boys to be trained by priests of the Celtic religious order, the Druids, as they had before the Romans came, the Iceni nobles now sent their older sons to train as Roman priests at the Temple of the Divine Claudius at Colchester. As a consequence, the tribe's east coast homeland was a peaceful backwater, with no Roman troops stationed in Iceni territory.

The Romans called the Iceni capital Venta Icenorum. It's the out-of-the-way village of Caister St. Edmunds today, just a few miles south of the city of Norwich, itself not settled until Saxon times. In A.D. 59, Caister's buildings would have been built from wood and mud. There would have been a forum with a weekly market and a Roman-style basilica, or meeting hall, and a small temple with an altar to the Roman counterparts of Celtic gods. Celtic religious habits, such as the maintenance of sacred groves and divining omens from rivers that were considered sacred, were officially discouraged.

Tacitus describes the home of the king of the Iceni as a villa, a country estate, which would have been on the best farmland outside Caister. It would have been built in the Roman style, with courtyards and a number of spacious wings plus stables and other outbuildings. Romans bathed every afternoon, commoners at public baths, the wealthy in baths in their own homes. Rigorous exercise was followed by a series of hot, warm, and cold baths. Dio indicates that cold baths were the norm for the hardy Iceni, of all ranks.

Boudicca would have grown up with servants around her, but no slaves. Tacitus complained that Britain's Celts had no interest in slaves, or in the monetary rewards to be gained from selling prisoners as slaves. Boudicca's clothes would have been ordinary by Roman standards, woolen for warmth in the harsh British winter. She had jewelry, of gold. She would have used toiletry articles—horsehair brushes made by her own people, other items imported from the Continent. The British were trading with France long before the Romans came on the scene. Now the British were also trading with Dutch and German tribes along the North Sea coast. Perhaps Boudicca used the face creams and perfumes of the East available, at a price, to any well-to-do Roman lady. But such feminine indulgences seem out of character with the Boudicca the Roman world would soon come to know.

Dio says Boudicca's hair was thick and tawny-colored, falling to her hips. Like all Celtic women, she let her hair grow long. Roman women went to great trouble to have their hair plaited and tied up in elaborate styles. The wealthier ladies had hairdressers on their staff and would spend hours every day on their coiffure. By comparison, Boudicca probably had maidservants who brushed her luxuriant long, reddish hair for her.

Most Iceni only saw Romans when the tax collectors made their annual visit in the summer, collecting a per-head poll tax and the death tax levied on the tribes, in gold and in grain, and when Roman army conquisitors came to assess young Iceni men for service as auxiliaries and to take recruits away. Otherwise, the Iceni were left alone.

The exception had been over the winter of A.D. 47–48. Lieutenant General Ostorius had only just arrived at Colchester to take up his appointment as Governor of Britain when a force of unidentified raiders broke into the territory of British tribes allied to Rome, knowing, says Tacitus, that the legions had gone into camp for the winter and that the new governor hadn't had a chance to familiarize himself with his command. After plundering farms and villages, the raiders had disappeared. General Ostorius wasn't sure which tribesmen were involved, but he had his suspicions. To show he wasn't to be messed with, he dispatched auxiliary units based at Colchester to disarm all the tribes of the region and to set up camps of occupation in every allied tribal area west to the Severn River and as far north as the Avon River. When young Iceni hotheads heard of Ostorius's heavy-handed order they sent messengers to surrounding tribes urging them to join the Iceni in armed resistance, naming an assembly point on their western border.

Tacitus says nothing about the king of the Iceni being involved in this. It seems that his young men took the action on themselves, against his advice. It also seems that as they rushed off to the congregation point, King Prasutagus sent a messenger south to Colchester to warn General Ostorius of what was taking place.

Determined to nip the revolt in the bud, the general didn't waste time summoning the legions from their camps on the western frontier, at least a week's march away. Collecting auxiliary units in the vicinity of Colchester, and putting his son Colonel Marius Ostorius "Scapula" in charge of his cavalry, he hurried north to the Iceni assembly point. It's clear that Ostorius had information that the revolutionaries numbered only a few thousand at most, and this convinced him he could handle the problem with auxiliaries alone. His force reached the rebel area undetected, and, leaving his troops a little way in the rear, Ostorius himself crept forward with scouts for a reconnaissance.

The general observed, says Tacitus, a tall bank of earth encompassing a large open area, reached by a narrow approach, with the surrounding countryside impenetrable to cavalry. Dikes of the Dutch kind were common in flat, low-lying Norfolk, with the Fens of western Norfolk then filled with hundreds of square miles of watery, boggy marshland. The rebels appear to have made their camp in the Fens, possibly at a place near Hilgay Fen called today Ten-Mile Bank. Returning to his troops, Ostorius made his dispositions, ordering the cavalry to dismount to fight on foot alongside the infantry.

On General Ostorius's signal a trumpet sounded and his troops splashed forward. The tribesmen, busy making weapons and ammunition, were taken by surprise. The auxiliaries climbed the sloping barrier's earth walls before the Britons had time to organize resistance. Only once the Roman troops were inside their camp did the warriors begin to put up a fight. Surrounded, many of the rebels refused to surrender or take a backward step, going down fighting, for which Tacitus was to commend them. At one point the Britons managed to launch a counterattack, their charge isolating the prefect of a cohort. Broad-shouldered young Colonel Marius Ostorius went to the rescue of his fellow colonel, an act for which he was to earn the highly prized Civic Crown on his father's recommendation, for saving the life of a fellow Roman citizen. We know it was a prefect he saved because the rank-and-file auxiliaries were all noncitizens.

We don't hear of reprisals being imposed on the Iceni for this short revolt. Survivors of the battle in the Fens would have been led away in chains to slavery, while King Prasutagus retained his throne. Now, aware of how tenuous his family's hold on power was, he made a will in the Roman fashion and deposited it with the priests at the Temple of Claudius at Colchester. In that will he left half his estate to the emperor, and half to his two daughters, in the hope of pleasing both the emperor and his family.

There was a basic problem with the terms of Prasutagus's last will and testament. Some British tribes, like the Iceni, were early women's liberationists, recognizing the rights of women. Celtic wives and daughters could inherit part of the estate of the deceased head of their household, and some tribes also allowed women to inherit their ancestral thrones. But under Roman law, while a woman could inherit the property of her mother or grandmother, she couldn't inherit the estate of her husband or father. At best, a Roman wife could expect to be refunded the dowry given to her husband by her family at the time of her wedding. So, under Roman law, the law now governing Roman Britain, King Prasutagus's will was invalid. That law said that without a male heir, a head of household's entire estate went automatically to the emperor. Prasutagus could have overcome the problem the same way many Romans did, by adopting a son and heir, in the way author Lew Wallace had his character Quintus Arrius adopt Judah ben Hur in his 1880 novel *Ben Hur*. Junius Gallio, elder brother of Seneca, Nero's chief secretary, had been adopted by Junius Gallio Sr. in this way; his original name had been Lucius Annaeus Novatus.

But, determined that his daughters should inherit his kingdom, the king of the Iceni wasn't prepared to adopt a male heir. It was a risky course, hoping that Nero would acknowledge his loyalty over the years and recognize the terms of his will; Augustus had set the precedent by, in special cases, allowing women to inherit from their menfolk. As it turned out, Nero may not have even had the opportunity to rule on the king's will.

It's likely that King Prasutagus died in the winter of A.D. 58–59, at a time when the province of Britain was without a governor. Two governors had succeeded General Ostorius—Didius Gallus for six years, and then, in A.D. 58, Quintus Veranius, who died in office the same year. Caught by suprise by Veranius's death, the Palatium scrambled to find a suitable replacement. They came up with the well-qualified Lieutenant General Gaius Suetonius Paulinus. A native of Fréjus, Roman Forum Julii, in southern France, General Paulinus was renowned for a crushing victory over Moors in Mauretania with a small force when Governor of Africa in A.D. 41–42. But in the many months between Veranius's death and his replacement's A.D. 59 arrival at Colchester, Britain was governed by the province's procurator, or chief financial administrator, Decianus Catus.

The name Catus can mean both wise and sly. This Catus was definitely not the former. King Prasutagus's will would have been opened in front of Procurator Catus, and he took a cold, hard financial administrator's view of it. The will was illegal; the king's property was now the emperor's. End of story. Following Prasutagus's funeral, Catus sent a party to take possession of the king's worldly goods.

Riding at the head of the party, carrying sidearms, were several legion centurions on attachment to the governor's staff, who exercised powers similar to our police today. They were followed by civil staff from the procurator's office, as many as two hundred of them, who would have been armed with wooden staffs. Catus's personnel were slaves. Men of Greek background were the usual choice for these gubernatorial staff positions, as the Greeks were considered the intellectuals of the Roman world. They went first to the late king's villa. There, Boudicca was stripped, then beaten with wooden rods, a traditional punishment for slaves that the procurator had the power to order. That Boudicca was punished indicates she had probably earlier defied an order to surrender her husband's property. The form of the punishment was designed to show that she was considered to only possess the status of a slave. For good measure, and apparently on their own authority, the procurator's men then raped Boudicca's two virgin daughters. After ransacking the house—as if its contents were the spoils of war, says Tacitus—they departed, no doubt using the king's own wagons to carry their plunder.

All the late king's male relatives were arrested, chained, and hauled away to be sold as slaves, to ensure that there could be no claimant to Prasutagus's throne. Remaining Iceni nobles were stripped of possessions that had been in their families for generations. When the procurator's men marched away, taking their prisoners and their loot, they left Boudicca and the Iceni in shock. As became clear from later events, in their wake, Boudicca, bleeding and outraged, clutched her violated daughters to her and made a vow to Andreste, Celtic goddess of war, to revenge herself, her family, and her people.

When Governor Paulinus arrived in Britain, the rape of the Iceni was a done deed. Tacitus indicates that Paulinus and Catus frequently argued, and perhaps the first argument broke out when the governor learned of his procurator's heavy-handed actions in East Anglia. But a tough, proud man, there was no way Paulinus could or would compensate the Iceni. The letter of the law had been observed. The fact that the servants of the law had exceeded their authority could not be corrected, for the Iceni were not Roman citizens, and without citizenship they had the same rights as slaves: none.

As General Paulinus turned his attention to subduing the tribes in Wales, the Iceni were forgotten. Now, like the Catuvellauni of Colchester, the Iceni were considered a subject people, not an allied tribe, without the right to their own leader. In the vacuum this created, Boudicca rose to the occasion. She called meetings of Iceni elders and told them of her vow to Andreste. The Iceni must wreak vengeance, she declared, and she was prepared to personally lead an uprising of the tribes of southern Britain that would utterly destroy the legions and throw the Romans out of Britain.

By her very physical stature she would have been a dominating presence, but that alone wouldn't have been enough to convince her people to go to war against the greatest military power on earth. Boudicca also had a fine tactical mind, and she shared a plan with her nobles designed to take advantage of the very way the legions worked. It would have been no secret that two of the four legions in Britain, the 9th Hispana and the 20th Valeria Victrix, were to undergo their twenty-year discharges the following year, A.D. 60, a year, coincidentally, when half of Rome's legions would reenlist. At markets throughout the region, tribesmen would have spoken of seeing the new enlistment of the 2nd Augusta arrive the previous year, remarking how green the fresh-faced recruits from the south of France looked as they marched through southern England to their bases in the west. The legionaries Britons were accustomed to seeing were mature, experienced soldiers, and many a budding British hero would have made a wine-soaked boast about how easy these new boy legionaries would be to cut down if the tribes had the will and the way. Here, said Boudicca, was the opportunity to turn boast into action. When the tough old soldiers of the two legions had left their legions, and their raw, untried replacements had barely pitched their tents in Britain, that was the time to strike.

The Iceni were excited. Not only would two of the four legions be reenlisting, but also, in the spring, General Plautius could be expected to lead his army on a campaign in the west as usual, leaving isolated auxiliary detachments in the east. If the tribes combined, they could sweep through England behind the governor's back and trap his legions between themselves and the Welsh. The Iceni had lost their possessions, their young men, their freedom. What else could they lose, apart from their lives? And what value was life without freedom? The Iceni voted to go to war, and elected Boudicca their war leader.

Invitations to join Boudicca and the Iceni in rising next spring went out to British tribes smarting at having to pay back a 40-million-sesterce personal loan from Chief Secretary Seneca, reputedly worth 300 million sesterces, who'd resorted to harsh repayment measures when he'd called in the loan early, says Dio. The Trinovantes, Iceni neighbors to the south, were the first to join Boudicca's rebel coalition. Soon, tribes throughout southern England were stockpiling wood, leather, iron, and bronze for arms manufacture. And to provide intelligence from in and around the governor's headquarters while the revolution was readied, Boudicca planted secret agents in Colchester.

But, Boudicca stressed, secrecy was imperative. According to Tacitus, the rebel leadership told the tribes: "We've already taken the most difficult step by starting to plan. In an enterprise like this there's more danger in being caught than in taking the plunge."

The tribes waited for Procurator Catus's tax collectors to pay their annual summer visit. Then, once Roman backs were turned and the wheat harvest was in, they began arming and training. They would not sow or reap in A.D. 60. Boudicca's strategic plan called for the seizure of government granaries at Colchester, the port of London, Roman Londinium, on the Thames, and the wealthy town of Verulamium, modern St. Albans, in Hertfordshire, north of London. This would permit the tribes, once the spring of A.D. 60 arrived, to ignore their fields and concentrate on arms and ammunition production.

A principal British weapon would be the war chariot. But, contrary to popular myth, Boudicca did not personally drive a chariot, nor did she possess a Roman-style chariot, like the one represented in the statue by Westminster Bridge near the Houses of Parliament in London today. Neither was the chariot she did use equipped with scything blades jutting from the wheels, like those of Middle Eastern kings. Boudicca did ride in a chariot, but one piloted by a driver who sat with his legs dangling over the open front. The rear also was open, and the sides were of wicker in a half-moon shape. Low and light, with wheels three feet across, British chariots were drawn by a pair of nimble ponies and were built for speed. Behind the driver stood a noble with an armory of light spears and a sword and shield. The British chariot was a mobile arms platform. As Julius Caesar had discovered, they were ideal for lightning dashes against legion formations, unleashing clouds of spears, and also could deliver their nobles to different hot spots in a battle, where they would jump down and fight on foot while their drivers waited nearby to speed them out of trouble if required.

How many chariots the tribes constructed in the arms buildup of A.D. 59–60 is not known, but the number probably was in the hundreds. Through the fall and winter, too, chariot crews trained, relearning old skills lost since the Roman invasion. As the spring of A.D. 60 approached, Boudicca and her war council listened to reports from their spies at Colchester with satisfaction. General Plautius had ordered logistical preparations to be made for a drive into North Wales in April, and over the winter the legions had been hard at work building small, flat-bottomed boats for the campaign. His new operation would involve the complete 14th Gemina Martia Victrix Legion, part of the 2nd Augusta, and a number of auxiliary infantry and cavalry units, including the 14th's Batavian consorts.

With Roman eyes fixed firmly on the west, the British rebel leaders made their final plans. Assembly points were agreed on. And the target for the first attack of the war was confirmed: a unanimous and popular choice, the symbolic and administrative heart of Roman occupation, the provincial capital, Colchester.

* * *

Colchester had grown into a handsome city since becoming the Roman capital of Britain fewer than seventeen years back. Now the former Catuvellauni capital boasted grand public buildings in stone: a fine local senate house; a public bathhouse; a theater in the Greek style where dramas, comedies, mimes, pantomimes, and musicals played to packed houses; and a massive colonnaded temple built to honor the late emperor Claudius, who, by decree of the Roman Senate, was now a god.

Like most Roman military colonies throughout the empire, Colchester was not surrounded by defensive walls. As Tacitus says, this was from a desire to do what was agreeable to Rome's local subjects rather than what was expedient. Colonies were located inside friendly territory, so, in theory, they had no need of defenses. Colonies were intended, not as symbols of occupation or domination, but as open communities that would blend into the local world, showcasing the benefits of cultivated and sophisticated Roman society. More than once, Roman colonists would pay the price for this policy of openness, a policy that rendered their hometowns defenseless.

The men of the 14th G.M.V.'s A.D. 51 discharge had made themselves at home at Colchester. Some had leased out their land grants—retired veterans weren't permitted to sell their grants for twenty years—and moved into the city, going into business, opening stores or taverns, becoming merchants or moneylenders. Other veterans came into town regularly from their farms, for the weekly market in the forum, for court sittings, for entertainment at the theater or chariot races and gladiatorial shows—the Senate at Rome permitted a set number of contests in each province annually. And they came for the religious festivals that occupied a third of the Roman calendar each year, festivals during which the former centurions of the 14th and legionaries awarded the top bravery decorations during their years in the legion led the processions in ceremonial dress.

Some of the veterans of the 14th had died by this stage, but upward of two thousand were living in and around Colchester. The youngest of them were around forty-nine in the spring of A.D. 60, while most of their second-enlistment colleagues were in their seventies. We know little of how the Evocati militia worked in peacetime, but like reserve units today, the veterans of the 14th G.M.V. probably had regular parades, and weapons drills to keep up their military skills. The cohort and maniple standards they'd marched behind while serving with the legion had come into retirement with them and were housed at an altar in the town's principal temple—in Colchester's case, the Temple of Claudius. The uniforms, weapons, and personal equipment they'd brought into retirement were stored at home, ready to be brought out in an emergency.

For the past nine years the retirees had led a quiet life. They'd married local British girls of the Catuvellauni, Trinovantes, and Iceni tribes and raised families, with none of their children being yet ten years of age. They'd enjoyed their postlegion days, with just an occasional hankering for the excitement of the past in hard-drinking reunions with their comrades. But the previous year, after the death of King Prasutagus of the Iceni and the lawlessness of Procurator Catus's men had set them an unsavory example, some of the veterans had found their old arrogance, and had made themselves unpopular with the locals by treating them no better than slaves. They were about to be repaid for their arrogance and unpleasantness.

In March, General Paulinus rode out of Colchester and headed west, to assemble the units allocated to the new year's campaign. After conducting the religious formalities of the Lustration Exercise, the purification of the legion standards that preceded every campaign, he invaded North Wales. The general left only a small auxiliary garrison back at Colchester's permanent military base, on the western outskirts of the city, most likely just a single cohort of infantry and a couple of squadrons of Thracian cavalry. We know from archaeological evidence that originally this fortified camp covered fifty acres. This was large enough to accommodate 12,500 men, which it would have done when much of the 20th V.V. and numerous auxiliary units had been based there. By A.D. 60 the camp had been scaled back with the transfer of units farther north and west. Within five years it would be closed altogether.

The absence of the governor had no impact on daily life at Colchester, which continued with its commercial bustle. Sometime after General Paulinus's departure for Wales, the city's statue of Victory, the winged Roman goddess based on the Greeks' Nike, one night tumbled from its pedestal in the town forum. It was found next day, face down on the paving stones and facing east. This was considered an ill omen by the townspeople, a portent of some dreadful event. But of what event, they could not know. The statue probably had been toppled by rebel agents in the town. Perhaps they were impatient for the uprising, or just intent on unsettling the highly superstitious Romans.

Finally, the day that Boudicca had been planning toward arrived, a day in the late spring of A.D. 60. The tribes would have waited until after an important Celtic fertility festival that took place in Britain at the beginning of May, turning it this year into a war festival. Dio says that when the tribes assembled, Boudicca used a form of Celtic divination, letting a hare escape from a fold of her gown. When the hare bounded off in an auspicious direction, this was a sign that the tribes could expect to be victorious.

"We have no fear of the Romans," Dio says Boudicca declared from an earthbank in the assembly area as she looked out over the massed warriors. "We'll show them that they are hares and foxes trying to rule over dogs and wolves!"

Full of confidence, the tribes marched on Colchester.

A bored, yawning auxiliary on sentry detail in a guard tower at the Colchester camp would have been the first to see signs that something was not right that morning, as smoke rose up from several different points on the northern horizon. Farmhouses of 14th G.M.V. veterans were going up in flames, strewn with the bodies of their occupants. Alerted by the guard centurion, the prefect commanding the Colchester garrison would have sent a cavalry detachment to investigate, and waited for their report. When the patrol failed to return, the colonel would have become worried. When the fields to the north and west began to darken with thousands of moving shapes generating a cloud of dust that rose into the hazy sky, he would have realized with sudden terror that his patrol wasn't coming back, and why. Ordering "To Arms" sounded, he sent men scurrying throughout the city and riders galloping to outlying farms to call the veterans of the Evocati militia to arms. And he ordered the camp's four gates closed.

The 14th G.M.V. retirees quickly grabbed their weapons and herded their families to the militia assembly point, the Temple of Claudius, a massive building on a rise that dominated the city and that Tacitus describes as a virtual citadel, there to form up behind their old legion standards, which were taken down from the altar. By the time the majority of veterans had assembled at the temple, thousands of civilians were milling around in their midst, in a state of panic and begging the militiamen to save them. By that time, the first elements of the army of the Britons had reached the city. Dio puts the number of rebel warriors following Boudicca at this early stage in the revolt at 120,000.

Boudicca would have established the priorities for the attack. The military camp was quickly surrounded and sealed off by one large group of warriors. Others went through the streets of Colchester, pulling down Roman statues, especially the statue of Marsyas, a naked figure bound to a column in the whipping position, a statue that stood in the Forum of

every Roman colony as a symbol of its autonomy. But most of all, the rampaging rebels were looking for blood, looking for Romans and their sympathizers. Civilians and militia latecomers were cut down wherever they
were encountered. Some rebels began looting stores and houses.

Arriving in her chariot, Boudicca was informed that the Roman militiamen were at the Temple of Claudius. She ordered it sealed off. At the
temple, the former first-rank centurions in charge would have planned to
force their way through the streets to the military camp and link up with
the garrison. But that would have left their families at the mercy of the
attackers. Deciding to make a stand where they were, the veterans began
to barricade themselves inside the temple.

The night sky above Colchester glowed orange. The buildings of the city
had been progressively plundered by the rampaging rebels during the day,
then set alight. Now, only the military camp and the Temple of Claudius
remained intact, still occupied by their defenders, and separated by flame
and smoke. The tribesmen erected their tents around Colchester, then
stood back, gleefully watching the city they hated burn fiercely.

As the Britons enjoyed the fiery show, the colonel in charge at the
camp was able to slip riders out the western gate in the darkness. Couriers
galloped south to London, where Procurator Catus was engaged in financial business. Others rode west for Wales and General Paulinus's campaigning army. Several rode hell for leather to the nearest legion station,
Longthorpe, rear base of the 9th Hispana Legion, to the north. Procurator
Catus was the first Roman official to receive news of the uprising, and
the first to react. From London, Catus sent two hundred men to aid the
defenders. Tacitus says they were without regular arms, suggesting these
were men from the procurator's own department, bailiffs, probably the
same men who had sparked this affair in the first place with the rape of
the Iceni, who were normally armed merely with wooden staffs. As soon
as these men were within sight of Colchester, the tribesmen gobbled them
up. The Britons probably didn't kill them all right away. As perpetrators of
the original crime against Boudicca and the Iceni, some would have been
reserved for special treatment.

For two days the 14th Gemina Martia Victrix veterans and the townspeople sheltering with them were surrounded at the Temple of Claudius,
without food, without water. Tacitus says the rebels were only interested

in plunder and slaughter and had neither the skill nor the desire to storm fortified positions. There would have been a few early attempts to break into the temple compound, but the tough old soldiers of the 14th G.M.V. stood firm and showered attackers with missiles, forcing them to withdraw.

Now, rebel fifth columnists inside the temple played their hand. We only know from Tacitus that the defenders were betrayed by British agents from within. These may have been townspeople who slipped out information. It's more likely the betrayers were priests of the temple, young men of the Iceni, whose parents, nobles of the tribe, had been deprived of their treasured possessions by Procurator Catus the previous year. Tacitus says the young British men who were chosen to serve as priests of the Claudian order were required to spend their personal fortunes on a religious cere-mony—probably public games to celebrate the inauguration of new mem-bers of the priesthood. Not surprisingly, new Iceni priests greatly resented this financial burden. These young men had every reason to want to revenge themselves on their foreign overlords, for their sakes and their families' sakes. Now opportunity knocked. With legion veterans holed up in their very temple, what better way to contribute to the Roman over-throw? The priests knew their temple intimately. If anyone was aware of the location of a secret entrance or entrances for the use of members of the priesthood only, they would have.

Now, two days into the siege, when Boudicca sent her tribesmen in a surprise attack, probably at night, they quickly stormed the defenses, prob-ably using entrances opened to them by priests. With the colonnades resounding to the screams of thousands of women and children cringing in the underground basement, which still exists today beneath the Nor-man castle built on the site, the temple fell. Overwhelmed by weight of numbers, doughty veterans from northern Italy, angry at betrayal by Britons they'd been protecting, threw down their weapons and surrendered, expect-ing to be treated as POWs.

Thousands of prisoners were taken, both militiamen and civilians. Now the Britons began exacting their vengeance on Romans and the Roman-ized Britons with them—native Britons who had chosen the Roman side and who were traitors in the eyes of the tribes. The worst traitors were local women who'd married retired Roman soldiers. And worst of all were those who'd married centurions.

As the temple was engulfed in flames, prisoners were led to the open expanse outside the military camp. What took place over the next few days was intended to be witnessed by the Roman auxiliaries in the camp. Tacitus says that some Roman prisoners suffered death by flame; others were hanged; others, crucified on wooden crosses the way the Romans executed slaves. Dio says that men and boys had their genitals cut off and thrust in their faces before the victims were boiled alive or impaled on red-hot skewers.

The fate of female prisoners was even worse. Dio says the Britons strung up the leading Roman women—the wives of retired centurions of the 14th G.M.V. would have been at the top of their list—then cut off their breasts and sewed them onto their mouths, to make the victims appear to be eating them. Not content with that, they then impaled the women on sharp skewers run lengthwise through the body.

These horrific tortures lasted for days, accompanied, says Dio, by sacrifices, banquets, and what he describes as wanton behavior—wild sex, it might be assumed—all in the name of Andate, Celtic goddess of victory. We don't know whether this barbarity was just a fun idea at the time or whether there was some genuine religious significance to it, just as the Germans grilled Roman officers over open flames after the Varus disaster of A.D. 9 as offerings to their gods. Human sacrifice did play a role in the religion of the Druids, but torture seems to have been for the gratification of the mobs, not the gods.

No one was spared. Children suffered the same fate as their parents. Tacitus commented on the stupidity of it all, quite apart from the barbarity. Anyone else would have retained prisoners, he said, to ransom them for gold, or to sell them to slave traders. But not the Britons. Boudicca's followers had embarked on an orgy of vengeance and destruction that transcended practical considerations. And they had only just begun.

Brigadier General Quintus Petillius Cerialis had only recently taken up his posting as commander of the 9th Hispana Legion, after spending more than a decade working his way up the promotional ladder through Rome's unique combined military and civil service ranks. Before this promotion he'd served as senior tribune, second in command, with another legion. It's probable that the previous year, when he'd entered the Senate, Cerialis had stood for election as a praetor and was one of three excellent candidates who, after failing to be elected, were compensated by Nero with legion commands.

Married to a cousin of Lieutenant General Vespasian, the Roman commander famous for conquering southern England with the 2nd Augusta in A.D. 43, thirty-one-year-old General Cerialis would have been eager to also make his name with a dashing victory. So when an exhausted courier reached him at his headquarters at Longthorpe on the Nene River, in the present-day county of Cambridgeshire, with an urgent request from the Colchester garrison for help, he didn't hesitate to order the assembly of a force that would march almost at once. He either wasn't informed of the size of the rebel forces, or he discounted the numbers and the threat the tribesmen posed. Cerialis, by one account a striking man with red hair and blue eyes, also had an impatient streak. He could have sent to General Plautius for orders, but as the general nearest to the scene of the uprising, Cerialis chose to act himself.

Longthorpe, near modern Peterborough, just to the west of the watery expanses of the Fens, was close by Ermine Street, the Roman military highway from London to the northern frontier and beyond, to Queen Cartimandua's realm of Brigantia. The 9th Hispana Legion's major permanent base at Longthorpe could house twenty-five hundred men, and it was here that young General Cerialis put together his relief force. Only days or weeks before, the latest enlistment of the 9th Hispana Legion had arrived in Britain from its recruiting ground in eastern Spain, and the unit's retiring veterans had left the island for land grants on the Rhine, probably using the same vessels of the Britannic Fleet that had brought the new enlistment to England. The recruits, youngsters with shiny new equipment and tired legs after marching through eastern Spain, over the Pyrenees, and through France to Boulogne, had barely completed basic weapons and formation training by the time the East Anglia emergency arose.

More than half the 9th Hispana's men were sitting in forts along the northern frontier. In his hurry, General Cerialis didn't even bother to send for the 1st Cohort of the legion, which normally accompanied the commander. His relief force comprised four cohorts of raw new 9th Hispana recruits, marching behind a cloth vexillum standard, plus some or all of his legion's 124 cavalrymen, and several squadrons of auxiliary cavalry. With two thousand heavy infantry and perhaps five hundred mounted troops, he set off at forced-march pace to travel the hundred miles to Colchester.

At best, the rider bringing General Cerialis the plea for help had taken fourteen hours to reach him, changing horses at outposts along the way. Taking several hours to assemble his troops, equipment, ammunition, food, and pack animals, the general would have set off in the middle of the afternoon of the second day of the Colchester siege. Without heavy baggage, the relief force could have made twenty-five miles a day by usual legion forced-march standards. Even so, by the time General Cerialis was into the second day of a four-day march, the Temple of Claudius at Colchester had already fallen.

The relief force tramped down the straight paved stretch of Ermine Street that the 9th Hispana recruits had marched up not long before, then swung hard left when they reached the Colchester road. As the relief column hurried east through Essex, Trinovantes locals on watch for Roman reinforcements would have kept them under surveillance all the way and sent messengers to Colchester to warn Boudicca that legionaries were coming. In response, tens of thousands of tribesmen stopped their victory celebrations and prepared a bloody greeting for the approaching Romans.

On the fourth day of their march, within an hour or two of Colchester, the relief column walked into a wall of screaming British warriors. On the rolling Essex countryside there was no opportunity for the legionaries to use the advantage of high ground. It appears that General Cerialis had no choice but to form an orbis, the legions' circular formation that the original draft of the 14th Legion had resorted to outside Atuatuca back in 54 B.C. Cerialis seems to have put the cavalry horses in the middle of the ring, ordering their riders to dismount and fight on foot. Surrounded by a sea of terrifying half-naked tribesmen sporting the heads of dead Romans on spears, the 9th's green Spanish youths went to pieces. Not in their units long enough to be instilled with the rigid discipline that made legions fighting machines, the young recruits became deaf to the orders of their experienced centurions. Many broke formation; others begged Britons for their lives. Only their centurions fought like soldiers, and with their entire force outnumbered twenty to one or more, they had no chance. The 9th Hispana recruits were progressively massacred.

As the defensive ring disintegrated around him, General Cerialis ordered his surviving cavalrymen to mount up. Bunched close together, hacking at uncovered British heads to left and right, and led by the young general, the riders drove their terrified horses through the British ranks. A number of them, including Cerialis, made it through, as the tribesmen surged over the remnants of the orbis behind them and annihilated the Spanish youths. Cerialis sent several troopers galloping south to London, carrying the news that two thousand men of the 9th Hispana Legion had been wiped out and that Cerialis himself was pushing on to Colchester to take command of whatever forces he found there.

General Cerialis and his troopers made it to Colchester. Probably approaching the capital's military camp at night, through fields littered with the gory corpses of men, women, and children the rebels had tortured and killed over the past few days, Cerialis identified himself to the terrified auxiliaries inside, and he and his men gained admittance through a gate that was quickly closed behind them. The Britons made no attempt to storm the camp, then or later. For now, General Cerialis was safe.

The riders whom Cerialis sent south succeeded in making it through to London. When Procurator Catus heard of the bloody fate of the men of the 9th Hispana relief force, and knowing how eager the rebels would be to lay hands on him in particular, he boarded a ship docked at London and ordered its master to get under way at once. Catus sailed the forty miles down the Thames to the North Sea and escaped to Gaul. It wasn't an inspiring act. All the merchants in the town followed his example, and before long not a single ship lay at London's normally bustling docks.

The east of England now lay open to Boudicca and her rebels.

XXII

LAST STAND ON
WATLING STREET

Lieutenant General Gaius Paulinus stepped from the small, flat-bottomed boat, scowled at the Roman troops lined up on the Welsh beach, and demanded to know what the men of the 14th Gemina Martia Victrix Legion thought they were doing.

Warriors of the Deceangli and Ordovice tribes had retreated ahead of the Roman advance without offering battle, but now, joined by the Insulae, the local population, they formed up on the southern shore of the island the Romans called Mona Insula, or Mona for short, the island of Anglesey just off the northwestern coast of Wales. The warriors waited in their clans, armed with shield and spear as the legionaries of the 14th G.M.V., the 2nd Augusta, and their auxiliary colleagues clambered from their small landing craft. Suddenly women came dashing through the assembled ranks of Welsh warriors, dressed all in black, their hair disheveled, waving burning firebrands and shrieking as if they were deranged. All around, Druid priests raised their hands to heaven and babbled pleas to their Celtic gods to bring the wrath of the heavens down on the heads of the invaders.

To the Roman troops, this was like a scene from hell. Dazzled, superstitious legionaries from northern Italy and southern France froze in their ranks, not even raising their shields to protect themselves as they watched with eyes wide. They'd heard this island was the home of heathen gods, and campfire tales of witches with supernatural powers and terrifying beasts lurking in the groves of Mona quickly filled their minds.

"The men are scared, General," a staff officer would have said. Maybe it was officer cadet Gnaeus Julius Agricola, who turned twenty on June 13 of this year. Born at Fréjus, Paulinus's hometown, Lieutenant Colonel Agricola had been taken under the general's wing and brought onto his personal staff that spring when he arrived in Britain for his first military posting. Agricola would command the 20th Valeria Victrix Legion in years to come, later returning to serve as governor of Britain for seven years. He also would become father-in-law of historian Tacitus, who describes what follows.

"Scared!" General Paulinus exploded. He strode out in front of the troops. "You mean to tell me your knees are knocking at the sight of a troop of frenzied women?" he called to them. "You? Men of the 14th Gemina? The 2nd Augusta? Scared of women?"

The legionaries laughed self-consciously, feeling suddenly ashamed. They began telling each other that there was nothing to be afraid of.

"Well, then?" Paulinus called. "What are you waiting for?"

"Come on, 14th Gemina!" yelled a standard-bearer, perhaps Standard-Bearer Marcus Petronius from Vicenza, before charging forward. Other standard-bearers followed suit, and then the entire legion surged past their commander in chief and charged the waiting tribesmen. The 2nd Augusta and auxiliaries swiftly followed.

Since marching into Wales in the spring of A.D. 60, General Paulinus had pushed all the way to the northwestern coast. Hardworking and sensible—in the judgment of his young aide Gnaeus Agricola—Paulinus also was ambitious. He had come to Britain in A.D. 59 with a big military reputation, popularity in Rome, and something to prove. As a young major general seventeen years earlier he'd cleared Mauretania of raiding Moors in a swift, bloodily effective campaign, and Tacitus says he was determined to use his new posting to challenge Field Marshal Domitius Corbulo, who had just recovered Armenia for Rome in the East, for the mantle of the empire's leading soldier.

To achieve his goal, Paulinus had to complete the conquest of Britain, just as his predecessor Quintus Veranius had hoped to do before he died in the middle of his first campaign. As he lay dying of natural causes, General Veranius had dictated his will, in which he'd lamented that if he'd lived another two years he would have overrun all of Britain for the emperor Nero. Paulinus knew it wouldn't be as easy as that. An essentially cautious, pragmatic, methodical man, like his rival Corbulo, Paulinus wasn't targeting British war leaders; he was going after the Druidic priesthood. Paulinus knew that there was one unifying strand running through the disparate tribes of England and Wales: the order of the Druids, who served the Celtic gods. All the tribes of Gaul and Britain appealed to the same Celtic gods to give them the power to defeat their enemies. Before the Romans came, the children of British nobles had been educated by

Druid priests, and many themselves became priests, while others went on to lead their tribes. The Druids were the lawgivers, recognized by the tribes as the final arbiters in the settlement of intertribal disputes, and this gave them great power and influence. To curb this seditious power, Augustus had made it illegal for Roman citizens to follow the Druidic religion. Claudius had gone a step farther and banned citizens and noncitizens alike throughout the empire from involvement with the order.

No longer could the British tribes send their young men to be educated by Druids, no longer could Gauls make pilgrimages to the sacred island of Anglesey, the order's spiritual home. Julius Caesar says Druidism was believed to have originated in Britain, and anyone in Gaul who wanted to make a profound study of the cult had gone there. Despite the imperial edicts, the Druids continued to strongly influence British tribes, with the priests encouraging the fight for independence and giving leading resistance fighters sanctuary on Anglesey. General Paulinus's A.D. 60 campaign was designed to seize the island and snuff out the Druidic fire at the heart of British resistance.

All through the winter the men of the 14th G.M.V. had been busy building boats to General Paulinus's design—small, flat-bottomed craft for river and in-shore work. These were carried in the task force's baggage train and unloaded each time they came to a river in their progress up through North Wales. As their jumping-off point they used the new legion base at Chester, Roman Castra Devana, or Deva, as it was soon known. After that there were several major waterways to cross—first the Dee, and later the Clwyd and the Conway. The task force that reached the narrow Menai Strait that spring launched its small boats once more and began the crossing to the island of Anglesey.

Although the strait is broader at its southern end, the sandbars here made for a much better landing place than the steep shore facing the shorter crossing to the north, opposite modern Bangor. General Paulinus's task force made the crossing in several places, the infantry rowing themselves across first, while some cavalry units searched out a shallow ford, and the squadrons of the Batavian Horse swam across with their horses.

Now, without waiting for the cavalry to join them, the men of the 14th G.M.V. charged forward after their initial hesitation on the beach and cut down the Welsh—warriors, witches, and priests alike. Traditionally, the people of Anglesey have always called the countryside that runs down to the strait from Porthamel Hall opposite Caernarvon the Fields of Blood, but there's no telling whether this was because it was the site of the 14th G.M.V.'s landing and the subsequent short, sharp, bloody battle.

Despite the pleas of the Druids, the gods of the Celts failed to come to the aid of their followers. Tacitus says that piles of British bodies were soon being consumed in the flames of funeral pyres lit by their own fire-brands. Roman troops ranged from one end of Anglesey to the other, capturing the rest of the priests and the island's population, and searching for the sacred groves of the Druids. They found the altars at the center of these forest clearings bathed in dried blood. Prisoners told them it was human blood, that it was the duty of the Druids to conduct human sacri-fices and to divine the future of their people by examining the entrails of human victims. The Romans were appalled. After all, they merely con-sulted the entrails of sacrificed animals to determine omens for the future!

Anglesey had been taken without a single Roman casualty. As General Paulinus was congratulating himself on his success and composing a report to Rome about the operation, a party of dirty, exhausted cavalrymen arrived from the mainland bearing an urgent dispatch. These were the messengers from the garrison commander at Colchester. How quickly the general's mood would have changed as he read the dispatch, then ques-tioned the troopers about the events of the first day of the rebel assault on his capital. He then summoned his senior officers to a council of war.

As his worried officers gathered around him in his *praetorium* tent, a grave General Paulinus told them what had taken place in the east and issued his marching orders. Everything points to his task force's three or four cohorts of the 2nd Augusta Legion being led by the legion's unnamed brigadier general and his deputy, a senior tribune. General Paulinus appar-ently left the two 2nd Augusta officers in charge on Anglesey. From Tac-itus we know that the Anglesey commander's orders were to garrison the island and prevent the tribes from reoccupying it, and to destroy the sacred groves and eliminate all traces of Druidism. To accomplish this task the brigadier general was given the men of his own legion and four cohorts of the 14th G.M.V.'s Batavian light infantry under prefects including Julius Civilis, plus a detachment of cavalry.

It's probable that at this stage General Paulinus didn't realize the scope of the rebel uprising in the east. If he had, every soldier he possessed would have marched with him. Taking the 14th G.M.V. Legion, the remaining four Batavian cohorts, and two cavalry wings, Paulinus recrossed the Menai Strait. At the same time he sent couriers galloping ahead. He sent to Col-chester to say he was on his way. He sent to Procurator Catus at London with a similar message, unaware that Catus had fled the province.

Another message, reaching Paulinus as he hurried through North Wales, revealed the fate of General Cerialis's 9th Hispana cohorts. How he must have cursed Cerialis, maybe using a Greek proverb popular in the past with the emperor Augustus: "Give me a safe commander, not a rash one." Realizing for the first time the full extent of the revolt, Paulinus dictated a flurry of orders for dispatch riders to take away. One dispatch was for the commander of the 20th Valeria Victrix Legion at Gloucester. Paulinus had allowed the 20th V.V. veterans being discharged this year to go into retirement a few months before, without waiting for their replacements to arrive. Those new 20th V.V. recruits were still somewhere between Britain and their recruiting ground in the Liguria and Transpadini regions of northwestern Italy. Perhaps storms on the English Channel had prevented them from sailing. Whatever the cause, the recruits had yet to reach their legion, which now consisted of just a few second-enlistment cohorts sitting in forts facing the fierce and as yet unsubdued Silures of South Wales. General Paulinus couldn't afford to pull those troops out of their garrisons; if the Silures were allowed to flood out of Wales behind his back he would be in real trouble.

Fortunately for Paulinus, while a thousand to fifteen hundred retiring men of the 20th V.V. had left Britain for retirement along the Rhine, two thousand had been given land grants in the west of England. Now the commander at Gloucester was ordered to round up the local veterans and send them marching behind their Evocati standards to meet Paulinus outside London. Paulinus would have consoled himself that at least these were mostly forty-year-old men who were still fit, had two decades of legion experience, hadn't lost their feel for military discipline, and wouldn't fold under pressure like rash young General Cerialis's raw 9th Hispana recruits.

The general also sent a dispatch to Exeter, to the officer in charge at the 2nd Augusta's headquarters, the legion's camp prefect, Major Poenius Postumus. The major was the youngest member of his family, and a native of the legion colony at Carthage in Africa initiated by Julius Caesar. And, as it turned out, he also was a coward. By the time he received the dispatch, Major Postumus also would have received reports from the east describing the rebel uprising in lurid detail. One of those reports, repeated by Cassius Dio, put the number of tribesmen now participating in the revolt at 230,000. When the major read General Paulinus's dispatch, he found himself being ordered to march with the 2nd Augusta's remaining cohorts to link up with the governor's main force outside London and take on the rebels. Major Postumus, a former first-rank centurion with a long career with the legions, burned the orders and pretended he'd never received them.

Out of Wales from the northwest, General Paulinus's task force came marching at the double, heading across country for Chester and then joining Watling Street, the stone-paved, cambered, drained Roman *via mili-taris* or military road that sliced across England all the way to London and the Thames. We don't know what the Romans called the road, as the name Watling Street was applied to it by later Anglo-Saxon settlers. The Roman military roads in Britain, principally Watling Street, Fosse Way, and Ermine Street, had been constructed to give a firm footing to legions on the move, so they could march rapidly from one part of the province to the other in all weather. Watling Street, carving through the English countryside straight and true, was so well sited that today its course from London to North Wales is still followed by the A5 highway.

Traveling light, without artillery, siege equipment, or the boats they'd taken into Wales, the 14th G.M.V. made record time on the march south. On Watling Street, they were met by the hastily recalled veterans of the 20th V.V. Legion—several cohorts, a total of two thousand men, marching behind their Evocati standards. Combined with the 14th G.M.V., which was close to full strength with a little over five thousand men, plus two thousand Batavian auxiliary infantry and a thousand cavalry, General Paulinus's force now numbered ten thousand fighting men, says Tacitus. The little army marched on, toward London. At the Ver River they passed through the town of St. Albans, which was in turmoil. The terrified Roman population there told General Paulinus that the rebels were now rampaging through Essex not far to the east and drawing other tribes from throughout southern England into their rebellion. They told him the rebel army had mushroomed to a quarter of a million men. Paulinus pressed on to London. When the general reached the Thames, he found that city in chaos, too.

London had grown out of the A.D. 43 forts of the 14th G.M.V. and the other legions that had camped beside the Thames following their landing in Kent. A wooden bridge had soon been built across the river by Roman engineers where the modern London Bridge stands today, and a settlement quickly blossomed on the northern side of the river opposite the bridge. Today's Gracechurch Street leads from the original Roman bridge site up to Cornhill, where the hub of the settlement lay. The Bank of England today occupies pretty much the center of Roman London, which by A.D. 60 had spread as far west as the hill where St. Paul's Cathedral now stands. At the site of the present-day Leadenhall Market on Gracechurch Street, a stone's throw from Lloyd's of London, the Romans built their basilica, the town's multipurpose meeting hall. On the eastern side of London Bridge the riverbank was lined with docks, which normally were crowded with trading vessels from Gaul and the Rhine. Even though the city had not been granted colony status, it had quickly attracted settlers,

merchants, and shipowners, and in the seventeen years since its foundation had become the main trading center of Britain.

When General Paulinus arrived at London from the northwest, the
docks were eerily deserted. All the merchants who could flee to the Continent had done so and put the rebellion at their back. Certain that the
governor would save them, most of the common people had stayed in
London in expectation of the arrival of the legions. Now they flocked
around Paulinus as his weary column filed into the city, urging him to put
his soldiers to work preparing defenses for the city, which, like Colchester,
had no walls. It had a small fort in the northwest, but London's first walls
wouldn't be built until a century later.

The general and his staff did a quick survey of the settlement. All
agreed that even when the men of the 2nd Augusta joined them it would
be impossible to defend London with the few troops at their disposal. And
the example of young General Cerialis was fresh in their minds. His
underestimation of the enemy had cost Rome several thousand men. Tacitus says that General Paulinus decided to sacrifice a town to save a
province. The people of London begged him to stay, but the general's
mind was made up. He sternly shook his head, offering a place in his column to anyone who wanted to leave. But that was all he was prepared to
do. Many tearfully accepted his offer, and as the 14th G.M.V.'s trumpets
sounded "Prepare to March," instant refugees bundled up those few
belongings they could carry and ran to fall in behind the soldiers. Others
remained in the city—women, the aged, people who couldn't bear to
leave their businesses or who refused to believe the atrocity stories that
were circulating. These local Celts and settlers from Gaul all hoped
Boudicca and her followers would do them no harm. After all, they would
have rationalized, they had never personally done harm to the Iceni or
their fellow Britons.

As General Paulinus pulled out of London and retraced his steps up
Watling Street, he would have anxiously sent cavalry scouts southwest to
find the approaching 2nd Augusta column and guide it to him. He quickly
passed through St. Albans again. As he had at London, he refused any
attempt to defend the town. Accepting frightened townspeople into his
train, he abandoned St. Albans and continued his withdrawal.

Back at London, shortly after the Roman column departed, Boudicca
and tens of thousands of Iceni, Trinovantes, and warriors from other tribes
who had joined their ranks descended on the city like a plague of rodents.
The rebel army had continued to grow with each passing day, as more
tribesmen arrived to join the uprising after hearing of the destruction of

Colchester. The rebels even brought their wives with them, in a baggage train of wagons and carts for booty, a train that stretched to the horizon.

None of the civilians who'd remained in London were spared, despite their pleas for mercy or pledges of allegiance to the cause of British independence or offers to support the rebels. Anyone in a Roman city was considered a collaborator—the tribesmen tortured and killed every soul they found, men, women, children, in another orgy of revenge, religious ritual, and personal pleasure-taking. They looted the city. And then they burned London to the ground. Charred remains from that fire have been found during building work and archaeological digs to this day. Once they had glutted themselves on all the pleasures and treasures that London had to offer, the rebels turned north. Following the retreating Roman troops up Watling Street, they fell on St. Albans and spent a day or two doing to it what they had done to London and Colchester, leaving it another smoking ruin strewn with mangled corpses.

In little more than a week, Boudicca and her followers had destroyed the three main Roman settlements in Britain. According to Tacitus, in the process they had killed seventy thousand Roman citizens and allies. Dio would put it at eighty thousand. Tacitus was to liken the Britons' killing frenzy to a man seeking vengeance for his own imminent execution.

As the tribes resumed a lumbering pursuit up Watling Street, cautious General Paulinus retreated farther and farther. Still there was no sign of the 2nd Augusta cohorts. By the time the general reached Warwickshire, it had dawned on him that these reinforcements weren't coming. As his officers urged him to send more messages to Exeter and to summon the garrison troops from the northern and western frontiers, he realized that there was no point in delaying the inevitable any longer. Within a day he would be at the Welsh frontier, and the rebels behind him would be in possession of virtually all of Roman Britain in the wake of his withdrawal. In a few weeks he would have gone from victor at Anglesey to the man who had lost an entire province. It was time to make a stand. General Paulinus called a halt to the retreat.

The exact Watling Street location of the confrontation between Paulinus and Boudicca is disputed. Some historians suggest it was near the present-day village of Fenny Stratford in Bedfordshire, not far north of St. Albans. Others believe it was where Watling Street dissects the Anker River in the vicinity of Mancetter, on the present-day Warwickshire/ Leicestershire border. The former site seems too close to St. Albans. The latter, fifty-five miles farther north, is not far from the Welsh border, and it's easy to imagine General Paulinus finally, resignedly stopping the retreat, with Wales, and enemy territory, just another day's march away. One more night on the run and there'd be nothing left to defend. Besides, the town of Mancetter, near the Anker River site, grew from a later settlement the Romans called Manduessedum—"Place of War Chariots."

Sending the thousands of civilians who'd been traveling with his column ahead to the fortress at Wall, just fifteen miles up the straight, paved highway, and probably also to Wroxeter a little farther on, General Paulinus decided to choose a place to face the barbarians and do battle, despite the huge odds against him. Better to die fighting and preserve a little honor than to keep running. With a strong cavalry screen in position some distance down Watling Street to give plenty of warning of the approach of the huge, slow-moving British column, General Paulinus and his staff rode around the local area while their legionaries built a camp for the night and the auxiliaries went foraging. Beside the Anker River, on the southern side of Watling Street, General Paulinus chose a battle site that would enable the Roman troops to take full advantage of the landscape. Tacitus tells us the location was approached by a narrow pass though the hills, closed in at the rear by a forest, and opening out onto a plain.

Boudicca and her army came up Watling Street, drawn on by the retreating Roman cavalry, and camped not far from the site chosen by Paulinus for the battle. Next morning, only after he had sent his cavalry out and made sure that not a single enemy warrior was in his rear, General Paulinus gave orders for his troops to form up for battle at the chosen place. The Britons would have laughed among themselves as they watched the Romans silently march out in their neat ranks behind their standards, assuring each other that the puny force would be swiftly annihilated, just like the cohorts of the 9th Hispana outside Colchester.

According to Tacitus, Paulinus placed the 14th G.M.V. Legion at the head of the defile in close order, facing the plain, with the veteran cohorts of the 20th V.V. joined with them. According to Dio, the Roman forces were in three divisions. Tacitus describes the 14th and the veterans of the 20th in one large group in close array in the center, with the auxiliary cohorts beside them, while the cavalry squadrons were equally divided on each wing, again in tight formation.

As the tribesmen massed expectantly for the battle, their wives came up in their booty-laden wagons and parked in a huge semicircle behind them, to watch the fun. Estimates of the number of warriors involved vary. By this battle, says Dio, the British war queen's forces had grown to 230,000 fighting men—odds of 23 to 1. Even if it was only the 120,000 he'd given her earlier in the revolt, the Roman troops were outnumbered

12 to 1. The warriors formed up in loose order in front of the wagons, separated into the clans of blood-related men in which the Britons, Gauls,
and Germans traditionally fought, which in turn were grouped by tribe.
Each clan was commanded by a leader, sometimes hereditary, sometimes
elected. The average British warrior was about the same size as the typical
legionary, and naked to the waist. In Caesar's time some had fought buck
naked. Many had painted their skins with woad in designs like Maori tattoos, but that custom had died out in southern Britain with the Romanization of the island.

The principal armament of the warrior was the spear, like the Roman
pilum, with stone, bone, or metal points. Each warrior carried a massive
shield, longer than the legionary counterpart. It was flat, rectangular, but
with curved corners, made of oak planks covered with hide, roughly five
inches thick at the center, thinner at the edges. The nobles of each tribe
were better equipped, and would have armed themselves with the armor
and swords of the 14th G.M.V. veterans who died at Colchester and of the
officers and men of the 9th Hispana who fell outside the town. The tribes
also had the famous British chariot in their arsenal. In design and purpose
it hadn't changed since Caesar first encountered it in 55 B.C. Back then,
four thousand chariots had been put into the field against him. How many
chariots were now in Boudicca's force we can only guess. In the time
available perhaps they'd been able to produce several hundred. There
were some British cavalrymen, too, using their own and captured Roman
mounts, and as they formed up on the wings in Roman fashion the chariots would have raced up and down in front of the massed infantry, their
drivers seated, a noble standing behind each brandishing spears, cursing
the Romans, and inciting their countrymen.

Boudicca appeared, in a chariot, her waist-length, red-brown hair flowing behind her like a cape. Her people cheered as, with her two defiled
daughters sitting or kneeling in front of her, the war queen cantered from
tribe to tribe, delivering a prebattle speech to her warriors. Folk tales would
come down through the ages that Boudicca's daughters had sliced off their
own breasts in protest at their rape by the Romans, or that the Romans
had done the evil deed to them. But these anecdotes grew out of Dio's
account of the atrocities inflicted on female Roman captives by the Britons.

The warriors fell silent as the queen's chariot drew to a halt in front of
them. According to Dio, she wore a multicolored tunic; a thick robe over
her shoulder was secured in place by a brooch. There was a large golden
necklace around her neck. And, Dio says, the tall woman shook a spear as
she addressed her warriors in a harsh voice and with a fierce, frightening

look in her eye. "I know it's unusual for Britons to fight under a woman's leadership," Tacitus says she called. "But forget that I am a woman or the member of a royal family. Now I am one of you, regaining my freedom, avenging my scourged body and the lost chastity of my daughters." As the massive crowd yelled its angry accord, she went on: "The gods are on the side of a righteous vengeance. In this battle you must conquer or die! This is a woman's resolve. As for you men, you can choose to live, and be slaves, if you wish."

A roar went up from the tribesmen. As the air filled with yells, chanting, and singing, across the field General Paulinus also was addressing his troops, riding from cohort to cohort with his staff. He had seen the wagons laden with booty across the plain, and so had his men. Now he applied a little psychology. Signaling total confidence in his troops' ability to win, Tacitus says he urged them to think about fighting, not looting. "That will come in due course," he went on. "First secure the victory. The enemy you see before you are more like women than warriors. Go forward, to the business of bloodshed and destruction, and win fame normally only accorded an entire army."

According to Dio, the general said to one unit, "It would be better for us to fall fighting bravely than to be captured and impaled." To another he said, "You've heard what atrocities these despicable Britons have committed against us." Among the troopers on one wing he'd spotted the men who'd brought him the first news of the revolt from Colchester. He nodded to them. "Some among you have witnessed those atrocities. It's your choice. All of you. Do you want to suffer the same treatment as our comrades? Or, by conquering, do you want to avenge those who've been killed, and at the same time set the rest of the world an example?"

With the cheers of his men ringing in his ears now, General Paulinus took his place between the lines with his staff. One of his officers, teenaged Lieutenant Colonel Agricola, would years later tell his son-in-law Tacitus that he and his comrades felt they had to fight for their lives before they thought about victory that day. But Paulinus seems confident he had what it took to win—the chosen ground, the tactics, the men for the job.

Those men included twenty-nine-year-old Standard-Bearer Marcus Petronius. Standing behind the 14th Legion's front line, with his bearskin cape of office over his helmet and shoulders, and with a small oval shield strapped to his left arm, Petronius held his standard high with two hands. The standard's bottom end was sharpened, so Petronius could jam it into the ground to make a stand and defend it with his life, or jam it into an enemy as a last resort. Petronius would have heard about Eagle-Bearer Calpurnius of the 1st Legion, famous for saving Senator Plancus's neck in Germanicus's Rhine camp in A.D. 14; Calpurnius had complained that during the Battle of Long Bridges against Hermann the ground had been too soggy for him to plant his standard and defend it with his sword. Here, today, the Anker plain in front of the 14th Gemina was firm and dry, solid enough for Petronius to plant his standard if worse came to worst. In the 14th's ranks behind Standard-Bearer Petronius stood Legionary Titus Flaminius as well as thirty-one-year-old legionary Lucius Naevius from Turin, and a little distance away, twenty-nine year-old Legionary Publius Cordus from Modena, with his best friend, Gaius Vibennius, right behind him, all thinking about home and loved ones, and offering a silent prayer to their gods.

Across the field, with a wave of her arm, Boudicca sent her chariots forward. Then she gave the infantry the signal to advance. British horns sounded, and, with a roar, the sea of warriors washed forward at the rapid walk in the chariots' wake. Boudicca had just launched the largest battle that would ever be fought on British soil. The noise from the mass of approaching Britons was deafening to the ears of the waiting men of the 14th.

"Stand your ground!" bellowed the centurions of the 14th. And instead of advancing to the attack, the men of their cohorts stood stock still. General Paulinus was deliberately keeping all his troops stationary, waiting for the enemy to come to him. While the legionaries occupied the foot of the hill pass it would be difficult for the Britons to maneuver around behind them.

Once the chariots had completed their missile pass, and with the British infantry breaking into a run as they came on, Paulinus gave an order. Trumpets blared. With drilled precision, the Roman troops moved into three large wedge formations, point to the fore, with the 14th G.M.V. wedge in the middle and the 20th V.V. and Batavians on either side. General Paulinus's standard dropped. Again trumpets sounded. "Advance!"

With a cheer, the three tightly knit wedges strode forward, and met the mass of oncoming warriors on the move. The wedge was just one of a number of formations that legionaries were trained to use. But on the receiving end, the Britons had never come across anything like it, and they didn't know how to counter it. With shields pumping in and out and swords slashing and jabbing over the top, the Roman wedges were like giant threshing machines, breaking up opposition lines and chewing up divided groups of men.

At the same time, the Roman cavalry went charging down the wings. The troopers were under orders to hold onto their javelins and use them as lances, moving into close quarters and thrusting them into the faces of the Britons. Riding down all who stood in their way, they closed off the flanks, hemming in the tribesmen. To many a cavalryman, such as Trooper Genialis from Frisia, it would have been like herding sheep.

In the face of the advancing wedges the bravest of the tribesmen tried to hold their ground. Britons were able to spear an infantryman here, to drag a cavalryman from his horse there, but, disoriented and unnerved by the unstoppable Roman wedges, the vast majority of warriors at the front of the sea of Britons tried to turn away, pressing into the men coming up behind them. The tribes' very numbers now told against them, as the turning tide at the front compressed against the huge mass pushing forward from the rear. There was no organization in the British ranks. This was no army, just a seething, uncoordinated crowd of humanity. Without leadership, training, or discipline, panic set in. Tribesmen began to break in terror, trying to escape, as, all the while, others farther to the rear strove to keep them going forward. Thousands were trampled by their own men.

On the flanks, the Roman cavalry bore in. Up front, the threshing machine came relentlessly, bloodily on. More and more warriors threw away their cumbersome shields and pushed back the way they had come. Even the most courageous Britons that day couldn't resist the tide of terror and were caught up in the crush toward the rear, a crush that met the semicircle of wagons, which acted like a prison wall. Tens of thousands of Britons were trapped, and fell victim to the legionary killing machine as it pressed all the way to the wagons, walking over a field of dead. The slaughter was terrible. And it wasn't confined to the warriors. Women with the wagons, desperately trying to disengage themselves from the turmoil, yet hell-bent on preserving their loot, also were cut down. Everywhere, too, lay their horses, drilled with Roman javelins.

It was over within an hour or two, as long as it took the men of the 14th Gemina Martia Victrix and their colleagues to kill seventy thousand British warriors and ten thousand of their women. Dio says that many Britons also were taken prisoner. Boudicca, seeing the day lost before her eyes, seeing the massacre, seeing once-boastful men discarding their weapons and fleeing, terrified, in their thousands, into the forest with Roman troops in hot pursuit, turned her chariot around, and with her daughters clinging on, urged the driver to speed them away from the site of the disaster.

The battlefield was littered with British dead. As Roman troops went from body to body, delivering the coup de grâce to severely wounded warriors and stripping the corpses of their weapons and valuables, General Paulinus was brought a report on Roman casualties. According to Tacitus, the combined total was four hundred dead among the 14th G.M.V., 20th V.V. militia, Batavians, and cavalry, with a similar number wounded.

According to Tacitus, too, Boudicca took poison following the British defeat on Watling Street, a battle that was never given a name by the Romans or by later British historians. Dio says that Boudicca's people gave her a costly funeral and that the tribes mourned her deeply. Ironically, the Boudicca statue on London's Thames Embankment today celebrates the woman who destroyed London. Her revolt had lasted only weeks. It had been, perhaps, what the Romans called "a senseless thunderbolt."

As British survivors of the Battle of Watling Street scattered back to their farms and villages, news of the Roman victory spread throughout the island, and beyond. When Camp Prefect Postumus of the 2nd Augusta Legion at Exeter learned of the victory, rather than face the wrath of General Paulinus, a court-martial, and an inevitable death sentence for disobeying orders, he took his own life, falling on his sword in the camp.

At Rome, the news of the victory on Watling Street was greeted with amazement and excitement by the general public as people realized how close the empire had come to losing Britain, and how a single legion had fought impossible odds to claim one of the most famous victories in Roman history. Overnight, from the markets to the baths, from the taverns to the crowds clustered around city notice boards and reading the Acta Diurnia, all talk was of the incredible bravery of the 14th Gemina Martia Victrix Legion. The 14th Gemina, as it became popularly known, was overnight the most famous legion of Rome. General Paulinus's 14th, people said, was braver than Caesar's legendary 10th or the famous 5th, the legion that had taken on Scipio's elephants at Thapsus.

Sensing the popular mood, the emperor Nero joined in the adulation by, Tacitus says, announcing that the 14th Gemina would henceforth be known as his "most effective" legion. Even Rome's enemies came to hear of how a single Roman legion had destroyed an army of 230,000. For centuries to come, the 14th Gemina would be known as "Conqueror of Britain." It was a reputation they were to carry proudly, even haughtily, a reputation that encouraged the men of future enlistments to stand their ground when others might have run as the going got tough, knowing that the clinging shame of Atuatuca had finally given way to everlasting fame.

But there was still work to be done. General Paulinus was determined to ensure that never again would there be a revolt by the tribes of southern Britain. After permitting his troops to claim the contents of the tribes' booty train as their own spoils, he marched the 14th Gemina east to clean up the mess left by the rebels. At Colchester, as tribesmen left on guard fled in all directions, Paulinus found a chastened General Cerialis and his auxiliary and cavalry companions, still sheltering behind the walls of the capital's military camp beside the blackened ruins of the city; Tacitus says they remained in the camp during the Watling Street battle. Before long, Cerialis was recalled to Rome.

General Paulinus took the British revolt personally. He probably felt responsible for all the death and destruction served up by the rebels, criticizing himself for not taking more precautions, for not being on his guard. From prisoners interrogated under torture he would have compiled a list of names of leading rebels who'd succeeded in fleeing the Watling Street battlefield. Tacitus says that many of the rebels didn't lay down their weapons after their escape, being conscious of their guilt and dreading what the avenging governor might do. They knew they were on Paulinus's blacklist.

Nero's Palatium moved quickly to make up for the military losses of the revolt and to bolster General Paulinus's efforts to keep a lid on the British province. While Paulinus himself recalled the troops he'd left on Anglesey, eight cohorts of auxiliary light infantry and a thousand cavalry were immediately dispatched to Britain from the Rhine. Tacitus says that two thousand legionaries also were sent to Britain from the Rhine. They came to join the 9th Hispana Legion and bring it back to full strength, a highly unusual step for any Palatium, but one required by highly unusual circumstances. These men were new recruits who'd just arrived on the upper Rhine from Spain to join the 21st Rapax Legion. Like the 9th, the 21st was a Spanish legion, with a similar recruiting ground. It underwent its reenlistment at the same time, making it the ideal source of replacements. As later events were to prove, fresh recruits weren't levied by the Palatium for the 21st Rapax—it would spend the rest of this enlistment four cohorts understrength.

General Paulinus's total victory over Boudicca, a victory snatched from the jaws of defeat, was to fire young Julius Agricola with a passion for military glory that would drive his later famous career, according to his son-in-law Tacitus. Paulinus kept his reinforced army in the field, under canvas, all through the summer and fall of A.D. 60 and then through the winter of A.D. 60–61, as he conducted a single-minded crusade to find every rebel and eradicate any potential for a repeat of Boudicca's revolt.

Procurator Catus, catalyst of the revolt, was dismissed from his post. We never hear of him again. His replacement, Julius Classicanus, fell out with General Paulinus almost as soon as he arrived in Britain. The new procurator felt that the governor was treating the Britons too harshly. The tribes would have readily agreed. Paulinus certainly didn't pussyfoot around with the British. Throughout southern England, any town or village that wavered or was hostile when General Paulinus came demanding the hand-over of locals on his long list of outlaws suffered the penalty—its leading men were executed and their homes and farms burned to the ground. Out-lawed rebels, faced with execution as the only option if they surrendered or were captured, continued to hide out and fight a hit-and-run guerrilla war in small groups.

The auxiliary infantry and cavalry newly arrived from the Rhine be-came forces of occupation, building new permanent camps in towns and villages throughout East Anglia and elsewhere, in areas that had never before seen Roman garrisons. Even as the locals tried to resume their old lives, mourning their dead and their lost freedom, they would have been hounded by edgy auxiliaries rigorously policing every movement on every road and suspiciously breaking up meetings of even a handful of tribes-people.

On top of all this, the Britons also had to contend with a famine that swept the countryside. Tacitus says this famine was the worst hardship of all for the Britons in the wake of Boudicca's revolt. The tribes had ne-glected to sow wheat so they could prepare for war. Now their people paid the price. And General Paulinus refused to help by dipping into the gov-ernment grain supply, much of it regained from the rebels after Watling Street. He preserved it instead for his troops and the surviving Roman settlers.

When the governor's new deputy argued that "high-spirited nations like those of the Britons inclined more slowly to peace" under martial law, General Paulinus told him to mind his own business. The seething Classi-canus began spreading word around the tribes that it would be to their benefit to wait for a new governor rather than enter into a peace deal with Paulinus. A new governor, said the procurator, would not possess Paulinus's thirst for vengeance or the pride of a conqueror, and would be more lenient in his terms. Procurator Classicanus then wrote a report to Rome saying that the revolt could not be expected to be wrapped up while Paulinus was still governor.

A surprised Palatium sent a senior secretary to Britain in the spring of A.D. 61 to check out the procurator's report, to settle differences between the governor and his deputy, and to pacify the Britons. Arriving with a huge entourage, Secretary Polyclitus was courted by both governor and procurator but was laughed at by the Britons, who had no idea how much power a former slave could wield at Rome when that former slave was a Palatium secretary. Polyclitus returned to Rome with a toned-down version of events for Nero, and General Paulinus was retained in his post by the emperor.

But shortly after, a rebel raiding party destroyed several ships of the Britannic Fleet as they lay beached in a British bay, and killed their crews. Seeing this as an opportunity to bring in new blood, the Palatium ordered Paulinus to hand over his army to one of the current consuls, Lieutenant General Petronius Turpilianus, and then return to Rome. General Turpilianus resigned his consulship and hurried to Britain to take over from Paulinus. Turpilianus terminated the hunt for rebels and the reprisals, and bloody Britain sighed with relief. As the legions went back to base and the new governor concentrated on rebuilding towns and relationships, the province lapsed into an uneasy but undisrupted peace.

Like the 14th Gemina, General Paulinus was famous now. Returning to Rome a national hero, within five years he would be appointed to his second consulship by a grateful emperor. But this was not the last the men of the 14th were to see of Paulinus. The general and the legion that had famously won the Battle of Watling Street for him would be reunited before the decade was out, in very different circumstances.

XXIII

THE YEAR OF THE
FOUR EMPERORS

T hree subjects always dominated talk at the taverns, in the baths, and on the barbers' stools of Rome, and all involved macho deeds—chariot races, gladiatorial contests, and legion battles. And when a Roman legion won a crushing victory, and against odds of 23 to 1, they became famous overnight, and their deed would be talked about and boasted of until this generation went to its grave, and looked back on by future generations with awe. What the 14th Gemina—as it was now commonly known—had achieved at Watling Street made the legion the Elvis, Arnold Schwarzenegger, John Elway, Tiger Woods, and Muhammad Ali of the Roman world all rolled into one. In their hometowns, relatives of 14th Gemina legionaries would have become minor celebrities.

Six years after the battle, the 14th was still as famous as the day its exploits against the Britons had made headline news. The fact that it had been way off in Britain all this time only enhanced the legion's mystique. So imagine the reception the men of the 14th Gemina received from every town it marched by on the way from Britain on a slow progress to a new temporary posting in the Balkans in late A.D. 66 and early A.D. 67.

All the way across Europe, deputations would have come from local councils bearing gifts of food, wine, and money. Like groupies plaguing rock stars, starstruck local girls would have trailed the legion for miles to admire the physiques of the supermen of the 14th, or joined their camp followers, or simply struck alluring poses as the legionaries passed, with centurions barking orders for their charges to keep their eyes to the front and their minds on the march, and doubling the marching camp guard at night to keep girls and soldiers apart. At Lyons, their delight increased when they received their latest pay, in gold freshly minted in the city at the imperial mint.

For some time, Nero's Palatium had been planning two major offensives. One was to be an expeditionary push south from Egypt. The other would be a drive into Parthia, aiming for the Caspian Gates passes in Iran, a variation of the operation on which Julius Caesar had been about to embark when he was killed. Units across the empire were ordered to join the buildup for the operations—legions and auxiliaries were transferred, Evocati militia units were called up and transported from Europe to the East. The legion chosen to lead the Parthian operation was the "most effective" 14th Gemina. It was ordered to Carnuntum in Pannonia, along with the 10th Gemina from Spain. Both were to prepare to march on Parthia as early as the following spring.

A new unit also was raised in A.D. 66 by Nero for the Parthian operation, the 1st Italica Legion—the first Roman legion recruited in Italy south of the Po since Augustus freed Italians from legionary service. According to Suetonius, the Italica's conscripts all had to be five feet eight and one-half inches or more. He says the unit was equipped as a Greek phalanx— the unit's twenty-one-foot spears were to be used to counter the infamous Parthian cavalry that had destroyed Marcus Crassus's legions at Carrhae in 53 B.C., cavalry still the backbone of the Parthian army. The 1st Italica went into training in Cisalpine Gaul.

After its triumphant march across Europe, the 14th Gemina arrived at Carnuntum beside the Danube and settled into camp, keyed up for the new year's operation. But dramatic events soon put Nero's two operations on hold. First, in the summer of A.D. 66, Jewish partisans rose up in revolt in Judea, inflicting heavy casualties on Roman forces in the region. By the beginning of A.D. 67, Jewish successes required significant resources to be diverted to a counteroffensive, under Vespasian, former commander of the 2nd Augusta and now a lieutenant general. It would take four years to put down the revolt.

Then, in February of A.D. 68, Julius Vindex, Governor of Gallia Lugdunensis in France, revolted against Nero. By April his forces had been routed in Gaul by the A.U.R. Nero's Palatium now shelved its Parthian and Ethiopian plans indefinitely. The 1st Italica was ordered to Gaul to restore order, and the 10th Gemina was sent back to Spain from Carnuntum. But the rot had set in. Servius Serpicius Galba, Governor of Nearer Spain, had supported Vindex. Now Galba raised the new 7th Galbiana Legion in Spain and marched on Rome to dethrone Nero. Overnight, the emperor disappeared. Suetonius wrote a highly colored and suspect account of Nero committing suicide on June 9 just outside Rome, but there is no confirmation as to how and when Nero died, and over the next twenty years reports of him turning up in the East abounded.

Galba reached Rome, having already been declared emperor by the Senate. Yet he had set a dangerous precedent. A man without connection to the imperial family of the Caesars had taken the throne. His claim was based on might alone, with the backing of the legions. Even the 14th Gemina, waiting impatiently for action at Carnuntum, initially swore loyalty to him. But after the dust of revolution had settled, the legions soon came to realize a simple fact: what an army can give, an army can take away.

"Prepare to March" was being trumpeted through the quarters of the 14th Gemina Legion at Carnuntum. It was late March in A.D. 69, and the legion had been summoned to the support of their new emperor. Not Galba. He was dead. On January 15, just weeks after he'd celebrated his seventieth birthday and seven months into his reign, Galba had been murdered in the Forum at Rome by Legionary Camurius of the 15th Primigeneia Legion. The celebrating soldiers with Camurius carried the dead emperor's head around the capital on the end of a pike.

Galba's gruesome end had been set in motion on New Year's Day, when the four legions of the Army of the Upper Rhine refused to renew their allegiance to him with the traditional January 1 oath. The A.U.R. legionaries were unhappy they hadn't received the financial rewards promised after supporting Galba, and angry that the Gauls who'd supported Vindex had been pardoned by the new emperor while the legions' friends, the neighboring Germans, Dutch, and Belgians west of the Rhine, had been treated like enemies. The four A.L.R. legions, led by Brigadier General Fabius Valens, commander of the 1st Legion, had then hailed their commander in chief as their emperor—the respected, fifty-three-year-old Lieutenant General Aulus Vitellius, whose uncle had been the General Vitellius who had served under Germanicus on the Rhine, and whose father had three times been consul. The A.U.R. immediately followed suit, and the disaffection had quickly spread to the troops Galba was keeping with him at Rome, including Legionary Camurius.

But instead of supporting Vitellius, the Praetorian Guard and German Guard at Rome had chosen their own emperor: thirty-six-year-old Marcus Salvius Otho, Nero's former best friend, until recently Governor of Lusitania, modern Portugal. Otho was endorsed by the Senate as the new emperor of Rome, and when the news reached the legions stationed in Pannonia—the 14th Gemina at Carnuntum and the 13th Gemina at Petovio in present-day Slovenia—both quickly swore allegiance to him, as did the two legions stationed nearby in Dalmatia, the 7th Galbiana and the 11th Claudia. While young Otho had no military reputation, he came from a famous and respected family. His father, a consul and lieutenant general, had been sent by Claudius to settle matters in Dalmatia after the A.D. 42 Scribonianus Revolt.

Tacitus says that the men of the 14th Gemina had long been faithful to Nero, and that this kindled their zeal for Otho, his former intimate friend. Now that allegiance to Otho was being put to the test. Lieutenant General Vitellius was sending two armies from the Rhine to invade Italy and take the throne from the new emperor. In response, Otho's Palatium sent orders for the legions in Pannonia, Dalmatia, and Moesia to march to Italy as quickly as possible and link up with forces being assembled at Rome by the emperor.

For speed, the two thousand or so men of the three senior cohorts of each of the 13th and the 14th would go on ahead at forced-march pace. The seven remaining cohorts of each legion would follow with their unit's baggage train as fast as they could. The two-thousand-man advance party of the 13th Gemina set off from Petovio, led by the legion's commander, Brigadier General Vedius Aquila. The remaining cohorts of the 13th Gemina would be brought on by the legion's second in command, Colonel Suetonius Laetus, father of the writer Suetonius, who was born this same year. Suetonius Jr. tells of his father often dining with Otho, so prior to promotion to the 13th the colonel would have served as a prefect of auxiliaries in Lusitania when Otho was governor between A.D. 58 and 68.

With farther to go, the three senior cohorts of the 14th Gemina marched from Carnuntum at the same time, apparently led by the legion's senior tribune, as no commander is mentioned for the 14th at this point. The 14th also marched to Italy without auxiliary support. The legion had split, violently, with its longtime auxiliary colleagues of the Batavian light infantry and Batavian Horse, back at the beginning of winter. The Batavians had been angry because their people had been harshly treated by Galba for opposing Vindex. They also were upset because one of their former cohort commanders, Colonel Julius Civilis, a member of the former Batavian royal house, had been arrested when he returned to the Rhine at the end of his twenty-five-year enlistment the previous year. Convicted of conspiracy against Galba, he'd been sentenced to death by A.L.R. commander Lieutenant General Fonteius Capito. But, on their own authority, although apparently with Galba's sanction, Brigadier Generals Valens and Aquinus, two of Capito's own legion commanders, had then arrested Capito on a trumped-up charge of conspiracy. In the fall Capito was executed by his own troops, with Civilis still in prison. As Capito's replacement, Galba chose General Vitellius, who, after arriving on the Rhine at

the end of November, set Civilis free and began extending cordial treatment to the people on the lower Rhine, including the Batavi. On hearing
this, the Batavian auxiliaries had naturally begun to feel favorably toward
Vitellius.

It's probable that the legionaries of the 14th Gemina hadn't agreed
with the freeing of Civilis. He'd served alongside the 14th for a quarter of
a century, and they knew he was superambitious and courted influential
friends. They would have felt that where there was smoke there was fire,
that if Civilis had been accused of sedition there was probably something
in it. And it hadn't helped Civilis's cause that his brother Claudius had
previously been executed by Capito for involvement in a conspiracy against
Rome. With these conflicting allegiances, arguments between Batavian
auxiliaries serving alongside the 14th Gemina and legionaries of the 14th
had subsequently become common. When Galba's Palatium was informed
that the Batavians were brawling with their legion companions, transfer
orders had gone to Pannonia. The Batavians were instructed to return to
Britain, still considered their long-term station. So in December, after
decades of marching and fighting alongside the 14th Gemina in Britain,
from the A.D. 43 invasion to the Caratacus chase, the taking of Anglesey,
and the defeat of Boudicca, the infantrymen of the eight Cohortes Batavior and the troopers of the famous Batavian Horse parted company with
their legion comrades, and on bad terms at that. The Batavians marched
out of Pannonia into Italy, then crossed the Alps into France.

As the Batavians arrived in the territory of the Lingones in southeast-
ern France they heard that Galba had been assassinated and that the Praetorians had placed Otho on the throne. The Lingone people around them
swore allegiance to Vitellius, and the Batavian troops did the same, sending riders from the Batavian Horse galloping north to the Rhine with a
message for Vitellius, declaring they were with him. Vitellius welcomed
them into his fold and instructed the Batavians to join with the army he
was sending to Italy from the lower Rhine under Brigadier General Fabius
Valens, when it reached France.

In early April, the separate 13th Gemina and 14th Gemina advance
columns marched into northeastern Italy from Pannonia. They were met
by dispatches from Rome ordering them to link up with Otho's forces at
the Po River. Within weeks, the contest between Vitellius and Otho would
erupt into a battle between Roman and Roman of the kind not seen since
the civil wars of the previous century.

XXIV

❦

BLOODY BEDRIACUM

O n March 14, a ragtag army had marched out of Rome and headed north in two columns to defend the throne of the new emperor, Otho. The first column comprised five Praetorian Guard cohorts, squadrons of Praetorian Guard cavalry, the sailors-turned-soldiers of Nero's 1st Legion of the Fleet, and two thousand gladiators from the capital's gladiatorial schools. Otho himself led the second column, on foot, bare-headed, wearing iron body armor, and accompanied by most of the members of the Senate, who were determined to show solidarity with their new emperor. In this second column marched more Praetorian Guard cohorts and handpicked men of the German Guard plus Evocati veterans brought back to Rome from Egypt by Nero, and a large number of seamen from the fleet at Ostia and Misenum who'd been pressed into service as light infantry. At the same time, warships of the Tyrrhenian Fleet set sail from Misenum to follow the Mediterranean coast to southern France in Otho's support.

Otho's tactical plan, conceived for him by others, called for a coordinated land and sea push into the south of France to forestall Vitellius's troops before they could cross the Alps into Italy. As he left Rome, Otho was unaware that the Cottonian Alps passes had already been secured for Vitellius by the 1st Italica Legion, which Nero had based at Lyons in France after the Vindex Revolt to protect the imperial mint there.

Only one of three Othonian advance parties, made up of men of the Praetorian Guard and City Guard, succeeded in crossing into southern France to link up with the Tyrrhenian Fleet. This force secured Fréjus for Otho, but it was too little, too late. As Otho moved north from Rome, word reached him that an army under Vitellius's brash young deputy, Brigadier General Aulus Alienus Caecina, until recently commander of the A.U.R.'s 21st Rapax Legion, had crossed the Alps, linking up with the 1st Italica. Caecina entered northwestern Italy with thirty thousand men, ruining Otho's plan to occupy southern France with his main force. Otho realized that now he would have to fight on home soil.

As Brigadier General Vestricius Spurinna hurried ahead with an Othonian flying column, including Praetorian Guards, to occupy Piacenza on the Po in Caecina's path, Otho, at the head of his main force with its long baggage train, followed as fast as he could. Reports soon came in that a forty-thousand-man force from Vitellius's Army of the Lower Rhine under Brigadier General Fabius Valens had entered northern Italy via Switzerland.

After Caecina reached Piacenza and began to assault the city, Otho sent elderly Lieutenant General Annius Gallus with the 1st Legion of the Fleet and a number of auxiliaries to support Spurinna. When, on the march north, Gallus learned that Caecina had been repulsed by Spurinna and had swung east, toward Cremona, he diverted to intercept him. Gallus's legion arrived at Bedriacum, a village on the road between Cremona and Verona, and made camp. They were soon joined by Spurinna's troops from Piacenza, and, during the night, more auxiliaries from Otho's main force.

Caecina's progress toward Cremona was hampered by skirmishes with Gallus's patrols. Each time, Caecina's troops suffered the heavier casualties. Annoyed by this, stung by his failure at Piacenza, and hearing that his colleague and rival Valens was approaching from the north with his army, Caecina decided not to wait for him. Leaving a third of his army in camp, Caecina moved out, planning to ambush Gallus's troops outside Cremona.

By this stage, Lieutenant General Gaius Suetonius Paulinus, consul for the second time in A.D. 66 and former governor of Britain, famous for his crushing victory over Boudicca with the 14th G.M.V. nine years before, had arrived at Gallus's Bedriacum headquarters. Gallus had been injured the day before in a fall from his horse, so Paulinus took charge of the infantry. Lieutenant General Marius Celsus, commander of the 15th Legion in Field Marshal Corbulo's second Armenian campaign, and a consul-elect, took over the cavalry. Tacitus says that no one at that time was considered a better soldier than Paulinus. Now fifty-eight going on fifty-nine, widely renowned as an energetic and practical general, if a little cautious, everyone knew that he hadn't panicked when faced with overwhelming odds in Britain, so everything pointed to him being a calm yet decisive leader now. As Napoleon Bonaparte was to say, a leader is a dealer in hope, and the famous Paulinus gave Otho's outnumbered, untested troops the hope of success.

Further boosting the confidence of Otho's men was the arrival at Bedriacum of the two-thousand-man 13th Gemina advance party from Petovio. When Paulinus asked where his famous 14th was, he was told by General Aquila that cohorts of the G.M.V. were coming, some way behind the 13th Gemina column; but no one knew when they might arrive. Tacitus says that the self-confidence of the men of the "most effective" 14th Gemina, "Conquerors of Britain," had "induced a tardiness of movement in them"—in other words, they were cockily coming down to the Po in their own good time.

General Paulinus was glad to include the three 13th Gemina cohorts in a force he now led west. From a deserter, he'd learned of Caecina's ambush plan, and twelve miles from Cremona he and General Celsus were able to turn the tables on Caecina. But then, at the moment of victory, General Paulinus had "Recall" sounded, apparently afraid that fresh troops might suddenly appear for Caecina. It was a prudent course, but it meant Paulinus let slip the opportunity to totally destroy two-thirds of Caecina's army. This skirmish was another victory for Otho. But not a complete one.

Caecina's fleeing troops regrouped just as General Valens's army arrived. Despite Caecina's heavy losses that day on the Bedriacum road, the now combined army of Vitellius that encamped on the plain near Cremona numbered more than sixty thousand men.

Otho slipped into his army's camp, bringing the last of his units, among them a new legion levied the previous year in southern France and since then camped south of Rome at the naval base of Misenum, the 1st Adiutrix Legion (1st Assistant or Supporter). It had been raised by the city of Vienne, supposedly in support of the 1st Italica Legion stationed nearby at Lyons, but in reality to prevent the Italica from looting Vienne—which the people of Lyons had urged the Italicans to do because of a long-standing intercity feud.

Otho called a council of war. At the praetorium tent, in the light of flickering, spluttering oil lamps, the emperor's chief advisers gathered: Generals Paulinus, Celsus, Spurinna, and Aquila; Praetorian Guard Prefects Colonels Licinius Proculus and Plotius Firmius; and the emperor's brother Salvius Titianus Otho, whom he'd made a consul in January. General Gallus was too unwell to attend. Otho heard General Paulinus counsel patience. All of Vitellius's troops had now arrived, Paulinus said, while Otho still had the men of four legions on the way—the 7th Galbiana and

11th Claudia from Dalmatia, and from Slovenia the remainder of the 13th Gemina and, most importantly, the 14th Gemina. The very presence of the famous 14th would bolster the confidence of the rest of Otho's troops, the general said. Besides, he would have reminded the emperor, this ground where they stood was the 14th's home turf, so its men could be expected to fight even more fiercely here. Wait for the legions, Paulinus urged. He was supported by General Celsus the cavalry commander, and also by General Gallus when his views were sought from his bedside.

But Otho was worried that Vitellius himself was on his way with more troops. Apart from his forces on the Rhine, Vitellius could draw on three legions in Spain, with two of the three in Britain also loyal to him. Otho was conscious of an old Latin saying, "There is danger in delay." In this case delay could give Vitellius the opportunity to arrive and decide matters with overwhelming numbers. Flattered by his brother and Colonel Proculus, Otho decided to go with his instinct, which was to strike on the heels of the day's victory and destroy the combined army of Caecina and Valens before Vitellius himself arrived and the reinforced opposition regained the initiative. His experienced generals reluctantly accepted the strategy, but Paulinus pushed for Otho to leave the actual battle in the hands of the commanders who'd been successful so far, and to personally go to the rear, for safety's sake. The emperor agreed.

As Otho prepared to withdraw to the town of Brixellum, seventeen miles away, taking with him a good part of the Praetorian Guard under Colonel Firmius, the German Guard cohorts, and a large cavalry detachment, the spirits of his remaining troops sank at the sight. Even worse for his cause, Otho's brother Salvius had been bending the emperor's ear—as Otho was about to leave the Bedriacum camp he put his inexperienced brother in overall command, to the horror of the generals.

As soon as Otho was out of sight, Colonel Proculus issued orders for the army to move camp and build a new one four miles from Bedriacum. Generals Paulinus and Celsus advised against the move, but Salvius ignored them. After a flaming row with the emperor's brother, the two generals went on strike. Unwilling to take responsibility for what they saw as impending disaster, Paulinus and Celsus stayed in their tents and refused to take any further part in the operation. The army moved west to the new campsite. Sixteen miles now separated the camps of the two sides.

Days passed without any further offensive action, until finally the exasperated Otho sent a message to his brother, ordering the immediate commencement of an offensive before reinforcements reached Vitellius's army. Now, as if sent by Providence, word arrived that the eagle of a legion was seen coming down the road from Verona. The troops at Otho's camp flooded to the ramparts, and began cheering wildly when the senior co-horts of the 14th Gemina Martia Victrix Legion came marching up to the camp's decuman gate. The boost for the spirits for Otho's troops was enor-mous. "The 14th Gemina is here!" they said excitedly, clapping each other on the back.

Now Salvius Otho found the confidence to finally accede to the emperor's wishes. He would go with what he had. The order was given for the army to advance on the enemy at dawn the next day, April 15.

In his thirties, a native of Vicenza like many men of the 14th Gemina, tall, handsome, and flamboyant General Aulus Caecina was supervising bridge works at the Po when scouts came galloping up with the news that Otho's army was coming down the road. Caecina quickly mounted up and rode back to camp. There, men were scurrying about, arming and forming up in units, while first-rank centurions of the legions threw dice to decide which legion would go where in their order of march. Without consulting Caecina, his rival General Valens now dispatched their cavalry to attack Otho's oncoming army.

As the cavalry came thundering toward them, Otho's advance guard, mostly the 1st Legion of the Fleet, halted and stood its ground. Expecting the seamen to run, the Vitellianist cavalry reeled back with frightened horses bleeding from javelin wounds, broke formation, and tried to retreat to their camp. In the path of the fleeing cavalry stood Caecina's 1st Ital-ica Legion. In unconventional Greek phalanx formation, the Italicans lowered their spears—projecting fifteen feet in front of them, counterbal-anced by six feet of spear behind—and refused to let their retreating troopers through. In the face of this "hedgehog," the cavalrymen had no choice but to turn around. Resuming the attack, they dispersed Otho's advance guard, chasing the infantry into the stony countryside.

The men of the three senior cohorts of the 14th Gemina would have had a bad, bad feeling in the pit of the stomach. The main body of Otho's army had been on the march for more than five hours, covering sixteen miles down the Cremona road, with noncombatants, camp followers, and parts of the baggage train intermixed with the cohorts. As the disorgan-ized column neared the Vitellianist camp, groups of inexperienced legion-aries who'd become separated from their standards began calling out for their comrades.

In the vanguard, marching with Salvius Otho, the men of the rigid formation of the 14th Gemina cohorts would have smarted at the lack of professionalism of it all. These were mature men with just two years to go of their second enlistments, the youngest of them around fifty-eight years old. Tough, scarred, cynical, they'd been marching with the legion since A.D. 31. They'd fought Germans east of the Rhine, they'd invaded Britain, thrashed Caractacus, and demolished Boudicca's rebel horde. Otho's ramshackle army would have been an insult to the proudest, most famous legion in the Roman army.

Now a rumor ran through the ranks of Otho's column that Vitellius's troops had mutinied and there wouldn't be a fight, so that when Vitellianist infantry came into view, some of Otho's men cheerily hailed them as fellow Romans and friends. There was a surprised, muted reply from the other side before "Charge" was sounded by the Vitellianist generals. Four miles outside their camp, the Vitellianist troops rushed Otho's outnumbered men, who, quickly overcoming their shock at the far from friendly reaction, ran to spread out and form a line on either side of the road. In Daily Orders that morning the dispositions for the coming battle had been announced. The 14th Gemina was to take the right wing, with the 13th Gemina beside it. Machinelike now, the 14th Gemina cohorts moved into position. To their left, the other units formed an extended battle line.

The ragged Othonian line not only held, it also repulsed the initial onslaught. The battle then began to break up into a series of separate fights, on the road as well as in the vineyards and woodlands bordering it. Here, men stood toe-to-toe, shield-to-shield, with flailing swords. There, groups many ranks deep threw javelins and other missiles at each other. Here, one side had the upper hand; there, the other. In the midst of battle, men recognized old legionary comrades and relatives in the opposing ranks. But no quarter was asked, and none was given.

As more units came up and became engaged, the battle spilled into the farmland of the open plain between the road and the Po River, where two very different legions met. For Otho, the Gallic recruits of the new 1st Adiutrix Legion. They'd never seen battle but were high-spirited and anxious to gain their first victory. For Vitellius, the tough Spaniards of the 21st Rapax Legion, the "Ravenous 21st," Caecina's own unit and "a legion of old and distinguished renown," as Tacitus puts it, whose origins went back to 49 B.C. The ranks of the 21st hadn't been replenished since two thousand of its recruits had been transferred to the 9th Hispana in Britain in A.D. 60, leaving it four cohorts understrength. Because of its lack of numbers, it had been Vitellius's only legion not to leave cohorts behind in the Rhine garrisons before the march to Italy.

The five thousand youngsters of the full-strength 1st Adiutrix ran forward to the attack. Perhaps the three thousand hardened legionaries of the 21st Rapax felt sorry for the Adiutrix's twenty-year-old farmboy conscripts, maybe they underestimated them, or maybe their weight of numbers told. Whatever the reason, the 21st's first ranks were overwhelmed by the impetus of the 1st Adiutrix's charge. The young soldiers of the Adiutrix cut their way through the opposing legion's 1st Cohort to the eagle of the 21st, killed the eagle-bearer, and with a cheer bore away the golden standard in triumph. The commander of the 1st Adiutrix, Brigadier General Orfidius Benignus, called to his men not to celebrate too soon. He urged them to hurry and re-form, as the fight wasn't yet won. He was right. Infuriated at losing their eagle, the remaining cohorts of the 21st Rapax regrouped, then charged the triumphant youngsters of the opposing legion.

The "Ravenous 21st" lived up to its name. In vicious fighting, it sliced its way through the center of the 1st Adiutrix's line, all the way to the legion commander. As General Benignus died urging on his men, and as numerous 1st Adiutrix standards were taken around him, his raw recruits lost their enthusiasm and their courage, and ran.

Not far away, on the right wing, Otho's most experienced legionaries, the men of the 14th Gemina and 13th Gemina, stood side by side. But the outnumbered 13th cohorts gave way to the charge of the recruits of the full-strength 5th Alaudae Legion. As the troops of the 13th Gemina fled, the two thousand men of the vaunted 14th Gemina Martia Victrix beside them found themselves suddenly exposed on one side.

But like Napoleon's embattled Old Guard at the Battle of Waterloo 1,746 years later, the 14th stood firm, despite superior numbers and an increasingly hopeless situation for their side. Vitellianist co-commander General Valens now gave orders for reserve auxiliary cohorts to attack the weakened right flank of Otho's struggling army and seal victory. Ironically, it was the men of the eight cohorts of the Batavian light infantry, former marching companions of the 14th Gemina for decades, who had been held in reserve and who now charged into the 14th to resume the argument they had started at Petovio, determined to settle that argument with blood. Still the 14th Gemina stood its ground, fighting off attacks to the front and on the flank.

The battle lasted all afternoon. But with the failure of the 1st Adiutrix and 13th Gemina to hold the Othonian line, Vitellius's troops broke through. More and more of Otho's men retreated from the battlefield. Some withdrew in relative order to the temporary safety of their fortified camp sixteen miles back down the road; others fled blindly south, toward

Rome. Holding its own till then, the 14th Gemina Martia Victrix had no choice but also to withdraw to the camp, to prevent themselves from being overwhelmed. Leaving their dead where they'd fallen, the three cohorts fell back, maintaining formation and holding off the exhausted Batavians. Now, considering the battle won and with the light fading, Caecina and Valens sounded "Recall."

As night fell, the road all the way to Bedriacum was so clogged with the corpses of troops and animals and abandoned wagons it was impassable. Otho's brother, as well as General Paulinus, General Celsus, and the Praetorian commander, Colonel Proculus, all escaped south in the darkness. Vitellius later arrested and imprisoned both Proculus and General Paulinus. Tried for treason in the fall, they would be acquitted and set free.

Only General Gallus, confined to his bed at the Bedriacum camp, stayed with the troops. He dragged himself from his tent and tried to rally legionaries as they flooded back into the camp in the dark. Now Brigadier General Aquila of the 13th Gemina blundered into the camp, and into the arms of the bloodied men of the 14th Gemina. Blaming him for his legion's desertion of them on the battlefield, the angry troops were ready to finish him off until old General Gallus convinced them to let him go.

With the 14th respecting Gallus's orders, and acting defiant and undefeated, even posting a camp guard detail as usual, panic among the other troops subsided. All in camp submitted to Gallus's authority, and order returned. Meanwhile, Caecina and Valens advanced their victorious army across country and pitched a new camp a mile away.

At Brixellum, the emperor had been receiving couriered updates of the battle. The first reports weren't encouraging. Then, in the night, came fugitives from the battle with news that all was lost at Bedriacum. Officers around Otho tried to convince him that he could still count on thousands of troops. Colonel Firmius reminded him the Praetorian Guard was still essentially intact there at Brixellum. On top of that, word had arrived that the advance guard of four thousand men from the 7th Galbiana and 11th Claudia had reached Aquileia, near present-day Venice, and were only days away. Otho still had the loyalty of the navy and all of southern Italy. And Rome and the Senate were behind him. His staff urged him to withdraw, to gather new strength, to fight another day.

But Otho was overwhelmed by depression. Unable to see a future for himself, he began talking about suicide, to end the slaughter and put the empire out of its misery. Vitellius was welcome to the throne, he said. He sent his distraught senior officers away and slept soundly that night, with two daggers under his pillow.

That same night, the remaining seven cohorts of the 14th Gemina and those of the 13th Gemina marched into Bedriacum township together with their baggage trains after the trek from Slovenia, only to receive the staggering news that a battle had been lost on the Cremona road that very day and that their legions had been forced to retreat.

The next morning at Brixellum, Colonel Plotius Firmius, co-prefect of the Praetorian Guard, found Otho dead in his tent, with a single stab wound to the chest. The Praetorian Guard hastily cremated their emperor. A swift cremation had been Otho's last wish, so his head couldn't be made a trophy by his enemies, the way that Galba's had.

That same morning of April 16, without consulting the men of the 14th G.M.V. or the other troops under his command, General Gallus sent envoys to the camp of Generals Valens and Caecina, who agreed to surrender terms for Othonian units at Gallus's camp and at Bedriacum itself, including all cohorts of the 14th. Gallus then ordered his troops to lay down their weapons, and once that had been done at his camp, he opened the gates.

With folded arms and furious scowls, the disarmed men of the 14th Gemina's senior cohorts watched as Vitellius's troops entered their camp, softening when they saw that Vitellius's legionaries came in not as victors, but as comrades in arms. Tears flowed as men found wounded friends and relatives in the camp. Vitellianists tended wounded on Otho's side. They even located the body of General Benignus of the 1st Adiutrix and gave him a cremation with full honors. The dead of the 14th weren't so lucky— a month later, when Vitellius arrived from the Rhine and surveyed the Bedriacum battlefield, the rotting corpses of the opposition dead still lay where they'd fallen.

While the battle was being fought, most senators had waited for news with a Praetorian detachment at Modena. When the first reports came in of the defeat near Bedriacum, these Praetorians refused to believe it. After fiery debate, the senators withdrew a little farther south, to Bologna. There, Coenus, a freedman previously in Nero's employ, raised false hopes when he arrived from the north with the story that the famous 14th Gemina Legion, fully intact, had linked up with Otho's guardsmen and cavalry at Brixellum and defeated Vitellius's army. Such was the reputation of the 14th that the story was instantly believed.

Coenus quickly continued on to Rome. He'd obviously seen the last cohorts of the 14th arrive at Bedriacum overnight as he fled south, and that had spawned his fiction. It turned out that his objective had been personal. Coenus carried an imperial safe conduct issued by Otho's Palatium. Without such a passport, it wasn't possible to travel the roads. But if Otho had been defeated and Vitellius was now emperor, all safe conducts issued in Otho's name, including Coenus's, were invalid. The ruse caused the safe conducts of Otho to be recognized for a little longer, until the truth of Vitellius's victory became indisputable. It was long enough for Coenus to reach the capital. But he paid the price; Vitellius later arrested and punished him.

Vitellius was now emperor of Rome. One of his first decrees was for the execution of the centurions of Otho's legions who had shown the most bravery at the Battle of Bedriacum. Centurions of the 14th topped the list. Tacitus says that this one act alone was enough to make the 14th Gemina and the 13th Gemina the sworn enemies of the new emperor.

Valens and Caecina dispersed the units that had fought for Otho. The 1st Adiutrix was sent to Spain. The 7th Galbiana and 11th Claudia, halted near Venice, were ordered to turn around and go back to their Dalmatian station. The Praetorian cohorts in Italy and southern France were at first disarmed. Those in Italy were then separated and distributed to various pro-Vitellius towns, but within months Vitellius would dismiss all their men from the Roman army, without benefits, and replace them with troops from his legions, who took over the Praetorian standards and their barracks at Rome. The German Guard was abolished and its men ordered home to Germany.

The men of the 13th Gemina, despised by both sides for the weak-kneed performance of their senior cohorts at Bedriacum, were forced to spend five weeks building wooden amphitheaters at Cremona and Bologna, where Caecina and Valens exhibited gladiatorial shows for their emperor when he arrived at the end of May, in celebration of the Bedriacum victory.

The brooding men of the 14th Gemina, their cohorts reunited once more, were initially kept in camp at Bedriacum. But the men of the legion's cohorts that hadn't participated in the battle, men such as Standard-Bearer Petronius and Legionaries Flaminius, Cordus, and Vibennius, refused to acknowledge that their legion had been defeated. Indignant, they complained that only men of the senior cohorts had been involved, and even then, none had yielded in battle and none had agreed to surrender, and that the legion should be treated with the respect its reputation deserved.

Troubled by the 14th Gemina's unbroken spirit, says Tacitus, Vitellius issued orders for it to be sent to Turin.

The legion packed up and, grumbling all the way, trooped west to Turin, the Roman town of Taurini Augusta, at the foot of the Alps. Matters became worse at Turin. The people of the city were strongly for Vitellius, and Otho's former troops weren't made welcome. A cohort of Otho's Praetorian Guard also had been sent there; this was before they were demobilized. Putting all his rotten apples in one barrel, Vitellius also ordered the troublemaking Batavian cohorts from his own army to Turin. Tacitus says Vitellius felt the Batavians would keep the 14th Gemina in line, due to their ongoing feud.

It was a recipe for disaster. In the Turin marketplace a Batavian alleged that a local artisan tried to cheat him. A soldier of the 14th Gemina, perhaps Legionary Naevius, a native of Turin, took the artisan's side. As an argument developed, legionaries and Batavians gathered around, and soon the affair went from words to blows. The resulting brawl was terminated only when the Praetorians stepped in and separated the two groups. Not surprisingly, the Praetorians now took the side of the 14th Gemina, and the legionaries continued to goad the Batavians until orders arrived from Vitellius transferring the Batavians to his own headquarters at Pavia and the 14th Gemina back to their old station, Britain.

As, in columns of two, the men of the 14th Gemina marched out through the vast red-brick gatehouse of Turin's Palatine Gate at dawn one day in May or June, fires sprang up throughout the city. The residents were left fighting blazes that quickly spread, and part of Turin was destroyed. Tacitus was in no doubt that the 14th was responsible. He says that the damage was eclipsed by the destruction suffered by other cities during the civil war and was soon forgotten by all but the people of Turin.

The 14th Gemina marched west, with very specific orders from Vitellius on the route they were to follow: across the Graian Alps, and avoiding the city of Vienne, whose loyalty Vitellius still suspected, especially after it had gone to great lengths to raise the 1st Adiutrix Legion for Otho. The city had actually raised the legion for Galba, but it had been commissioned too late to serve him and marched for Otho by default. When the city fathers realized that Vitellius distrusted them, Vienne set about raising yet another legion in their province, calling it the 2nd Adiutrix; the 2nd Augusta Legion was normally recruited in their territory, and the Adiutrix was ostensibly created to support it. Ironically, the 2nd Adiutrix wouldn't be commissioned in time to march for Vitellius, but before long would play a leading role for another emperor, alongside the 14th Gemina.

Once it crossed the Alps, the 14th Gemina came to a crossroads. To the left lay Vienne. To the right, northern France and Boulogne, their embarkation point for the return to Britain. Some in the ranks wanted to turn left and march to Vienne, which they felt sure would finance them if the 14th led a revolt against Vitellius on the strength of their name and their fame. But wiser heads prevailed. The 14th Gemina turned right.

The Batavian cohorts had joined Vitellius at Pavia, the Roman Ticinum, on the left bank of the Ticino River twenty miles above its junction with the Po. There, while the new emperor enjoyed a banquet, the unarmed troops were entertained by a wrestling match between a soldier from the 5th Alaudae Legion and a Gallic auxiliary. Drinking heavily, spectators became involved in the contest. The brawl became a riot, with auxiliaries on one side and legionaries the other. The Batavians joined in on the side of the Gauls.

The guard cohorts of Vitellius's legions subdued the riot. In doing so, they killed a thousand auxiliaries. An all-out battle between legionaries and auxiliaries was averted only when the cry went up that the 14th Gemina Legion was approaching in battle order to challenge Vitellius. Such was the power of the name of the legion that panic set in. As "To Arms" was sounded by the trumpets of various units, legionaries and auxiliaries rushed to arm, find their standards, and man the ramparts of the emperor's camp. The storm finally abated when the approaching troops were identified as the last of Vitellius's troops coming down from the Rhine, not the 14th Gemina.

The next day, as the fat, treble-chinned Vitellius surveyed the bodies littering the camp, he was full of praise for his legionaries. But he heaped scorn on the auxiliaries, all noncitizens and foreigners. He wanted no more to do with them. The Gallic auxiliaries were now ordered home to France and Belgium. The Batavians were transferred to the Army of the Upper Rhine. Bitterly regretting their decision to support Vitellius, the Batavian units left Pavia and marched for the Rhine.

XXV

STORM ON THE RHINE

To the men of the 14th Gemina, it was natural justice. The story of how it ended reached them in Britain a few weeks after the event. It had taken place on December 20, A.D. 69. Seven months after he'd taken the throne, the emperor Vitellius was alone inside the vast, echoing Palatium, deserted by even his closest servants. An army was at the gates of Rome. Vitellius's best general, Valens, was dead. General Caecina was a prisoner. Caecina's legions had been defeated in a fierce two-day battle at Cremona. The German Guard had left the palace and was making a last stand at the Castra Praetoria. Half of Vitellius's Praetorian Guard had surrendered at Narni, north of Rome. The other half was in Campania, to the south, with his brother Lucius, too far away to help him now.

In July, even before Vitellius entered Rome, the legions of the East had hailed Field Marshal Vespasian—commander in Judea and onetime commanding officer of the 2nd Augusta Legion—as their emperor. Other legions had swiftly followed suit, in Moesia, Pannonia, and Dalmatia. As an army marched from Syria to depose Vitellius, troops in Slovenia loyal to Vespasian had set out for Italy under a brigadier general, Primus Antonius. Joined by more and more supporters, Antonius's small force had grown into an army that defeated Caecina's legions at Cremona and was now fighting its way into Rome.

Vitellius tried to close the massive doors to his Palatium apartments, but couldn't. Terrified, he concealed himself in what Tacitus calls "an unseemly hiding place." Suetonius says it was a janitor's room and that he chained a dog outside the door. Taking Suetonius's lead, the equally colorful Dio says it was a doghouse, with the dogs still in it, and they bit him. The emperor was hauled from his hiding place by Colonel Julius Placidus, a cohort commander with the City Guard or Night Watch, and dragged from the Palatium, through the Forum, to the Gemonian Stairs. There, days before, the severed head of the commander of the City Guard and Night Watch, Lieutenant General Flavius Sabinus, brother of Vespasian and former commander of the 14th Gemina, had been displayed after his execution. Sabinus had tried to engineer a bloodless transition of power from Vitellius to Vespasian, but the German Guard had arrested and killed him.

Vitellius, hands bound, surrounded by angry City Guard and Night Watch troops and a mob baying for his blood, stunned more than frightened, looked around the hate-filled faces in disbelief. In days, the closer Vespasian's legions had come in their march on Rome, Vitellius had gone from feared emperor to despised tyrant. There, at the foot of the stairs, a dozen swords were plunged into him. And so died Rome's fourth emperor in fifteen months. The following day, December 21, the Senate met and confirmed the absent Vespasian as the new emperor of Rome.

It had been a typically icy, damp autumn and winter on the Welsh border for the men of the 14th Gemina Legion, with the weather quickly deteriorating as early as September. Since returning to Britain in the summer, they'd been sitting at fortresses along the frontier in present-day Shropshire, their cohorts separated, facing the bleak hills and mountains of North Wales, which were still to be conquered by Rome, hearing via occasional dispatches about the exploits of other units involved in the fighting in Italy.

The legion's main fortress was at Viroconium, the former capital of the Cornovii tribe. At that time one of the largest towns in Britain, it mutated into the present-day small village of Wroxeter. The fortress, capable of holding half the legion, was just north of the town, a short way from the east bank of the snaking Severn River. Men of the 14th had been based here before they were sent to Pannonia three years back, so they knew the place well enough. It's likely there would have been one or two local ladies more than happy to see them again, and others who grieved when they learned that this centurion or that legionary had died at Bedriacum.

There at Wroxeter, huddled around the fires of their damp wooden barrack buildings over the fall and winter of A.D. 69–70, playing board games, and jawing as soldiers do, the men of Rome's most famous legion would have celebrated Vitellius's demise and cheered each other with reminders that they had little more than eighteen months left to go before their twenty-year enlistments were up. After all they'd been through since they'd joined in A.D. 51 or A.D. 31, they would have been ready to call it quits when the time came, and they would have been thinking about a few acres of their own, preferably someplace hot and dry, with a buxom wife to warm the bed and healthy children to warm the heart. But there were one or two battles for them to fight before they enjoyed the pleasures of retirement. One was with a hidden enemy.

For it seems that a fatal illness hit the 14th Gemina at Wroxeter, as early as the fall. Possibly a strain of influenza or viral pneumonia, the epidemic took the lives of several men, legionaries as well as auxiliaries of the Thracian Equitatae combined cavalry and infantry unit now serving with the legion in place of the Batavians. Their bodies were laid in a military cemetery on the main road into the town, northeast of the fortress.

We know that these were men who died from natural causes because Roman troops killed in battle were buried or cremated where they fell, if at all. Besides, the legion saw no action on its return to Britain. The other three legions in the province had verged on mutiny throughout this war of succession, and the current governor, Vettius Bolanus, merely kept his head down, gave no orders, and commissioned no military expeditions against the tribes during his tenure. For his legions, his period of command was one long vacation.

Among those who died in this epidemic at Wroxeter and were commemorated with tombstones that survive to the present day were Legionary Titus Flaminius and Standard-Bearer Marcus Petronius of the 14th Gemina. In eighteen years with the 14th, thirty-eight-year-old Petronius had fought Caratacus and Boudicca. With fewer than two years of his enlistment to go, Petronius had been back at the Wroxeter base only months before he died in the late fall or early winter.

In the spring of A.D. 70 the men of the legion packed their gear to leave Wroxeter—for good, as it turned out. Vespasian, their new emperor, had work for them. The legion was to take part in a major operation in Belgium and Germany. It would have given the men of the 14th great satisfaction to hear their orders. They were to go after the Batavians who'd once been their friends and now were their implacable enemies. More than just upsetting an emperor, as the Batavians had done in Italy, now they had started a revolt on the Rhine against Rome. And it was the 14th Gemina's job to finish it.

The revolt was led by Colonel Julius Civilis, a man the legionaries of the 14th knew all too well. The Batavian, a descendant of King Chariovalda, resented the execution of his brother and his own imprisonment. He resented seeing often inept Roman youths go from the Juvena Collega training school to officer cadet, prefect, tribune, legion commander, senator, praetor, and consul while he remained a mere cohort commander for twenty-five years. And then he saw a golden opportunity.

It had begun as a diversion. Civilis, who in A.D. 69 had been released from custody by Vitellius and resumed command of a Batavian cohort on the Rhine, had years before formed a friendship with Vespasian when the pair served in Britain. In the summer, supposedly to help Vespasian's cause by tying up Vitellianist troops on the Rhine, Civilis had led Batavian auxiliaries in an uprising that had soon been joined by other German and Gallic auxiliary units. Before long the affair had embroiled all seven legions that had left elements on the Rhine when Generals Caecina and Valens and then Vitellius himself had marched on Italy. By early A.D. 70, with some of their generals dead and the rest captured, the men of the Rhine legions had either been killed or gone over to the rebels, as Civilis declared an "Empire of Gaul," with him as its emperor. Every Roman base on the Rhine from the North Sea to Switzerland had been taken by the rebels, and German tribes beyond the Rhine were sending Civilis reinforcements. With the tribes of central and southern Gaul considering joining Civilis's Gallic Empire, Rome was on the verge of losing all its territories in France, Belgium, Luxembourg, Holland, and western Germany.

With Vitellius dead, once Vespasian's chief deputy, Field Marshal Licinius Mucianus, had reached the capital from Syria, Rome was able to turn its undivided attention to Civilis. Commander of the task force sent by the Palatium to the Rhine in the spring of A.D. 70 was Lieutenant General Annius Gallus, the same General Gallus who had surrendered the 14th Gemina at Bedriacum. As Gallus's deputy, Mucianus chose Major General Quintus Cerialis, the same General Cerialis who'd led two thousand men of the 9th Hispana to their deaths at the hands of Boudicca's rebels outside Colchester in A.D. 60. Back in December, Cerialis had slipped out of Rome and joined General Antonius and his Vespasianist army north of the city. When word had arrived that after a failed attempt to negotiate Vitellius's abdication, General Sabinus had holed up on Capitol Hill with his son Clemens and Vespasian's youngest son, Domitian, supported by Sabinus's men of the Night Watch, but surrounded and under siege by three cohorts of Vitellius's German Guard, Cerialis had led a thousand cavalry from General Antonius's army galloping south to save them. While smoke billowed from the burning Capitol in the distance like a distress beacon, Cerialis and his troopers had been repulsed at the city's Colline Gate by Vitellius's troops. As Cerialis was forced to withdraw, Sabinus was captured and killed.

Despite these two significant failures, Cerialis was entrusted with the job of second in command of Gallus's army on the strength of the fact he was married to the new emperor's cousin. With General Gallus unwell and being carried to the Rhine in a litter, General Cerialis eagerly headed off with an advance force—the 21st Rapax Legion, auxiliary infantry, and cavalry, including the Singularian Horse, the elite German unit created by Vitellius to replace the Praetorian Cavalry. Simultaneously, movement orders went out to legions in Italy, Spain, and the 14th Gemina in Britain, telling them to head to the Rhine.

Shipped across from England by the Britannic Fleet, the 14th Gemina and their supporting auxiliary cohorts landed at Boulogne and were met by Brigadier General Fabius Priscus, the legion's new commander, sent by Field Marshal Mucianus. General Priscus immediately marched the force into Belgium. As Priscus's troops moved northeast, ships of the Britannic Fleet shadowed it up the coast to provide close support.

The 14th Gemina had heard that General Cerialis had retaken Mainz and then, as legionaries previously with the rebels came back over to Rome, he'd defeated the Treveri tribe of Belgium and Luxembourg in a battle at Rigodulum near their capital, Trier, on the Moselle River. They'd also heard how Civilis had made a surprise attack on Trier itself, which General Cerialis had only just repelled. As the rebels withdrew up the Rhine toward Batavia, Cerialis followed. The 14th Gemina marched with orders to subdue central Belgium, then link up with General Cerialis's main force at Cologne.

The Canninefates, allies of the Batavians on the Dutch coast, were determined to resist the 14th Gemina's push north. Excellent seamen, with a sizable fleet of small craft, they sailed south as the Roman fleet drew nearer. The admiral commanding the Britannic Fleet was taken completely by surprise as little craft swarmed around his cruisers like angry bees stinging lumbering bears. More than half the Roman vessels were either sunk or boarded and captured by the Canninefates. The rest of the Britannic Fleet turned tail and fled back to Boulogne, leaving the troops onshore to their own devices.

Undaunted, General Priscus slogged on with the 14th Gemina. Crossing the Scheldt River, he swung the legion due east and pushed into the heart of Belgium, accepting the surrender of two tribes that had been supporting Civilis since early in the revolt. First it was the Nervii of central Belgium. Then it was the turn of the Tungri, former Germans who had made their home in King Ambiorix's Eburone lands, with their capital at Atuatuca Tongrorum, today's Tongres, the same Atuatuca remembered by every enlistment of the 14th as the spiritual birthplace of their legion back in 54 B.C.

As the 14th Gemina continued east, heading for Cologne, the Nervians, eager to prove their renewed loyalty to Rome, sent their young men to punish the Canninefates for attacking the Roman fleet. The Nervian youths were quickly wiped out by Civilis's allies.

While General Cerialis awaited reinforcements at Cologne, he dispatched his cavalry on a probe up the Rhine. Near Neuss, rebel cavalry under Civilis's deputy Julius Classicus sent the Roman troopers, including the proud Singularians, reeling in bloody retreat.

The 6th Victrix Legion, a unit that hadn't seen action in decades, now joined General Cerialis after marching from Nearer Spain, where it had been based for the past hundred years. To put some backbone into the Singularian Horse, the 6th Victrix's second in command, Colonel Gaius Minicius, was transferred to the command of the unit's 1st Wing. On the heels of the 6th Victrix, the brand-new 2nd Adiutrix Legion arrived from Ravenna, where it had been training. Its young French recruits were as green as grass but determined to show the shamed veterans of the Rhine legions how to fight. And then Brigadier General Priscus arrived from Belgium with the crack troops of the famous 14th Gemina, their appearance boosting already high spirits in Cerialis's army. These legions doubled the size of Cerialis's force, to more than fifty thousand men.

The Roman general resumed the advance. As his legions came up the Rhine, the rebels pulled back. Cerialis found the former legionary fortress at Neuss a blackened ruin. Approaching Old Camp, he saw that the rebels had dammed the Rhine, flooding his path. Advancing across the waterlogged river plain, the Roman army was attacked on the flanks by Germans who were at home in the marshy terrain, dashing in for hit-and-run attacks before splashing away again. Roman officers kept formations together, reined in panicking horses, calmed young soldiers, and collected their wounded as they went. The army made slow, plodding, painful progress, taking casualties all the way, until they reached high ground not far from Old Camp, where a marching camp was pitched.

At Old Camp, over the remains of four thousand Roman soldiers of the 5th Alaudae and 15th Primigeneia Legions massacred by the rebels only months before, Civilis had built a new fortress; here he prepared to make a stand. In the day's twilight, German skirmishers returned to the Old Camp redoubt in high spirits, boasting to their comrades how they'd made General Cerialis's Romans bleed every step of the way north.

At sunset, at the marching camp in the hills, as they cooked their dinner bread and patched their wounds, the Roman legionaries could hear Germans singing down beside the Rhine in celebration of their day's work. In the early evening, the word was quickly spread around the tents of the 14th Gemina by their guard sergeants as they took around the watchword for the next twenty-four hours: prepare for battle. General Cerialis was determined to have it out with the rebel army come the new day.

XXVI

THE GEMINA'S REVENGE

At dawn on an overcast morning, General Cerialis's crimson standard was raised in the Roman camp. Trumpets sounded "Assembly." The legions fell in, and the redheaded, blue-eyed Cerialis and his adjutant stepped up onto the raised turf of the camp tribunal. The adjutant announced the general's orders. The legions would march down to the Rhine and give battle to the rebels. Once the order of march and of battle was announced, the trumpets sounded "Prepare to March," followed by "Battle Order."

Civilis's scouts had seen the Roman general's standard go up. They knew what it meant, and so did Civilis when they reported back to him at Old Camp. He and his fellow rebel leaders had already agreed that their men were ready for a full-fledged fight to destroy the notoriously ill-starred General Cerialis. Civilis himself had been in Britain when Cerialis had fouled up against Boudicca, and he'd heard all about his Colline Gate failure in December. As the Roman army marched silently out of camp and tramped down from the hills to raised, dry ground outside Old Camp, Civilis sent his troops out to take up battle positions. Tacitus says Civilis was impatient for a decisive battle. The Batavian knew that the longer he put off a major confrontation, the more time he gave for additional legions to arrive on the Rhine. He himself was expecting a few more German reinforcements from the Chauci tribe east of the Rhine, but not enough to justify waiting.

Separated by a marsh, the two armies faced off. The rebels extended in battle order from the river, looking south. Civilis formed his men in columns, with gaps between each. His Batavians and a German tribe, the Gurgerni, occupied the right wing. Belgian tribesmen occupied his center, along with Canninefates, Frisians, and Treverans, with the marsh in front of them. Germans from east of the Rhine, including Tenctheri and Bructeri, took the left flank beside the river.

257

General Cerialis formed two north-facing lines. In his front line he placed his auxiliary infantry and, on the wings, cavalry. The legions occupied the second line, with the general keeping back one group as a reserve—probably the six cohorts of the 21st Rapax, which had played a key role in his victory at Rigodulum on the Moselle. It's likely the 6th Victrix took the left wing. Men of the seven Rhine legions, the former deserters, were bunched together, undoubtedly in the center. Where the 14th Gemina was located we aren't told, but indications are the legion was assigned the key right wing, beside the Rhine, with the untested youngsters of the 2nd Adiutrix next to it.

Both commanders gave pep talks. General Cerialis was to say he wasn't much of a public speaker. Instead of the traditional formal speech to the entire army, he rode from unit to unit, addressing each individually and succinctly. He started with the 14th.

"'Most effective' 14th Gemina, Conqueror of Britain," Tacitus says he began. This brought a proud roar from the men of the 14th. After the humiliation of Bedriacum, it was a tonic to be recognized for their glorious record. "Today," General Cerialis went on, "in destroying forever our treacherous, cowardly, and beaten enemy, I want you to not just fight a battle, I want you to execute a punishment!"

Again the 14th Gemina sounded its approval. The general moved on. To the men of the 2nd Adiutrix, fresh-faced and keen, he said, "Here, today, make the most of the opportunity to consecrate your new standards and your new eagle in battle."

Galloping to the far wing, he called to the Spanish legionaries of the 6th Victrix Legion: "You held Spain for Galba, who recruited you. It was your powerful influence that helped make him emperor. You have the old glory of the Roman name to live up to, the glory of countless victories by the legions of Spain, as recently as the victory of your countrymen of the Rapax at Rigodulum. Your wait for glory ends here!"

Another roar filled the air. The general moved to the center. He stopped in front of the cohorts of the legions that had disgraced themselves, and Rome, by deserting to the rebels the previous year. Tacitus says that with his arm outstretched, he pointed to the dammed river and then to Old Camp, saying, "Here is your bank of the Rhine. Here is your former camp. Both are yours to recover today, by the slaughter of the rebels!"

A deafening roar went up from the Rhine legions. Cerialis and his staff returned to his command position between the battle lines.

Across the watery field, Civilis, in full armor and looking fierce with his battle-scarred face, was in full voice. Tacitus says he reminded his

Batavians and Germans that Old Camp was the site of a great Roman defeat at their hands. "You are standing on the monument to your glory. Under your feet lie the remains of Roman legions." Referring to Hermann's famous victory in the Teutoburg Forest, he said, "Today will either rate with the greatest German glories of the past or will be infamous in the eyes of history. It is up to you. All precautions that a skillful general should take have been taken. The Rhine and the gods of Germany are in your sight. Give battle under their auspices, and remember your wives, remember your parents, remember your fatherland!"

In response, a roar went up from the Batavians, Belgians, and Germans.

From across the battlefield the legionaries of the 14th Gemina watched and listened in silence. Tacitus says that men like those in the 6th Victrix Legion couldn't wait for the fight to begin. Enlisted two years back, they'd been sitting in Spain while other legions fought the battles of the war of succession and while three emperors had won and lost their thrones. They were more than ready for their share of the action, and the fame. But according to Tacitus, others—in particular the men of the 14th Gemina—were weary of war. With retirement just a year away for the 14th, Tacitus says its men were thinking about the financial bonus they would be paid for putting down the rebellion, and of a well-earned rest. But first they had not only to win this battle, they also had to survive it.

Men of the 14th Gemina such as thirty-nine-year-old legionary Publius Cordus from Modena and his good friend Gaius Vibennius had seen plenty of bravado from barbarian tribes opposing them over the years, and would have watched with growing impatience as the Germans and Batavians rapped weapons on raised shields and chanted their deep-voiced war song, the "Barditum." Tacitus says some Germans even did crazy dances to intimidate the Romans.

The combatants didn't have to wait long for the battle to begin. Civilis launched it with a signal to the missile throwers he'd stationed at the front of each of his columns. When his standard dropped, the slingers let loose. Now, as the missiles began to fly, even tough old campaigners of the 14th Gemina would have joined the inexperienced and the fearful in the newer legions in private renditions of the legionary's prayer. Auxiliaries in the front line raised their oval shields to protect themselves as stones and lead pellets came whizzing over the marsh, rattling, bouncing, and ricocheting off leather, wood, and metal, scoring a hit here and there on exposed flesh and bringing cries of pain. The Roman front line stood firm as the rebels maintained the barrage. Occasionally groups of Germans would run out in front of their stationary columns, jumping and splashing and gesticulating as they tried to entice the Roman auxiliaries into the marsh. But Cerialis's front line didn't budge.

Once the missile-throwers ran out of ammunition, they retired through gaps in the columns. Now Civilis ordered an advance. Tall Germans lowered their twelve-foot spears, then came on at the march, weapons extended. Reaching the Roman front line, they were able to wound auxiliaries with impunity because they didn't have to close with them, standing out of the range of auxiliary swords. The auxiliary line wavered, but held.

Now a column of Bructeri Germans from north of the Lippe River appeared on the far side of the Rhine and ran out onto the dam constructed by Civilis. Plunging into the water, they swam upriver a little way before landing beside the Roman army. Dripping wet and half naked, yelling, screaming, the wild, hairy Bructeri went straight into the attack against the nearest auxiliaries, like wolves tearing at sheep. Under fierce assault, many shaken and some demoralized, the auxiliaries began to give ground.

General Cerialis quickly ordered two of his legions to the rescue. Trumpets sounded, and the 14th Gemina and 2nd Adiutrix advanced at the march. Auxiliaries gladly parted to let them through. It was the youngsters of the 2nd Adiutrix who made first contact with the Bructeri, pushing ahead of the 14th in their eagerness to taste first blood. Coming to an abrupt halt at the end of German spears, they faltered. Then the 14th Gemina came up, like a machine, shield lines as solid as rock. The Germans were checked. Then, as the cohorts of the 14th bore in like Sherman tanks, the Bructeri were pushed back, until they retreated in disorder to their own lines. The 14th held its position.

Several hours of fighting passed, with neither side making major gains. In the afternoon, as the darkening sky threatened rain, a Batavian deserter was brought to General Cerialis. Swearing allegiance to Cerialis, the emperor Vespasian, and Rome, the former auxiliary guaranteed that if given a force of cavalry he would lead an outflanking move against the rebels using a route through the marsh that offered solid ground. Cerialis, frustrated by lack of progress, gambled on the deserter, and detached some 240 troopers from his cavalry. Almost certainly men of the Singularian Horse, tall, bearded Germans with hexagonal shields sporting their unit motif of four scorpions, they would have been led by the commander of their 1st Wing, young Colonel Gaius Minicius, who hailed from Aquileia in the home territory of the 14th Gemina. Colonel Minicius would soon receive major bravery awards from his new emperor, Vespasian—a Golden Crown, and the Ancient Spear. General Cerialis gave the colonel his orders, wished him well, then sent him on his way.

Giving the impression that they were deserting the battlefield, the cavalry detachment galloped away. Once out of sight, they skirted around the marsh to the west, guided by the Batavian deserter. True to his word, the deserter led the troopers over firm ground. The Gurgerni, the obscure German tribe posted on the right wing, hadn't bothered to put out pickets to guard against surprise attack. Now they were surprised! With a loud cheer, the Roman cavalry charged the Gurgernians' exposed flank, and with Colonel Minicius heroically leading the fight, the vastly outnumbered force broke the rebels' right wing.

As soon as General Cerialis heard his cavalry cheering from across the battlefield, he ordered a full frontal charge by his legionary second line. Trumpets sounded the "Charge," standards inclined to the front. The auxiliaries let the legionaries pass through their ranks as they went forward at the run, as, on the rebels' right, the Roman cavalry was cutting swaths through the Gurgerni and coming to grips with the Batavians.

The legions collided with rebel formations, which gave way, falling back toward the river. The legions pressed after them. Rain began to fall as, fighting all the way, the rebels continued to give ground. The rain grew heavier, bogging down legionaries and cavalry alike and reducing visibility. In the gloom, many rebels, including Civilis and fellow tribal leaders, escaped, some downriver, some across the dam.

With nightfall close, General Cerialis knew it was pointless pursuing the remnants of the shattered rebel army. He sounded "Recall," and his triumphant troops retired to their camp. They had won a resounding victory. Thanks to the firmness of the 14th on the right wing, the deserter, and the cavalry, the back of the rebel resistance had been broken.

The next morning, the elated men of the 14th Gemina were still patching wounds, telling tales about their part in the Battle of Old Camp, and delighting in the defeat of their old friends become foes, the Batavian cohorts, when the 10th Gemina Legion arrived, having just marched all the way up from its long-term station in Spain, via Mainz.

The Spaniards brought news that ailing Lieutenant General Gallus had finally reached the Rhine from Italy, accompanied by the 8th Augusta Legion. Installing himself at the Mainz A.U.R. headquarters, Gallus, Cerialis's superior, sent Cerialis orders with the 10th Gemina—send him back the 14th Gemina now that the 10th had arrived to replace them. The old general would feel much more secure with Rome's most famous legion in his camp rather than a unit that hadn't seen action in living memory.

Reluctantly, Cerialis gave the men of the 14th their marching orders: return to Mainz at once.

Maybe, as they marched away, the men of the 14th Gemina felt they were being cheated out of the final victory over Civilis and their old rivals the Batavians. But then again, maybe they felt they'd done enough. Now they could retire with a major victory under their belts, and with the legion's conquering reputation restored.

The drama of the Civilis Revolt was nearing its end, but there were still a few scenes to play out, a few surprises before the curtain fell. At Leiden, Civilis, his deputies Classicus and Tutor, and his last supporters collected what belongings they could transport, set fire to the rest, then retreated into the Batavian "island." General Cerialis continued a steady pursuit, supported now by the Germanic Fleet, which had come back down the Rhine, from where it had fled into Switzerland at the height of the rebel success. To counter him, Civilis divided his remaining fighters into four raiding parties led by himself, his nephew Verax, and Classicus and Tutor. At Arnhem, Roman Arenacum, they struck the 14th's replacement, the untried 10th Gemina Legion, which in fierce fighting lost its camp prefect and five first-rank centurions before the raiders withdrew. Simultaneously, at Leiden, the overconfident 2nd Adiutrix youngsters were stung by another raiding party.

At a riverside town the Romans called Vada, Civilis himself led an attack on auxiliary infantry and cavalry. Colonel Briganticus, commander of the Singularian Horse and nephew of Civilis, was killed in this engagement. The highly mobile General Cerialis arrived on the scene, but too late to help Briganticus. Cerialis had gained a reputation for galloping from one Roman encampment to the next, impatiently urging his men to push the rebels farther and farther back toward the North Sea and wrap up the campaign before winter set in, as it was now late in the fall and the weather was deteriorating daily. Without hesitation the general plunged into the fighting on the riverbank, to support the dead Briganticus's struggling Singularians. As German and Batavian attackers were driven into the water, Civilis was recognized, on his horse, trying to rally his troops, until, abandoning his mount, he swam for it like his men. His nephew Verax also was spotted in the water, as both swam to the other side of the river and escaped.

Going back upriver to Neuss and Bonn to inspect the work of troops rebuilding the camps destroyed there by the rebels, General Cerialis decided to spend several nights at Bonn. As was the usual practice, the ships of the Germanic Fleet, now based here, were dragged up onto the riverbank bow first. The admiral in command offered his flagship for use as the general's quarters, and as General Cerialis's servants moved his belongings on board, the general's standard was run up the warship's flagstaff.

That afternoon, just before sunset, when the tribunes of the watch of each legion camped at Bonn came to General Cerialis aboard ship to pass on the register of able-bodied men in camp and to receive the new watchword, the general told them he wanted a peaceful night. The trumpet calls that normally sounded the change of watch every three hours outside his headquarters were to be suspended, he said, and the sentries were to refrain from demanding the watchword. No doubt raising their eyebrows among themselves, the young lieutenant colonels went back to their units and passed on the instructions to their guard sergeants. After dark, the general quietly slipped ashore and disappeared.

The Bonn camp had been under observation all day by German tribesmen across the Rhine. Sometime after eight o'clock that night, when the first change of the watch took place at the camp, the Germans noticed with surprise that none of the usual trumpet calls took place outside the camp *praetorium*. When, three hours later, the same thing occurred, the attention of the Germans became rooted on the sentry posts. Before long, in the moonlight, they saw Roman sentries nodding off to sleep. After midnight, as thick clouds rolled in, blanketing the moon and making the night as black as pitch, the Germans moved to capitalize on the apparent laxity of the Roman guards on the far bank.

From upriver, the Germans launched small boats. Using the current so they only had to paddle a little, reducing noise, they came gliding into the western shore beside the Roman camp. While one German commando party concentrated on ships of the fleet, throwing grappling hooks over sterns, another slipped ashore, crept up to a guard post, slit the throats of sleeping sentries, then slithered into the camp.

In camp, there was silence but for the snoring of thousands of troops and the occasional whinny of a horse. Torches flickered at legion altars and on the camp's main streets. Creeping to the nearest tentline, the Germans cut tent ropes. As eight-man tents collapsed, the raiders let out a terrifying war cry, then began stabbing through the canvas at the men trapped beneath. Down at the water's edge, their comrades let out a yell in reply and set about dragging frigates and double-banked light cruisers of the bireme class out into the river, rowing their own little craft furiously. At the same time, several Germans noticed the square crimson standard of a praetor hanging on the staff of the largest Roman cruiser. Climbing aboard, they went on a vain search for General Cerialis.

With confusion and panic reigning in the camp, the raiders slipped away. As half-dressed legionaries ran around with sword in hand, General Cerialis appeared in their midst, almost naked, according to Tacitus. The historian was to say it was believed that Cerialis had been spending the night in the bed of a German girl, Claudia Sacrata, a native of the Ubi tribe from the west bank.

On this occasion, General Cerialis's willfulness had saved his life. But there was still the matter of his reputation. Quintus Petillius Cerialis was not only a married man, he also was the husband of the emperor's cousin. The scandal could have ruined his career, but it wasn't allowed to. The event was hushed up, the disgrace hidden. A later inquiry to determine the reason for the success of the German raid put the blame on the officers of the guard, despite their testimony that they'd only been obeying orders.

The next day, just as order was being restored to the camp, the Germans had the audacity to row their captured ships past Bonn. They even sent the general's flagship up the Lippe River as a gift to the German prophetess Veleda. Shortly after, where the Meuse met the Rhine, the rebel "navy" confronted more Roman vessels of the Germanic Fleet, but after a brief exchange of missiles the craft parted. It was Civilis's last hurrah.

General Cerialis now doubled his efforts to occupy Batavian territory north and south of the Waal. As his legions pushed on through heavy autumnal rains, rivers began to flood, and much of the low-lying Batavian land between the Waal and the Meuse was inundated. Soon there would be nowhere left for the rebels to run.

Within several days of Civilis's naval demonstration on the river, the rebel leader learned that General Cerialis had sent secret emissaries to leading Batavians, and even to the influential prophetess Veleda. The Roman general promised peace for the Batavi and a pardon for Civilis if the rebels capitulated at once. Civilis also discovered that some of his followers were convening meetings among themselves, without him and without telling him, to discuss a possible surrender. Tacitus says that tribal leaders were now holding Civilis solely responsible for the Rhine war, blaming their now adverse situation on his lust for power. They'd lost their homes, they were out of food, they were at the end of their tether. They began talking of repenting, and of punishing the guilty.

Civilis realized that if he didn't act quickly and contact the Romans, other Batavians would beat him to it—maybe even deciding to deliver

Civilis's head to Cerialis as a sign of their good intent. General Cerialis received a Batavian messenger. Reading the message the rider carried, Cerialis would have smiled—the rebel leader proposed a peace conference involving just the two of them. A bridge across the Waal River had been cut down at his instruction, said Civilis. At an appointed time, he would walk to one end of the broken bridge, Cerialis to the other. They would then talk across the gap.

On the agreed day, probably overcast and cold, at the agreed time, the two leaders walked to the ends of the bridge from opposite riverbanks. As their nervous escorts hung back, the pair stood looking at each other across the fast-moving floodwaters. Redheaded General Cerialis, in his armor and scarlet general's cloak. Battle-scared Civilis, in his best Roman armor, his hair color close to normal now after the red dye he'd been adding since the year before in emulation of ancient German warrior custom had faded, just as his dreams of Batavian independence had faded.

There at the bridge, the two leaders struck a deal, and Civilis surrendered. His followers soon did the same. Josephus, commenting on the end of the Civilis Revolt, says that General Cerialis forced the rebels "to abandon their madness, and to grow wiser."

XXVII

GOOD-BYE AND
APPLAUD US

At Mainz, the men of the 14th Gemina heard about General Cerialis's night with his girlfriend at Bonn. The story would have generated lurid remarks, bawdy ditties, and ribald barrack room laughter. And they heard, too, that the Civilis Revolt was over.

The 14th Gemina soldiers knew what happened to Civilis after his surrender, but we don't—Tacitus's account breaks off at the bridge meeting. Pardoned, Civilis probably ended his days under house arrest in an island mansion at the naval base city of Ravenna, often the repository of surrendered foreigners. We never hear of him again.

The Batavian people didn't suffer long-term as a result of the revolt. New Roman bases were built in their territory, and they would enjoy tax-free status for continuing to supply their young men as auxiliary recruits. Existing Batavian units weren't disbanded, despite having been at the core of the rebellion—infantry cohorts were split, four going to Britain, others to the Danube frontier; the Batavian Horse continued to be an elite unit.

In the wake of Civilis's revolt, fourteen legions now had all or some of their cohorts on the Rhine—the 1st Adiutrix also had arrived from Spain, to where Vitellius had exiled it after Bedriacum. For now, the trusted 14th Gemina was transferred down to Lyons in France, guarding the imperial mint until the Palatium could sort out who went where long-term. By year's end the 14th was sent back to Mainz, its new permanent station. There, the legion underwent its twenty-year discharge in the new year of A.D. 71. Retirees collected savings from the legion bank and received their discharge certificates and their retirement bonuses in gold. Attending a final assembly, their general would have told them that theirs had been the most heroic enlistment in the legion's history.

It's most likely that these veterans were sent to Britain to repopulate the Colchester area allocated to their ill-fated 14th G.M.V. predecessors. As they marched off into civilian life, subject to civil law for the first time in decades and responsible for their own keep, their recent commander in chief, General Cerialis, also was embarking on a new career chapter. Not only had he been made a consul that year by Vespasian for his success on the Rhine, he was now Governor of Britain. Taking the 2nd Adiutrix Legion with him to replace the 14th Gemina in Britain, Cerialis arrived well into A.D. 71. He found the three legions already stationed in Britain lethargic and morose after three inactive years as spectators on the fringe of the war of succession. Things quickly changed under General Cerialis.

Tacitus tells us, in a brief passage in his *Agricola*, that the Brigantes had gone on the warpath in A.D. 71, inspired by the recent passivity of the legions in Britain and incited by the creation of a new Roman colony on their doorstep. The town of Lincoln, on the southern fringe of Brigantia, was granted colony status this year. Retiring Austro-Swiss legionaries of the 16th Gallica Legion from the Rhine, which discharged and reenlisted this year along with the 14th, probably settled there.

Tacitus says the Brigantes—led by their queen, Cartimandua—burned a Roman colony on their frontier, which could only be the new colony of Lincoln. Plus, unlike Boudicca during her uprising, they stormed a military camp—no doubt an auxiliary fort. The Brigantes relaxed after this success, says Tacitus. It seems that this took place prior to Cerialis's appointment, and probably generated it. The Brigantic raid gave new governor General Cerialis an excuse to embark on a major campaign of conquest, with the dual aims of punishing the Brigantes—the largest tribe in all of Britain, according to Tacitus—and of changing Yorkshire's status from allied kingdom to part of the province of Britain.

He launched a full-scale drive north, using the 20th V.V.—commanded by newly promoted Brigadier General Gnaeus Agricola—and probably also the 2nd Adiutrix and 2nd Augusta, leaving the 9th Hispana in the south. Quickly taking York, over the next four years Cerialis would occupy all Yorkshire, fighting a number of battles and extending the province's boundary another hundred miles north, to the Tyne River. Queen Cartimandua, who had survived a coup attempt by her own husband, disappears from the record, possibly committing suicide. She was the last sovereign of the Celtic kingdom of Brigantia.

At Mainz in A.D. 71, before General Cerialis launched his British campaign, the 14th Gemina's latest recruits came marching up from the north of Italy to take the places of the men who'd gone into retirement. The new men included eighteen-year-old Quintus Faustus from Pollentia; short, stubby Gnaeus Musius from Veleia, a future eagle-bearer of the 14th Gemina, and his brother Marcus, who would become a centurion; and Gaius Valerius Secondus, who would die at Mainz just a year before his enlistment expired. As these new recruits arrived, the legionaries who'd volunteered to sign on for another twenty years moved up into the legion's senior cohorts in the usual fashion. Among those who chose to stay with the legion, signing up for new enlistments and being promoted several cohorts, were Legionary Cordus from Modena and his friend Gaius Vibennius, and Lucius Naevius from Turin, who now also had a brother in the legion.

Now one of the four legions of the Army of the Upper Rhine, the 14th Gemina was joined at its Mainz base by the 1st Adiutrix Legion. Both units had come in from the outside to put down Civilis's insurrection, both had proven their loyalty to Vespasian. The units they replaced, the 4th Macedonica and 22nd Primigeneia, had sided with Vitellius, while their Rhine contingents had gone over to Civilis, and they were split up: one legion went to Dalmatia, the other to the A.L.R. The other legions now assigned to the A.U.R. also had marched for Vespasian; they were based farther up the Rhine—the 8th Augusta at Strasbourg, the 11th Claudia at Windisch, in Switzerland.

This same year, the Senate decreed that for their conquest of Judea and the taking of Jerusalem after a brutal siege, Vespasian and Titus were to be awarded Triumphs. That summer of A.D. 71, youngsters of the 14th Gemina's new enlistment would have read the *Acta Diurnia* the day it reported the emperor's Triumphal procession through the streets of Rome. Vespasian, who'd arrived at Rome from Alexandria by October of A.D. 70, shared the day with Titus, with nineteen-year-old Domitian riding a white horse behind them, followed by seven hundred Jewish prisoners from the ninety-seven thousand taken during and after the siege of Jerusalem.

The costs involved in this celebration would have been kept to a minimum. When he arrived at Rome, Vespasian declared that three times the current revenue of the empire was needed to cover the expenses his predecessors had incurred during the war of succession. To pay the bills, he introduced higher taxation throughout the empire. At the same time, he looked at the Military Treasury. In A.D. 68, before Nero disappeared, there had been twenty-seven legions; now there were thirty-two. Nine new legions had been raised over the past thirty years—five of them in fewer than eighteen months during the war. Clearly, Rome didn't need thirty-two legions. It certainly couldn't afford them.

Vespasian was able to immediately abolish the two Legions of the Fleet because their men weren't citizens and had no legal entitlements. He also combined the understrength 7th Galbiana and 18th Legions to create the 7th Gemina. But still more cuts were required. Vespasian's Palatium set in motion the first planned legion abolition of the imperial era. The 1st Legion, Pompey's onetime personal unit, sometimes called the 1st Germanica—apparently for its service in Germany—and also briefly titled the 1st Augusta, and one of the first legions to have gone over to Civilis in A.D. 69, was not reenlisted when its A.D. 74 discharge came around. Five years later, when the A.D. 79 discharge of the 15th Primigeneia Legion, another Civilis turncoat, fell due, it was likewise abolished.

Eighteenth-century historian Edward Gibbon wrote that the strict economy of Vespasian was the source of his magnificence. Vespasian's economic reforms turned Rome's finances around so well that within a few years he could embark on building programs at home and abroad, restoring the gutted Capitoline complex, commencing new temples and Rome's Hunting Theater, the so-called Colosseum, and, from A.D. 73, converting the wooden buildings at legion bases around the empire to stone and brick.

Over the two decades following the A.D. 71 enlistment, the 14th Gemina Legion would perform a policing role while based at Mainz. From A.D. 74, Vespasian extended the German frontier past the Agri Decumates region, taking in the Black Forest, between the Rhine and Danube, and the 14th Gemina helped build a line of forts, the *limes*, along the new border, as new Roman settlers flooded in from Gaul and Upper Germany.

Two members of the legion who didn't take part in this work were Legionaries Publius Cordus and Lucius Naevius, who died at Mainz in A.D. 74, apparently from natural causes and probably over the winter. Their gravestones tell us that forty-three-year-old Cordus had put in twenty-three years with the legion before he was buried by his friend Gaius Vibennius, while Naevius, who was forty-five, was commemorated by his brothers.

Vespasian died in the arms of his attendants in A.D. 79, at age sixty-nine, after a decade of strong rule in which he'd proven to be Rome's best administrator since Augustus. Titus succeeded him but outlived his father by only two years, dying at forty-one. During his brief and benign reign Titus opened the Colosseum and had to contend with a fire at Rome almost as devastating as the Great Fire of A.D. 64, and the eruption of Mount Vesuvius, which buried Pompeii, Herculaneum, and other Campanian towns.

In A.D. 81, Vespasian's second son, Domitian, came to power as the eleventh emperor of Rome. His would be a fifteen-year reign of terror.

In January of A.D. 89, a revolt against him by Lieutenant General Antonius Saturninus, A.L.R. commander, was put down by two of Saturninus's
own legions that he'd initially embroiled in his scheme. As a result,
Domitian decreed that no two legions could share the same base anywhere
in the empire, to limit the opportunity for legions to combine in revolt.

Many legions now had to find new bases. The 14th Gemina's companion legion marched off to a new station in Pannonia, leaving the 14th
at Mainz with just its auxiliary support units. The identity of the auxiliary
light infantry with the 14th now is unknown. Batavians were never again
billeted with the legion. According to Suetonius, another upshot of the
Saturninus Revolt was a decree by Domitian restricting legionary savings
kept in their legions' banks to 1,000 sesterces per man, because General
Saturninus had dipped into his legions' savings to pay big up-front fees to
German mercenaries who were to take part in his rebellion. By doing this,
Domitian sought to reduce the temptation the banks offered other gener-
als around the empire as sources of revolutionary funds.

In Domitian's reign, the 5th Alaudae and 21st Rapax Legions would be
wiped out in Moesia, during incursions by the Dacians, Sarmatians, and
Iazyge Germans from across the Danube. The Dacians achieved their victories wielding their fearsome scimitar curved swords which sliced through
legionary helmets like butter. Domitian would raise one new legion, the
1st Minervia, and increase the salary of every Roman legionary to win
rank-and-file loyalty, from the 900 sesterces a year paid since the time of
Julius Caesar—there had been no such thing as economic inflation all
through this time—to 1,200 sesterces a year.

In A.D. 91, the 14th Gemina underwent its latest discharge and reenlistment and prepared to move home. As the winter of A.D. 91–92
approached, the new senior cohorts of the 14th Gemina marched out of
Mainz and headed for Pannonia, where they would link up with the
recruits of the latest enlistment. The legion settled into a new base at
Mursa, modern Osijek in Croatia, on the Drava River in A.D. 92. Here, at
the legion fortress, built on the heights overlooking town and river, the
legion sat out the next six years, fuming at not being able to revenge
Roman losses to the Dacians. Domitian's inept leadership saw the fighting
end with a humiliating peace treaty favoring the Dacians. But the 14th
Gemina would be one of the units used in Rome's avenging Dacian Wars
beginning in A.D. 101.

Domitian was assassinated by members of his and his niece's staff in
A.D. 96, and the Senate replaced him with the elderly senator Nerva, who
did no more than stabilize the empire and maintain order for the next two
years, as something of an imperial janitor for the next tenant of the Pala-

tium, Trajan. Spanish-born, the son of a renowned general who'd commanded the 10th Legion during the Jewish Revolt, Trajan, himself a general, had been commanding on the upper Rhine at the time Nerva died of old age. Trajan had rankled at the way Domitian allowed the Dacians to get away with the annihilation of Roman legions and detested the subsequent peace treaty in which Rome actually paid reparations to the Dacian king, Decebalus. As soon as he became emperor, Trajan began planning an invasion of Dacia, today's Romania. Before taking up residence in Rome, he spent a year on the Rhine making long-range military plans, which would include raising two new legions—the 2nd Traiana, named after himself, and the 30th Ulpia, named after his family. As part of this buildup, in that year, A.D. 98, the 14th Gemina was posted across Pannonia from Mursa to Vindabonna, today's Vienna, in Austria. There it began intense training.

In the spring of A.D. 101, once the latest enlistment of the Praetorian Guard joined him, Trajan launched his first offensive across the Danube, with ten legions. The second in command of one of his legions, the 5th Macedonica, was Trajan's cousin by marriage, twenty-five-year-old Colonel Publius Hadrianus, or as we know him, Hadrian.

A peace treaty with Decebalus the following year, A.D. 102, ended hostilities. As most of the Roman army recrossed the Danube, the 14th Gemina returned to base in Vienna. But the treaty was broken by the Dacian king within three years, and in A.D. 105–106 the 14th Gemina was a part of Trajan's army of twelve legions that swept into Dacia in two columns. Hadrian, a brigadier general now, commanded the 1st Minervia Legion.

This time, Trajan was determined to conquer Dacia completely. The 14th Gemina was involved in bloody fighting through perilous passes and along mountain ridges in the drive for the heart of Dacia. Trajan's pincer movement resulted in the capture of the Dacian capital, Sarmizegethusa, and saw King Decebalus take his own life after he was trapped in the snow-covered hills to the east by pursuing Thracian Horse cavalry.

In A.D. 107, Trajan proclaimed Dacia a province of Rome, with a garrison of two legions. The 14th Gemina returned to Vienna, as Trajan split the legion's province in two. The western half, the 14th's half, became Upper Pannonia, with Carnuntum its capital. Aquincum, the future Budapest, became capital of the eastern half, Lower Pannonia—with newly promoted Major General Hadrian briefly appointed its first governor. The legion was in Vienna when it underwent its A.D. 111 discharge and reenlistment.

When Trajan died in August, A.D. 117, Hadrian succeeded him as emperor. But Hadrian didn't follow Trajan's policy of expanding the frontiers with offensive military operations. He immediately pulled back and consolidated Rome's borders. His policy of consolidation was illustrated by the seventy-three-mile barrier the Vallum Hadriani, Hadrian's Wall, built from coast to coast across northern England starting in A.D. 122 to keep out barbarian tribes from the north. From now on, legions such as the 14th Gemina would be mostly confined to defending the borders of their provinces against outside incursion and putting down occasional uprisings within them.

In A.D. 117—within months of Hadrian taking the throne—the 14th Gemina was transferred from Vienna twenty miles east to the provincial capital, Carnuntum, moving into the base it had occupied briefly from A.D. 67 to 69. The Carnuntum legion camp, built opposite a river crossing near modern Petronell in Austria, at the crossroads of several trade routes, had much changed since the last time the 14th was there. It had begun as a temporary camp created by Tiberius in A.D. 6. The first permanent base, constructed in A.D. 14, was extensively upgraded in A.D. 73, with its timber buildings replaced by Vespasian's Palatium with solid structures of stone, brick, and tile. The men of the 14th Gemina found they even had an elaborate bathhouse for their exclusive use. As it turned out, Carnuntum was to be home base for the legion for hundreds of years to come.

If Hadrian was a disappointment to his legionaries, who wanted offensive campaigns for action, glory, promotion, and booty, he did have one lasting influence on them. Up to this point Romans had been clean-shaven, shaving every day with a semireligious fervor. Legionaries had been excused shaving for days or even weeks at a time while on campaign, but were always expected to later clean themselves up. Hadrian began the fashion of wearing a beard—to hide an ugly scar, according to Dio—which was taken up by all levels of society and followed by most emperors who succeeded him well into the fourth century. Increasingly, from this time on, legionaries wore short beards. Some emperors curled their hair and beards artificially with curling tongs, but within a few decades the fashion, adopted by legionaries, was for short, neatly trimmed beards.

From its base at Carnuntum, the A.D. 131, 151, and 171 enlistments of the legion were intimately involved in the grueling A.D. 166–180 wars waged by the emperor Marcus Aurelius against the Germanic tribes flooding across the Danube, the Quadi, Iazyges, and Marcomanni, wars depicted in the movie *Gladiator,* in which the Germans killed and took hostage hundreds of thousands of Roman settlers. Marcus prosecuted these wars with what he himself described as his "undeviating steadiness of purpose," and to be closer to the front between A.D. 174 and 176 he based himself and his popular wife, Faustina, at Carnuntum, living in a temporary Palatium complex built a mile downriver from the 14th Gemina's base. While there, Marcus found time to pen at least one of the twelve books of his philosophical *Meditations*.

At one point during these wars German tribes forced the legions back from the Danube, and the 14th Gemina's base at Carnuntum was evacuated. Severely damaged by the invaders before the Marcomanni Wars ended in 179 with the tribes submitting to Marcus, the fortress was reoccupied and repaired by the 14th Gemina.

Marcus died shortly after, in March 180, aged just fifty-nine. Ill for some time, he passed away at Vienna, within miles of the 14th Gemina. He'd rarely been in Rome, spending most of his reign fighting to keep the barbarians at bay. Now his nineteen-year-old son and successor Commodus did a Hadrian and pulled back, terminating the legions' offensive operations on the Danube frontier.

By 192, the Governor of Upper Pannonia was forty-six-year-old Lieutenant General Lucius Septimius Severus, who'd been a consul two years earlier and who probably took up his Pannonian appointment in 191 just as the 14th Gemina was undergoing its latest reenlistment. He sat on his hands when the tyrannical Commodus was assassinated in December 192 by a wrestler employed by members of the Senate. But when Commodus's successor, the respected general Pertinax, was murdered by the Praetorian Guard the following March, Severus acted. On April 13, 192, the 10th Gemina arrived from Vienna to join the 14th Gemina at an assembly at Carnuntum. Here, General Severus announced Pertinax's murder, blamed the Praetorian Guard, and demanded that the emperor be avenged, promising his men a hefty bonus if they marched on Rome with him. His young troops, who had only recently undergone reenlistment, not only swore to avenge Pertinax, they also hailed Severus as their new emperor.

Combining the 14th Gemina and the 10th Gemina with the legions stationed in Lower Pannonia, the 1st Adiutrix and the 2nd Adiutrix, plus auxiliaries, Severus marched on Rome, making record time, and surrounded by a bodyguard of his legionaries. At Rome, meanwhile, the Praetorians had auctioned the throne to a multimillionaire senator, Marcus Didius Julianus. As the Danube legions approached, the Praetorians deserted Julianus, who was executed in his Palatium bathroom on the Senate's orders. Severus took Rome without a fight and was officially appointed emperor by the Senate in June 193. One of his first acts was to line up the men of the Praetorian Guard, disarmed and surrounded by his legions, and dishonorably discharge every man for Pertinax's murder. From then on, the Praetorian Guard's ranks were filled by men from the legions. Over the next four years, the 14th Gemina would have served in Severus's campaigns against rivals for his throne, before going back to garrison duty in Upper Pannonia.

Augustus's Palatium had initiated the convention whereby no legion could be based in its home province, but by the end of the second century, as Rome struggled to maintain the increasingly ragged frontiers of its empire, the legions began to be recruited in or near the provinces where they were based. This was partly for convenience but also because it was felt that legionaries would fight hardest when they were defending their own turf.

In about 193, Septimius Severus changed the regulation that had prevented legionaries from marrying during the twenty years of their enlistment, and also upped their salaries. Before long, legionaries at frontier postings were being encouraged to become involved in local agriculture and business when not on duty, to integrate them into local communities. How the old-timers of the first century would have sneered had they seen their successors three centuries later—locally recruited garrison troops, bearded, two inches taller than them on average but probably not as fit, part-time businessmen with legal wives and children living on their doorstep. Heaven forbid!

Hadrian had made Carnuntum a municipality, and Severus granted it colony status, and it's probable the men of the 14th Gemina's discharge of 211, the year Severus died, took up land grants in the district. Apart from the flourishing town a mile or so west, a separate, less salubrious community grew along the road leading south from the legion base, first populated by camp followers, now by legion wives and children.

During Severus's reign, too, historian Cassius Dio was made a consul, and within a decade he came to Carnuntum as Governor of Upper Pannonia. He was already composing the eighty books of his *Roman History*. Neither Dio nor his legions saw any action of note during the term of his governorship in Pannonia. It's there, in Pannonia still, with the 10th Gemina, that we find the 14th Gemina Legion in about 233 when Dio penned a list of the thirty-three legions then serving with the Roman army.

In 270, with the empire fast eroding at the edges, a new emperor, Aurelian, skillfully used the Danube legions—no doubt including the 14th Gemina—to throw back an army of Goths who had penetrated into Pannonia from the province of Dacia. The emperor then secured the frontier at the river by permanently abandoning Dacia to the Gothic tribes, resettling the province's Roman inhabitants south of the Danube. The 14th Gemina would have subsequently served with other Danube legions in a 271 campaign by Aurelian, which recovered Rome's eastern provinces from the armies of dynamic Syrian monarch Queen Zenobia of Palmyra.

The 14th Gemina would remain in Pannonia for the next century and a half, primarily as a border defense unit battling regular German incursions. Its new commander in chief in 293 was General Gaius Galerius, a future emperor. From 375 the boy emperor Gratian spent large sums upgrading legion facilities in the two Pannonias after the legions there proclaimed his four-year-old brother Valentinian II his co-emperor. As a part of this program the 14th Gemina's Carnuntum base was totally and lavishly rebuilt. But, long-term, this was a waste of time and money. Twenty years later the two Pannonian provinces were abandoned by the western emperor Honorius in the face of advancing Visigoth hordes from Dacia. Combatting incessant attacks all along the empire's northern frontier for decades, the Roman army had been hemorrhaging away. It seems that just twenty-four of the thirty-three legions of Cassius Dio's day remained in existence by this time.

As the four legions stationed in Pannonia—still the 14th and 10th Geminas in Upper Pannonia and the 1st Adiutrix and 2nd Adiutrix in Lower Pannonia—fell back in stages to defend Italy, two of the three legions in Britain also were being pulled out. The last legion in Britain, the 6th Victrix, would come out in 406, and the Britons, like the Pannonians, would be on their own. The Italians would fare little better: the barbarians would be at the gates of Rome itself within four years of Britain's final desertion.

In the spring of 395, as the 14th Gemina's lead elements marched away from the Danube and the legion's Carnuntum home of the past three hundred years, trailed by a sad refugee train of legionary family members and their possessions, legionaries with burning torches would have lit tubs of pitch spread throughout the complex. As the rear guard disappeared over the southern horizon, the legion's new Carnuntum base burned to the ground.

From there, it was all downhill for the Roman Empire in the West. Once the brilliant general Flavius Stilicho, Rome's Marshal of the Armies, was executed in 408 by Honorius, legions were soon overrun as barbarian tribes flooded into western Europe, down into North Africa, then across the Mediterranean to Italy. Alaric's Visigoths were looting Rome by August 410. The 14th Gemina Martia Victrix Legion ceased to exist in the fifth century, swamped and wiped out fighting losing battles against the Visigoths, the Vandals, the Alans, the Lombards, and the Huns. Only one of the old-style legions would still be on record within a hundred years of Alaric's sacking of Rome.

Since its foundation in 58 B.C., the 14th Legion had served Rome for upward of five centuries. What a variety of characters had inhabited the

14th Legion stage and played a role in its fortunes during that time. What a cast list to contemplate:

Julius Caesar, who raised it, and Generals Sabinus and Cotta, who died with it. The heroes of Atuatuca—Chief Centurion Balventius, who went down fighting, Centurion Lucianus, who died trying to save his son, Standard-Bearer Petrosidius, who heaved his eagle over the wall, then turned to fight, and die. The men of the second Atuatuca disaster, and young Colonel Trebonius, with his life-saving wedge formation.

Centurion Fulginus, whose ambitions died with him at Lérida. Greedy Governor Cassius, who went down with his gold. The anonymous centurion of the 14th who challenged Scipio before the Battle of Thapsus and paid for his audacity with his life.

Tragic, talented Germanicus Caesar, who led the legion on a quest for revenge, and who in death gave Rome the emperors Caligula, Claudius, and Nero. And Germanicus's adversary Hermann, the young German freedom fighter destroyed by his own people.

General Sabinus, who took the 14th ashore in Britain and through the Battle of the Medway, only to perish in Rome trying to negotiate Vitellius's abdication. Standard-Bearer Petronius, leading the way on the Severn, on Anglesey, and at the Anker, buried beside the Rhine after twenty-three years with the legion. Legionary Cordus, who survived the Battle of Watling Street only to meet a miserable death in wintry Wales. And their opponents—wily Caratacus, who led the 14th a dance for years, and Boudicca, whose gory vengeance lasted just weeks yet would be remembered for two thousand years.

General Paulinus, who led the 14th to stunning success and turned the legion into Nero's feared killing machine, but who couldn't repeat the performance at Bedriacum. General Gallus, who surrendered the 14th, only to claim the famous legion for himself after it had taken revenge on the Batavians. Civilis, whose revolt rocked Rome. And General Cerialis, famous and honored at last, twice a failure but the third time lucky with the help of the 14th, despite a rash streak and a German girl named Claudia.

But most of all, the 14th G.M.V. itself was the star of the show. Romans would always remember it as the legion that overcame its shame to seize everlasting fame.

When actors in the Roman theater had finished their performance, they would all come onstage and call to the audience, "*Valete et plaudite,*" which means "Good-bye and applaud us." Say good-bye to the cast of the story of the 14th Gemina Martia Victrix Legion. Their performance is at an end. Applaud them if you will.

APPENDIX A

THE LEGIONS OF ROME,
30 B.C.–A.D. 233

According to Cassius Dio, legions marked with an asterisk were still in existence in A.D. 233.

Augustan Legions

1st Legion: Founded by Pompey the Great in 84 B.C. Briefly held title "Augusta," bestowed by the emperor Augustus c. 25 B.C. for Cantabrian War service, taken away by Marcus Agrippa in 19 B.C. for cowardice. In early first century had the unofficial title "Germanica" for service in German campaigns, but this soon fell into disuse. Believed to have been abolished by the emperor Vespasian at the time of its A.D. 74 discharge.

2nd Augusta Legion: Founded by Pompey the Great in 84 B.C. Granted "Augusta" title, meaning "Augustus's," by the emperor Augustus, c. 25 B.C., for Cantabrian War service.*

3rd Augusta Legion: Founded by Pompey the Great in 65 B.C. Granted "Augusta" title by the emperor Augustus c. 25 B.C.*

3rd Cyrenaica Legion: Origin unclear. Served under both Caesar and Lepidus in 40s B.C. Its title suggests that it was raised in the province of Cyrenaica.*

3rd Gallica Legion: Originally one of Pompey's legions, surrendered to Caesar in Spain; discharged in Transalpine Gaul in 48 B.C. and reenlisted there for Caesar, with a title apparently designed to differentiate it from the existing 3rd Legions.*

4th Macedonica Legion, later *4th Flavia Legion:* Founded by Pompey the Great in 65 B.C. Could have taken title "Macedonica" in 33 B.C. when its recruitment was transferred from Spain to Macedonia. Another theory is that it took "Macedonica" title for its performance at 42 B.C. First Battle of Philippi, where it was almost wiped out. Renamed *4th Flavia* by the emperor Vespasian in A.D. 70, reason unknown.*

4th Scythica Legion: In Mark Antony's army in Macedonia in 31–30 B.C. Raised in the East by him or by Brutus and Cassius. Taken into Octavian's forces 31–30 B.C. Origin of Scythica title unknown.*

5th Alaudae Legion: Founded by Caesar in Transalpine Gaul in 52–51 B.C. Title is from Celtic for "Crested Larks." Caesar apparently gave it the number 5 after discharging Pompey's 5th in 49 B.C. Wiped out prior to A.D. 93, in Domitian's reign. Not reenlisted.

5th Legion, later *5th Macedonica Legion:* Founded by Pompey the Great in 65 B.C. Reenlisted by Caesar in Spain in 47 B.C. to replace the legion's Pompeian enlistment he disbanded in 49 B.C. "Macedonica" title may stem from the Battle of Philippi.*

6th Ferrata Legion: Founded by Pompey the Great in 65 B.C. Loaned to Caesar in 52–51 B.C., then went back to Pompey's forces in Spain. Part that went over to Caesar after Pharsalus in 48 B.C. adopted "Ferrata" title, meaning "Ironclad."

6th Victrix Legion: Part of above legion that was split at Pharsalus. This component continued to fight for Pompey until it surrendered to Caesar at Thapsus in 46 B.C., after which he reenlisted it as his own. "Victrix," meaning "Conqueror," title apparently granted c. A.D. 9 by the emperor Augustus for Pannonian War service.*

7th Claudia Pia Fidelis Legion: Founded by Pompey the Great in 65 B.C. Granted "Claudia Pia Fidelis" title, meaning "Claudius's Loyal and Patriotic," following the Scribonianus Revolt, by the emperor Claudius in A.D. 42. The "Pia Fidelis" fell into disuse.*

8th Augusta Legion: Founded by Pompey the Great in 65 B.C. Granted "Augusta" title by the emperor Augustus, c. 25 B.C., apparently for Cantabrian War service.*

9th Hispana Legion: Founded by Pompey the Great in 65 B.C. "Hispana" title, meaning "Spain's," awarded for service in the Cantabrian War. Ceased to exist in reign of the emperor Hadrian, apparently wiped out, c. A.D. 122 in Britain.

10th Legion: Founded by Julius Caesar in 61 B.C. Had unofficial title "Fretensis," said to mean "of the Strait of Messina" and relating to Octavian's 38–36 B.C. Sicilian battles with Sextus Pompey.*

10th Gemina Legion: Created in 31 B.C. combination by Octavian of a non-Italian 10th Legion of Antony with an unidentified non-Italian legion. Title means "Twin."*

11th Claudia Pia Fidelis Legion: Founded by Julius Caesar in 58 B.C. Granted "Claudia Pia Fidelis" title along with the 7th by the emperor Claudius in A.D. 42. The "Pia Fidelis" fell into disuse.*

12th Fulminata Legion: Founded by Julius Caesar in 58 B.C. According to Dio, it was granted "Fulminata" title, meaning "Thunderbolt," by the emperor Marcus Aurelius in A.D. 174 for a victory in a thunderstorm against Germanic tribes, but its men were using the title in the late republic, and its coins bore the thunderbolt logo in the first century.*

13th Gemina Legion: Founded by Julius Caesar in late 58 B.C. Gained "Gemina" title, meaning "Twin," by the emperor Augustus in 31–30 B.C., when combined with an unidentified legion.*

14th Gemina Martia Victrix Legion: Founded by Julius Caesar in late 58 B.C. Believed to have gained the "Gemina Martia" title in combination with the Martia Legion in 31–30 B.C., and granted the additional "Victrix" title by Augustus c. A.D. 9 for service in the Pannonian War. The "Martia" and "Victrix" had fallen into disuse by the middle of the first century.

15th Legion: Founded by Julius Caesar in 54 B.C. For a time took the title "Apollinaris," meaning "of [the god] Apollo."*

16th Legion, later called the *16th Gallica Legion,* and later still the *16th Flavia Legion:* Founded by Julius Caesar in 54 B.C. in Gaul. Granted "Flavia" title by the emperor Vespasian in A.D. 70, reason unknown.*

17th Legion: Founded by Julius Caesar in 49 B.C. Believed wiped out in Africa in that year. Reformed in 42 B.C. by Antony, and then was one of Varus's three legions lost in the A.D. 9 Teutoburg disaster. Never re-formed.

18th Legion: As above, except the legion was re-formed, apparently by Nero in A.D. 66, for his planned Egyptian operation. Four cohorts then served in the Judean offensives of A.D. 67–70, and six on the Rhine during the Civilis Revolt. Believed to have been combined by Vespasian in A.D. 70 with the 7th Galbiana to create the 7th Gemina.

19th Legion: Founded by Julius Caesar in 49 B.C. Wiped out by Germans under Arminius (Hermann) in Teutoburg Forest, A.D. 9. Never re-formed.

20th Valeria Victrix Legion: Started as two legions. The 20th was founded by Julius Caesar in 49 B.C. The Valeria Legion, meaning "Powerful," recruited by Pompey in 84 B.C., was given the vacant 20th number by the emperor Augustus in 31–30 B.C. Augustus apparently granted it the "Victrix" title c. A.D. 9 for Pannonian War service.*

21st Rapax Legion: The 21st was founded by Julius Caesar in 49 B.C. Indications are that the Rapax Legion, meaning "Rapacious," was founded in Spain for Pompey the same year, and originally called the Indigena, the "Native" or "Home-Grown" Legion. Given the vacant 21st number by the emperor Augustus in 31–30 B.C. One of two legions wiped out by the Dacians and Germans prior to A.D. 93 during the reign of Domitian. Never re-formed.

22nd Deiotariana Legion: The Deiotariana Legion was formed by Julius Caesar in 47 B.C., from remnants of two legions of King Deiotarus of Galatia. It was given the vacant number 22 by Augustus in 30–31 B.C. Ceased to exist during the reign of Hadrian; said to have been wiped out in the East in A.D. 135.

Post-Augustan Legions

(In order of creation)

15th Primigeneia Legion: Raised by the emperor Caligula in A.D. 39, apparently for his aborted British campaign. The title said to have been bestowed by the next emperor, Claudius, seemingly in relation to the goddess Fortune, a leading military deity. No reason known for use of the number 15. Ceased to exist in the reign of Vespasian; apparently abolished in A.D. 79 because of its poor record during the Civilis Revolt.

22nd Primigeneia Legion: Same origin of legion and of name as for the 15th Primigeneia. No known reason for use of the number 22.*

1st Italica Legion: Founded by the emperor Nero in A.D. 66, for his planned but never executed invasion of Parthia. Originally equipped as a Greek-style spear phalanx. Took its name as the first legion recruited in Italy south of the River Po in almost 120 years.*

1st Classica Legion (Legion of the Fleet): Recruited by Nero from sailors of the Roman navy in A.D. 68. Saw civil war action in A.D. 69. Abolished by Vespasian in A.D. 70.

1st Adiutrix Legion: Raised by the city of Vienne in Gaul for the emperor Galba in A.D. 68, as a supporter of, or assistant to, the 1st Italica Legion, then stationed nearby at Lyons.*

7th Gemina Legion: Originally a second 7th Legion, founded by Galba in the Spanish recruiting grounds of the original 7th in A.D. 68 and called for a time the 7th Galbiana, "Galba's 7th." Apparently combined by Vespasian with the 18th Legion in A.D. 70; as a result, took the "Gemina" title.*

2nd Adiutrix Legion: Raised by the city of Vienne for the emperor Vitellius in A.D. 69, as a supporter of, or assistant to, the 2nd Augusta Legion, which had its recruiting grounds in the same province. Even adopted the 2nd Augusta's emblem, the flying horse Pegasus.*

2nd Classica Legion (Legion of the Fleet): Recruited by the emperor Vitellius from sailors of the Roman navy in A.D. 69. Surrendered without a fight to forces of Vespasian, who abolished it in A.D. 70.

1st Minervia Legion: Founded by the emperor Domitian c. A.D. 82. Named after his patron deity, the war goddess Minerva.*

2nd Traiana Legion: Raised by the emperor Trajan in A.D. 100–102 to release an existing legion for his Dacian Wars, and named after him.*

30th Ulpia Legion: Raised by the emperor Trajan in A.D. 100–102 for service in his Dacian Wars, and given the number 30 because it would be Trajan's 30th legionary unit, together with his family name.*

2nd Italica Legion: Raised in Italy south of the Po River by the emperor Marcus Aurelius c. A.D. 165, for his Germanic Wars.*

3rd Italica Legion: Same as for the 2nd Italica Legion.*

1st Parthicae Legion: Founded by the emperor Septimius Severus c. A.D. 197 for eastern operations, apparently gaining its title for defeating Parthians invading Mesopotamia.*

2nd Parthicae Legion: Same as for the 1st Parthicae Legion.*

3rd Parthicae Legion: Same as for the 1st Parthicae Legion.*

APPENDIX B

IMPERIAL ROMAN MILITARY RANKS AND THEIR MODERN-DAY EQUIVALENTS

(IN ORDER OF PRECEDENCE)

Army

Rank	Description	Equivalent
Miles gregarius	Literally, a "common soldier" of the legion.	Private
Signifer	Standard-bearer for legion cohort and maniple. No real authority. Unit banker.	Corporal
Aquilifer	Eagle-bearer of the legion. Most prestigious post for a standard-bearer.	Corporal
Tesserarius	Orderly sergeant; sergeant of the guard.	Sergeant
Optio	Second in command of a century and of a cavalry squadron. Unit training, administration, and records officer.	Sergeant major
Decurio	Decurion. Cavalry officer, commanding a squadron of legion cavalry. Several grades, based on length of service.	Second lieutenant
Centurio	Centurion. Officer commanding a century, maniple, and cohort. Sixty to a legion, including six *primi ordines*. Eleven grades, including *primi ordines* and *primus pilus*. Seniority usually determined by length of service.	First lieutenant

Primi ordines	Six most senior "first rank" centurions of a legion, serving in the first, double cohort.	Captain
Primus pilus	Literally the "first spear," a legion's most senior centurion, one of the *primi ordines*.	Captain
Praefectus castrorium	Camp prefect. A former centurion, the third in command of a legion; quartermaster, and officer in charge of major detachments separated from the legion.	Major
Tribunus angusticlavius	Tribune of the thin stripe, a staff officer, serving a six-month officer cadetship.	Lieutenant colonel
Praefectus	Commander of an auxiliary cohort or wing.	Colonel
Tribunus laticlavius	Tribune of the broad stripe, second in command of a legion and commander of Praetorian/City Guard cohorts. Also called military tribune. Because of limited vacancies, Claudius appointed "supernumerary" tribunes, who didn't serve but still moved up the promotional ladder.	Colonel
Praefectus praetoria	One of two commanders of the Praetorian Guard, of equal rank. While, nominally, prefects of the Guard held the rank of colonel, some rose through the ranks and were former centurions, while others were ex-generals. On occasion they commanded field armies.	Colonel
Legatus legionis	Legate of the legion. Legion commander. Of senatorial rank.	Brigadier general
Praetor	A senior magistrate at Rome, second only to the consuls. Praetors and former praetors could command a legion and armies in the field.	Major general
Consul	The highest official at Rome after the emperor. The two consuls for the year shared the presidency of the Senate and gave their names to the year. Consuls or former consuls normally commanded Roman field armies. Seniority was determined by the number of consulships held and when.	Lieutenant general

Propraetor	Governor of an imperial province. A former consul. (See the glossary for details.)	Lieutenant general
Proconsul	Governor of a Senatorial Province. A former consul. (See the glossary for details.)	Lieutenant general

Navy

Miles classicus	A soldier in the marine corps.	Marine
Centurio classicus	Centurion of marines.	Lieutenant
Navarchus	Commander of a warship in the Roman navy.	Captain (naval)
Praefectus classis	Commander of Roman navy squadron or fleet.	Admiral

APPENDIX C

THE PRAETORIAN GUARD,
THE CITY GUARD,
THE NIGHT WATCH

1. The Praetorian Guard and City Guard Cohorts

From the reign of Augustus the Praetorian Guard was Imperial Rome's criminal and political police force, occasionally also serving in military campaigns. The City Guard and Night Watch were the civil police and fire brigades of the city of Rome, with City Guard detachments sometimes also serving at other centers. During the first century B.C. and first century A.D. the emperor's personal body-guard was provided by another unit, the German Guard, a separate and elite legion-strength unit of handpicked German auxiliaries, based, up to four cohorts at a time, at Rome's Palatium—their ten cohorts rotated regularly between Rome and several Italian towns outside the capital.

Men of the Praetorian Guard enjoyed the most prestige and the highest pay of any unit in the Roman army. For hundreds of years during the early imperial era theirs was the only regular army unit permitted by law to be stationed in Italy south of the Po River.

The Praetorian Guard was the oldest unit in the Roman army. After the creation of the Republic in 509 B.C., it accompanied the praetor, the most senior elected Roman official before the post was superseded by that of consul, and the unit's task was protection of the praetor and the city of Rome. Later, it was answerable to the consuls.

The Praetorian Guard fell into disuse during the first half of the first century B.C., and played no part in Roman history when Pompey the Great and Julius Caesar were making their mark. In 44 B.C., following Caesar's death, Mark Antony, as sole remaining consul, recruited a new Praetorian Guard at Rome as a personal protection unit. The initial strength of Antony's Guard was six thousand men. His Guard had one thousand men per cohort, setting the pattern for the future.

Appian says Antony's guardsmen were former legion centurions, but this was impossible, being the equivalent of all the centurions from one hundred legions. They would have been retired veterans of a variety of ranks. Unlike legionaries, who were signed up for sixteen-year enlistments at that time, Antony enlisted his Praetorians for twelve years.

In October 44 B.C., Antony left these six Praetorian cohorts at Rome and formed a new Praetorian cohort from his legions at Brindisi. This 'Brindisi cohort' stayed with him for the rest of his career. The combined Praetorian cohorts marched for Antony and Octavian during the war against Cassius and Brutus. In early October 42 B.C., on the day the first Battle of Philippi was fought in Macedonia, two thousand men of the Guard were with the Martia Legion and another legion being shipped in as reinforcements for Octavian and Anthony. In a lightly escorted troop convoy bound from Italy to Greece, they were caught by 130 warships loyal to Brutus and Cassius and suffered heavy casualties.

Following the division of the empire after Philippi, it seems the Praetorians, apart from the Brindisi cohort, remained based at Rome when Antony took command in the East, and they came under Octavian's control. By 32 B.C., the Praetorians' enlistment had expired. But as Octavian declared war on Cleopatra that year, while he recruited new men to the Guard he also retained a number of Praetorian vets, being reluctant to let go of his best troops. He finally allowed these men to retire seven years later, providing land grants and setting up a colony for them in 25 B.C. at Merida (Augusta Emerita), in Spain, and settling others near the later city of Aosta (Augusta Praetoria), in northwestern Italy. But not before they'd fought for him against Antony and Cleopatra, then in a campaign against Illyrian tribes, followed by the first two years of the Cantabrian War in northern Spain, finally subduing the troublesome Celts of the Salassi tribe in northwestern Italy. Among the tombstones of some of his retired Praetorians found at another colony in northern Italy, at Ateste, were those of men such as Titus Fannius of the 1st Praetorian Cohort and Marcus Gellius of the 2nd.

In 30 B.C., after defeating Antony and Cleopatra, Octavian (the later Augustus) reorganized the Praetorian Guard, giving it the task of protecting and maintaining order at Rome. In that year, he ordained that the unit's command should always be split between two commanders, each with the rank of prefect, or colonel. In 2 B.C. those prefects were Quintus Ostorius Scapula and Publius Salvius Aper. At Augustus's death in A.D. 14 the prefects were Sicilians, Lucius Aelius Sejanus and his father Seius Strabo.

By A.D. 23, Strabo had been sent to Egypt, leaving his son as sole colonel of the Guard. Sejanus, like many of his successors, was to use his solitary power to further his own political ambitions. One of Sejanus's first steps was to bring all the Praetorian Guard cohorts under the roof of a single new fortified barracks, the massive Castra Praetoria, in the 4th Precinct of Rome on the city's northeastern outskirts, at a site beyond the old city walls. Prior to this, the cohorts had been quartered separately at Rome.

Many emperors followed the Augustan practice of appointing dual Praetorian Prefects, but the number varied between one and two throughout the Praetorians' existence. For example, early in his reign Claudius had two Praetorian Prefects, Lusius Geta and Rufrius Crispinus, but replaced them with a single commander, Sextus Afranius Burrus, on the insistence of his wife Agrippina the Younger. Nero retained Burrus, but on that prefect's death in A.D. 62 reverted to two: Faenius Rufus, who was later replaced by Nymphydius Sabinus after being involved in the A.D. 65 Piso Plot against Nero, and Ofonius Tigellinus. The emperor Septimus Severus, who reigned A.D. 193–211, used one Praetorian Prefect at a time, first Fulvius Plautianus then Papinian, but extended the prefect's powers to the control of State finances and all Italian courts outside Rome.

After the abolition of the Praetorian Guard by Constantine the Great in the fourth century, two Praetorian Prefects continued to be appointed by subsequent emperors, with their duties confined to finances and administration. The dual posts were still being used by the A.D. 393–423 reign of Flavius Honorius—both Praetorian Prefects were murdered in an uprising of the army that also killed most of the rest of Honorius's cabinet, just prior to the death in A.D. 408 of Honorius's best general, Marshal of the Armies Stilicho.

It was the custom of the emperors to present each new Praetorian commander with a sword, as a symbol of the Guards' right to bear arms in the capital. An old law made it illegal for the ordinary citizen to go armed within the city of Rome. There were three exceptions to this rule. The first was the emperor himself, and some emperors wore a ceremonial dagger representative of their power over the life and death of every subject, often around their neck. As his badge of office, the emperor's Chief Secretary wore a sheathed dagger at the waist. Third, men of the Praetorian Guard, City Guard, Night Watch, and German Guard were authorized to wear swords in the city.

Normally, the prefect's ceremonial sword was handed over sheathed, but in A.D. 110 when the emperor Trajan presented the sword to new Praetorian Prefect Colonel Saburanus, he unsheathed the weapon, held up the blade, and said to the colonel: "Take this sword in order that, if I rule well, you may use it for me, but if I rule badly, against me."

While the equivalent modern rank of colonel nominally went with the job of Praetorian Prefect, men of higher rank sometimes occupied the post. Vespasian's son and successor, Titus, a successful commander in chief during the Judean offensives, subsequently held the post for some years. On the other hand, men sometimes came up through the ranks from common soldier to become Prefect of the Guard. Men the like of Gaius Silpicius Similis, a centurion, briefly held the post during Trajan's reign. The length of the term of office of Praetorian Prefects was open-ended, although not for life as proposed to Augustus early in his reign, and was terminated at the emperor's discretion.

One of the most famously industrious colonels of the Guard was Quintus Marcius Turbo, a prefect during Hadrian's reign. A former general, Turbo always worked into the early hours of the morning. When, in A.D. 136, the emperor urged him to take life a little easier, Colonel Turbo replied, paraphrasing the emperor Vespasian, that a Prefect of the Guard should die on his feet.

In Augustus's day the Praetorians numbered nine thousand men in nine cohorts. These cohorts were organized along similar lines to the double-strength 1st cohort of each Imperial legion, and were officered by six centurions. As Praetorian cohorts operated independently of one another, there was no chief centurion or camp prefect of the Guard. Each Praetorian and City Guard cohort was commanded by a tribune, a broad-stripe colonel who had served his years on the army's promotion ladder and qualified for deputy legion commander status. Guard tribunes shared the task of Tribune of the Watch at Rome on rotation. There are instances of Praetorian tribunes who were still serving in the Guard in their forties. There is no record of junior tribunes serving officer cadetships with the Guard in Imperial times as they did with the legions.

From the reign of Augustus the Praetorian Guard was required to provide a detachment that surrounded the building where the Senate was sitting—usually the Senate House, but on special occasions sittings took place in one temple or another—to prevent members of the public from entering. Following an A.D. 33 edict of the Senate, they also searched all senators for weapons before they were allowed to enter the Senate House. In addition, the Praetorian Guard provided a cohort for guard duty to keep order at the circus on chariot racing days and during public spectacles, at the amphitheater during public spectacles, and at the theater during musical and dramatic performances. During a riot at a theater at the capital in A.D. 15 a Praetorian centurion and several guardsmen were killed and their tribune injured.

The Praetorian Guard also operated the city prison, which was on the Street of the Banker, beside the Gemonian Stairs and a short distance from the Forum, and carried out sentences imposed by the emperor, Senate, and courts, including implementing exile and execution any place in the empire. There are accounts on record of centurions of the Guard traveling to remote provinces and distant islands with details of up to 60 guardsmen to carry out the capital punishment of condemned individuals on the spot.

A typical execution assignment took place in A.D. 66 when Nero sent a centurion and Guard detachment to northwest Italy to execute Marius Ostorius Scapula, who had won the Civic Crown in Britain as a young cavalry colonel twenty years before while serving with his father, the governor, and who had been found guilty of conspiracy to murder the emperor. Ostorius barricaded himself inside his villa and took his own life. The Praetorian centurion subsequently decapitated him—the heads of executed men were returned to Rome as proof the sentence had been carried out.

Heads of offenders executed outside Rome were exhibited on the rostra in the Forum and/or the Gemonian Stairs. The bodies of those executed at Rome were thrown down the Stairs, a custom said to have originated with Tarpaeia, daughter of the commander of the Capitol during the Sabine War, who betrayed Rome to the Sabines and was thrown from the Tarpaeian Rock in punishment. It was illegal to bury or cremate the bodies of executed men and women; they were tossed into the Tiber after public display.

The City Guard was Rome's beat police force. Formed by Augustus in A.D. 10 and in three cohorts through to the time of Tiberius, later growing to four, the City Guard provided the sentries at the city gates and did the everyday police work of the capital, in daylight hours, including patrolling the deserted streets on days when chariot races and public spectacles were being conducted at one arena or other, to discourage burglars. The City Guard also acted as a fire brigade during daylight. City Guard cohorts, with a strength of 1,500 men each, were commanded by tribunes, who reported to the City Prefect. Like the Praetorian Prefect, the City Prefect had the nominal rank of colonel, but the post was frequently held by men of general rank.

The cohorts of Augustus's Praetorian Guard and City Guard were numbered 1 through 12, the first nine being Praetorian cohorts, the last three being City Guard cohorts. One cohort, the 12th, later the 13th and subsequently the 18th when the Guard expanded, was permanently stationed in France at Lyons (Lugdunum), capital of the province of Gallia Lugdunensis, to guard the Imperial mint that Augustus set up there to replace the old Republican mint beneath the Temple of Juno Moneta at Rome. A new central mint was established at Rome from A.D. 64, and once the Lyons mint was eventually phased out no City Guard cohort was stationed outside Rome.

Caligula added three more Praetotian cohorts. By Nero's reign, there were fourteen Praetorian cohorts and four City Guard cohorts. They were numbered 1 through 18, with the last four being City Guard cohorts. In A.D. 66 the strength of the 18th Cohort at Lyons was down from 1,500 to 1,200 men; Vindex may have taken 300 of these guardsmen to the Rhine as his personal bodyguard. Josephus indicates the unit was back to full strength by A.D. 68 following riots at Lyons in the wake of Nero's demise.

Claudius stationed a cohort of the City Guard at Ostia and another at Puzzuoli, Rome's two main west coast ports. Their first duty was to act as firemen, to protect the ports' vast grain warehouses. The length of the Puzzuoli posting is uncertain, but during the reigns of Nero and Galba and into the reign of Otho the 17th Cohort of the Guard was stationed at Ostia. From the reign of Vespasian, a fire brigade of barefoot Tyrrhenian Fleet marines served Ostia and Puzzuoli, allowing the City Guard cohorts to return to normal duties at the capital.

After coming to power in A.D. 69, Vitellius sacked all guardsmen (experienced men with under two years to run on their enlistments), replacing them with twenty thousand men from the legions he'd brought with him from the Rhine, creating twenty new Praetorian cohorts. He would live to regret it—the fired guardsmen joined his rival Vespasian. Once Vespasian became emperor he reduced Praetorian numbers, recruiting the new A.D. 71 enlistment in Italy, as in the past. In his reign there were seven thousand Praetorians in fourteen cohorts. By the reign of Alexander Severus, 150 years later, the Praetorian Guard numbered ten thousand men.

Until A.D. 69 there was also a Praetorian Cavalry. Vitellius replaced it in July of A.D. 69 with the newly created Singularian Horse, an elite unit made up of Rome's best German auxiliary cavalrymen, in several wings. Their unit emblem was the scorpion, they used hexagonal shields, and they had their own barracks and stables complex at Rome in the 5th Precinct, below the Esquiline Hill. The Singularians were still in existence late in the second century, as attested by tombstones of the unit's troopers at Rome, but by the early third century had been superseded as the household cavalry by the Batavian Horse.

Praetorian Guard and City Guard soldiers were Roman citizens and natives of Italy. During the reign of Tiberius, A.D. 14–37, recruits for Praetorian and City Guard cohorts were levied in Etruria, Umbria, Latium, and the old Roman colonies in Italy. Centurions could be both transferred to Guard cohorts from the legions and promoted from within Guard ranks.

From 27 B.C., Praetorians were paid substantially more than legionaries— 4 sesterces per day. When Tiberius came to the throne in A.D. 14 he doubled Praetorians' pay to win their support, to three times what legionaries were paid. In 13 B.C., Augustus established set retirement bonuses for his troops. Praetorian guardsmen received 20,000 sesterces on retiring, as opposed to legionaries' 12,000 sesterces each.

Unlike legionaries, Praetorians rarely had the opportunity to profit from the spoils of war, but they were compensated by receiving larger financial legacies than legionaries in the wills of various emperors, and new emperors paid them a bonus when they took the throne. There were various other sources of income. For example, Tiberius paid each of his Praetorians a 1,000-sesterces bribe to stay in barracks when he had Naevius Sertorius Macro, then commander of the German Guard, forcibly remove their prefect Sejanus in A.D. 31. (Macro was subsequently given Sejanus's job by the emperor.)

The twelve-year enlistment period for members of the Praetorian Guard instituted by Mark Antony in 44 B.C. was increased to sixteen years by Augustus in A.D. 5, in line with the increase in the legion enlistment period from sixteen to twenty years that he introduced between 6 B.C. and A.D. 11.

Almost always, the Praetorian Guard only left Rome if it was to accompany the emperor of the day as he traveled or campaigned outside the capital. The Guard played a prominent role in the Dacian Wars between A.D. 101 and 106, when the emperor Trajan personally led the campaigns. He apparently waited for the latest Praetorian reenlistment to be completed in early A.D. 101 before launching his invasion. There were occasional exceptions to this rule. In A.D. 14 Tiberius sent Praetorian cohorts with his son Drusus to put down a mutiny of the three legions stationed in Pannonia. He also sent two Praetorian cohorts to his adopted son Germanicus Caesar for his last German campaign in A.D. 16.

Following Vitellius's death the men of his Praetorian Guard became PoW's, but that didn't stop them clamoring for their discharge rights. Licinius Mucianus offered them land only, but they hung on for their retirement bonus. The Senate authorized a state loan from private businessmen to pay them out, with a former consul appointed to administer the fund, but Mucianus subsequently discharged them without benefits.

2. The Night Watch

For the hours of darkness there was a separate Night Watch at Rome during much of the Imperial era. The *Cohortes Vigilum*, literally "the cohorts that stay awake," were seven in number. Augustus divided Rome into fourteen administrative regios or precincts, and each Night Watch cohort of one thousand men covered two regios and was quartered in barracks in their precincts. These district Night Watch headquarters were the forerunners of police precinct houses of modern times. The Night Watch was commanded by its own prefect, an officer of Equestrian rank who reported to the City Prefect.

The Night Watch was formed by Augustus in A.D. 6, as a temporary night time police force and fire brigade following extensive fires in the city. The Watch proved so useful that he kept them on and they became a permanent fixture. In Augustus's day Night Watch men were always freedmen, former slaves. Later, they came from other classes of society, as well. They were paid from the public treasury. Their rate of pay is unknown, but would have been similar to that of auxiliaries, as would their length of service.

Prior to the formation of the Night Watch, the wealthier inhabitants of Rome employed night watchmen to patrol their blocks. These watchmen carried bells to warn residents of fire, and Night Watch patrols most likely did the same.

To relieve congestion and prevent accidents in the narrow streets of Rome by day, in 59 B.C. Julius Caesar banned wheeled transport from Rome during daylight hours, giving the Night Watch plenty to do as traffic police by night. Augustus exempted Imperial chariots, carriages of the Vestal Virgins and the empress, and the carts of construction workers from this regulation. This meant that all wagons bringing in produce for sale in the capital and taking out exports could only move at night. Hence Imperial Rome's reputation as the city that never slept.

The nocturnal Night Watch troops never left the capital and were considered inferior in quality and status to both Praetorian and City Guard soldiers.

3. Uniforms, Arms, Standards, and Equipment

The Praetorian Guard, City Guard, and Night Watch were armed and uniformed in the same manner as the legionary. The curved Praetorian shield was a little more rounded at the top and bottom than that of the legionary, and Praetorian standardbearers wore lion skin capes as opposed to the bearskin capes of legion standardbearers.

The Praetorian Guard did not march behind an eagle standard like a legion. As each Guard cohort was in effect an independent unit, guardsmen rallied behind the standards of their cohorts, all of which were topped by the symbol of the open right hand.

A law promulgated by Augustus permitted men of Guard units to go about the city of Rome armed only with swords. Their shields and javelins were stored in the barracks armory, and were brought out for parades outside the old city walls, for emergencies, and when the Praetorians and City Guard served outside the city of Rome.

4. Reorganization and Decline

The Praetorian Guard was reorganized by Septimus Severus in A.D. 193. The recruiting ground of the Guard had been broadened by this time by Severus's predecessors to take in not only Italy but Spain, Macedonia, and Noricum—central Austria and part of Bavaria. Severus had marched on Rome with his Pannonian legions to avenge the murder by men of the Guard of the new emperor Pertinax, a famous and respected soldier, and the Guard was made to pay. After taking Rome bloodlessly in June of A.D. 193, Severus had the Praetorians form up on the Field of Mars and then ceremoniously stripped them of bravery decorations and dishonorably dismissed them. He ordered that any former member of this Praetorian enlistment who came within one hundred miles of Rome in the future be executed. Severus formed a new Guard with fifteen thousand men from his legions, with the most meritorious legionaries at frontier garrisons transferred to Praetorian service.

Severus took his Praetorian Guard against rivals Niger in the East and Albinus, Governor of Britain, in France. In February 197, near Lyons, when Severus led his Guard to shore up his right wing, they broke, and Severus only just managed to reform them. Then, with the help of cavalry, they routed Albinus's left wing and won the day.

A typical Praetorian of the third century was Lucius Titius Celer. A member of the 9th Cohort, commanded by a Centurion Montanus, he died at Rome aged thirty-four. Celer, a native of Zuglio in Italy, had served for fifteen years.

The emperor Diocletian had no great liking for Rome or its institutions—he lived out most of his reign in the East. When he became emperor in A.D. 285 he disbanded the existing Praetorian Guard and City Guard cohorts and brought in two legions from the Balkans, forming them into two Praetorian Guard divisions with a combined strength of ten thousand men. Diocletian appointed a co-emperor, Maximianus, giving himself the title Jove and Maximianus that of Hercules, and the two new Praetorian divisions were called the Jovia and the Herculiana. This new Guard served on the same pay and length of service conditions as the legions.

Maxentius, emperor from A.D. 306, reverted to the old Praetorian system. Abolishing Diocletian's two divisions, he recruited Praetorians from all the legions and lifted their numbers to eighteen thousand, also reinstating their old service period and pay privileges.

The end of the Praetorian Guard came abuptly in A.D. 312. General Constantine, who governed Spain, Gaul, and Britain, marched into Italy with forty thousand men to challenge Maxentius, his brother-in-law. After defeating Maxentius's larger army outside Verona, Constantine won the Battle of the Milvian Bridge at Rome; here thousands of Praetorians were killed standing their ground as the rest of Maxentius's army was overrun.

Constantine sent Maxentius's surviving Praetorians to his legions, banishing them to frontier garrison posts. Decreeing the abolition of the Praetorian Guard, he forbade the creation of any new force to replace it and had the Praetorian barracks torn down. When Constantine departed Rome several months later he turned his back on the city, returning only twice in his twenty-five-year reign. He made his capital at Constantinople, the later Istanbul in Turkey.

A number of emperors were made by the Guard, notably Claudius, Nero, Otho, Diocletian, and Gordian III. More were unmade by the Praetorians, murdering, dethroning, or deserting them—Caligula, Nero, Galba, Pertinax, Julianus, Elagabalus, Balbinus, and Maximus included.

The demise of the Guard reflected the course of the Roman military, then on a downhill slide. Within another eighty-three years the legions were being withdrawn from the frontiers. Two hundred years later the Senate would also disappear. No Senate, no Praetorian Guard, no Augustan legions. The fall of Rome can be charted by the end of her most enduring institutions.

APPENDIX D

SOURCES

Primary Sources

Novelists are professional liars. And we praise them for their fabrications. Historians, on the other hand, are expected to be faithful to the facts. The books in this series are based primarily on classical texts and inscriptions. Some epigraphic material is on stone monuments, some inscribed on metal, vellum, and papyrus, such as the discharge notices of legionaries and citizenship certificates of retired auxiliaries, and the pleas of soldiers to the gods on temple offerings. There are even letters of officers' wives on the British frontier, exchanging gossip and dinner invitations, and the letter from an Egyptian cavalry officer to his mother at home in Egypt asking her to send him more money.

Inscriptions and written records can generally be taken at face value. Classical texts, however, have to be approached with the eye of a historical detective, for some classical authors hovered between the worlds of novelist and historian, spicing up their narratives with exaggeration and invention. Many speeches in classical texts were invented by their authors—even if basing them on firsthand sources—and few writers could escape coloring their writings with personal prejudices and preferences. So in trawling classical sources for the facts, comparison, analysis, and objectivity are essential.

In the thirty-two years of research and writing that went into this book, the classical and contemporary written sources listed below were consulted. Primarily, this work was made possible by the following classical sources, listed alphabetically.

(*Acts of the Apostles* from the Bible also provides a contemporary insight regarding several aspects of legion activity during the first century.)

Appian. Born in about A.D. 95 in Alexandria, Appian, a lawyer at Rome and later a financial administrator in the provinces, wrote Roman histories, including his *Civil Wars*. He is the least well regarded of the Greek historians of the Roman Empire, but for historical events between 133 B.C. and 70 B.C. he is the only reliable continuous source.

Recommended English translations: *Appian: Roman History*, trans. H. White (1889), rev. for Loeb series by I. Robison (London: Loeb, 1913); and *Appian: The Civil Wars*, trans. J. Carter (London: Penguin, 1996).

Julius Caesar. *The Gallic War* and *The Civil War*, together with *The Alexandrian War, The African War, and The Spanish War* by other hands. The first volumes of Caesar's memoirs, covering the period 58–51 B.C., were published in his lifetime. He was still working on his account of the Civil War when he was murdered in 44 B.C. These works were collated by Caesar's loyal staff officer Aulus Hirtius after the dictator's death. Hirtius combined them with additional material, some of which he wrote himself, the rest apparently penned by officers who had been on the scene for the the Civil War's last battles.

Caesar's writings are in the third person, as if produced by an independent observer, and strive to paint him in the best light possible while denigrating his opponents. In the associated material, Hirtius tried to emulate and praise his master. Another of Caesar's former officers, Gaius Asinius Pollio, felt that Caesar's memoirs showed signs of carelessness and inaccuracy, and that he had been either disingenuous or forgetful in describing his own actions.

Recommended English translations: Among the best are *The Commentaries of Caesar*, trans. W. Duncan (London: Dodsley, 1779); *Caesar: Commentaries on the Gallic and Civil Wars*, trans. W. A. M'Devitte and W. S. Bohm (London: Bell, 1890); *Caesar: The Gallic War & The Civil War*, trans. T. Rice Holmes, Loeb series (London: 1914–1955); *Caesar: The Conquest of Gaul*, trans. S. A. Handford (1951), rev. J. F. Gardner (1967) (London: Penguin, 1967); and *Caesar: The Civil War*, trans. J. F. Gardner (London: Penguin, 1967).

Cassius Dio. This Greek historian, whose full name was Cassius Dio Cocceianus, was born in the Roman Bithynia in about A.D. 150. He joined the Senate under the emperor Commodus. Twice a consul, he was governor of Africa, Dalmatia, and Upper Pannonia. His history of the Roman empire in eighty books, completed just before his death in about A.D. 235, often used the works of other authors, including Tacitus and Suetonius, for source material, although some of his errors are glaringly original. From Dio we glean much of what we know about Claudius's invasion of Britain.

Recommended English translations: *Dio's Roman History*, trans. C. Cary, Loeb series (London: Loeb, 1914–1927), and *Cassius Dio, the Roman History: The Reign of Augustus*, trans. I. Scott-Kilvert (London: Penguin, 1987).

Cicero. Marcus Tullius Cicero (106–43 B.C.) was one of the most noted orators of his day, a leading senator, and a prodigious author. Cicero's letters provide insight into Caesar's invasion of Italy and Mark Antony's quest for power on the death of Caesar.

Recommended English translations: *Cicero: Letters to Atticus,* trans. O. E. Winstedt (Cambridge, Mass.: Harvard University Press, 1912–1958); *Cicero: Letters to his Friends,* trans. W. Glynn Williams, M. Cary, and M. Henderson, Loeb series (Cambridge, Mass.: Harvard University Press, 1912–1958); *Letters of Cicero,* trans. L. P. Wilkinson (London: Hutchinson, 1949); and *Cicero: Selected Letters,* trans. D. R. Shackleton Bailey (London: Penguin, 1986).

Josephus. Born in A.D. 37, Joseph ben Matthias commanded Galilee for the partisans during the first year of the Jewish Revolt of A.D. 66–70 and later took the Roman name Flavius Josephus after being captured and becoming a Roman collaborator. Josephus's *Jewish War* provides in-depth coverage of the A.D. 66–70 Jewish Revolt.

Recommended English translations: *The Jewish War,* trans. H. St. John Thackery, R. Marcus, and L. H. Feldman (London: Loeb, 1926); also, the trans. of G. A. Williamson (London: Penguin, 1959, rev. 1970); *The Complete Works of Josephus,* trans. W. Whiston (1737; repub. as *The New Complete Works of Josephus* [Grand Rapids, Mich.: Kregel, 1999]).

Pliny the Younger. Gaius Plinius Caecilius Secundus, nephew and heir of Pliny the Elder, was a consul in A.D. 100 and later Governor of Bithynia-Pontus. His correspondence with the emperor Trajan gives a fascinating insight into Roman provincial government.

Recommended English translations: *The Letters of Pliny the Consul,* trans. W. Melmoth (1746; rev. W. M. Hutchinson [London: Loeb, 1915]); *Pliny's Letters,* trans. A. J. Church and W. A. Brodribb (Edinburgh: Blackwood, 1872); and *The Letters of the Younger Pliny,* trans. B. Radice (London: Penguin, 1963).

Plutarch. Plutarchos (A.D. 46–c.120) was a Greek scholar who wrote in the reigns of Roman emperors Nerva, Trajan, and Hadrian. Shakespeare used Plutarch's *Parallel Lives* as the basis for his plays *Julius Caesar* and *Antony and Cleopatra.* Plutarch's great work provides biographies of key players in the history of the legions: Sulla, Marius, Lucullus, Sertorius, Cato the Younger, Crassus, Pompey the Great, Julius Caesar, Mark Antony, Brutus, Cassius, Cicero, and the emperors Galba and Otho.

Recommended English translations: Sir Thomas North's 1579 translation can be heavy going with its Tudor English. Easier reads are John Dryden's *The Lives of the Noble Grecians and Romans* (1683–1686; reprint, Chicago: Encyclopaedia Britannica, 1952); *Plutarch's Lives of Illustrious Men,* trans. J. and W. Lanhome

(London: Chatto & Windus, 1875); and *Plutarch's Lives*, trans. B. Perrin, Loeb series (London: Loeb, 1914–1926).

Polybius. This Greek historian, who lived between 200 and 118 B.C., was an adviser to Scipio Aemillianus, the Roman general who conquered Carthage. Polybius's *History of Rome* deals with authority about the army of Republican Rome.

Recommended English translations: *The Histories of Polybius*, trans. E. Shuckburgh (London: Macmillan, 1889); *Polybius: Histories*, trans. W. R. Paton (London: Loeb, 1922–1927); and *Polybius: The Rise of the Roman Empire*, trans. I. Scott-Kilvert (London: Penguin, 1979).

Suetonius. Biographer Gaius Suetonius Tranquillus was born in A.D. 69, in the middle of the war of succession that followed Nero's demise. Suetonius was briefly in charge of the imperial archives at Rome. He became senior correspondence secretary to the emperor Hadrian, but was fired for disrespect to the empress Sabina while Hadrian was away. He must have begun researching his *Lives of the Caesars* while running the archives, for his biographies of Julius Caesar, Augustus, and Tiberius are filled with detail that could only come from official sources.

Recommended English translations: *Lives of the Twelve Caesars*, trans. P. Holland (1606; reprint, New York: New York Limited Editions Club) (1963; rev. trans., London: F. Etchells and H. Macdonald, 1931). A 1796 translation by A. Thompson, reprint, Williamstown, Mass: Corner House, 1978; Loeb series, trans. J. C. Rolfe (London, 1914); and *The Twelve Caesars*, trans. R. Graves (1957; rev. M. Grant [London: Penguin, 1979]).

Tacitus. Living between A.D. 55 and 117, Publius Cornelius Tacitus was a consul in A.D. 97 and Governor of Asia in A.D. 112. With access to the official sources, he filled his *Annals*, *Histories*, *Agricola*, and *Germania* with facts, making him an unrivaled authority on the legions of the first century.

Recommended English translations: *Annals & Histories*, trans. A. J. Church and W. J. Brodribb (1869–1872); reprint, Chicago: Encyclopaedia Britannica, 1952; also trans. W. Peterson, Loeb series (1914–1937); reprint, Franklin, Pa.: Franklin Library, 1982; *Annals*, trans. M. Grant (London: Penguin, 1966); *Annals*, trans. D. R. Dudley (New York: Mentor, 1966); *History*, trans. A. Murphy (London: Dent, 1900); *The Agricola and the Germania*, trans. A. J. Church and W. J. Brodribb (London: Macmillan, 1869–1872); *Tacitus*, trans. H. Mattingly and S. A. Handford (London: Penguin, 1948); *Tacitus*, a combination of all his works, trans. C. H. Moore and J. Jackson (London: Heinemann/Putnam, 1931).

Additional Sources: A Selected Bibliography

Abbott, F. F., and Johnson, A. C. *Municipal Administration in the Roman Empire.* Princeton, N.J., Princeton University Press, 1926.

Arrian. *History of Alexander, and Indica*. Translated by P. Brunt. Loeb series. Cambridge, Mass.: Harvard University Press, 1976.

Aurelius, M. *Meditations*. Translated by G. Long. Chicago: Encyclopaedia Britannica, 1952.

Azzaroli, A. *An Early History of Horsemanship*. London: E. J. Brill, 1985.

Birley, A. *Marcus Aurelius*. London: Eyre & Spottiswoode, 1966.

Birley, E. *Roman Britain and the Roman Army*. Kendal, U.K.: Titus Wilson, 1953.

Boardman, J., J. Griffin, and O. Murray. *The Oxford History of the Classical World*. Oxford, U.K.: Oxford University Press, 1986.

Bouchier, E. S. *Spain under the Roman Empire*. Oxford, U.K.: B. H. Blackwell, 1914.

Boyne, W., with H. Stuart Jones. *A Manual of Roman Coins*. Chicago: Ammon, 1968.

Brogen, O. *Roman Gaul*. London: Bell, 1953.

Broughton, T. R. S. *The Romanization of Africa Proconsularis*. New York: Greenwood, 1968.

Bryant, A. *The Age of Elegance*. London: Collins, 1954.

Buchan, J. *Augustus*. London: Hodder & Stoughton, 1937.

Caracalla. *Historia Augusta*. Loeb series. Cambridge, Mass.: Harvard University Press, 1923.

Carcopino, J. *Daily Life in Ancient Rome*. London: Pelican, 1956.

Casson, L. *Ancient Egypt*. Alexandria, Va.: Time-Life, 1965.

Cave, W. *Lives, Acts, and Martyrdoms of the Holy Apostles*. London: Hatchard, 1836.

Chevalier, R. *Roman Roads*. Translated by N. H. Field. London: Batsford, 1976.

Church, A. J. *Roman Life in the Days of Cicero*. London: Seeley, 1923.

Clausewitz, C. P. G. von. *On War*. Translated by J. J. Graham. New York: Penguin, 1968.

Colledge, M. A. R. *The Parthians*. Leiden: E. J. Brill, 1986.

Collingwood, R. C. *Roman Britain*. Oxford, U.K.: Oxford University Press, 1932.

Cottrell, L. *The Great Invasion*. London: Evans, 1958.

——— . *Enemy of Rome*. London: Pan, 1962.

Cowell, F. R. *Cicero and the Roman Republic*. Harmondsworth, U.K.: Penguin, 1956.

Croft, P. *Roman Mythology*. London: Octopus, 1974.

Cunliffe, B. *Rome and Her Empire*. Maidenhead, U.K.: McGraw-Hill, 1978.

——— . *The Celtic World*. London: Bodley Head, 1979.

——— . *The Roman Baths at Bath*. Bath, U.K.: Bath Archeological Trust, 1993.

De La Billiere, Gen. Sir P. *Looking for Trouble*. London: HarperCollins, 1994.

Delbruck, H. *History of the Art of War*. Translated by J. Walter Renfroe Jr. Lincoln: University of Nebraska Press, Bison Books, 1990.

Depuy, R. E. and T. N. *The Encyclopedia of Military History: From 3500 B.C. to the Present*. London: Military Book Society, 1970.

Divine, A. *Secrets and Stories of the War: Miracle at Dunkirk*. London: Reader's Digest Association, 1963.

Duff, J. D. *Lucan*. Cambridge, Mass.: Harvard University Press, 1977.

Emile, T. *Roman Life under the Caesars*. New York: Putnam, 1908.

Forestier, A. *The Roman Soldier*. London: A. & C. Black, 1928.

Frank, T., ed. *An Economic Survey of Ancient Rome*. Paterson, N.J.: Pageant, 1959.

Frere, S. S. *Britannia: A History of Roman Britain*. London: Routledge & Kegan Paul, 1987.

Frontinus, S. J. *Stratagems and Aqueducts*. Translated by C. E. Bennet and M. B. McElwain. London: Loeb, 1969.

Fuller, J. *Julius Caesar: Man, Soldier, and Tyrant*. London: Eyre & Spottiswoode, 1965.

Furneaux, R. *The Roman Siege of Jerusalem*. London: Rupert Hart-Davis, 1973.

Gardner, J. F. *Family and Familia in Roman Law and Life*. Oxford, U.K.: Oxford University Press, 1998.

Gibbon, E. *The Decline and Fall of the Roman Empire*. Chicago: Encyclopaedia Britannica, 1932.

Grant, M. *Gladiators*. Harmondsworth, U.K.: Penguin, 1967.

————. *Julius Caesar*. Harmondsworth, U.K.: Penguin, 1969.

————. *Cleopatra*. Harmondsworth, U.K.: Penguin, 1972.

————. *The Jews of the Roman World*. Harmondsworth, U.K.: Penguin, 1973.

————. *The Army of the Caesars*. Harmondsworth, U.K.: Penguin, 1974.

————. *History of Rome*. Harmondsworth, U.K.: Penguin, 1978.

————. *The Roman Emperors*. Harmondsworth, U.K.: Penguin, 1985.

————. *Roman History from Coins*. New York: Barnes & Noble, 1995.

Graves, R. *I, Claudius*. London: Arthur Barker, 1934.

Haywood, R. M. *Ancient Greece and the Near East*. London: Vision, 1964.

————. *Ancient Rome*. London: Vision, 1967.

Highet, G. *Juvenal the Satirist*. Oxford, U.K.: Clarendon, 1954.

Hill, W. T. *Buried London*. London: Phoenix House, 1955.

Home, G. C. *Roman London*. London: Eyre & Spottiswoode, 1948.

Jimenez, R. *Caesar against the Celts*. Conshohocken, Pa.: Sarpedon, 1996.

Jones, A. H. M. *Augustus*. New York: W. W. Norton, 1972.

Keppie, L. *Colonisation and Veteran Settlement in Italy, 47–14* B.C. London: British School at Rome, 1983.

————. *The Making of the Roman Army: From Republic to Empire*. Totowa, N.J.: Barnes & Noble, 1984.

————. *Roman Inscribed & Sculpted Stones in the Huntorian Museum University of Glasgow*. London: Society for Promotion of Roman Studies, 1999.

Ker, W. C. A. *Martial*. London: Loeb, 1919–1920.

Laking, G. F. *A Record of European Armour and Arms Through Seven Centuries*. New York: A.M.S., 1934.

Leach, J. *Pompey the Great*. New York: Croom Helm, 1978.

Livy. *The War with Hannibal*. Translated by E. de Selincourt. Harmondsworth, U.K.: Penguin, 1965.

MacArthur, B., ed. *The Penguin Book of Twentieth-Century Speeches*. London: Penguin, 1992.

MacMullen, R. *Soldier and Civilian in the Later Roman Empire*. Cambridge, Mass.: Harvard University Press, 1967.

Mannix, D. P. *Those About to Die*. London: Mayflower, 1960.

Margary, I. D. *Roman Roads in Britain*. London: Phoenix House, 1957.

Marsden, E. W. *Greek and Roman Artillery*. Oxford, U.K.: Oxford University Press, 1969.

Mattingly, H. *Roman Coins from the Earliest Times to the Fall of the Western Empire*. London: Methuen, 1927.

Merrifield, R. *London: City of the Romans*. London: Batsford, 1983.

Mommsen, T. *The Provinces of the Roman Empire*. Edited by T. R. S. Broughton. Chicago: University of Chicago, Phoenix Books, 1968.

Morton, H. V. *In the Steps of the Master*. London: Rich & Cowan, 1934.

Mothersole, J. *In Roman Scotland*. London: John Lane the Bodley Head, 1927.

Napthali, L. *Life in Egypt under Roman Rule*. Oxford, U.K.: Clarendon, 1983.

Parker, H. D. M. *The Roman Legions*. New York: Barnes & Noble, 1958.

Payne-Gallwey, Sir R. *The Crossbow: Mediaeval and Modern, with a Treatise on the Ballista and Catapults of the Ancients*. 1903. Reprint, London: Holland Press, 1995.

Peterson, D. *The Roman Legions Recreated in Colour Photographs*. London: Windrow & Greene, 1992.

Petronius Arbiter, G. *The Satyricon*. Translated by M. Heseltine. London: Loeb, 1913.

Philo Judaeus. *The Works of Philo*. Translated by C. D. Yonge. Peabody, Mass.: Hendrickson, 1993.

Plato. *The Dialogues*. Translated by B. Jowlett. Reprint, Chicago: Encyclopaedia Britannica, 1952.

Pliny the Elder. *Natural History*. Edited and translated by H. Rackman. London: Loeb, 1938–1963.

Raven, S. *Rome in Africa*. London: Longman, 1969.

Robertson, D. S. *Greek and Roman Architecture*. Cambridge, U.K.: Cambridge University Press, 1943.

Robinson, H. R. *The Armour of Imperial Rome*. Oxford, U.K.: Oxford University Press, 1975.

Romer, J. *Testament: The Bible and History*. London: Michael O'Mara, 1988.

Rossi, L. *Trajan's Column and the Dacian Wars*. London: Thames & Hudson, 1974.

Rostovtzeff, M. I. *The Social and Economic History of the Roman Empire*. New York: Biblio & Tannen, 1957.

Salway, P. *Roman Britain*. Oxford, U.K.: Oxford University Press, 1981.

Schwarzkopf, General H. N. *It Doesn't Take a Hero*. New York: Bantam, 1992.

Seager, R. *Tiberius*. London: Eyre Methuen, 1972.

Seneca. *Letters from a Stoic*. Translated by R. Campbell. Harmondsworth, U.K.: Penguin, 1969.

Sherwin-White, A. N. *The Roman Citizenship*. Oxford, U.K.: Oxford University Press, 1939.

Simkins, M. *Warriors of Rome*. London: Blandford, 1988.

Smith, F. E. *Waterloo*. London: Pan, 1970.

Starr, C. G. *Roman Imperial Navy, 31 B.C.–A.D. 324*. Ithaca, N.Y.: Cornell University Press, 1941.

Statius. *Collected Works*. Translated by J. H. Mozley. Cambridge, Mass.: Loeb, 1928.

Strabo. *The Geography of Strabo*. Translated by H. L. Jones. Cambridge, Mass.: Loeb, 1924.

Sulimirski, T. *The Sarmatians*. New York: Praeger, 1970.

Syme, R. *Ammianus and the Historia Augusta*. Oxford, U.K.: Oxford University Press, 1968.

————. *History in Ovid*. Oxford, U.K.: Oxford University Press, 1979.

————. *Historia Augusta Papers*. Oxford, U.K.: Clarendon, 1983.

Times (London). *Concise Atlas of World History*. London: Times, 1982.

Todd, M. *The Northern Barbarians, 1000 B.C.–A.D. 300*. New York: Blackwell, 1987.

————. *The Early Germans*. Oxford, U.K.: Blackwell, 1992.

Trench, C. C. *A History of Horsemanship*. Garden City, N.Y.: Doubleday, 1970.

[U.K.] War Office. *Field Service Regulations*. London: H. M. Stationery Office, 1914.

Utley, R. M. *The Lance and the Shield*. New York: Henry Holt, 1993.

Vernam, G. R. *Man on Horseback*. Garden City, N.Y.: Doubleday, 1964.

Waldeck, C. *Secrets and Stories of the War*. London: Reader's Digest Association, 1963.

Wallace, L. *Ben Hur*. London: Ward, Lock, 1880.

Ward, G. C., with R. and K. Burns. *The Civil War*. New York: Alfred A. Knopf, 1991.

Warmington, E. H. *Nero*. Harmondsworth, U.K.: Penguin, 1969.

Warry, J. *Warfare in the Classical World*. London: Salamander, 1989.

Watson, G. R. *The Roman Soldier*. Ithaca, N.Y.: Cornell University Press, 1969.

Webster, G., and D. R. Dudley. *The Rebellion of Boudicca*. New York: Barnes & Noble, 1962.

————. *The Roman Conquest of Britain*. London: Pan, 1973.

Webster's New Twentieth-Century Dictionary of the English Language. Cleveland: World, 1953.

Weigall, A. *Nero: Emperor of Rome*. London: Butterworth, 1930.

Wheeler, R. M. *Rome beyond the Imperial Frontiers*. London: Bell, 1954.

White, K. D. *Greek and Roman Technology*. Ithaca, N.Y.: Cornell University Press, 1983.

Wightman, E. M. *Roman Trier and the Treveri*. New York: Praeger, 1970.

Wiseman, F. J. *Roman Spain*. New York: Bell, 1956.

GLOSSARY

ACTA DIURNIA Rome's *Daily News,* world's first newspaper. Handwritten daily by the Palatium at Rome and sent around the empire. Founded by Julius Caesar in 59 B.C.

A.L.R. (Roman) Army of the Lower Rhine.

AQUILIFER Standard-bearer who carried the *aquila,* the legion's eagle.

A.U.R. (Roman) Army of the Upper Rhine.

AUXILIARY Noncitizen serving in Roman army. Light infantry and cavalry. Recruited throughout empire. In imperial times served twenty-five years. Paid less than legionary. From first century, granted Roman citizenship on discharge. Commanded by prefects.

BATAVIAN HORSE Elite auxiliary cavalry unit of Roman army. Recruited in present-day Holland.

BATTLESHIP Roman warship of Deceres class.

BOLT Large metal-tipped arrow fired by archers and *scorpio* catapults.

CAMP PREFECT *Campus praefectus.* Legion officer, third in command after commander and senior tribune. Promoted from centurion. Quartermaster, commander of major legion detachments.

CAMPAIGNING SEASON Traditionally, early March to October 19, when legions conducted military campaigns, after which they went into winter quarters.

CENTURION Legion, Praetorian/City Guard, and Marines officer, sixty to a legion. Equivalent to lieutenant and captain. Enlisted man promoted from ranks.

CENTURY Legion subunit made up of ten squads. In republican times, of a hundred men. In imperial times, of eighty men. Commanded by a centurion.

CHIEF CENTURION *Primus Pilus* (first spear). Legion's most senior centurion.

CIVIC CROWN Crown of oak leaves for saving the life of a Roman citizen in battle.

COHORT   Battalion. Ten to a legion. In Caesar's time, of 600 men. In imperial times, cohorts 10 through 2 had 480 men, the senior 1st Cohort, 800.

CONQUISITOR   Roman army recruiting officer.

CONSUL   Highest official at Rome; president of Senate. Two held office annually. Also commanded Roman armies, with equivalent rank of lieutenant general. The minimum age in the republic was forty-two; in the imperial era the minimum age was thirty-seven, except for members of the imperial family.

CONTUBERNIUM   Legion subunit; the squad. In the republic, of ten men. In the empire, of eight men.

CRUISER   Midsize warship, including bireme, trireme, and quinquereme.

CURSUS PUBLICUS   "The State's very fast runner." Imperial Rome's courier service. Used carriages and mounted couriers. Horses changed at way stations every six to ten miles.

DECIMATION   Literally, to reduce by a tenth. Legions punished for mutiny or cowardice by one man in ten being clubbed to death by their comrades after drawing lots.

DECUMAN GATE   The main gate of a legion camp, it faced away from the enemy.

DECURION   Legion cavalry officer. Four to each squadron.

DICTATOR   Temporary supreme chief of republican Rome, supposedly for six months.

EAGLE   The *aquila*, sacred standard of a legion; originally silver, later gold.

EQUESTRIAN   Member of Roman order of knighthood. Required net worth of 400,000 sesterces. Basic qualification for service as senior military and civil officer.

EVOCATI   In the imperial era, militia corps of retired legion veterans.

FASCES   Symbol of Roman magistrate's power, an ax head protruding from a bundle of wooden rods. Carried by lictors; quaestors had one, legates five, praetors six, consuls and most emperors twelve, dictator and some emperors, twenty-four.

FIRST-RANK CENTURIONS   *Primi ordines*, legion's six most senior centurions.

FORUM   Open space, usually rectangular, in all Roman cities and towns where law courts, meeting halls, temples, markets, and speakers' platforms were located.

FREEDMAN   Former slave, officially granted freedom.

FRIGATE   *Liburnan*, light, fast warship.

FURLOUGH FEES   Fees paid to centurions to allow one legionary in four to take leave.

GEMINA LEGION   "Twin" legion formed by merger of two existing legions.

GERMAN GUARD   Elite bodyguard unit of emperor; handpicked German auxiliaries.

GLADIUS   Roman legionary sword twenty inches long, double-edged, with a pointed end.

IMPERATOR   Title. Literally, chief or master. Highest honor for a general. Became reserved for emperors after their armies' victories. Title "emperor" grew from *imperator.*

IMPERIAL   Relating to the period of Roman history from 27 B.C. to the fall of the empire.

IMPERIAL PROVINCE   Armed frontline province. Garrisoned by legions plus auxiliaries. Governed by a propraetor, a former consul appointed by the emperor.

JUVENA COLLEGA   Young men's guild, for sons of Roman nobility in Italy.

LEGION   Regiment. From *legio* (levy, or draft). In 10 cohorts. Republican legion nominal strength, 6,000 men: imperial, 5,180 enlisted men and 72 officers, including own cavalry unit of 120 men.

LEGIONARY   Soldier of a legion. Mostly a draftee, a Roman citizen. Most recruited outside Italy in imperial era. Republican recruits served sixteen years; imperial, twenty years.

LUSTRATION   The *Lustratio Exercitatio,* legion religious ceremony performed in March. Standards were purified with perfumes and garlands prior to each new campaign.

MANIPLE   Company. Legion subunit, of 160 men in imperial times. Three to a cohort.

MANTLET   Wooden shed, on wheels, used in siege works.

MARCHING CAMP   Fortified camp built by legions at the end of every day's march.

MARINE   Roman naval soldier. Freedman. Served twenty-six years. Paid less than auxiliary.

MURAL CROWN   Crown of gold awarded to first Roman soldier over enemy city wall.

OPTIO   Sergeant major. Deputy to centurion and decurion. Unit records and training officer. One to a century, four to legion cavalry units.

ORBIS   The Ring; the Roman legion's circular formation of last resort.

OVATION   Lesser form of a Triumph. Celebrant rode on horseback through Rome.

PALATIUM Origin of the word "palace." Residence and military headquarters of emperors at Rome. First established by Augustus on Palatine Hill, from where name derived. All emperors' headquarters were thereafter called the Palatium, even when new palaces were built.

PALUDAMENTUM General's cloak. Scarlet in republican times. In imperial times, legion commanders wore a scarlet cloak; commanders in chief, a purple cloak.

PILUM A Roman legionary's javelin. Metal-tipped, weighted end, six to seven feet long.

PRAETOR Senior magistrate and major general. Could command legions and armies.

PRAETORIAN GATE Gate of a legion camp that faced the enemy.

PRAETORIAN GUARD Elite unit founded in the republic to guard Rome. Elite military police force in imperial times.

PRAETORIUM Headquarters in a legion camp.

PREFECT Commander of auxiliary units, Praetorian Guard, City Guard, naval fleets. A citizen of equestrian status. Prefects governed Egypt and, between A.D. 6 and 41, Judea.

PROCONSUL Literally, "as good as a consul." See SENATORIAL PROVINCE.

PROCURATOR Provincial official of equestrian rank, deputy of governor, superior to prefect. Financial administrator and tax gatherer. Sometimes governed small provinces.

PROPRAETOR Literally, "as good as a praetor." See IMPERIAL PROVINCE.

QUADRIGA Roman chariot drawn by four horses. Golden quadriga used in Triumphs.

QUAESTOR "Investigator." Lowest-ranking Roman magistrate. Assistant to consuls and governors. Responsible for treasury matters, military recruiting, and special commissions.

SARDONYCHIS Emperor's personal seal, introduced by Augustus in 27 B.C.. Used by most subsequent emperors. Bore image of Augustus cut by the artisan Dioscurides. Also Palatium's outbound correspondence department, because the seal went on outgoing letters.

SATURNALIA Festival of Saturn in December. Slaves could dress like their masters, dice games were legal, and patrons gave clients gifts. Origin of Christian Christmas festival.

SCORPION *Scorpio,* quick-firing artillery, using metal-tipped bolts; fifty to each legion.

SECOND ENLISTMENT MEN   Legionaries who voluntarily served another six-teen- or twenty-year enlistment with their legion when their first enlistment expired.

SENATE   Rome's most powerful elected body. Members, needing a net worth of 1 million sesterces, qualified for legion commands, praetorships, and consul-ships. Minimum age thirty in imperial times. Augustus limited it to six hundred members.

SENATORIAL PROVINCE   In imperial era, a province with a proconsul, a gover-nor appointed by the Senate for a year from its members. Garrison usually of aux-iliaries.

SIGNIFER   Literally a signaler; the standard-bearer of legion subunits.

SINGULARIAN HORSE   *Equus Singulares.* Elite household cavalry unit formed in July A.D. 69 by the emperor Vitellius to replace the Praetorian Cavalry.

SPATHA   Roman cavalry sword. With round end, and longer than the *gladius.*

TESSERA   Small wax sheet on which was inscribed the legion watchword for the day.

TESSERARIUS   Legion guard/orderly sergeant. Distributed the *tessera* to his men.

TESTUDO   "Tortoise" formation. Legionaries locked shields over their heads and at their sides.

THIRD ENLISTMENT MEN   Legionaries voluntarily serving a third enlistment.

TORQUE   Neck chain of twisted gold. Roman army bravery award.

TRIBUNAL   Reviewing stand in a legion camp; built in front of tribunes' quar-ters.

TRIBUNE   Legion, Praetorian Guard, and City Guard officer. Six in republican legions shared command. In an imperial legion, a "thin stripe" junior tribune was an officer-cadet serving a mandatory six months; five to a legion. One "broad stripe" senior tribune (a so-called military tribune) per legion was a full colonel and legion second in command. Senior tribunes commanded Praetorian and City Guard cohorts. From the reign of Claudius, twenty-five senior tribunes were appointed annually, but not all were given legion or Guard posts.

TRIUMPH   Parade through Rome in a gold quadriga by a victorious general, fol-lowed by his soldiers, prisoners, and spoils. He also received T.D.s and a large cash prize.

TRIUMPHAL DECORATIONS (T.D.S)   A crimson cloak, crown of bay leaves, laurel branch, and statue in the Forum for generals celebrating a Triumph; and in lieu of a Triumph.

VEXILLUM   Square cloth banner of auxiliary units and legion detachments.

V.V.   *Valeria Victrix*. Title of the 20th Legion after c. A.D. 9.

WATCH   Time in Roman military camps was divided into watches of three hours, at the end of which sentries changed, on a trumpet call. The officer of the watch was a tribune.

WATCHWORD   Password in a Roman military camp. Daily, just prior to sunset, the tribune of the watch presented the most senior officer in camp with a register of the number of men fit for duty, and in return was given the watchword for the next twenty-four hours. This was distributed to the sentries by the guard cohort's *tesserari*. In imperial times the watch tribune of the Praetorian Guard obtained the Guard's watchword from the emperor.

WINTER CAMP   A permanent base where a legion usually spent October to March.

INDEX